Global Entrepreneurship

Shawn M. Carraher
Cameron University

Dianne H. B. Welsh
The University of North Carolina
Greensboro

Kendall Hunt
publishing company

Book Team

Chairman and Chief Executive Officer   *Mark C. Falb*
President and Chief Operating Officer   *Chad M. Chandlee*
Vice President, Higher Education   *David L. Tart*
Director of National Book Program   *Paul B. Carty*
Editorial Manager   *Georgia Botsford*
Editor   *Melissa M. Tittle*
Assistant Vice President, Production Services   *Christine E. O'Brien*
Senior Production Editor   *Mary A. Melloy*
Senior Permissions Editor   *Colleen Zelinsky*
Cover Designer   *Suzanne Millius*

Cover Credits
Globe image © Digitalife, 2009
Used under license from Shutterstock, Inc.

www.kendallhunt.com
Send all inquiries to:
4050 Westmark Drive
Dubuque, IA 52004-1840

◎ Dedication

Shawn M. Carraher

I dedicate this book to my wife Sarah, sons Shawn Jr. and Charles, and to the glory of God.

Dianne H. B. Welsh

I dedicate this book to my husband, Ted Shalek, and my daughter, Shannon D. Welsh-Cole.

◎ Brief Contents

Part 1 Introduction

Part 2 Specialized Topics

Part 3 Area Studies

Part 4 International Case Study

⊘ Contents

PART TWO—SPECIALIZED TOPICS   85

◎ Preface

This book focuses on what you need to know about global entrepreneurship. It explains the principles that come from entrepreneurship, international business, cross-cultural management, strategy, exporting, international education, international economics and environmental concerns, and leadership. This book summarizes what we believe are the most significant core principles that will help you to succeed as a global entrepreneur or develop your global entrepreneurship strategy. Besides the introductory chapters establishing the principles of global entrepreneurship, we also include topical specialized chapters, area studies, and a case study on a company going international.

We live in a world with countless opportunities, and the vast majority of those opportunities are international. As electronic mediums expand, ideas that may be opportunities will multiply by the thousands. This book was developed with the entrepreneur in mind that wants to identify ideas that may be opportunities beyond their borders. We believe we provide the essential background and knowledge that will give the entrepreneur the skills he or she needs to operate globally. The world economy will benefit from entrepreneurs that contribute internationally, both economically and socially.

This text presents the basic principles of global entrepreneurship and explains how to apply them. It focuses more on practical applications than on statistical surveys and empirical research. We also include examples of specific area studies that the reader may use as an example in a part of the world where they would like to develop a particular product or service to export or import. As a general rule, only the essential elements of global entrepreneurship have been included. We welcome feedback on the text that was developed from the lack of accessible material available in one place and from teaching the topic for many years and compiling our own materials.

We would like to thank Dr. Kevin Lowe, Department of Business Administration Chair, for suggesting Kendall Hunt Publishing, Melissa Tittle, our editor at Kendall Hunt for her guidance, and for the editorial assistance of those who eliminated many errors to make this a more readable text. We are grateful for Drew Robb's assistance with the teacher's manual. Also, we would like to thank our colleagues who contributed to this text and to the field of global entrepreneurship.

Shawn M. Carraher
Dianne H. B. Welsh

◎ Introduction

This book is organized into four sections that explain global and international entrepreneurship. The first section includes the introductory chapters which are designed to provide the reader with a broad overview of the topic and how the material can/should be used. The second section includes more specialized and focused topics on specific aspects of international and global entrepreneurship. The third section includes area studies chapters. The final section includes a case.

This book is designed so that it could be used at the undergraduate or graduate levels and should be used along with experiential exercises and written assignments. The chapters were chosen based upon a detailed study undertaken by the International Entrepreneurship Division of the U.S. Association for Small Business & Entrepreneurship as to what educators in the areas of international and global entrepreneurship believed should be included in such a course. In addition to studying the materials in this book it was also recommended that students should prepare an in depth country profile for a selected country focusing on the entrepreneurial opportunities within that country. A second recommended project is that students complete an organizational project for a client seeking to move internationally. Alternatives to this project could include supplementation with other case studies, completion of an international business plan, or an actual field project. Suggested experiential projects include an international joint venture negotiation [exercise available from CIBER of the University of Maryland], completion of a cross cultural interview where someone from a culture different from one's own is interviewed, BaFa BaFa—a cross-cultural exercise, available from www.stsintl.com, Simulation Training Systems, or even language tag in which students are asked questions in one language and must respond in a different language.

Please let us know of suggestions that you have for future editions of this book.

◎ About the Authors

Shawn M. Carraher received his Ph.D. in Business Administration from the University of Oklahoma. He is the Virginia Brewczynski Endowed Chair and Director of the Small Business Institute® and academic Director of the Center for Emerging Technology & Entrepreneurial Studies at Cameron University. He has served as President of the SouthWest Academy of Management, Division Chair of the Management History Division, Division Chair elect of the Technology & Innovation Management Division, and PDW Co-Chair and Board member for the Careers Division and the Southern Management Association. He has also served as the President of the Small Business Institute®, the Association for Small Business & Entrepreneurship, and the Association for Entrepreneurship, Family Business, & Franchising as well as an officer of six Divisions of the U.S. Association for Small Business & Entrepreneurship. He has published over 100 journal articles, his most recent publications having appeared in the *Journal of Applied Psychology, Journal of International Business Studies, Journal of Occupational & Organizational Psychology, Organizational Research Methods, Decision Sciences, Educational and Psychological Measurement, Journal of Managerial Issues, Journal of Vocational Behavior, Journal of Quality Management, Journal of Applied Management and Entrepreneurship, Career Development International, Polymeric Materials: Science and Engineering, Global Business and Finance Review,* and the *Journal of Business Strategies* and has directed research projects in over 100 countries. His research focuses on a variety of international entrepreneurship topics in the health care and tourism industries and he has worked with over 30,000 SME owners from around the world. Shawn has also worked as a consultant specializing in performance enhancement and management development. He co-owns a 116-year old family business.

**Dianne H. B. Welsh** is the Charles A. Hayes Distinguished Professor of Entrepreneurship at the Bryan School of Business and Economics at the University of North Carolina Greensboro. Dianne earned her Ph.D. in Business Administration from the University of Nebraska. A recognized scholar in international entrepreneurship and franchising; she is co-editor of the first comprehensive volumes on global franchising in emerging and industrialized markets. Dianne is the author of over 100 published manuscripts that have appeared in the *Academy of Management Journal, Journal of International Business Studies, Entrepreneurship Theory & Practice, Journal of Business Venturing, Journal of Small Business Management, Family Business Review,* and others. From an early age, Dianne had the opportunity to work in many different roles in her family's business, Boyt Division Welsh Sporting Goods. Her father, Holden Welsh, Sr. revolutionized the luggage industry when he created the first soft-sided luggage in 1963. From 2000–2005, Dr. Welsh founded and directed the programs in entrepreneurship while fostering partnerships with local business and outreach efforts at John Carroll University in Cleveland, Ohio as the Kahl Chair in Entrepreneurship and Family Business Center while holding the Walter Chair in Entrepreneurship. At The University of Tampa, she founded and directed the Florida Entrepreneurship Family Business Center while holding the Walter Chair in Entrepreneurship from 2005–2008. She is the Past President for the U.S. Association for Small Business & Entrepreneurship (USASBE) and was a Presidential Appointee to the Board of Visitors for the U.S. Air Force Academy, a member of the Defense Advisory Committee for Women in the Services (DACOWITS), and the Executive Board of the Entrepreneurship Division of the Academy of Management for eleven years. She currently serves on the Executive Board of the Global Consortium of Entrepreneurship Center Directors' Association (GCEC). She has owned three of her own successful businesses. Dr. Welsh is President of Family Business First International, Inc., a worldwide strategic planning firm focusing on succession planning in the public and private sectors, entrepreneurial leadership, and employee reward systems.

◯ About the Contributors

Ilan Alon

Dr. Ilan Alon is Harvard Kennedy School Visiting Scholar and Fellow, Jennifer J. Petters Professor of International Business, and the Executive Director of the China Center at Rollins College, Winter Park, Florida (ialon@rollins.edu; ilan_alon@ksg.harvard.edu). Among his recent books are:

- Globalization of Chinese Enterprises (Palgrave McMillan, 2008)
- Service Franchising: A Global Perspective (Springer, 2005)
- Chinese Economic Transition and International Marketing Strategy (Praeger, 2003)
- International Franchising in Industrialized Markets: Western and Northern Europe (CCH Inc., 2003)
- International Franchising in Emerging Markets: Central and Eastern Europe and Latin America (CCH Inc., 2001)

Nadia Ballard

Nadia Ballard has over ten years experience in international marketing and research and has taught international business and marketing classes. She has worked in entrepreneurial and corporate environments in several countries and has provided consulting services to a number of small and medium enterprises looking to expand internationally. She holds an MBA degree from the Crummer Graduate School of Business at Rollins College and a B.A. degree in English, Technical Writing specialization from University of Central Florida.

Madeline M. Crocitto

Madeline Crocitto (Ph.D., City University of New York) is a professor at the State University of New York, College at Old Westbury. Her research focuses on careers and pedagogy, appearing in the *Journal of Management Education, Journal of International Business Studies,* and *Career Development International.* Madeline has held leadership positions including Board Member of the Careers Division of the Academy of Management, Director, Eastern Academy of Management, and VP Special Projects, International Entrepreneurship Education Track United States Association of Small Business & Entrepreneurship, from which she received the 2006 Outstanding Educator award. Currently, she is on the editorial board of *Career Development International* and the *Academy of Management Learning Journal.*

Dale R. Funderburk

Dale R. Funderburk has a B.A. in economics from East Texas State University. He also holds the M.S. and Ph.D. in economics from Oklahoma State University. He has over thirty years' experience in teaching at the university level. He is a professor of economics at Texas A&M University-Commerce, where he teaches graduate and undergraduate courses in the areas of macroeconomic theory and policy, money, banking and financial markets, and monetary theory. Dr. Funderburk has published articles in such journals as *The Appraisal Journal, Journal of Economics, Journal of Forensic Economics, The Real Estate Appraiser and Analyst,* the *National Social Science Journal, Antitrust Law and Economics Review, Trial, Advances in Global Business Research* and even *The Quarter Horse Journal.* He has presented papers and guest lectures at conferences and universities as far away as China, India and Lebanon. In 2004 he was named the "AGBA Global Educator of the Year" by the Academy for Global Business Advancement in New Delhi, India.

Joan F. Gillman

As Director of Special Industry Programs, Executive Education, for the University of Wisconsin-Madison School of Business, Joan's office acts as a conduit between University resources and the business community. In this role, she currently co-hosts a daily radio show, In Business with Jody and Joan on Madison 1670 from 6–7 PM, focusing on local business issues.

Joan's duties span Executive Education from small business and entrepreneurship to teaching managers and designing executive programs. She has taught in both the Small Business Development Center (Business Planning) and Executive Education for the Supervisory Management Series. She was co-director of the Agribusiness Executive Management Program that assisted farmers and agri-businesses in Wisconsin. As founder of The Family Business Center, a regional membership program which addresses the special needs of the family business dealing with succession, communication, and strategic planning issues, she successfully completed succession planning for the center.

Gillman currently serves on the School of Business Advisory Board, Edgewood College, Madison School District's Business & Education Partnership, and as secretary for the Board of Directors—International Center for Entrepreneurial Studies, JJ Strossmeyer University, Osijek, Croatia.

Gillman has two children and enjoys traveling whenever possible. Her most recent travels have been in Croatia, Macedonia and Bulgaria for the Open Society Institute, the nonprofit foundation of George Soros, where she is starting centers for Entrepreneurship. She is also the second woman ever to publicly address men in Saudi Arabia. She is active in many local organizations.

Kira Henschel

With a background in international relations, geology, and engineering, as well as more than a decade living abroad and working in the international commerce arena, Kira Henschel has supported the endeavors of entrepreneurs, as well as small and large organizations, in realizing their ambitions of becoming active international companies. In addition to serving as Honorary Commercial Attache for Wisconsin in Austria from 1985–1990, she held leadership roles in local, national and international non-profit organizations focused on business, environmental and women's issues. She is currently on the faculty of Cardinal Stritch University College of Business in Milwaukee, Wisconsin.

Frank Hoy

Frank Hoy is Director of the Centers for Entrepreneurial Development, Advancement, Research and Support (CEDARS) at the University of Texas at El Paso (UTEP). Dr. Hoy is also a professor of management and entrepreneurship and holds the endowed Chair for the Study of Trade in the Americas. He is a past editor of *Entrepreneurship Theory and Practice* and for Latin America for the *Journal of World Business*. His most recent book is *Franchising: An International Perspective*, co-edited by John Stanworth of the University of Westminster.

Lan-Ying Huang

Lan-Ying Huang is an Associate Professor of the Department of Business Administration at National Changhua University of Education in Taiwan. She holds a Master of Business Administration from Cleveland State University (1994), and Doctorate in Business Administration from Nova Southeastern University in the U.S. (2002). Her research interests lie in the areas of international business strategy and investment, global marketing and logistics. Dr. Huang has co-authored several chapters in books as well as articles in journals such as *Journal of American Academy of Business; International Journal of Family Business; The Asia Pacific Journal of Economics* and *Business;* and *Journal of Business & Entrepreneurship*.

Alvin J. Jackson, Jr.

Alvin J. Jackson, Jr. is a graduate of Texas A&M University with a B.S. in Civil Engineering, and MBA in Marketing and Masters of Science in Management from Commerce School of Business & Technology, and has been a marketing and sales executive for the past ten years. His experience has included serving both private and public sectors including real estate and construction, higher education and working for a Fortune Top 10 corporation in the telecommunications industry.

Mr. Jackson works closely with local, regional and national real estate executives and several construction, engineering and governmental agencies to ensure the right product and lifestyle is delivered in residential, commercial and mixed-use acquisitions. He brings marketing stewardship and an interconnection with several different governmental agencies throughout the region.

Nir Kshetri

Nir Kshetri is Assistant Professor at University of North Carolina-Greensboro. He holds a Ph.D. from University of Rhode Island; an MBA from Banaras Hindu University; and an M.Sc. (Mathematics) and an M.A. (Economics) from Tribhuvan University.

Nir's book *The Rapidly Transforming Chinese High Technology Industry and Market: Institutions, Ingredients, Mechanisms and Modus Operandi* (Chandos: Oxford) was published in 2008. He has published about 30 journal articles, 20 book chapters and presented 70 conference papers. Nir's awards include the 2008 Meheroo Jussawalla Research Paper Prize, Association of ACR/Sheth foundation dissertation award, first place in PTC paper competition in 2001 and second place in 2000.

John N. Odel

John Odel is the director of the International Management Concentration of the School of Management at Rhode Island College. He has also served as the Director of the Study Abroad program of the College. He has also been active in the United States Association for Small Business and Entrepreneurship (USASBE) where he had served as director of the International Division. Previously, Dr. Odel has taught at the Institute of Economics I of the Jagiellonian University in Krakow, and Riga Technical University, in Riga, Latvia.

John A. Parnell

John A. Parnell is the William Henry Belk Professor of Management at the University of North Carolina at Pembroke. He is the author of over 200 basic and applied research articles, published presentations, and cases in strategic management and related areas. Dr. Parnell earned the BSBA, MBA, and MA degrees from East Carolina University, the Ed.D. degree from Campbell University, and the Ph.D. degree in Strategic Management from The University of Memphis. He has authored textbooks in strategic management, crisis management, and organizational theory, and is the founding editor of the *International Journal of Sustainable Strategic Management*.

George M. Puia

George M. Puia is the Dow Chemical Company Centennial Chair in Global Business at Saginaw Valley State University. His primary teaching and research areas are in the areas of global business, innovation and technology management, and international entrepreneurship. He holds a Ph.D. in Strategic Management from the University of Kansas. Prior to his appointment to the Dow Chair, Puia served in faculty positions at Indiana State University and the University of Tampa (UT), where he was director of the nationally recognized UT Small Business Institute. Dr. Puia has served in a variety of marketing management and general management roles both domestically and abroad. He is a leader in academic and professional organizations that promote business internationalization.

Yvonne Pendleton

Yvonne Pendleton, Director, Corporate Heritage, Mary Kay Inc. is an award-winning journalist and author. She is responsible for book properties, academic outreach and executive speechwriting as well as national efforts outside the company such as the A&E–produced broadcast of Mary Kay's Biography televised worldwide and a *New York Times* best-selling book. Pendleton, who worked closely with the legendary founder, led the 2008 re-publication of a classic Mary Kay Ash best seller. Prior to joining Mary Kay Inc., she was a newspaper editor at both Newhouse and Times Mirror corporations. Voted outstanding journalism graduate at the University of Alabama, Pendleton and her husband have two children and three grandchildren.

Sherry E. Sullivan

Sherry E. Sullivan (Ph.D., Ohio State University) has published in journals including: *Journal of International Business Studies, Journal of Management,* and the *Academy of Management Executive.* She was Chair of the Academy of Management's (AOM) Career Division, served on the AOM's Gender and Diversity in Organizations Board, twice served on the Board of Southern Management Association, served as Treasurer and track chair for Midwest Academy, Secretary and track chair for Southwest Academy, and Chair of USASBE's International Division. She is a recipient of GDO's Chusmir Outstanding Service Award and Southwest Academy's Outstanding Educator Award, as well as named a Fellow of the Southern Management Association.

Barbara M. Weiss

Barbara M. Weiss is an Assistant Professor of International Business at The University of Tampa. Dr. Weiss received her bachelor's degree in History from Northern Michigan University. She has a Master of International Business Studies (MIBS) degree from the University of South Carolina. Her master's degree in International Relations and Ph.D. in International Political Economy were conferred by the University of Tsukuba, Japan where she was a Japanese Ministry of Education (Monbusho) scholar. She worked in the area of international finance in the U.S., Canada, and Japan before entering academia. Dr. Weiss has also taught at the University of Applied Sciences Cologne (Germany) where she developed an International MBA program and was the Assistant Director of the university's Business Institute Gummersbach (Betriebswirtschaftliches Institut Gummersbach). Her research is in international business risk, investment theory, business-government relations, global entrepreneurship, and the economic basis of security. She is currently revising a book manuscript for publication titled, *Risk and Security: The Political Economy of Investment and Market Integration.*

Anatoly Zhuplev

Anatoly Zhuplev is a Professor of International Business at Loyola Marymount University (Los Angeles, California). He taught for ten years at the Moscow Management Institute, and subsequently at the Advanced Training Institute of the State Committee for Printing and Publishing in Moscow; in Bonn, Germany; in Warsaw, Poland (as a Fulbright scholar), Paris, France, and at Northeastern University in Boston, Massachusetts. His books and articles on International Management, International Entrepreneurship, International Business, and Corporate Governance have been published in the U.S., Canada, Western Europe, Russia, and the former USSR. He received his Ph.D. from the Moscow Management Institute, Russia, in 1981, and his B.S. from the Moscow Engineer-Economics Institute in 1974.

Part One

Introduction

Chapter One

INTERNATIONAL ENTREPRENEURSHIP AND INTERNATIONAL BUSINESS

George M. Puia, *Dow Chemical Company Centennial Chair in Global Business*
Saginaw Valley State University, Saginaw, Michigan

Learning Objectives

Upon completion of this chapter, students should be able to:

- Define international entrepreneurship and differentiate it from domestic and global entrepreneurship.
- Describe how government policies can influence a nation's entrepreneurial capacity and the entrepreneurial opportunity environment.
- Describe two evolutionary approaches to business internationalization.
- Understand the born-global model and how it differs from the evolutionary approaches.
- Understand the role that the GEM and World Bank studies play in improving our understanding of comparative international entrepreneurship.

Key Terms

born-global firms
comparative entrepreneurship
entrepreneurial capacity
GEM studies
international intrapreneurship

internationalization/internationalized
liberalization/trade liberalization
necessity and opportunity entrepreneurs
opportunity environment
Uppsala Model

After a long day at sea off the Atlantic coast, a fishing vessel landed a prized 710-lb bluefin tuna (they can grow as large as 1,500 lbs). The fishing community in Nova Scotia has fished tuna from these waters for generations, dividing the catch into tuna for stores, restaurants, and food processing plants. There is little production capacity for premium tuna in the regional market—most locally fished tuna finds its way into cans for serving in either sandwiches or cat food.

Most boats took their catch to a local seafood processor, yet a few entrepreneurs developed a global business perspective. Using satellite phones, fishers kept aware of tuna prices in world markets. Tuna is much more valuable in cities like New York, Paris, and, especially, Tokyo, where it is a central ingredient in sushi and sashimi. The Nova Scotia team checked their sources and then carefully packed their catch in dry ice for an overnight flight to the Tokyo fish auction.

The Tokyo tuna auction begins well before dawn with rapid bidding similar to a stock trading floor in the U.S. (though in polite Japanese fashion). Moving from pallet to pallet, the entire auction takes less than two hours. The Tokyo Central Wholesale Seafood Market (Tsukiji) is the largest seafood market in the world, handling 2.3 million kilograms of seafood every day.[1] While local markets pay about $40 to $50 per pound, the Tokyo auction often pays more than double that amount. The Nova Scotia 710-lb tuna reached an auction price of $117 per pound, selling for a little over $83,000. While it was a great price for their team, it was well below the record $370 per pound.[2]

If the story ended here, it would be a good story about smart exporting; our global fish story does not end there. The chef who purchased this fish divided the 710-lb tuna into 2,380 servings of sushi. Because of his international reputation, the chef could sell his sushi to diners in New York and Boston in elite restaurants for about $75 a serving. After spending its life in Nova Scotia's waters, this one tuna would travel over 35,000 miles in two days to sell as sushi for $178,500! Welcome to the world of international entrepreneurship.

⊚ Defining International Entrepreneurship

The opening story gives us a glimpse of international entrepreneurs. They compete in many of the same arenas as other businesses, but they are quick to spot unmet customer needs. When international entrepreneurs observe a need, they pull together resources; in this case, a blend of very old and very new technologies, to satisfy the customer. Most of all, they assume the risks and start a new venture.

International entrepreneurs share a number of characteristics with domestic entrepreneurs. They discover and evaluate opportunities; they take risks, organize resources, and create new goods and services of value to customers. What makes international entrepreneurs different from their domestic counterparts is their inclination to operate on the global stage. International entrepreneurs create businesses with the intent to function across borders. To do this international entrepreneurs must be able to identify opportunities in international contexts, assess unique risks inherent in cross-border businesses, evaluate opportunities with specific target countries in mind, and marshal human and financial resources from across the globe.[3,4] Considering these distinctions, we define international entrepreneurship as *the discovery and evaluation of opportunities and the organization of resources to exploit opportunities across national borders to create fundamentally new goods and services.*

Within this definition are several different types of entrepreneurship and entrepreneurs. One distinction is the difference between opportunity and necessity entrepreneurship. *Opportunity entrepreneurs* form new ventures because they see the opportunity for potential rewards. *Necessity entrepreneurs* create ventures for self-employment to make up for the lack of other job opportunities in their environment. There are also *family-based entrepreneurs* who create businesses with a view to employing family members and *social entrepreneurs* who create ventures with the primary goal of creating public good.

Differentiating International Entrepreneurship from International Business

There is much in common between the study of international entrepreneurship and international business. After all, both small and large businesses face similar contextual challenges as they cross borders to conduct business. Since both entrepreneurs and multinational firms share the same environments, there is obvious overlap in their interests. International business as a field tends to focus on the institutional and contextual influence on multinational corporations. International entrepreneurship differs in both scale and content. Table 1.1 compares the domain of international business and international entrepreneurship.

TABLE 1.1 Comparing International Entrepreneurship and International Business

	INTERNATIONAL ENTREPRENEURSHIP	INTERNATIONAL BUSINESS
Firm History	New, emerging	Established
Scope	Varies—usually focused on early stages of business development	Comprehensive
Firm Size	Small, start-ups, and born-global	Large, multinational
Finance	Angel and venture capital, competitiveness, exchange rates, trade financing	Balance of payments, international financial institutions, capital markets
Operations	Exporting, sourcing	Global sourcing, foreign direct investment
Intellectual Property (IP)	IP creation (patents, proprietary knowledge), IP exploitation	Technology transfer, foreign sourcing of research and development

While there is some obvious overlap between the two fields, in the past two decades international entrepreneurship has established itself as an independent field of study; it is not a subset of international business.

◎ Why Study International Entrepreneurship?

We study international entrepreneurship because there is always more opportunity in the world than there is in any one country. Additionally, changes in technology, transportation, and trade liberalization have made international trade more accessible to companies, especially new entrepreneurial firms.

A defining characteristic of our millennium is the presence of a global economy. As the opening story illustrates, in a global economy, consumers worldwide choose from a wide variety of goods and services. Manufacturers purchase materials and equipment from the world's most productive and qualified suppliers. Employees can increasingly bring their knowledge to bear in new and unfamiliar countries. Technology creates new levels of information interconnectedness. Investment capital crosses national borders in record flows. Collectively, this movement of goods, labor, and capital across national borders is part of a growing trend toward globalization—the creation of an integrated interdependent world economy. Much of the growth in international business activity in the last 50 years has been the result of the globalization of the business environment. Entrepreneurs are on the cutting edge in creating international businesses; they are often the first movers into new markets, products, and services.

The sheer volume of international trade is staggering. In 2003 alone, global exports totaled nearly $7.3 trillion.[5] In the decade from 1994 to 2004, trade grew from 19% to 26% of global economic output.[6] Given the size of the global economy in terms of potential customers, firms that choose to remain domestic miss great opportunities and often face increased risks. For example, a company that has achieved the enviable position of having one-third of the U.S. consumer market for its products has only a 1.5% share of the global market; 98.5% of the market is still available.

Explosion of Growth in the Field

Just as international trade has grown, so has entrepreneurship. Over the last ten years, new business incorporations have averaged 600,000 businesses per year in the U.S. alone. At any point in time, about 16% of U.S. firms will have been in existence less than one year. These newly formed businesses are engines of local economic growth, creating the vast majority of new jobs. Since 1980, Fortune 500 companies have lost more than 5 million jobs. At the same time, small entrepreneurial firms created 34 million new jobs. We refer to the fastest growing of these start-ups as high-expectation entrepreneurs, or *gazelles*. Gazelles represent only 9.8% of the world's entrepreneurs but account for an astounding 75% of job creation by new ventures.[7]

It is well documented that small entrepreneurial firms are central to economic growth. What is less well known is that entrepreneurs are the primary source of innovation; smaller firms create 67% of all new inventions. These innovations play an integral role in the economic renewal process, creating jobs as mature industries decline, while birthing entire new industries. Entrepreneurial firms are also the major method by which the disenfranchised, minorities, and immigrants become part of the mainstream economy.

Just as the practice of entrepreneurship has grown, so has entrepreneurship as a field of study. Entrepreneurship curriculum first began to appear in the early 1970s at the University of Southern California. By the early 1980s, over 300 universities were reporting courses on entrepreneurship and by the 1990s that number had grown to 1,050 schools. As of 2005, there are more than 2,200 entrepreneurship courses offered at over 1,600 schools.[8] There are nearly 300 endowed positions in entrepreneurship and over one hundred established and funded entrepreneurship centers at American universities. In addition, organizations like the Entrepreneurship Division of the Academy of Management, European Council for Small Business (ECSB), and International Council of Small Business (ICSB) and its American counterpart, the Association of Business and Entrepreneurship help develop a strong and rapidly emerging knowledge base for the field. In addition, organizations like the North American Small Business International Trade Educators (NASBITE) and the Forum for International Trade Trainers (FITT) have been working to provide tools and certification for international entrepreneurs to succeed in global markets.

Liberalization of World Markets Creates New Opportunities

In a broad sense, the global economy has existed since the early 1300s when Marco Polo and the Dutch traders fanned out to sell their goods in far-off lands. Yet, Polo faced a world where states were almost entirely independent. There were few agreements or institutions in place to integrate economic life across borders. Today, there is a high level of interconnection and integration among national economies. This new interconnected economy, facilitated by air travel, telecommunications, and computers, is one in which informed citizens and successful executives monitor events not only in their own community or nation but also worldwide.[9] Driving the increase in world trade is trade liberalization of national economies.

We characterize *liberalization* as the decreased role of government in the economy, such as the privatization of government owned industries. *Trade liberalization* refers to policies that reduce government interventions into trade, such as the removal of tariffs or other trade barriers. While these liberalization policies have an effect on domestic economic growth, they also have a substantial positive effect on trade. Simply stated, when other economic factors such as education, or level of natural resources are equal, countries with liberal trade regimes experience higher levels of trade.

Trade liberalization can be a very difficult process for a country to undertake. As the World Bank noted in its annual report, "successful trade reform requires reallocating resources among economic groups, and that adjustment can be costly for some."[10] Despite this difficulty, dozens of governments have undertaken trade reforms.

The most common form of trade liberalization is the reduction of trade barriers like tariffs. Tariffs are a tax the host government places on imports to make them more expensive than locally produced goods. This of course favors local businesses at the expense of international entrepreneurs. Trade liberalization increases competition, improving the quality and value of goods and services in local markets.

Governments often try to help their local businesses by negotiating favorable trade agreements with other countries. We commonly refer to these negotiated pacts as bilateral agreements. Negotiating bilateral agreements with 200 countries would be extraordinarily time consuming. As a result, trading countries have chosen to enter multilateral agreements—trade agreements between large groups of countries. The largest such multilateral agreement is administered by the *World Trade Organization* (WTO). The WTO, established by the nations involved in a predecessor arrangement, the *General Agreement on Tariffs and Trade* (GATT), was created to monitor and control the international trading system. WTO members include the developed countries as well as 110 of the 152 developing countries.

Membership in the WTO requires adherence to a generally liberal set of trade arrangements that facilitate the expansion of orderly world trade. The early results have been impressive. In 1950, Great Britain and Germany had tariff rates of 23% and 26%, respectively. Now both countries hold to the WTO tariff rate of 3.9%. To put those figures in perspective, an American auto sold in the United States for $20,000 would cost an additional $780 under the current tariff. Under the 1950s tariff, the same U.S. auto would cost an additional $4,600 in Great Britain, and an extra $5,200 in Germany. One can easily see how consumers (and therefore international entrepreneurs) can benefit from trade liberalization.

The Rise of Small-Firm Supply Chain Networks

Companies produce goods and services in a value-chain, a sequence of value-added steps. Consider an auto manufacturer. They would purchase raw materials, manufacture sub-assemblies, assemble complete cars, transport them to markets, sell, and service them. Historically, businesses conducted these steps at a single location, but not any longer. With transaction costs and trade barriers falling (Figure 1.1), firms could begin to move parts of their value chain to different locations, locations where entrepreneurs could offer more innovative or cost effective solutions than local suppliers.

There are two primary methods of internationalizing a firm's inputs: global sourcing and global supply chain management. *Global sourcing* is the process of purchasing from suppliers worldwide to provide customers with the best quality product or service at the best possible cost. One of the easiest ways to discover the breadth of global sourcing is to read the manufacturer's label on items in your own home or apartment. It may be difficult to find items manufactured in your home country. Global sourcing also represents an interesting career opportunity for students of international business. Careers in global sourcing include

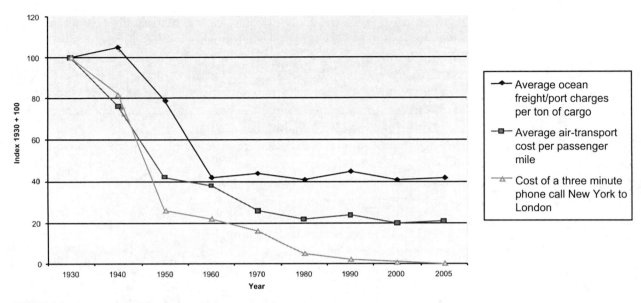

FIGURE 1.1 Transportation communication costs, 1930–2005.

purchasing specialists, negotiators, contract manufacturing supervisors, and logistics specialists, among others. Global sourcing is a critical tool for firms in developed countries as it allows them to lower the average labor cost by mixing high paying knowledge jobs in the developed economy with lower paying, lower skilled jobs in the lesser developed country.

Global supply chain management is more comprehensive than global sourcing. In global supply chain management, firms integrate their entire supply chain globally—from raw materials to finished delivered goods—to provide high levels

 TABLE 1.2 Moving to a Global Supply Chain

SUPPLY CHAIN ELEMENT	TYPICAL REGIONAL SUPPLY CHAIN	FUTURE GLOBAL NETWORK
Product design	Products tailored to local and regional markets	Common standards and design principles
Procurement	Regional sourcing of materials and supplies	Global commodity sourcing
Manufacturing strategy	Plants produce to meet local requirements—capacity often duplicated across borders	Location decisions made on production and logistics costs with a view to regional and global exporting
Supply-chain planning	Inventory, forecasting, and supply controlled at the local level	Global resource planning

(Adapted from Mainardi, C. R., Salva, M., and M. Sanderson. "Label of origin: Made on earth." *Strategy & Business* 15, 1999:42–53.)

of customer satisfaction and higher profits. Firms increasingly rely on supplier networks around the globe to improve their quality and efficiency.

For small entrepreneurs to succeed in a global supply chain environment, they often interconnect with dominant buyers and suppliers across the globe. They also need to cost effectively transport their goods and services to distant markets. Many international entrepreneurs find a productive niche as a member of the global supply chain of a multinational enterprise.

It is easy to take for granted the enormous changes that have occurred in the last half of the twentieth century. For example, just two generations ago in the global transportation infrastructure, commercial airfreight did not exist; firms calculated the average time to ship goods globally in months, not hours. Today, for a wide array of products from fresh flowers to electronic components, air cargo is the most reliable and cost effective means of shipping. Many modern production management practices, including the just-in-time inventory techniques so important to multinational corporations, rely heavily on global air cargo.

Ocean shipping operations have undergone a transformation no less dramatic than that of airfreight. Ocean shipping costs have fallen by as much as 80% over the last 50 years. Supertankers holding up to 500,000 tons displacement have replaced tankers one-fifth their size *without* an increase in crew size. Similarly, containerized cargo ships are now thirty times larger than the old merchant steamers they replaced. Firms can now use advanced technology to load and unload ships with only a minimal crew, replacing expensive unionized labor in large industrialized ports. Finally, sea freight can seamlessly integrate with domestic rail and truck transportation; firms can now ship goods as easily across the globe as they once did across town. By using intermodal transportation, a firm can load a container at their site, attach it to a semi-truck for shipment to a rail yard, then to a sea port, and finally by truck to the final destination. With intermodal shipping, the cargo never leaves its container. This reduces labor costs and greatly improves shipping security.

A similar revolution has taken place in telecommunication. Because of deregulation and new technologies, telecommunication costs have dropped significantly. The explosion of new competitors in both voice and data transmission have kept pressure on prices, which continue to fall sharply. In the old economy, it was common to attempt to keep production processes under one roof. In that setting, management could physically supervise all of the steps in the production process to assure they added value. New communications technologies have made it cost efficient to separate value-adding steps of production and use in ways that were not previously feasible.

With new communication technologies, we feel the change in value chain management across a wide range of industries. For example, software entrepreneurs in India or Ireland create program modules for U.S. firms, e-mailing their results back to their U.S. customers. In health care industries, hospitals can transmit MRI images for remote diagnosis by phone or Internet. Financial service industries transfer assets electronically, greatly reducing the cost of global commerce. It is now increasingly common to design computer chips in Silicon Valley for production implementation in East Asia. The aggregate value of these individual company transactions is staggering. Chinese companies alone exported over $23 billion in electronics, semiconductor, and information technology in 2005.[11] This rapid and extreme reduction of communication costs has broad implications for international trade, particularly the trade of services.

These dramatic improvements in information and communications technology (ICT) created new opportunities for global entrepreneurs. In New York, an Indian MBA student was using the Internet to keep in touch with friends from his home country. He learned they were not as excited about the Spider-Man comic series as were his American friends. Sharad Devarajan understood their concerns: Spider-Man was based on U.S. cultural values. The fact that Spider-Man gains his power after being bitten by a high-tech spider, or that Mary Jane rejects Peter because he is a geek, are features that do not necessarily work in the rest of the world. Devarajan's answer was to create Spider-Man in India. Set in Mumbai, the Indian Spider-Man, a boy named Pavitr Prabhakar, receives his power to fight evil from an ancient yogi, wears traditional garb, leaps around rickshaws and scooters in Indian streets, and swings from monuments such as the Gateway of India and the Taj Mahal. Devarajan creates and manages each new comic in New York for production and distribution in South Asian markets.[12]

The Internet has certainly been a driving force in interconnecting businesses and consumers into a global economy. Recent data shows over 1.4 billion people use the Internet worldwide—about 22% of the world's population. The Internet has become a dynamic force in both business-to-consumer (B2C) and business-to-business (B2B) markets. E-commerce is not just for large businesses—Evertek Computer Corporation, which sells new and refurbished computers and parts, has business in more than eighty countries booked through internet portals.

The Cross Border Movement of Intellectual Property

Intellectual property—patents, trademarks, copyrights, and other proprietary processes—represent the top of the economic food chain. A heart surgeon may make thousands of dollars per hour, but he or she can only make money when they are physically working. An entrepreneur, on the other hand, can collect rent from their intellectual property. Intellectual property can move across borders without transportation costs, giving it high profit potential. By every measure, the transfer of intellectual property across borders is increasing at record rates.

◎ Two Streams of Research

Two important streams of international entrepreneurship inform our field: internationalization and comparative entrepreneurship.[13] Internationalization is the transformation of a domestic entrepreneur into one who does business in more than one country. Comparative entrepreneurship investigates the similarities and differences between international entrepreneurs based on their country of origin. Both streams give greater understanding of this dynamic field. The balance of this chapter explores each of those streams to give a better picture of international entrepreneurship.

Moving Ventures across Borders

A firm has *internationalized* when it moves from being a domestic firm to providing goods or services overseas. An entrepreneurial firm is global if it is simultaneously operating in all the key regions of the world (no one demands a company to do business in all 190+ countries). The difference between an international entrepreneur and global one is largely an issue of scope. In some cases, firms are global because they provide essentially the same product or service worldwide. They are global by virtue of the global universality of their goods—oil, metal fasteners, tires—we use these products the same way in every country. Other industries feel consumer pressure to adapt their product or service to meet local conditions. Companies that produce processed foods, advertising, certain items of clothing, and types of entertainment are among businesses that feel a constant pressure toward local adaptation to each market. The more extensive the need for adaptation, the greater the time required to adapt to local conditions.

Discovery of International Opportunities

One of the distinguishing characteristics of entrepreneurs is their ability to recognize opportunities. The great management writer Peter Drucker once lamented that managers of large corporations never properly understood opportunities, warning that businesses could only grow by exploiting opportunities.[14]

In practice, opportunity finding takes two forms: reactive and proactive. International opportunities confront *reactive* entrepreneurs in ways that force them to respond.[15] For example, a firm may have an international customer who discovers the company on the Internet. An existing customer may open an overseas operation and require service overseas. A guest to a trade show may ask to represent their country.

What the three previous examples have in common is that they represent reactive international entrepreneurship. There is little planning or strategy involved. The major problem with a reactive approach is that the entrepreneur may miss outstanding opportunities by focusing on immediate ones. A proactive strategy, one where the entrepreneur plans their international activity in advance, is far more likely to achieve success.

Internationalization Models

Internationalization is a business response to globalization that occurs when a domestic firm begins to sell or operate across national borders. It can also describe the activities a company undertakes to expand its limited international activities to more countries. With internationalization, new business practices, laws, regulations, and cultures confront the entrepreneur. A firm can internationalize without operating off-shore; many international firms are importers—firms that acquire their products or services abroad. More often, internationalization describes a company's first attempts at exporting or licensing. We will now explore several models that attempt to describe how firms internationalize.

The Uppsala Model

The Uppsala Model is named after the Swedish University where researchers Johansen and Vahlne developed a process theory of internationalization. In their model, businesses progress through a series of discrete steps as a company evolves from a domestic to an international firm.[16,17] Firms tend to expand domestically first, followed by incremental international expansions. It is essentially a "learning curve" model; as the manager or entrepreneur develops extensive new experiential knowledge, they are able to make new international commitments.

The acquisition of new knowledge helps the entrepreneur discover new opportunities abroad. Researchers developed the Uppsala Model before the current wave of globalization. At that time, countries varied more greatly in the extent to which their own internal markets were internationalized. While the Uppsala Model predicted an evolutionary approach to internationalization, it recognized that some entrepreneurs were "early starters" in internationalizing their business. These entrepreneurs made their decision to move more quickly, independent of whether the markets they wished to serve were more or less internationalized.[18]

Other Models of Evolutionary Internationalization

An alternative evolutionary model of firm internationalization is the "Innovation Model." The Innovation Model tracked the international product life cycle—a model developed to explain the internationalization process of large businesses. If you could measure internationalization as the ratio of export sales to total sales, you would see the firm change in discreet steps. Like Uppsala, the model predicted incremental change based on management decisions. In Stage 1, a firm would be entirely domestic; in Stage 5, more than 40% of its sales would come from foreign markets.[19,20] In the Innovation Model, the focus is on the learning sequence of senior managers in adopting an innovation; the theory treats internationalization as an innovation.[21]

As markets evolved they became more global; the Internet, CNN, and other global media helped consumers in developing markets discover the best goods and services available worldwide. In many industries, it became impractical to consider the possibility of delaying entry to foreign markets because, if you did, you might cede the market to a new competitor.

There are other challenges to the Evolutionary Model. While manufacturing firms tended to start in domestic markets, than internationalize by moving to psychologically-"near" markets before attempting distant ones, it was not so for service firms. Service firm internationalization did not follow a traditional evolutionary model.[22]

Management Capacity to Internationalize

Because it takes unique skills to internationalize a venture, it is not surprising that the experience of the top management team is a critical issue. Research has shown that ventures whose managers had overseas work experience influenced the speed and depth of internationalization.[23,24]

Students can prepare themselves now for international entrepreneurship careers. Research indicates that firms whose managers studied abroad were far more likely to internationalize.[25]

Born-Global Firms

Born-global entrepreneurs are more recent phenomena in international entrepreneurship. *Born-global entrepreneurs* are early adopters of internationalization; they apply knowledge-based resources to sell outputs in multiple countries from at or near their founding.[26] Several features make these entrepreneurs unique. They have a global focus, a commitment to explore proactively international markets, and a knowledge base that facilitates these activities. Not surprisingly, born-global firms first appeared in countries with relatively small domestic markets and, despite limited resources, they rapidly progressed to international markets.[27]

Since born-global ventures often start with small teams, it makes sense to examine the background of the top management team. Do the characteristics entrepreneurs' possess lead to born-global companies? One recent study examined Australian born-global ventures. Their research found managers had mindsets that greatly influenced the speed and efficacy of internationalization. They labeled the most effective mindset a strategist. The strategist is more benevolent and collaborative, seeking to maintain key relationships. Unlike other born-global types, the strategist maintains a long-term view of the firm and is able to avoid some of the competitiveness that can divide top management teams from each other and from their customers.[28]

The knowledge to become born-global comes from a variety of sources. Some knowledge might be industry specific; experience in a particular industry might introduce the nascent firm to foreign market opportunities. Other management teams have academic knowledge. Their formal education and study abroad experiences have exposed them to foreign opportunities.[29] Both industry and academic experiences can accelerate an entrepreneur's exploration of foreign markets. Last, opportunity finding is not sufficient for international success. Born-global entrepreneurs need to have an orientation toward cross-cultural collaboration and the complementary skills needed to make collaboration work.[30]

How Entrepreneurship Differs across Countries

Comparative entrepreneurship is the study of how entrepreneurial practice differs across nations. Comparative entrepreneurship draws attention to two sets of characteristics: *entrepreneurial capacity*—the ability of entrepreneurs to respond to new opportunities, and the *entrepreneurial opportunity environment*—the in-country conditions that create opportunities for entrepreneurs.[31]

Government programs influence entrepreneurial capacity through the strength of the educational system, the availability of entrepreneurship training programs, as well as by the general cultural and legal environment. One can think of each country as a laboratory; each laboratory is experimenting to develop a system that creates the most dynamic and entrepreneurial economy. By comparing countries, we can identify best practices for nurturing and supporting entrepreneurship. Each country has unique environmental characteristics that shape the opportunity set for entrepreneurs. Among the factors that shape opportunities are government regulations, financial resources, commercial and legal infrastructure, market openness, physical infrastructure, and cultural and societal norms. In general, countries with an independent legal-judicial system, open markets, adequate physical and financial resources, and limited regulations generate more opportunities for new business creation. International entrepreneurs then identify and analyze these opportunities to create new business models.

The Global Entrepreneurship Monitor Studies

One systematic approach to comparing entrepreneurship across nations is the Global Entrepreneurship Monitor (GEM) studies. Operated by a consortium of universities, GEM started in 1999 by exploring entrepreneurship in ten countries and, in 2008, it researched forty-two countries. It is the largest survey-based study of entrepreneurship in the world. The GEM program has three major goals:

- to measure differences in the level of entrepreneurial activity among countries,
- to uncover factors determining the levels of entrepreneurial activity, and
- to identify policies that may enhance the level of entrepreneurial activity.[32]

At the heart of the GEM study is an adult population survey that explores entrepreneurial attitudes and experiences in the general population. Each national team collects its data in exactly the same manner at the same time of year to assure comparability findings.[33] The GEM studies present entrepreneurship as a complex phenomenon, where no one measure or metric can capture its richness or complexity. One recent GEM study explored high-potential, opportunity, and necessity entrepreneurs across nations and found that only high potential entrepreneurs had a significant impact on economic growth.[34]

The GEM data has facilitated a wide range of studies across the globe that examine entrepreneurial capacity and the entrepreneurial opportunity environment. GEM researchers in New Zealand, one of the top six countries in the world for entrepreneurial activity, discovered a highly networked context. This level of networking made it easier for entrepreneurs to discover opportunities and engage needed resources.[35] A practical implication of this finding is that programs that improve entrepreneur networking will positively correlate with their success. While similarities are intriguing, the differences between countries are also informative. Most research suggests that larger markets are positively related to new business starts. A South African study using GEM data found the opposite result; smaller markets were more attractive to entrepreneurs.[36] It is hard to overestimate the impact of the GEM studies. As of 2008, over 120 refereed journal articles have appeared in the English language and another seventy-six in non-English languages.

Analyzing the Environmental Context

Scholars have paid much attention to the role regulation plays in shaping business opportunities.[37] There is a consensus that there is an inverse relationship between business regulation and new venture creation; countries with burdensome regulations stifle entrepreneurship. Several groups have looked at the opportunity environment for entrepreneurs. One of the most widely used sources for comparison is the World Bank data set, "Doing Business."[38]

The Doing Business studies track regulations of interest to all businesses but particularly entrepreneurs. Table 1.3 compares five countries on three measures for ease of starting a business. The complete Doing Business annual report covers dozens of measures on more than 180 countries.

Countries differ in the ways in which they regulate or restrict the entry of new business. Some regulation of entry is valuable to both the country and the firm. Official registration or licensing for example may make a firm more reputable. Most trade scholars often adhere to an alternative model, referred to as the "tollbooth model."[39] In the tollbooth model, politicians and bureaucrats encourage regulation as it adds to their power. Some research has gone as far as to infer that public officials create regulations as means of incentive, a form of official bribery; firms will pay the official fees needed in order to receive a permit.[40] Regulatory policies influence business investment and entry choices—countries with higher levels of regulation make it more difficult for entrepreneurs to exploit opportunities.

The GEM studies and World Bank share some findings; countries that have liberal trade regimes, government policies that support the protection of intellectual property, and availability of capital providing mechanisms have higher levels of international entrepreneurship. There is also evidence that formal programs, whether sponsored by governments or universities can influence an entrepreneur's international orientation.

TABLE 1.3 The Regulation of Entrepreneurial Activity in Five Countries

COUNTRY	NUMBER OR PROCEDURES TO START A BUSINESS	DURATION TO START A BUSINESS (DAYS)	COST (% OF GROSS NATIONAL INCOME PER CAPITA)
Brazil	18	152	8.2
China	14	40	8.4
Finland	3	14	1.0
India	13	30	70.1
United States	6	6	0.7

(Adapted from The World Bank Group. *Doing Business 2009: Measuring Business Regulation.* Washington, DC: World Bank, 2009.)

Culture and Entrepreneurship

Each day conversations, radio and television programs, Internet sessions, music, art, and architecture bombard us with information. We would be overwhelmed and unable to function without a framework for interpreting this constant stream of information. Yet, most days, we function pretty well. *We have been taught how to make sense of our context.* We have learned the rules for living in our setting by observing our elders and other successful actors, through our various religions, language, the sound of our music, and even the design of our buildings. We have learned our *culture.*

Defining Culture

Culture is the shared set of beliefs, values, and norms passed from one generation to another that structure a member's perceptions of the world. It is the acquired knowledge that people use to experience and interpret their own behavior and the behavior of others. If our minds are the *hardware* of intelligence, then culture is the software of the mind.[41]

In a cultural context, members express culture through the behaviors they exhibit, the artifacts they craft, and the politico–economic philosophies they embrace. Members base their expressions on the values and beliefs they hold about the world around them. Social structures like family, religion, language, and education transmit these values and beliefs from generation to generation. In turn, culture influences a country's business practices. Figure 1.2 provides a graphic representation of the complex interrelated set of cultural characteristics.

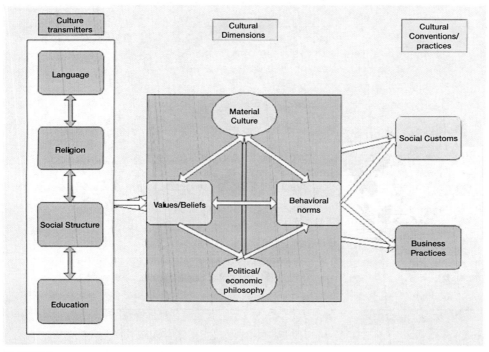

FIGURE 1.2 A model of culture.

Culture's Influence on Management Practices

In addition to finding opportunities and obtaining resources, entrepreneurs must manage their ventures; international entrepreneurs must manage in a cross cultural context. Management texts describe the basic tasks of management as planning, leading, organizing, and controlling. These *basic* management tasks are difficult, even when practiced in a single country. Managing across national borders can be especially complex. Recent scholarship, for example, demonstrates the impact of culture on employee attitudes toward benefits and other compensation.[42] Table 1.4 helps us examine some of the ways that culture influences the four primary tasks of managers.

While only a partial list, it is easy to see that culture greatly influences the management process.

In addition to shaping management practices, national culture influences a nation's level of innovation. Understanding how culture shapes innovation can help the entrepreneur be more effective in cross-border settings. Further, there is emerging research that suggests that cultural diversity also has a positive influence on innovations. By definition entrepreneurs are innovators, they must learn to work in a culturally diverse setting.[43–45] Culture shapes the processes by which international entrepreneurs identify opportunities, organize resources, and manage implementation of new ventures.

TABLE 1.4 **The Cultural Dimensions of Entrepreneurial Management**

MANAGEMENT TASK	CULTURAL DIMENSION
Planning	• Controls whether planning will be undertaken • Influences which stakeholders are involved in planning • Influences the time horizon of the process
Leading	• Greatly influences the communication process • Establishes standards for motivation • Determines the accepted role of leadership • Limits the number of leaders
Organizing	• Influences the structure of organizations • Relates the natures of tasks to the types of individual who can perform those tasks • Determines the appropriateness of certain types of alliances or partnerships
Controlling	• Determines the extent to which groups or individuals are responsible for organizational control • Influences the corporate governance system
Risk Assessment	• Influences which behaviors one considers "risky" • Introduces emotional moderation or implication of perceived risks (e.g., the concept of fate)

Summary

International entrepreneurship is the discovery and evaluation of opportunities and the organization of resources to exploit opportunities across national borders to create fundamentally new goods and services. Opportunity entrepreneurs form new ventures because they see the opportunity for potential rewards. Necessity entrepreneurs create ventures for self-employment to make up for the lack of other job opportunities in their environment. There are also family-based entrepreneurs who create businesses with a view of employing family members and social entrepreneurs who create ventures with the primary goal of creating public good. The study of international entrepreneurship is important because it is a driving force in the creation of new jobs, it improves the quality of life and economic opportunities where it operates, and it provides better quality goods and services to customers worldwide.

Two important streams of research in understanding international entrepreneurship are the internationalization literature and comparative entrepreneurship. The internationalization model has two competing theories. In one, firms gradually evolve from domestic firms, undergoing a process of internationalization. In the other, firms are born-global and able to exploit knowledge resources in ways that help them to enter overseas markets from nearly the point of their founding.

Comparative entrepreneurship helps identify emerging trends and techniques that make businesses more competitive. Two large scale studies dominate the comparative landscape: the GEM studies and the World Bank research. The GEM studies help us understand why and how people from different countries become entrepreneurs. The World Bank studies focus our attention on the contextual environment within which international entrepreneurs must operate. Last, no study of international entrepreneurship would be complete without exploring the role of cultural difference. Culture shapes the processes by which we identify opportunities, organize resources, and manage implementation of new ventures.

Discussion Questions

1. What changes have taken place in world markets in the last twenty years that make it easier for domestic entrepreneurs to spot opportunities in foreign markets?
2. Can an entrepreneur afford to internationalize slowly, or must their firm be "born-global"?
3. How does the level of regulation within a country affect the creation of new ventures?
4. In what ways is the study of international entrepreneurship unique from the study of international business?
5. In what ways do the GEM and World Bank studies improve our knowledge of international entrepreneurship?

Endnotes

1. Bestor, T. C. 2004. Tsukiji: The fish market at the center of the world. *California Studies in Food and Culture* 11.

2. Associated Press. Premium tuna fetches $100,000 at auction. *MSNBC* 6 January 2009.

3. Oviatt, B. M., and P. P. McDougall. 2005. Defining international entrepreneurship and modeling the speed of internationalization. *Entrepreneurship: Theory & Practice* 29(5):537–553.

4. Zahra, S., and G. George. (2002). International entrepreneurship: the current status of the field and future research agenda. In *Strategic Entrepreneurship: Creating an Integrated Mindset*, edited by Hitt, M. A., Ireland, R. D., Sexton, D. L., and S. M. Camp. Oxford: Blackwell Publishers: 255–228.

5. World Trade Organization. Stronger than expected growth spurs modest trade recovery. *Press Release*, 5 April 2004.

6. International Monetary Fund. 2004. *International Monetary Fund World Economic Outlook*. Washington, DC: IMF Publications.

7. Autio, E. 2005. GEM high-expectation entrepreneurship summary report. *Global Entrepreneurship Monitor*.

8. Zwaniecki, A. 2008. Entrepreneurship spreads across US university campuses. *Economics and Trade*.

9. Brown, S. 1998. America and the global economy: International trade and investment. *Vital Speeches of the Day*: 293–296.

10. Wolfensohn, J. D. 2000. *World Development Report, 1999–2000*. Washington, DC: Oxford University Press: 33.

11. National Trade Data Base. 2005. *Global Patterns of US Merchandise Trade*.

12. Desmaris, M. Devarajan's Gotham Entertainment swings deal for Spider-Man in India. *India Business Journal* 1 July 2004.

13. Wright, R. W. 1994. Trends in international business research: Twenty-five years later. *Journal of International Business Studies* 25: 687–701.

14. Drucker, P. 1974. *Management Tasks, Responsibilities, Practices*. New York: Harper & Row.

15. Foley, J. F. 2004. *The International Entrepreneur, 2nd ed*. Chicago: Dearborn Financial Publishing.

16. Johanson, J., and J. Vahlne. 1977. The internationalization process of the firm—a model of knowledge development and increasing foreign market commitment. *Journal of International Business Studies* 8:23–32.

17. Johanson, J., and J. Vahlne. 1990. The mechanism of internationalization. *International Marketing Review* 7:11–24.

18. Johanson, J., and L.G. Mattson. 1988. Internationalization in industry systems—a network approach. In *Strategies for Global Competition,* edited by N. Hood. London: Croom Helm.

19. Andersen, O. 1993. On the internationalization process of firms: a critical analysis. *Journal of International Business Studies* 24:209–231.

20. Cavusgil, S. T. 1980. On the internationalization process of firms. *European Research* 8:273–281.

21. Andersson, S., and I. Wictor. 2003. Innovative internationalisation in new firms: Born globals: The Swedish case. *Journal of International Entrepreneurship* 1:249–276.

22. Bell, J., McNaughton, R., Young, S., and D. Crick. 2003. Toward an integrative model of small firm internationalization. *Journal of International Entrepreneurship* 1:339–362.

23. McDougall, P. P., Shane, S., and B. M. Oviatt. 1996. New venture internationalization, strategic change, and performance: a follow-up study. *Journal of Business Venturing* 11:23–40.

24. Burgal, O., and G. C. Murray. 1998. The international activities of British start-up companies in high-technology industries: differences between internationalizers and non-internationalizers. In *Frontiers of Entrepreneurship Research*, edited by Reynolds, P.D., Byrave, W. D., Carter, N. et al. Babson Park, MA: Babson College: 447–463.

25. Bloodgood, J. M., Sapienza, H. J., and J. G. Almeida. 1996. The internationalization of new high potential U.S. ventures: Antecedents and outcomes. *Entrepreneurship Theory and Practice* 20:61–76.

26. Knight, G. A., and S. T. Cavusgil. 2004. Innovation, organizational capabilities, and the born-global firm. *Journal of International Business Studies* 35:124–141.

27. McDougall, P., and B. Oviatt, 2000. International entrepreneurship:the intersection of two research paths. *Academy of Management Journal* 43:902–906.

28. Freeman, S., and S. T. Cavusgil. 2007. Toward a typology of commitment states among Managers of born-global firms: A study of accelerated internationalization. *Journal of International Marketing* 15(4):1–40.

29. Nordman, E. R., and S. Melén. 2008. The impact of different kinds of knowledge for the internationalization process of born globals in the biotech business. *Journal of World Business* 43(2):171–185.

30. Karra, N., Phillips, N., and P. Tracey. 2008. Building the born global firm: Developing entrepreneurial capabilities for international new venture success. *Long Range Planning* 41:440–458.

31. Acs, Z. J., Arenius, P., Hay, M., and M. Minniti. 2005. *Global Entrepreneurship Monitor: 2004 Executive Report*. Babson Park, MA: Babson College and London: London Business School.

32. Harding, R., and N. Bosma. 2007. *GEM Global Reports—2006*. Babson Park, MA: Babson College.

33. Quill, M., Bosma, N., and M. Minniti. 2007. *Globe Entrepreneurship Monitor: 2006 Data Assessment*. Babson Park, MA: Babson College.

34. Wong, P. K., Ho, Y. P., and E. Autio. 2005. Entrepreneurship, innovation and economic growth: Evidence from GEM data. *Small Business Economics* 24(3):335–350.

35. Cruickshank, P., and D. Rolland. 2006. Entrepreneurial success through networks and social capital: Exploratory considerations from GEM research in New Zealand. *Journal of Small Business & Entrepreneurship* 19:63–80.

36. Naudé, W., Gries, T., Wood, E., and A. Meintjies. 2008. Regional determinants of entrepreneurial start-ups in a developing country. *Entrepreneurship & Regional Development* 20(2):111–124.

37. Puia, G.M., and W. Minnis. 2007. The effects of policy frameworks and culture on the regulation of entrepreneurial entry. *Journal of Applied Management and Entrepreneurship* 12.

38. The World Bank. 2008. *Doing Business, 2008: Comparing Regulation in 178 Countries*. Washington, DC: The World Bank.

39. DeSoto, H. 1990. *The Other Path*. New York: Harper & Row.

40. Shleifer, A., and R. W. Vishny. 1993. Corruption. *Quarterly Journal of Economics* 153:599–617.

41. Hofstede, G., and G. J. Hofstede. 2008. *Cultures and Organizations: Software of the Mind*. New York: McGraw-Hill.

42. Carraher, S. M., and M. R. Buckley. 2005. Attitudes towards benefits among SME owners in western Europe: An 18-month study. *Journal of Applied Management and Entrepreneurship* 10:45–57.

43. Shane, S. A. 1993. Cultural influences on national rates on innovation. *Journal of Business Venturing* 8:59–73.

44. Shane, S. A. 1992. Why do some societies invent more than others? *Journal of Business Venturing* 7:29–46.

45. Puia, G. M., and J. Ofori-Dankwa. 2005. Intra-cultural variation and entrepreneurship: Exploring the effect of diversity on national levels of innovation. *Review of Small Business and Entrepreneurship Research* 31:8–20.

Chapter Two

Environmental and Contextual Sources of Global Variation in Entrepreneurial Activities

Nir Kshetri
The University of North Carolina, Greensboro, North Carolina

Learning Objectives

Upon completion of this chapter, students should be able to:

- Provide a review of environmental and contextual factors affecting entrepreneurial activities in an economy by focusing both on the demand and supply sides.
- Examine the demand and supply sides of entrepreneurships in the international context.

To achieve the chapter objectives, we divide environmental and contextual factors as discussed above into two major categories: economic factors and institutional factors.

Key Terms

culture
demand-side perspective
economic factors
institutional factors
political stability
supply-side perspective

This chapter examines economic and institutional factors affecting entrepreneurial activities. Factors analyzed include entrepreneurial opportunities, skills, access to capitals, incentives, and culture, as well as overall macro-economic environment and institutional contexts. The focus is thus on the demand-side as well as the supply-side perspectives of entrepreneurship. We also discuss examples of measures taken by various governmental and non-governmental agencies to change some of the institutional factors to stimulate entrepreneurship.

⊚ Introduction

A constellation of factors linked to economic and institutional environments influence a country's entrepreneurship trajectory. The Danish National Agency for Enterprise and Construction's Division for Research and Analysis (FORA) has proposed five main categories related to business environment indicators that affect entrepreneurial activities in a country: opportunities, skills, capital, incentives and culture.[1] In addition, FORA also argued that contextual factors, such as those related to the macroeconomic environment and institutional context like unemployment rate and gross domestic product (GDP) growth, are tightly linked to a country's entrepreneurial landscape. These factors can be studied under the demand-side and the supply-side perspectives of entrepreneurship.

The supply-side perspective of entrepreneurship focuses on the individual traits, attributes, and characteristics of entrepreneurs.[2] Some of the important issues examined under the supply-side perspective include how culture,[3] social class, and ethnic group[4] are related to individuals' entrepreneurial behavior. According to this logic, differences in entrepreneurship depend on the differences in individuals. Put differently, the personality or social group of an individual entrepreneur determines how, why, and where new businesses are founded.[2]

The demand-side perspective of entrepreneurship, on the other hand, focuses on rates, or the context in which entrepreneurship occurs[2] and thus deals with sources of opportunities and the entrepreneurial roles that need to be filled in an economy.[5] According to the demand-side perspective, some of the important ways to examine entrepreneurship include creation of new ventures by organizational hierarchies,[6] the activity of the professions,[7] the policy of nation-states,[8] the development of markets,[9] and the advent of technological change.[10]

⊚ Economic Factors

Economic factors influencing entrepreneurship in an economy are related to indicators such as physical and financial infrastructures, access to capital, gross national product, balance of payment and balance of trade situation, debt and servicing costs, inflation rate, interest rate, exchange rate, and exchange rate stability.

Physical and Financial Infrastructures

Availability of physical infrastructures such as roads, ports, water, telecommunications, and power play a critical role in facilitating entrepreneurial activities.[11] Most industrialized countries have well-developed physical infrastructures in place to support entrepreneurial activities. In the United States, for instance, the government has played a central role in infrastructure such as roads, rural electrification, and public schooling, which led to increased productivity among small businesses.[12] A lack of well-developed physical infrastructures has been a barrier hindering entrepreneurship development in many developing countries. Among developing countries, China's entrepreneurial performance has been phenomenal, which can be partly attributed to the country's investment in infrastructure. China had 78,000 kilometers of railway track by 2007 and is estimated to spend $42 billion in railways in 2008.[13] China's success has also encouraged neighboring countries such as Vietnam and India to improve infrastructure.[14] In 2005, U.S. Treasury Secretary John Snow called on India to allow more foreign investment in its financial sector to help pay for the huge infrastructure upgrades needed to encourage entrepreneurship.[15]

Financial infrastructures such as stock exchanges, credit guarantees, payment systems, insurance companies, banks and microfinance organizations, and other lending institutions are equally important in promoting entrepreneurship. It is argued that due to increasing globalization of capital markets, finance is no longer a big problem for promising entrepreneurs in emerging economies. The real problem concerns the lack of channels linking finance with potential entrepreneurs.[16]

Access to Capital

Research has indicated that only small proportions of latent entrepreneurs, or those who would prefer to be entrepreneurs rather than being paid employees, starts their own businesses. A lack of access to capital is often the biggest roadblock for latent entrepreneurs to materialize the goal of starting their own business.[17] For most potential entrepreneurs in many developing countries, a village loan shark is the only available source of capital, whose interest rate is 200% to 300% a year.[18]

A Country's Credit Rating

A country's credit rating captures most of the economic indicators discussed above. Note that credit rating agencies (CRAs) analyze and evaluate the creditworthiness of corporate as well as sovereign issuers of debt securities.[19] A sovereign rating is aimed at measuring the risk that a government may default on its own obligations in either local or foreign currency. It takes into account both the ability and willingness of a government to repay its debt in a timely manner.[20] Standard and Poor's ratings, Moody's ratings, and Fitch's ratings are among the most widely used credit ratings.

Studies conducted by international economists for both developed and developing economies have indicated that a small number of variables explain 90% of the variation in the ratings.[21-25] They include GDP per capita, GDP growth, inflation rate, the ratio of non-gold foreign exchange reserves to imports, the ratio of the current account balance to GDP, default history, and the level of economic development.[19]

In the mid-1990s, some European countries such as Italy and Belgium spent over 12% of their GDP for debt servicing. Credit rating agencies and investors perceived the situation as a symptom of major financial weakness, hindering entrepreneurship.[26] Likewise, in January 2008, the credit rating agency Moody's warned that the United States was at a risk of losing its triple-A credit rating, which has been held since 1917.[27] The January 11, 2008 issue of *Financial Times* noted that "the credit crisis triggered by the growth in risky mortgage lending, which has affected banks and investors around the world, has dispelled the myth that a triple-A credit rating is a guarantee of security."

⟲ Institutional Factors

Granovetter forcefully argued that "the anonymous market of neoclassical models is virtually nonexistent in economic life and that transactions of all kinds are rife with the social connections described."[28] Note that economic factors are embedded in formal and informal institutions.[29] Thus, an examination of relevant institutional factors would shed some light on the growth of entrepreneurship in a society.

Laws, Policies, and Regulations to Promote Entrepreneurship

Countries differ significantly in their regulations related to supporting entrepreneurial development. For instance, in the early 2000s, to start a business an entrepreneur in Mozambique was required to complete nineteen procedures, which took more than 149 business days and cost $256 in fees to meet government requirements. This compared with sixteen procedures, sixty-two business days, $3,946 in Italy and two procedures, two days, $280 in Canada.[30] Likewise, to get a business license in India, it takes up to 159 days in Bhubaneshwar but 522 days in Ranchi. To register property, it takes thirty-five days in Hyderabad and 155 days in Calcutta.[31]

Some developing countries, however, have made considerable progress in establishing regulative institutions that are conducive to entrepreneurship development. The four Visegrad countries (Czech Republic, Hungary, Poland, and Slovakia) are remarkable examples of economies that have successfully promoted the growth of small and medium sized enterprises (SMEs). In the early years of transition, programs related to SME promotion got higher priority in these countries' national strategies, which led to the development of entrepreneurship in these countries.[32] The Visegrad countries have a more favorable environment for entrepreneurship compared to other economies in Eastern Europe. In Romania, for instance, starting a business is difficult and time-consuming. There are at least thirteen institutions involved in the process in the country. In 1999 Poland had about 2 million small businesses, which compared with 850,000 in Russia that year. Note that Russia's population is about four times that of Poland.

Formal institutions associated with policies and regulations in areas such as science, technology, intellectual property rights (IPR), and labor mobility are linked to a country's entrepreneurial performance.[33] In the absence of strong property rights, investment and entrepreneurship face a number of roadblocks.[34]

In many emerging economies, the rule of law is often weakly developed or sometimes ignored with impunity.[35] Most of the wealth in these economies is in the form of informal ownership outside of the formal legal system, and, hence, is not recognized or enforced in the form of legal titles.[36] Most obviously, because of ineffective legal enforcement of private property rights, entrepreneurs have to acquire political and administrative protection or depend on informal networks for security.[37] The absence of institutions to protect property rights and strong judicial system thus hinders the growth of private entrepreneurship. For instance, insecurity of property rights hindered entrepreneurship in China[38] and private entrepreneurs lacked legal protection in the country.[37]

Political Stability

External and internal conflicts in a country increase the costs and uncertainty for businesses in the country. More to the point, political instability hampers the implementation of coherent policy to foster entrepreneurship.[32] For example many foreign businesses show little interest in Africa because of political instability and corruption.[39] Analysts also argue that Russia needs to gain political stability for the faster development of entrepreneurship in the country.[40] On the other hand, the rapid growth of local entrepreneurship in China can be attributed to the country's ability to maintain political stability.[41]

Skills

One of the most important barriers to entrepreneurship in developing countries centers on poorly educated and unskilled labor force.[39] Educational programs are of particular importance to develop entrepreneurial skills in the society.[42] For instance, in the post-socialist economies, experience and training gained under the communist system contributes very little for the management and business skills needed for free market entrepreneurship.[43] This is powerfully illustrated in many Chinese entrepreneurs' lack of understanding of practical distinctions between various types of financing.[44] Likewise, "soft" concepts of management, such as marketing and consumer behavior, are not integrated into Chinese thinking,[45] which has hindered entrepreneurial development in the country. Beyond all that, many Chinese managers' cognitive framework reflects a "government takes care of everything" culture.[46]

Values and Norms

A society's cultural norms and values are tightly linked to the growth of entrepreneurship. Prior researchers have recognized that cultural norms, beliefs, and values influence attributes required for successful entrepreneurial venture, such as attitude toward risk taking and hard work.[47] These factors are also framed as normative institutions that influence the degree to which a country's citizens admire entrepreneurship.[48]

A lack of modern entrepreneurial culture and anti-entrepreneurship norms and values are identified as major problems hindering the growth of entrepreneurship in post-socialist Russia.[49] In China, entrepreneurship as an occupation was often considered for individuals not able to find other jobs (e.g., those with criminal records).[50] Likewise, accumulating a huge amount of wealth is a delicate subject in China[51] and some consider entrepreneurs as selfish or "avaricious peddlers."[52] Yet, it is also apparent that more entrepreneurship-friendly institutions are developing in China.

One important aspect of societal norms and values that makes them interesting is the fact that private businesses can take measures to change some of them. In Sweden, for instance, the think tank Timbro is working to bring a long-term shift in the "public opinion in favor of free markets, entrepreneurship, private property, and an open society."[53] Timbro is funded mostly by large Swedish corporations.

Risk-Taking Behavior

Entrepreneurial activities inherently involve risk-taking behaviors. Societies across the world vary greatly in their risk-taking behavior. In the Arab world, for instance, large corporate bureaucracies are found to be risk averse.[54] The lack of a tradition of private entrepreneurship in central and eastern European countries is also related to an underdeveloped risk-taking culture in the absence of local norms and social networks providing support for such a culture.[43] For example, Russian managers with experience in state-owned enterprises tend to avoid risk.[55] Likewise, it is suggested that Chinese tend to lack characteristics needed to be successful entrepreneurs, such as risk taking.[56,57] Consider, for example, the Chinese venture capital (VC) landscape. Most VC funds in the country are linked to the government and can be considered as a loan.[58] Enterprises that are able to obtain VC funds feel an obligation not to lose the resources. Moreover, an incubator losing the government-owned money also becomes a target of official criticism. Chinese government VC funds thus cannot accept the Western level of risk taking.[58]

Summary

This chapter provided an overview of environmental and contextual factors affecting entrepreneurial activities in an economy. We discussed how economic and institutional factors facilitate and hinder the development of entrepreneurship in an economy. The discussion focused on demand and supply factors.

An important point to keep in mind is that economic and institutional factors related to entrepreneurship are changing in emerging economies. For instance, Chinese citizens with educations and entrepreneurial experience in the industrialized world, who are more similar to managers from the Western world, are returning to China. Likewise, there has been a rapid increase in the inflow of foreign VC to China thanks mainly to dense networks of Chinese people overseas.[59] A similar point can be made about other emerging economies such as India and Russia.

Developing economies have made considerable progress on the institutional front as well. Central and eastern European transition economies, for instance, are creating institutions to promote democracy. At the same time, new social norms, values, and beliefs are evolving to support entrepreneurship in these economies.[60] For instance, about 80% of young Russians surveyed said that they have "successfully adapted to capitalism."[61] Likewise, China is arguably shifting from top-down, state-directed technology policies to more flexible, market-oriented approaches that foster innovation and entrepreneurship.[62] Cetron and Owen note that "On average, institutions are growing more transparent in their operations and more accountable for their misdeeds."[63]

We also provided some examples to demonstrate that societal and institutional factors, such as the government and associations funded by private businesses, can change most of the factors discussed in this chapter. A related point is that some factors are easier to change than others. From the national policy maker's standpoint, for example, enactment of financial legislation to develop local linkage to global capital market development of entrepreneurial skills may be easier than changing the culture of the society.

Discussion Questions

1. Among the various factors discussed above, which one do you think is the most important in facilitating and hindering the growth of entrepreneurial activities in an economy?
2. Can environmental and contextual factors be changed by the state or non-state actors?
3. Why is political stability important for the growth of new businesses?
4. Select a developing country and critically examine how various environmental and contextual factors discussed in this chapter have influenced entrepreneurship in the country.

Endnotes

1. The National Agency for Enterprise and Construction's Division for Research and Analysis International Consortium for Dynamic Benchmarking of Entrepreneurship, Denmark. 2006. Quality assessment of entrepreneurship indicators, 2(16).

2. Thornton, P. H. 1999. The sociology of entrepreneurship. *Annual Review of Sociology* 25(1):19–46.

3. Weber, M. 1904. *The Protestant Ethic and the Spirit of Capitalism.* New York: Routledge.

4. Aldrich, H., and R. Waldinger. 1990. Ethnicity and entrepreneurship. *Annual Review of Sociology* 16:111–135.

5. Shane, S., and S. Venkataraman, 2000. The promise of entrepreneurship as a field of research. *Academy of Management Review* 25(1):217–226.

6. Freeman, J. 1986. Entrepreneurs as organizational products: Semiconductor firms and venture capital firms. *Advances in the Study of Entrepreneurship, Innovation, and Economic Growth* 1:33–52.

7. Wholey, D. R., Christianson, J. B., and S. M. Sanchez. 1993. The effect of physician and corporate interests on the formation of health maintenance organizations. *American Journal of Sociology* 99(l):164–200.

8. Dobbin, F., and T. J. Dowd. 1997. How policy shapes competition: Early railroad foundings in Massachusetts. *Administrative Science Quarterly* 42:501–529.

9. White, H. C. 1981. Where do markets come from? *American Journal of Sociology* 87:517–547.

10. Shane, S. 1996. Explaining variation in rates of entrepreneurship in the United States: 1899–1988. *Journal of Management* 22(5):747–781.

11. Commission on the Private Sector & Development, United Nations Development Program. 2004. Constraints on the private sector in developing countries. In *Unleashing Entrepreneurship: Making Business Work for the Poor.* http://www.undp.org/cpsd/report/index.html#english.

12. Plastrik, P. 1991. Global competitiveness and small business. *Harvard Business Review* 69(1):174–176.

13. China's infrastructure splurge: Rushing on by road, rail and air. *The Economist* 14 February 2008.

14. Sheridan, B., and D. Gross. Here's the Good News; Forget Headlines—The World Economy Has Never Been Better. *Newsweek* 150(26): 24 December 2007.

15. Larkin, J. Snow presses India to open financial sector. *Wall Street Journal* A14: 9 November 2005.

16. Florence, E. 2006. Private equity finance as a growth engine: What it means for emerging markets. *Business Economics* 41(3):7–21.

17. Blanchflower, D. G., Oswald, A., and A. Stutzer. 2001. Latent entrepreneurship across nations. *European Economic Review* 45(4-6):680.

18. Gross, D. Poverty: Cheap loans at insanely high rates? Give us more. *Newsweek* 20 September 2008. http://www.newsweek.com/id/160074.

19. Elkhoury, M. 2008. Credit rating agencies and their potential impact on developing countries. Discussion Paper No. 186, United Nations Conference on Trade and Development. http://www.unctad.org/en/docs/osgdp20081_en.pdf.

20. Moody's Special Comment. A guide to Moody's sovereign ratings. August 2006: 1.

21. Bhatia, A. V. 2002. Sovereign credit ratings methodology: an evaluation. *IMF Working Paper* 02/170.

22. Cantor, R., and F. Packer. 1995. Sovereign credit ratings, Federal Reserve Bank of New York. *Current Issues in Economic and Finance* 1(3).

23. Cantor, R., and F. Packer. 1996. The credit ratings industry, Federal Reserve Bank of New York. *Quarterly Review.*

24. Haque, N. U., Kumar, M., Mathieson, D., and N. Mark. 1996. The economic content of indicators of developing country creditworthiness. *IMF, Staff Paper* 43(4).

25. Reisen, H., and J. Von Maltzan. 1999. Boom and bust in sovereign ratings. *OECD Technical Papers* 148. http://www.oecd.org/pdf/M00006000/M00006204.pdf.

26. Fairlamb, D. 1995. Europe confronts the inevitable. *Institutional Investor* 29(4): 85–89.

27. Moody's puts U.S. on credit watch. *Wall Street Weather* 11 January 2008. http://www.wallstreetweather.net/2008/01/moodys-puts-us-on-credit-watch.html.

28. Granovetter, M. 1985. Economic action and social structure: The problem of embeddedness. *American Journal of Sociology* 91(3):481–510.

29. Parto, S. 2005. Economic activity and institutions: Taking stock. *Journal of Economic Issues* 39:1,21–52.

30. Djankov, S., La Porta, R., Lopez-De-Silanes, F., and A. Shleifer. 2002. The regulation of entry. *Quarterly Journal of Economics* 117(1):1–37.

31. World Bank 2007. Doing Business 2008: India, Bhutan, and Sri Lanka Lead South Asia's Jump in Reform, Washington, D.C.: World Bank, http://web.worldbank.org/wbsite/external/countries/southasiaext/0,,contentMDK21487753~pagePK:146736~pipk:226340~thesitepk;223544,00.html?eid=3001

32. Forst, M. 1996. Helping small business in eastern Europe. *OECD Observer* 198:51–54.

33. Groenewegen, J., and M. van der Steen. 2006. The evolution of national innovation systems. *Journal of Economic Issues* 40(2):277–286.
34. Fukuyama, F. 1996. Against capitalism. *Foreign Affairs* 75(6):145.
35. Bratton, M. 2007. Formal versus informal institutions in Africa. *Journal Democrat* 18:96–110.
36. De Soto, H. 2003. *The Mystery of Capital: Why Capitalism Triumphs in the West and Fails Everywhere Else.* New York: Random House.
37. Yang, K. 2002. Double entrepreneurship in China's economic reform: An analytical framework. *Journal of Political & Military Sociology* 30(1):134–148.
38. Djankov, S., Qian, Y., Roland, G., and E. Zhuravskaya. 2006. Who are China's entrepreneurs? *American Economic Review* 96(2):348–352.
39. Aworuwa, O. E. 2004. A bootstrap model for microenterprise development of a distressed community. *Journal of Third World Studies* 21(1):79–96.
40. Matthews, C. H., Qin, X., and G. M. Franklin. 1996. Stepping toward prosperity: The development of entrepreneurial ventures in China and Russia. *Journal of Small Business Management* 34(3):75–85.
41. Cardos, E., Yusuf, S., and A. Challenge. 1994. Red capitalism: Growth and inflation in China 37(3):49–56.
42. Florence, E. 2006. Private equity finance as a growth engine: What it means for emerging markets. *Business Economics* 41(3):7–21.
43. Warner, M., and C. W. Daugherty. 2004. Promoting the 'civic' in entrepreneurship: The case of rural Slovakia. *Journal of the Community Development Society* 35(1):117–134.
44. Kambil, A., Long, V. W., and C. Kwan. 2006. The seven disciplines for venturing in China. *MIT Sloan Management Review* 47(2):85.
45. Borgonjon, J., and W. R. Vanhonacker. 1992. Modernizing China's managers. *The China Business Review* 19(5):12–17.
46. Lynch, D. J. 2005. China's management pool is shallow. *USA Today*:1B
47. Weber, M. 1930. *The Protestant Ethic and the Spirit of Capitalism.* New York: The Citadel Press.
48. Busenitz, L. W., Gomez, C., and J. W. Spencer. 2000. Country institutional profiles: Unlocking entrepreneurial phenomena. *Academy of Management Journal* 43(5):994–1003.
49. Seawright, K. W., Mitchell, R. K., and J. B. Smith. 2008. Comparative entrepreneurial cognitions and lagging Russian new venture formation: A tale of two countries. *Journal of Small Business Management* 46(4):512–535.
50. Nair, S. R. 1996. Doing business in China: It's far from easy. *USA Today* 124(2608):27–29.
51. R. Flannery, 2006. China's 40 Richest, November 13, *Forbes*, http://www.forbes.com/global/2006/1113/067.html
52. Hsu, C. 2006. Cadres, Getihu, and good business-people: Making sense of entrepreneurs in early post-socialist China. *Urban Anthropology & Studies of Cultural Systems & World Economic Development* 35(1):1–38.
53. Lehrer, E., and J. Hildreth. 2002. Scandinavia's surprising turn from socialism. *The American Enterprise* 13(8):42–44.
54. Graham, E. M., Lewis, J. A., De Marino, D. N., and W. A. Reinsch. 2006. How can the U.S. reopen for business to the Arab world? *Middle East Policy* 13(2):71–89.
55. Taylor, T. C., and A. Y. Kazakov. 1997. Business ethics and civil society in Russia. *International Study of Management of Organization* 27:5–18.
56. Holt, D. G. 1997. A comparative study of balues among Chinese and U.S. entrepreneurs: Pragmatic convergence between contrasting cultures. *Journal of Business Venturing* 12(6).
57. Anderson, A. R., Li, J. H., Harrison, R. T., and P. J. A. Robson. 2003. The increasing role of small business in the Chinese economy. *Journal of Small Business Management* 41(3):310.
58. Harwit, E. 2002. High-technology incubators: Fuel for China's new entrepreneurship? *China Business Review* 29(4):26–29.
59. United Nations Development Program. 2001. *Human Development Report.* http://www.undp.org/hdr2001/completenew.pdf.
60. Roland, G. 2002. The political economy of transition. *The Journal of Economic Perspectives* 16(1):29–40.
61. Nikitina, O. 2004. Changing times, changing attitudes: What do Russians really think about the transition to capitalism? *RussProfile* 1(4):26–27.
62. Segal, A. 2004. Is America losing its edge? *Foreign Affairs* 83(6):2.
63. Cetron, M. J., and O. Davies. 2005. Trends shaping tomorrow's world. *Futurist* 42(3):35–50.

Chapter Three

GLOBAL ENTREPRENEURSHIP STRATEGY

John A. Parnell
University of North Carolina, Pembroke, North Carolina

Learning Objectives

Upon completion of this chapter, students should be able to:

- Understand and explain the theoretical underpinnings of global entrepreneurial strategy.
- Understand how changes in the global landscape and created opportunities for global entrepreneurship.
- Understand how the global landscape influences the mission of entrepreneurial enterprises.
- Understand the nature of corporate-level and business-level entrepreneurial strategy formulation at the global level.
- Understand the challenges associated with strategy execution and control—including crisis management—within the context of global entrepreneurship.

Key Terms

contingency theory

crisis management

economies of (global) scope

General Agreement on Tariffs and Trade (GATT)

industrial organization (IO)

outsourcing

resource-based view (RBV)

self-reference criterion

strategic control

World Trade Organization (WTO)

With recent moves toward democratization throughout the world during the last two decades, global entrepreneurial strategy is more important than ever before. Entrepreneurial opportunities occur when new products or services can satisfy the needs of a particular market. In its simplest form, entrepreneurship involves identifying these opportunities and mobilizing to pursue them. The prevalence of such opportunities outside of a firm's host country is more prevalent today than ever.[1,2]

The process of entrepreneurship is often associated with small business activity. It also occurs within large firms as corporate entrepreneurship, or intrapreneurship. Successful entrepreneurship in any size organization requires both intellectual capital and an innovative mindset.[3] While it can be difficult to develop the latter in large firms, the existence of intellectual capital in many large firms can serve as a key advantage for them relative to their smaller counterparts, especially in global environments. Hence, entrepreneurial activity is a salient issue for all firms, regardless of size.

The international environment offers a number of applications to strategic management in entrepreneurial firms.[4–6] Historically, the reasons for moving toward globalization are clear. The majority of the world's technological advances are no longer introduced in the United States. Many of these developments come from developed nations such as Japan and countries within the European Economic Union. Further, this growth has extended to developing nations that now account for approximately one-half of the world's output.

Strategic planning, however, is much more complex in global environments for several reasons. The external environment—including political and economic instabilities—can vary substantially from one nation to another. Competition can be intense and control of the enterprise quite difficult when operations are geographically dispersed.

Culture is a key consideration and has been posited as one of the key determinants of differences in the level of entrepreneurial activity across nations.[7] Nonetheless, clear and linear links between cultural attributes and entrepreneurial activity are often difficult to identify. For example, countries whose firms are more likely to be entrepreneurial tend to have moderately high levels of individualism. However, extremely high individualism can actually hinder the development of teamwork, a key ingredient in the entrepreneurship process.[8] Hence, clear and simple rules and relationships seem elusive.

Following a commentary of theoretical perspectives, the remainder of this chapter examines how globalization affects each broad step of the strategic management process within entrepreneurial firms: (1) analysis of the external environment, (2) analysis of the internal environment, (3) strategy formulation, and (4) strategy execution and strategic control. Business activity occurring outside of a firm's host country can be viewed as a continuum from international (the most limited) to multinational to global (the most aggressive). These options are discussed in greater detail later within the strategy formulation section.

Theoretical Perspectives on Entrepreneurial Strategy

The theoretical and philosophical underpinnings of entrepreneurship differ somewhat from those of strategic management within less entrepreneurial, mature firms.[9,10] Specifically, three theoretical perspectives warrant discussion. First, *industrial organization* (IO), a branch of microeconomics, emphasizes the *influence of the industry environment* on the firm. The central tenet of industrial organization theory is the notion that a firm must adapt to influences in its industry to survive and prosper; thus, its financial performance is primarily determined by the success of the industry in which it competes. Industries with favorable structures offer the greatest opportunity for firm profitability.[11] Following this perspective, it is more important for a firm to choose the correct industry within which to compete than to determine *how* to compete with a given industry.[12]

IO assumes that an organization's performance and ultimate survival depend on its ability to *adapt* to industry forces over which it has little or no control rather than to *create* change. According to IO, strategic managers should seek to understand the structure of the industry and formulate strategies that feed off the industry's characteristics.[13,14] Because IO focuses on industry forces, strategies, resources, and competencies are assumed to be fairly similar among competitors within a given industry. If one firm deviates from the industry norm and implements a new, successful strategy, other firms will rapidly mimic the higher performing firm by purchasing the resources, competencies, or management talent that have made the leading firm so profitable. Hence, the IO perspective is more prominent in the strategic management of large firms operating in mature industries.[15,16]

Perhaps the opposite of the IO perspective, the *resource-based view* (RBV) sees performance primarily as a function of a firm's ability to utilize its resources. Although environmental opportunities and threats are important, a firm's unique resources comprise the key variables that allow it to develop a distinctive competence, enabling the firm to distinguish itself from its rivals and create competitive advantage. Resources include all of a firm's tangible and intangible assets, such as capital, equipment, employees, knowledge, and information.[17] An organization's resources are directly linked to its capabilities, which can create value and ultimately lead to profitability for the firm. Hence, resource-based theory focuses primarily on individual firms rather than on the competitive environment, a perspective consistent with the notion of new venture creation and innovation within entrepreneurial firms.

Contingency theory represents a third theoretical perspective. According to this approach, the most profitable firms are likely to be those that "fit" with their environments. In other words, a strategy is most likely to be successful when it is consistent with the organization's mission, competitive environment, and resources. Contingency theory assumes that an established firm can increase or decrease entrepreneurial activity over time in order to adjust to the characteristics of its environment. Firms can become proactive by choosing to operate in environments where opportunities and threats match the firms' strengths and weaknesses.[18] Should the industry environment change in a way that is unfavorable to the firm, its top managers should consider leaving that industry and reallocating its resources to other, more favorable industries. From the contingency perspective, entrepreneurs should seek to fill market gaps when their strengths and resource base enable them to do so effectively.

Within the strategic management of mature organizations, each of these three perspectives may contribute somewhat equally to the overall strategic orientation of the firm. In contrast, the resource-based and contingency views tend to be dominant in entrepreneurial firms bent on innovation and creativity. Entrepreneurial firms, be they small or large, tend to emphasize the firm's unique combination of resources and capabilities in an effort to create change in the environment or align the organization with existing external trends.

External Environment

The first step of the strategic management process, analysis of the external environment, includes a look at a firm's industry structure as well as the macroenvironmental (i.e., political, legal, social, economic, and technological) forces that affect its operations. External analysis creates the context for business activities. The issue of protectionism and free trade is a central concern in the global environment and creates a context for thinking about global entrepreneurship, as shifts toward greater free trade can create a number of business opportunities for entrepreneurial firms.[19,20]

At the global level, the period from World War II to the late 1980s was marked by increased trade protection. Many countries protected their industries by imposing tariffs, import duties, and other restrictions. Import duties in many Latin American countries ranged from less than 40% to more than 100%.[21] However, this trend was not limited to developing nations. Countries in Europe and Asia—and even the United States—have imposed import fees on a variety of products, including food, steel, and cars. In the 1980s, the United States also convinced Japanese manufacturers to voluntarily restrict exports of cars to the United States in lieu of a tariff. Interestingly, this particular tariff may be largely responsible for Japanese automobile manufacturers establishing a large number of production facilities in the United States.

During this time, however, many nations desired to eliminate trade barriers. In 1947, twenty-three countries entered into the cooperative *General Agreement on Tariffs and Trade* (GATT). Expanding to over 110 nations over several decades, GATT has assisted in relaxing quota and import license requirements, introducing fairer customs evaluation methods, and establishing a common mechanism to resolve trade disputes.

As momentum for GATT grew, a major shift in U.S. policy occurred in the late 1970s and the 1980s in favor of deregulation, eliminating a number of legal constraints in such industries as airlines, trucking, and banking, but not all industries were deregulated. By 1990, a reversal of trade protectionism and strong governmental influence in business operations began to take place. In the United

States, new economic policies reduced governmental influence in business operations by deregulating certain industries, lowering corporate taxes, and relaxing rules against mergers and acquisitions. This trend has continued into the twenty-first century, although not as forceful as in the late 1990s.

A GATT agreement led to the formation of the *World Trade Organization* (WTO), an international body designed to supervise and liberalize global trade. Launched in 1995, the WTO has over 150 nation members representing an estimated 95% of world trade. WTO agreements attempt to forge common ground in trading requirements across nations.

The move toward free trade has also been seen in Europe, where a number of nations banded together to develop a trade-free European Community. Today, Europe is fast becoming a single market of 350 million consumers. The European Union (EU) represents the largest trading bloc on earth, accounting for more than 40% of the world's gross domestic product (GDP).[22] Meanwhile, the United States, Canada, and Mexico established the North American Free Trade Agreement (NAFTA) to create its own strategic trading bloc. A number of analysts believe that world business will eventually be divided into several such blocs, each providing preferred trading status to other nations within the bloc.

This trend toward less regulation has even extended to the former communist countries. As new governments formed in the former Soviet bloc nations of Eastern Europe, such as Poland, Czechoslovakia, and Hungary, they began to open markets and to invite foreign investment.[23] In addition, China officially remains a communist nation, but its economic development policies have taken a distinctively free market approach since the late 1990s.

Trade restrictions have always existed in market economies to some extent, especially in politically sensitive areas. For example, the United States and other Western countries have banned the export of advanced technology in certain circumstances. The United States prohibits the export of certain electronic, nuclear, and defense-related products to many countries, particularly those believed to be involved in international terrorism. Many of these restrictions were revised and strengthened following the terrorist attacks of September 11, 2001.[24]

Nonetheless, the notion of globalization has gained steam in recent years. The *New York Times* foreign affairs correspondent Thomas Friedman's 2005 bestseller presented his spin on this phenomenon. In *The World is Flat*, Friedman argued that the period of American world economic domination has ended because changes during the last two decades have leveled or "flattened" the economic playing field for those in other countries, most notably India and China.[25]

The dot-com boom and subsequent bust around the turn of the century contributed significantly to the emergence of Friedman's "flat world." During the bubble, telecommunications companies were replete with cash and invested hundreds of millions of dollars to lay fiberoptic cables across the ocean floors, cables that currently and inexpensively connect countries like India and China to the United States. The dot-com bust resulted in significant stock market losses, forcing companies to cut spending wherever possible. Hence, many turned to opportunities for cost-cutting created by the fiberoptic cables and began to offshore jobs as a means of addressing a new economic reality. As Indian entrepreneur Jerry Rao explained, any work that can be digitized and moved from one location to another will be moved. Indeed, approximately half a million U.S. Internal Revenue Service (IRS) tax returns are actually completed by accountants in India each year.[25]

The notion of a level economic playing field creates a number of challenges for Western firms and societies, one of which is the debate over free trade. Supporters contend that a flatter world is here to stay and that efforts to thwart it will only stifle growth in economic powers like the United States, an argument Friedman echoes. Proponents charge that the unbridled global trade drives down wages and will ultimately result in a reduced standard of living in developed nations.

Nonetheless, the flat world has created a plethora of global business opportunities for entrepreneurial firms in both developed and emerging nations. The issue of free trade and protectionism aside, operating outside of one's host country can enable a firm to access key resources, develop economies of scale, and lower production costs. It can also create opportunities for mutually beneficial partnerships. The host country's government may even offer tax and investment incentives.

There remains significant opposition to Friedman's flat world, however. For example, *outsourcing*—contracting out a firm's non-core, non-revenue-producing activities to other organizations primarily (but not always) to reduce costs—has become more widespread in the United States in recent years. Many consumers and activists have become increasingly concerned about trade deficits with other nations and job losses that occur when a firm moves a production facility abroad or a retailer stocks its shelves with imported products.[26] A number of American firms have closed production facilities in the United States and opened new ones in Mexico, China, India, and other countries where labor costs are substantially lower and regulations are less inhibitive.[27-30] When implemented properly, outsourcing can cut costs, improve performance, and refocus the core business.

These opportunities notwithstanding, there are many threats associated with international activities.[31] A firm may face trade barriers, cumbersome regulations, or a learning curve when it comes to serving customers abroad. There may also be a backlash if the unpopular political actions of a firm's host country are generalized to the firm.

Internal Environment

The mission of an entrepreneurial organization—the reason for its existence—may be closely connected to its international operations in several ways. For instance, a firm operating in one country may need inputs from firms in other nations. Virtually all of Japan's industries would grind to a halt if imports of raw materials from other nations ceased, since Japan is a small island nation and its natural resources are quite limited.

A firm's mission and its international operations are also connected through the economic concept of comparative advantage, the idea that certain products may be produced more cheaply or at a higher quality in particular countries due to advantages in labor costs or technology. Chinese manufacturers, for example, enjoy some of the lowest global labor rates for unskilled or semi-skilled production. As skills rise among Chinese workers, however, some companies have succeeded in extending this comparative advantage to a number of technical skill areas as well. The annual salary for a successful engineer in China was less than $20,000 in 2002, a level well below those in more developed parts of the world.[32]

For global entrepreneurs, involvement outside of a firm's host country may also provide advantages not directly related to costs. For political reasons, it is often necessary for a firm to establish operations in another country, especially if its products are widely distributed there. Doing so can also provide other advantages, however, such as gaining expertise about local market conditions. For example, Ford operates a number of plants in Western Europe, where manufacturing has helped its engineers design windshield wipers for cars engaged in high-speed driving on the German autobahns.[33]

Strategy Formulation: Issues at the Corporate Level

Deciding to pursue international opportunities is a strategic decision generally made at the corporate level. In a small firm, this level is not easily distinguished from the business, or competitive, level of the firm. In a large firm, however, the corporate level may be somewhat removed from the business level, potentially stifling international entrepreneurial activity. If a firm is involved beyond its domestic borders, it may compete abroad at one of three levels: international, multinational, or global. A number of small, entrepreneurial firms operate successfully at the international level, whereas their larger counterparts often pursue a multinational or global approach. Effective operations at any of these levels often—but not always—necessitates economies of scale and a relatively high market share.[34]

International Orientation

The first option is the most conservative of the three. Some entrepreneurial companies choose to be involved on an international basis by operating in various countries, but limiting their involvement to importing, exporting, licensing, or global partnerships with other firms. Exporting alone can significantly benefit even a small company. However, international joint ventures among firms may be desirable even when resources for a direct investment are available. For example, in 2001, General Motors (GM) launched a $333 million joint venture with Russian firm OAO Avtovaz. GM provides technological support to the struggling holdover from Soviet-era industry to engineer a stripped-down version of an SUV currently offered by the Avtovaz. The vehicle will be offered for about $7,500. By engaging in the joint venture, GM gains immediate access to the market, but places its reputation on the line by putting its "Chevy" name on a product produced by a technologically weak automobile producer.[35] This move can be considered entrepreneurial (or intrapreneurial) for both GM and its Russian partner.

Although firms with global objectives may choose to invest directly in facilities abroad, there are a number of reasons why global strategic alliances may be more attractive, especially among small entrepreneurial firms. However, due to the complexities associated with establishing operations across borders strategic, alliances may be particularly attractive to firms seeking to expand their global involvement. Companies often possess market, regulatory, and other knowledge about their domestic markets, but may need to partner with companies abroad to gain access to this knowledge as it pertains to international markets.

International strategic alliances can also provide entry into a global market, access to the partner's knowledge about the foreign market, and risk sharing with the partner firm. They can work effectively when partners can learn from each other, when neither partner is large enough to function alone, and both partners share common strategic goals but are not in direct competition.

A number of problems can arise from international joint ventures, however. These challenges include the potential for disputes and lack of trust over proprietary knowledge, cultural differences between the partnering firms, and disputes over how to share the costs and revenues associated with the partnership.

Other conservative options are also available to a firm seeking an international presence. Under an international licensing agreement, a foreign licensee purchases the rights to produce a company's products and/or use its technology in the licensee's country. This arrangement is common in the pharmaceutical industry, where drug producers in one nation typically allow producers in other nations to produce and market their products abroad.[36,37] However, licensing tends to be best in large firms with combinations of strategic activities, as well as firms with standardized products in narrowly defined market niches.

In contrast to international licensing, international franchising is a longer term arrangement whereby a local franchisee pays a franchiser in another country for the right to use the franchiser's brand names, promotion, materials, and procedures.[38] Whereas licensing tends to be pursued primarily by manufacturers, franchising is more commonly employed in service industries, such as fast-food restaurants. Led by companies such as Burger King, KFC, Avis, and Coca-Cola, American firms now franchise to over 50,000 local entrepreneurs abroad.

Multinational Orientation

The second option, involvement at the multinational level, is more aggressive than the first. Under this approach, a firm pursues direct investments in other countries, and their subsidiaries operate independently of one another. For example, Colgate-Palmolive has attained a large worldwide market share through its decentralized operations in a number of foreign markets.

In some respects, the multinational orientation represents a transition structure as a firm moves from minimal international involvement to a global orientation. For some firms, however, it provides a fixed strategic position, offering the advantage of greater strategic control.

Global Orientation

The third option, global involvement, is the most aggressive of the three. Globally involved firms pursue direct investments and interdependent subdivisions abroad. Effectively, global firms approach the international marketplace with relatively standardized products.

A global orientation is often associated with established, mature firms. For example, some of Caterpillar's subsidiaries produce components in different countries, while other subsidiaries assemble these components, and still other units sell the finished products. As a result, Caterpillar has achieved a low-cost position by producing its own heavy components for its large global market. If its various subsidiaries operated independently and only produced for their individual regional markets, Caterpillar would be unable to realize these vast economies of scale.[39]

Selecting the Proper Orientation

Firms shift from a domestic mindset to a global mindset for numerous reasons. Pursuing global markets can reduce per-unit production costs by increasing volume. A global strategy can extend the product life cycle of products whose domestic markets may be declining, as U.S. cigarette manufacturers did in the 1990s. Establishing facilities abroad can also help a firm benefit from comparative advantage, the difference in resources among nations that provide cost advantages for the production of some but not all goods in a given country. For example, athletic shoes tend to be produced most efficiently in parts of Asia where rubber is plentiful and labor is less costly. A global orientation can also lessen risk because demand and competitive factors tend to vary among nations. There are a number of factors to consider, including the similarity of customer needs abroad to those in the firm's domestic market, differences in production and distribution costs, and regulatory and tariff concerns.

A global orientation brings about three key advantages for firms adopting a global perspective, the first of which centers around economic concerns. The multinational corporation (MNC)—contrasted with a firm operating only in domestic markets—can increase production levels, thereby fostering standardization and economies of scale.[40,41] When a firm produces more, it may also enjoy greater efficiencies in marketing and distribution, a phenomenon known as *economies of (global) scope.* The importance of scope economies relative to scale economies has increased in recent years.[42]

The second advantage of globalization is related to cultural change. Global media and the pervasiveness of the Internet have created a global consumer culture, one where distinct localized preferences for particular goods and services have been replaced by higher quality and cheaper offerings bearing global brands.[43] This shift has enabled firms to address the needs of customers in different markets with common products, services, and marketing approaches. Because consumers are more familiar with the products and services available in other countries, they are likely to be more open to uniform offerings, as opposed to those tailored to the specific needs of a given locale.

Third, a globalization perspective can also foster growth outside of a firm's host country. Given the intense competition in most markets in the developed world, organizations seeking to grow must remain abreast of opportunities that may exist, especially in emerging economies. "Thinking global" enables a firm to seek out, recognize, and pursue such opportunities with greater effectiveness.[44,45]

Whether a firm should pursue international involvement and if so to what extent depends on a number of factors.[46] The following questions may shed light on the appropriateness of a global approach for a firm:

1. Are customer needs abroad similar to those in the firm's domestic market? If so, it may be possible for the firm to develop economies of scale (discussed in greater detail in a future chapter) by producing a higher volume of the same good or service for both markets.
2. Are differences in transportation and other costs abroad favorable and conducive to producing goods and services abroad? Are these differences favorable and conducive to exporting or importing goods from one country to another?
3. Are the firm's customers or partners already involved in global business? If so, it may be necessary for the firm to become equally involved.
4. Will it be difficult to distribute goods and services abroad? If competitors already control distribution channels in another country, expansion into that country will be difficult.
5. Will government trade policies facilitate or hinder global expansion? For example, NAFTA facilitates trade among firms in the United States, Canada, and Mexico. Similar trading blocks, such as the EU, occur in other parts of the world.
6. Will managers in one country be able to learn from managers in other countries? If so, it is possible that global expansion can improve efficiency and effectiveness, both abroad and in the host country.

◎ Strategy Formulation: Issues at the Business Level

Innovation—the process of transforming an invention into a commercially viable product or service—is central to the development of competitive strategy in the entrepreneurial firm. Opportunities for innovation are prevalent in the international arena. However, developing a competitive strategy for a business operating in global markets can be a complex task.[47,48]

There is no simple formula for developing and implementing successful business strategies across national borders. Broadly speaking, there are two basic approaches to global strategy orientation, the first of which is associated with the common advice "think globally, act locally." Following this logic, a business organization would emphasize the synergy created by serving multiple markets globally, but formulate a distinct competitive strategy for each specific market that is tailored to its unique situation. Others argue that an alternative approach—consistency across global markets—is critical, citing examples such as Coca-Cola, whose emphasis on quality, brand recognition, and a small world theme has been successful in a number of global markets. These two approaches represent distinct perspectives on what it takes to be successful in foreign markets.

The first approach, localization (i.e., acting local), implies that a firm gives its primary attention to issues at the local level. For a domestic firm, this simply means that its managers are concerned only with domestic issues and do not actively entertain activities outside of the host country. Indeed, globalization may not be appropriate for every firm. Demand for the firm's products or services may not be sufficient to justify global expansion. Rivals in other countries may already be serving the relevant markets effectively in those locales. Channel complexities abroad may necessitate packaging, manufacturing, or distribution changes that are too costly for the firm. Even differences in the availability of ingredients or preferences for styles or flavors associated with the firm can create roadblocks.[49] Hence, "acting local" is all that is required for organizations whose strategies suggest that managers "think local." For a firm operating across borders, localization suggests that strategies reflect a strong effort to tailor firm activities to the specific needs of each location.

In contrast, a firm can "act global" by adopting a global perspective on strategy. A number of scholars and practitioners have argued for such an approach. Levitt, Ohmae, and others have long contended that international firms can only survive if they develop global strategies that reflect the growing similarities across disparate markets.[50,51] Such firms typically have direct investments and interdependent subdivisions abroad. For example, some of Caterpillar's subsidiaries produce components in different countries, while other subsidiaries assemble these components, and still other units sell the finished products. As a result, Caterpillar has achieved a low-cost position by producing its own heavy components for its large global market. If its various subsidiaries operated independently and produced only for their individual regional markets, Caterpillar would be unable to realize these vast economies of scale and enjoy the benefits of a global strategy.

A localization strategy also has its challenges. Tailoring a business strategy to meet the unique demands of a different market requires that top managers understand the similarities and differences between the markets from both industry and cultural perspectives.[52-55] This can be difficult, as a revisit to China as an example illustrates. When a Western firm seeks to conduct business with one of its Chinese counterparts, managers from both firms must recognize the cultural differences between the two nations. Recently, a number of consulting and management development organizations in both China and the West have been busy training managers to become aware of such differences and take action to minimize misunderstandings that can arise from them. For example, Chinese managers are more likely than Americans to smoke during meetings and less likely to answer e-mail from international partners. In the United States, it is more common to emphasize subordinate contributions to solving problems, whereas Chinese managers are more likely to respect the judgment of their superiors without subordinate involvement.[56]

Consider Coca-Cola's global approach to marketing the popular soft drink, one that has been relatively consistent across borders. Some product differences exist, however, due to availability and cost factors. In Mexico, for example, Coke contains readily available cane sugar. In the United States, where customers are not believed to perceive a major difference in sweeteners, Coke changed to high-fructose corn syrup, a less expensive alternative.[57]

Compared to Coca-Cola, Yum Brands takes a more localized approach with its KFC business unit. KFC emphasizes chicken in its host country—the United States—but added fish sandwiches to menus at its Malaysian outlets in early 2006. According to KFC Holdings (Malaysia) executive director and chief operating officer To Chun Wah, "As much as our customers love our chicken products, they also want a greater variety of meat products at KFC. Our market surveys show that our customers want more than just tasty, high quality, and affordable chicken but are also constantly on the lookout for new and interesting things to eat." This move reflects a clear move to "localize" business strategies along the lines of taste. Outlets in Malaysia are not required to carry the fish sandwich if they prefer not to, however. Fish sandwiches had already proven to be successful in other Asian markets, such as Beijing, Shanghai, and Taipei.[58,59]

Yum Brands took localization another step further in 2004 when it launched East Dawning, a bright, clean fast-food restaurant in Shanghai. East Dawning operates like Yum's KFC restaurants except that its menu and décor are Chinese. Menu offerings include Chinese favorites such as noodles, rice, soy milk, fried dough, and plum juice. Yum hopes to turn East Dawning into China's largest fast-food restaurant one day. Yum is also considering launching an Indian fast-food restaurant in India.[60]

Tailoring a business strategy to meet the unique demands of a different market requires that top managers understand the similarities and differences between the markets from both industry and cultural perspectives. For example, since the 1970s, Japanese automobile manufacturers have sought to blend a distinctively Japanese approach with a concern for North American and European values. Honda, the first Japanese manufacturer to operate a facility in the United States, has been successful in this regard. In 2000, Mitsubishi aggressively redesigned the Montero Sport to make it a "global vehicle" that could sell effectively in world markets. In 2001, however, the carmaker dropped its "one size fits all" approach and began to emphasize design factors unique to the critical American market.[61]

Given the intense competition in most markets in the developed world, strategic managers in many entrepreneurial firms attempt to remain abreast of opportunities that exist in emerging markets. While emerging economies such as China, Brazil, South Africa, Mexico, and parts of Eastern Europe are attractive in many respects, poor infrastructure (e.g., telecommunications, highways, etc.), cumbersome government regulations, and/or a poorly trained workforce can create great challenges for the firm considering expansion. The advantages notwithstanding, growth through global expansion should be considered carefully before pursuing expansion into any emerging market.

China, for example, boasts the world's largest population and has been tabbed as a world economic leader within the next few decades. Its entrance into the WTO, declining import tariffs, and increasing consumer incomes suggest a bright future for the nation. At present, China remains a mix of the traditional lifestyle based in socialism and its own form of a neo-Western economic development. Nowhere is this friction seen best than on the roads of Beijing, where crowds of bicycles and pedestrians attempt to negotiate traffic with buses and a rapidly increasing number of personal automobiles. American-style traffic reports have even become pervasive in a country where the world's largest automakers are fighting for a stake in what seems to have become a consumer automobile growth phase of mammoth proportions.[62,63]

Western manufacturers such as Eastman Kodak, Procter & Gamble, Group Danone of France, and Siemens AG of Germany have already established a strong presence in China. A number of Western restaurants and retailers have also begun to expand aggressively into China, including U.S.-based McDonald's, Popeye's Chicken, and Wal-Mart. As the CEO of Yum, owner of KFC, Pizza Hut, and Taco Bell, put it: "China is an absolute gold mine for us."[64] French-based Carrefour has been one of the most successful with thirty locations by 2003. Product mixes in the Chinese stores tend to be similar to those in the domestic market, with adjustments made for local preferences.[65,66]

⊙ Strategy Execution and Strategic Control

A number of execution issues are critical to the success of firms pursuing global entrepreneurial opportunities. Culture is a key concern in strategy implementation in any organization, but takes on additional importance within entrepreneurial enterprises. Cultural differences generally represent a major consideration for firms operating abroad, especially in strategy implementation efforts. In many respects, an organization's culture can be viewed as a subset of the national culture. Operating outside one's own country must overcome obstacles in areas such as leadership and maintaining a strong organizational culture. For example, leaders of some nations resist innovation and radical new approaches to conducting business, whereas others welcome such change. Such national tendencies often become a part of the culture of the organization in those countries.[67]

The *self-reference criterion* also presents a potential problem. Managers often believe that the leadership styles and organizational culture that work in their home country should work elsewhere. However, like each nation, each organization has its own unique culture, traditions, values, and beliefs. Hence, organizational values and norms must be tailored to fit the unique culture of each country in which the organization operates, at least to some extent. This can create special challenges when firms from different countries become partners or even merge their organizations.

Strategic control, an extension of the execution process, consists of determining the extent to which the organization's strategies are successful in attaining its goals and objectives. Within strategic control efforts, adjustments to the strategy are made as necessary.[68] The need for strategic control is brought about by two key factors, the first of which is the need to know how well the firm is performing. Without strategic control, there are no clear benchmarks and ultimately no reliable measurements of how the company is doing.

A second key factor supporting the need for strategic control is organizational and environmental uncertainty. Because strategic managers are not always able to accurately forecast the future, strategic control serves as a means of accounting for last-minute changes during the implementation process. The notion of strategic control has recently added a "continuous improvement" dimension, whereby strategic managers seek to improve the efficiency and effectiveness of all factors related to the strategy. This is particularly important within the realm of global entrepreneurship where uncertainty is high and constant strategic change is often required.

One key strategic control consideration is that of crisis planning. Indeed, any organization can be faced with a *crisis*, any substantial disruption in operations that physically affects an organization, its basic assumptions, or its core activities.[69] Such crises can include any low-probability, high-impact event that threatens the livelihood of the organization. Crises are typically characterized by ambiguity of cause, effect, and means of resolution and a belief that the organization must respond quickly.[70] *Crisis management* refers to the process of planning for and implementing the response to a wide range of negative events that could severely affect an organization. Some potential crisis events are more likely than others in certain types of firms. Airlines, for example, may focus crisis preparations on prospective events such as spikes in fuel prices and hijackings, whereas a small hardware store may plan for events such as the abrupt loss of a key employee or a natural disaster. The nature of the global environment, including economic and political instabilities, suggests that crisis planning should be a key concern of global entrepreneurs. Simply stated, entrepreneurial firms can and should prepare for the ones they are most likely to face.

Summary

Global opportunities abound for entrepreneurial organizations. However, the turbulence, rapid pace of change, and often unpredictability of the global environment can create roadblocks for many firms. Executives in entrepreneurial enterprises, small and large, should take special care to understand the intricacies of the international arena before formulating its corporate and business strategies. Those who do can greatly improve the prospects for their firms' success in the global arena.

Global strategy formulation can be challenging for entrepreneurs. For example, the common advice to "think globally, act locally" has merit, but not all successful firms in global markets have followed this approach. Entrepreneurs should understand both their own resources and the intricacies of their global markets before crafting a strategy.

Discussion Questions

1. What can entrepreneurs and prospective entrepreneurs learn from the resource-based view (RBV)?
2. How have global economic changes in the last two decades created opportunities for entrepreneurs?

3. What is the thesis of Thomas Friedman's bestseller *The World is Flat?* What is the link between the flat world and global entrepreneurship?
4. Should global entrepreneurs follow the "think global, act local" advice? Why or why not?
5. How can the self-reference criterion create a challenge for global entrepreneurs? What can be done to overcome this challenge?

Endnotes

1. Kuratko, D. F. 2007. Entrepreneurial leadership in the 21st century. *Journal of Leadership & Organizational* Studies 13(4):1–11.
2. Hessels, J., van Gelderen, M., and R. Thurik. 2008. Entrepreneurial aspirations, motivations, and their drivers. *Small Business Economics* 31(3):323–339.
3. Koellinger, P. 2008. Why are some entrepreneurs more innovative than others? *Small Business Economics* 31(1):21–37.
4. Barringer, B. R., and A. C. Bluedorn. 1999. The relationship between entrepreneurship and strategic management. *Strategic Management Journal* 20:421–444.
5. Hitt, M. A., Nixon, R. D., Hoskisson, R. E., and R. Kochlar. 1999. Corporate entrepreneurship and cross-functional fertilization: activation, process, and disintegration or a new product design team. *Entrepreneurship Theory and Practice* 23(3):145–167.
6. Shane, S., and S. Venkatraman. 2000. The promise of entrepreneurship as a field of research. *Academy of Management Review* 25:217–226.
7. Parnell, J. A., and T. Hatem. 1999. Cultural antecedents of behavioral differences between American and Egyptian Managers. *Journal of Management Studies* 36:399–418.
8. Morris, M. H., Davis, D. L., and J. W. Allen. 1994. Fostering corporate entrepreneurship: cross-cultural comparisons of the importance of individualism versus collectivism. *Journal of International Business Studies* 25:65–89.
9. Parnell, J. A. 2006. Generic strategies after two decades: a reconceptualization of competitive strategy. *Management Decision* 44:1139–1154.
10. Parnell, J. A., and D. L. Lester. 2007. Reevaluating the entrepreneurship-management conundrum: challenges and solutions. *Journal of Applied Management and Entrepreneurship.* 2007;12(4):74–88.
11. Porter, M. E. 1981. The contributions of industrial organization to strategic management. *Academy of Management Review* 6:609–620.
12. Hawawini, G., Subramanian, V., and P. Verdin. 2002. Is performance driven by industry- or firm-specific factors? A new look at the evidence. *Strategic Management Journal* 24:1–16.
13. Bain, J. S. 1968. *Industrial Organization.* New York: Wiley.
14. Scherer, F. M., and D. Ross. 1990. *Industrial Market Structure and Economic Performance.* Boston, MA: Houghton-Mifflin.
15. Seth, A., and H. Thomas. 1994. Theories of the firm: implications for strategy research. *Journal of Management Studies* 31:165–191.
16. Barney, J. B. 1986. Strategic factor markets expectations, luck, and business strategy. *Management Science* 42:1231–1241.
17. Barney, J. B. 1995. Looking inside for competitive advantage. *Academy of Management Executive* 19:49–61.
18. Zajac, E. J., Kraatz, M. S., and R. K. F. Bresser. 2000. Modeling the dynamics of strategic fit: a normative approach to strategic change. *Strategic Management Journal* 21:429–453.
19. Bjornskov, C., and N. J. Foss. 2008. Economic freedom and entrepreneurial activity: some cross-country evidence. *Public Choice* 134(3–4):307–328.
20. McMullen, J. S., Bagby, D. R., and L. E. Palich. 2008. Economic freedom and the motivation to engage in entrepreneurial action. *Entrepreneurship Theory and Practice* 32(5):875–895.
21. International Monetary Fund. 1989. *International Financial Statistics Yearbook.* Washington, DC: International Monetary Fund.
22. Rapoport, C. Europe looks ahead to hard choices. *Fortune* 14 December 1992: 145.
23. Raiszadeh, F. M. E., Helms, M. M., and M. C. Varner. 1993. How can eastern Europe help American manufacturers? *The International Executive* 35:357–365.
24. How September 11 changed America. *Wall Street Journal.* 8 March 2002: B1.
25. Friedman, T. L. 2005. *The World is Flat.* New York, NY: Straus and Giroux.

26. Ansberry, C., and T. Aeppel. Surviving the onslaught. *Wall Street Journal* 6 October 2003: B1,B6.

27. Dean, J. Long a low-tech power, China sets its sight on chip making. *Wall Street Journal* 17 February 2004: A16.

28. Morse, D. In North Carolina, furniture makers try to stay alive. *Wall Street Journal* 20 February 2004: A1,A6.

29. Luhnow, D. As jobs move east, plants in Mexico retool to compete. *Wall Street Journal* 5 March 2004: A1,A8.

30. Millman, J. Blueprint for outsourcing. *Wall Street Journal* 3 March 2004: B1,B4.

31. Aidis, R., Estrin, S., T. 2008. Mickiewics. Institutions and entrepreneurship development in Russia: a comparative perspective. *Journal of Business Venturing* 23(6):283–310.

32. Wonacott, P. China's secret weapon: smart, cheap labor for high tech goods. *Wall Street Journal* 14 March 2002: A1.

33. Eiben, T. U.S. exporters on a global roll. *Fortune* 29 June 1992: 94.

34. Geringer, J. M., Tallman, S., and D. M. Olsen. 2002. Product and international diversification among Japanese multinational firms. *Strategic Management Journal* 21:51–80.

35. White, G. L. GM trusts former Soviet auto maker to build car with the Chevy name. *Wall Street Journal Interactive Edition* 20 February 2001.

36. Merchant, H., and D. Schendel. 2000. How do international joint ventures create shareholder value? *Strategic Management Journal* 21:723–737.

37. Powers, T. L., and R. C. Jones. 2001. Strategic combinations and their evolution in the global marketplace. *Thunderbird International Business Review* 43:525–534.

38. Chan, P., and R. Justis. 1990. Franchise management in East Asia. *Academy of Management Executive* 4:75–85.

39. Wright, P., Kroll, M., and J. A. Parnell. 1998. *Strategic Management: Concepts*. Upper Saddle River, NJ: Prentice Hall.

40. Fletcher, D. 2000. Learning to 'Think global and act local': experiences from the small business sector. *Education & Training* 42(4/5):211–220.

41. Trompenaars, F. 1993. *Riding The Waves of Culture: Understanding Cultural Diversity in Business*. London: Brealey.

42. Harvey, M., Kiessling, T. S., and M. Novicevic. 2003. Staffing marketing positions during global hyper-competitiveness: a market-based perspective. *International Journal of Human Resource Management* 14:223–245.

43. Oliver, R. W. 2000. New Rules for Global Markets. *Journal of Business Strategy* 21(3):7–9.

44. Fletcher, D. 2000. Learning to 'Think global and act local': experiences from the small business sector. *Education & Training* 42(4/5):211–220.

45. May, A. S. 1997. Think globally—act locally! Competences for global management. *Career Development International* 2(6):308–309.

46. Parnell, J. A. 2003. *Strategic Management Concepts*. Cincinnati, OH: Atomic Dog Publishing.

47. Lester, D. L., and J. A. Parnell. 2006. The complete life cycle of a family business. *Journal of Applied Management and Entrepreneurship* 11(3):3–22.

48. Menefee, M. L., and J. A. Parnell. 2007. Factors associated with success and failure among firms in high technology environments: a research note. *Journal of Applied Management and Entrepreneurship* 12(4):60–73.

49. Asher, J. 2005. Capturing a piece of the global market. *Brandweek* 46(25):2.

50. Levitt, T. 1983. The globalization of markets. *Harvard Business Review* 83(3):92–102.

51. Ohmae, K. 1989. The global logic of strategic alliances. *Harvard Business Review* 89(2):143–154.

52. Allio, D. J., and R. J. Allio. 2002. Coors Light in Puerto Rico: battling for local dominance in a global market. *Strategy & Leadership* 30(6):13–17.

53. Farley, J. U., and D. R. Lehman. 2001. The important role of meta-analysis in international research in marketing. *International Marketing Review* 18(1):70 –79.

54. May, A. S. 1997. Think globally—act locally! Competences for global management. *Career Development International* 2(6):308–309.

55. Shirouzu, N. Tailoring world's cars to U.S. tastes. *Wall Street Journal* 15 January 2001: B1.

56. NEW: Fong 2004

57. Terhune, C. U.S. thirst for Mexican cola poses sticky problem for coke. *Wall Street Journal* 11 January 2006: A1,A10.

58. Nambiar, P. Grab a fish sandwich—at KFC. *New Strait Times* 5 January 2006: B24.

59. Parnell, J. A., and J. Ruzita. 2008. Competitive strategy and performance measurement in the Malaysian context: an exploratory study. *Management Decision* 46:5–31.

60. Adamy, J. One U.S. chain's unlikely goal: pitching Chinese food in China. *Wall Street Journal* 20 October 2006: A1,A8.

61. Shirouzu, N. Tailoring world's cars to U.S. tastes. *Wall Street Journal* 15 January 2001: B1.

62. Leggett, K., and T. Zaun. World car makers race to keep up with China boom. *Wall Street Journal* 13 December 2002: A1, A7.

63. Chen, K. Beyond the traffic report. *Wall Street Journal*. January 2, 2003: A1, A12.

64. Chang, L., and P. Wonacott. Cracking China's market. *Wall Street Journal* 26 November 2002: B1.

65. Chang, L. Western stores woo Chinese wallets. *Wall Street Journal* 26 November 2002: B1,B6.

66. Saporito, B. Can Wal-Mart get any bigger? *Time.* January 13, 2003: 38–43.

67. Pretorius, M., Millard, S. M., and M. E. Kruger. 2006. The relationship between implementation, creativity, and innovativeness in small business ventures. *Management Dynamics* 15(1): 2–13.

68. Picken, J. C., and G. G. Dess. 1997. Out of (strategic) control. *Organizational Dynamics* 26(1):35–48.

69. Burnett, J. 2002. *Managing Business Crises: From Anticipation to Implementation*. Westport, CT: Quorum.

70. Pearson, C., and J. Clair. 1998. Reframing crisis management. *Academy of Management Review* 23:59–76.

Chapter Four

GLOBAL BUSINESS PLAN

Joan Gillman, *University of Wisconsin–Madison, Madison, Wisconsin*
Kira Henschel, *Association of Equipment Manufacturers, West Allis, Wisconsin*

Learning Objectives

Upon completion of this chapter, students should be able to:

- Understand the concepts of business planning.
- Understand the key differences between a domestic business plan and an international one.

Key Terms

culture	logistics
finance	marketing
investors	planning

Introduction

You're not just building a business plan to seek funding or get started. You're building a strategic roadmap for your business for years to come. It's a living, dynamic document that you can go back to year after year. It will be adjusted and changed, based on the realities of the marketplace, but it's a great document to work from.

—*Don Kuratko, Professor, Ball State University*

◎ International Business Plans

Planning is the act that makes all subsequent action go well, whether you're taking a trip, writing a book, or building your business internationally. Business plans are not just tools for start-up businesses; they are dynamic documents that serve as guidelines throughout the life of your enterprise, whether you remain domestic or seek to do business abroad.

Business planning is a two step process: first you do the strategic work of research and planning, *then* you document the plan in writing. The purpose of a global business plan is to prepare your business for entering or expanding in the international marketplace. Deciding to operate outside of the United States adds a whole new level to the business planning. Each section of your business plan has its own research needs, so you can break your plan down into manageable chunks, rather than dealing with the whole daunting process at once. This is particularly important when you become involved in the international arena because, in addition to the global opportunities that may exist, you must now include potential barriers to entry, such as:

- the stability of the government
- language(s)
- cultural differences
- banking and finance systems
- customs (product entry/exit issues)
- international tax issues
- legal and regulatory issues (product registration, environmental compliance, etc.)
- operational structure (own, lease, subsidiary, branch, utilities, plant and equipment)

How much is enough when creating your global business plan? A typical plan will run twenty-five to fifty pages in length, probably somewhat longer when taking into account nondomestic information. Back up your narrative with facts and cite your sources. Do your homework and show your audience that you know the business you're in.

Know Your Audience

First and foremost, you are writing this plan for YOU and your company! If you are an entrepreneur with a small company, your plan provides a roadmap for you to follow. Or perhaps you are creating this plan for a larger organization to expand abroad. Whatever the case, other audiences for your plan are:

- the financial community, who will want to see the feasibility of your business substantiated by facts and figures, especially if you're seeking funding
- potential investors

- potential managers and other key personnel
- potential joint venture partners
- potential landlords
- potential vendors
- advisors like your accountant, lawyer, or spouse
- agencies in the country/countries in which you wish to do business

What Business Are You Really In? Can It Be Taken Abroad?

Answering these questions is particularly important when deciding to become involved in the international business arena. Large or small companies and the individuals who run them are in the same business—figuring out what their customers need and want and what they can do to provide some portion of that better than any competitor can. Are you also working with other businesses (business-to-business transactions) or business-to-consumer?

Other questions that need to be considered include: Are you importing, exporting, or both? What are the market opportunities for your goods or services? Most importantly, will they be viable over the long term? Becoming an international business takes time and, above all, patience.

Regardless of your product or service, you are also in the technology business. Crossing borders, time zones, and cultures means using today's technology to better serve your business and your customers. Part of your plan must be staying current on technological developments and maximizing them in your operations.

What Are Your Plans for Growth?

Steven Covey's adage "start with the end in mind" is particularly true in international business. Your plan should include concepts for the evolution of your business. Even in this ever-changing world, you may discover strategic opportunities by focusing on your particular strengths and your unique position, product, or service. Are you already operating a successful business domestically and wish to expand by going abroad, or is your business internationally oriented from the start? This will play a significant role in your international business plan.

How far into the future should you plan? Like the captain of a ship, you need to keep your eye on a point far enough out that, if you see a threat or an opportunity, you have time to react to it. The planning horizon is the time required to put a strategic plan in place. It is typical for businesses to form detailed plans for the next twelve months, somewhat less detailed plans for the subsequent year or two, and then simply define visions and values that will guide your choices beyond that horizon. International business development may take considerably longer than building the same company or operation domestically. The questions to ask yourself: Where do I want to be in ten years, twenty years, and thirty years? Do I want to grow this business to sell? To pass on to future generations? How big do I want to be?

The ancient philosopher Heraclitus once said, "You never step into the same river twice." In a business, like a river, the environment is fluid. Even if your goal is to remain the same, you must work to stay where you are, or you will find yourself swept along by the current.

Components of Your Global Business Plan

An international business plan should include the following main components: front matter, marketing, personnel, financial data, and a closing.

Front Matter

This should be the last part of your plan that you write. It should include:

- cover letter
- nondisclosure statement
- title page
- table of contents
- executive summary
- business description
- vision and mission statements

Potential investors, lenders, employees, customers, and vendors all want to know what your vision of the business is and, more importantly, you want to know. Because of the complexity of operating internationally, this may be the most important work you do in your business. It will continually guide you on what to do and what not to do.

Marketing

The marketing section of your international business plan is the blueprint that keeps you building upward toward customer satisfaction and business success. It should cover, at a minimum, a:

- Market analysis (industry analysis, competitive analysis, customer analysis)
- Description of products/services offered
  - Are your products/services culturally appropriate?
  - Does the name of your product/service work in the country/countries in which you seek to do business?
- Marketing plan
  - Discuss the different aspects of marketing with your particular international markets in mind (product, price, packaging, position, presentation)
  - Are there legal restrictions for your product/service? Some countries are stricter than others with regard to components, packaging, etc. Do your research! Don't assume that because your product/service is acceptable in your home country it will be successful in your target market.

Personnel

A global business plan is only as strong as the people who execute it. The purpose of the personnel section is to build faith in the business's management team. It helps demonstrate that you and your team have the skills to run your marketing, operations, and financial functions domestically and/or abroad. It is important to provide backgrounds for all key personnel. Depending on the country/countries in which you wish to operate, you may also need to include foreign personnel, either from an operational standpoint or to comply with national requirements.

- management team
- staff team
- plans for growth

Financial Data

Financial data is how the game of business is scored. This important information indicates the life or death of your business. The financial section reports on how the company has done in the past and projects how it will perform in the future, about three to five years down the road. This section should include some or all of the following:

- profit and loss statement
- cash flow forecast
- balance sheet
- break-even analysis
- assumptions and comments

A soundly conceived and well-prepared financial section is crucial to anyone seeking to secure investors or lenders. For international businesses, exchange rate fluctuations and differing banking and accounting systems add an additional level of complexity. Get the advice of professionals who are familiar with the financial culture of the country or countries with which you wish to be involved.

Summary

This section rounds up the key facts and presents the final statement of purpose for the global business plan. Most bankers will flip to the back of a plan to assess how well thought out and thorough the plan is. A typical final section of a business plan might include the following:

- closing summary statement
- applications and effects of loans
- supporting documents (personal financial statements, resumes, positive newspaper articles about the business, and other credibility builders)

Writing a global business plan requires a substantial investment of your time and thought, even more than a domestic business plan. To help guide the process, a checklist is provided for you below. Involve others in the process. Get advice and feedback on your plan. Share it with your accountant, your banker, and others you feel would contribute valuable information and support.

A word of advice: *Writing* a global business plan is not enough. You've got to move on it, to take action. Plan, write, line up resources, then go! An ideal business plan will be accompanied by a presentation in person by the business owner. It's important to have a positive attitude and learn how to leverage your best characteristics to make everything come together. It's essential to believe in what you can do and that confidence needs to come through in the writing of the plan and in its presentation to others.

A closing thought on creating your international business plan, or planning in general: creating a plan forces you to set goals. The Cheshire Cat in Lewis Carroll's *Alice in Wonderland* asked a lost Alice, "Where are you going?" when she asked directions. "I don't know," answered Alice. The Cat replied, "If you don't know where you're going, it doesn't matter which way you go." Defining goals and means of achieving them is what planning is all about.

Global Business Plan Outline

I. **Cover Sheet**

    A. Title of the document

    B. Presented to

    C. Applicant

    D. Date

II. **Table of Contents**

III. **Executive Summary** (usually written last; not more than two pages). This is an important section of the plan because it should provide a concise overview of the complete plan. Often a lender or prospective investor may read only this section and the financial plan.

    A. Brief Description of the Business

        1. Products/services

        2. Legal structure

        3. Background/history of the business

        4. Is business new to international business or this plan for the international expansion of an existing business?

    B. The Opportunity

        1. Market

        2. Industry

        3. Competition

        4. Niche/strategy

    C. Financials

        1. Sales projections

        2. Profit potential

        3. Growth potential

    D. The People. Identify owners, officers, and other key personnel as well as management team

    E. The Offering

IV. The Business

    A.   Nature of the Business (type and legal structure)
1. Start up or existing business
2. Type of business (manufacturing, wholesale, retail, service)
3. Legal structure (proprietorship/partnership, LLC, corporation)
4. General information (location[s], hours of operation)

    B.   Product/Service
1. What is the product/service?
2. What are you selling?
   a. price
   b. selection
   c. service
   d. quality
   e. convenience
3. How will the product/service be produced/marketed?
4. Who will buy it?
5. Proprietary information

    C.   History of the Business
1. Date the business began operations
2. Chain of ownership
3. Significant changes in the business product/service line, location/facilities, marketing strategy, capitalization
4. Summary of sales and profit history

    D.   The Business Opportunity
1. Sales by size/dollars/units
2. Profitability
3. Market share
4. Based on market analysis

V. The Industry

    A.   Present Status

    B.   Trends Impacting the Business/Industry
1. Technology
2. Economy
3. Political
4. Legal
5. Demographic
6. Social

    C.   Characteristics of Firms in the Industry
1. Average firm size
2. Cost structure
3. Typical profit margins, gross and net
4. Seasonal sales patterns
5. Other important characteristics

    D.   Industry Outlook/Forecast

    E.   Data Sources

VI. The Market

    A.   Define the Market

      1. Customer category (consumer, business, industrial, institutional, government)
      2. Define *need* for product/service
      3. Geographic coverage (distance, time, traffic patterns, topographic considerations, social and cultural considerations)
      4. Demographic target (age, income, gender, employment, education, residence, family status, race, religion)
      5. Psychographic characteristics

   B. Quantify the Market
      1. Size
      2. Trends
      3. Local issues
      4. Based on demographic and geographic definition of the market

   C. Profile the Competition
      1. Who are your competitors?
      2. Where are they located?
      3. How do they/you compare?
      4. Nature and status of each competitor

   D. Marketing Strategy
      1. Competitive focus (price, quality, service, selection, convenience)
      2. Marketing methods
      3. Marketing channels
      4. Channels of distribution
      5. Advertising/promotion plan

VII. Location

   A. Site
      1. Size
      2. Physical character
      3. Legal constraints on use

   B. Facilities
      1. Buildings
      2. Storage

   C. Linkages
      1. Traffic
      2. Accessibility
      3. Convenience
      4. Exposure
      5. Parking
      6. Suppliers
      7. Competitors
      8. Market

VIII. Business Objectives

   A. Annual Profit Targets
   B. Annual Sales Growth Rate
   C. Rate of Return on Investment
   D. Rate of Return on Equity

IX. **Technical Considerations**

    A. Process/Technology
        1. Present
        2. State-of-the-art
        3. Special applications, considerations, constraints
        4. Trends

    B. Raw Materials/Inventory
        1. Requirements
        2. Sources/availability
        3. Suppliers

    C. Proprietary Information
        1. Patents/tradenames/trademarks/copyright
        2. Process
        3. Product

X. **Management/Personnel**

    A. Organization
        1. Organizational chart
        2. Major responsibilities of key managers
        3. Ownership structure
        4. Board of directors

    B. Management Team
        1. Resumes of key management personnel
        2. Strengths and weaknesses
        3. Personnel
        4. Compensation (wages and salaries, benefits; legal requirements in countries)
        5. Level of investment by managers

XI. **Potential Risks and Problems**

    A. What potential problems could arise?

    B. How likely are they to occur?

    C. Plan to meet or overcome problems/risks

XII. **Financial**

    A. Projected Income Statement
        1. Three years, minimum
        2. Assumptions

    B. Projected Balance Sheet
        1. Three years, minimum
        2. Assumptions

    C. Cash Flow Statement
        1. First year monthly; second and third years quarterly
        2. Assumptions

    D. Business Valuation
        1. Methodology
        2. Assumptions
        3. Estimated value

    E. Break-Even Analysis

F.   Sensitivity Analysis
    1.   Assumptions
    2.   "What if" analysis

XIII. The Offering

A.   Capitalization

B.   Terms

C.   Sources and Uses of Funds

D.   Ownership Structure

E.   Projected Return to Investors

XIV. Supporting Documents

A.   Organization

B.   Credit Reports

C.   Letters of Intent or Sales Agreements

D.   Lease and Purchase Agreements

E.   Options

F.   Copies of Leases

G.   Contracts

H.   Permits and Licenses

I.   Insurance (domestic, international as appropriate for countries)

J.   Letters of Reference

K.   Business Development Schedule

L.   Resumes

M.   Other Issues

Discussion Questions

1.   Why is a business plan important when moving a client organization internationally?
2.   What is the most important part of the business plan for your client?
3.   Why is financial information important in a business plan?
4.   How might the triple bottom line of sustainable strategic management come into play when developing a business plan?
5.   What client might you want to work with in this class?
6.   Given the introduction to business plans given in this chapter, what might you want to focus upon with your client?
7.   How might an international business plan differ from one done for a similar domestic firm?

Suggested Reading

Alterowitz, R., and J. Zonderman. 2002. *Financing Your New or Growing Business*. Irvine, CA: Entrepreneur Press.

Gillman, J. 2001. *Business Plans that Work*. Cincinnati, OH: Adams Media.

Schroeder, C. 2007. *Specialty Shop Retailing, How to Run Your Own Store, Revised*. Hoboken, NJ: Wiley.

Internet Sites

1. Information and tools for small business. www.entrepreneur.com

2. **Small Business Administration.** The U.S. Small Business Administration provides a plethora of information on exporting, international business plans, and other aspects of international business. www.sba.gov/oit/info and www.sba.gov/starting/indexbusplans.html

3. **Small Business Advisor.** www.isquare.com

4. **U.S. Commercial Service, Department of Commerce.** The U.S. Department of Commerce, the U.S. Small Business Administration, and the Export-Import Bank formed a unique partnership to establish Export Assistant Centers, a network of one-stop shops which deliver a comprehensive array of export counseling and trade financing services to export-ready firms in one convenient location. The sole purpose of these offices is the promotion of U.S. exports. www.export.gov.

5. **Strategies.** Canada's most comprehensive Internet site. This site provides a plethora of information for exporting companies, including trade facts, market research reports, industry sector analyses, trade statistics, and foreign investment information. Strategies offer many of the services that the U.S. Department of Commerce Commercial Service offers and is a useful site concerning doing business in Canada. http://strategis.ic.gc.ca/engdoc/main.html.

6. **North American Industrial Classification System.** The North American Industry Classification System (NAICS) is replacing the U.S. Standard Industrial Classification (SIC) system. NAICS will reshape the way we view our changing economy. NAICS was developed jointly by the U.S., Canada, and Mexico to provide new comparability in statistics about business activity across North America. www.census.gov/ftp/pub/epcd/www/naics.html.

Chapter Five

BUSINESS OPPORTUNITIES FOR GLOBAL ENTREPRENEURSHIP

Alvin J. Jackson, Jr.
Texas A&M University–Commerce, Commerce, Texas

Learning Objectives

Upon completion of this chapter, students should be able to:

- Understand entrepreneurial compatibility.
- Understand global opportunities for small businesses.
- Understand corporate culture as it relates to entrepreneurship.
- Understand economic challenges, including global market integration and inflation.
- Understand political systems and perspectives.
- Understand social and cultural differences.
- Understand technological effects.
- Understand market entry approaches.

Key Terms

e-commerce and technological change   intrapreneurial culture
global market integration   protectionism

The last decade of the twentieth century has shown that modern changes can occur in a short period of time in our modern economic history. If we take a look in our rear view mirror, we will notice our bridges for travel no longer constrain us to a limited portion of a specific state, county, or governing country. The roadmap has been extended beyond borders, which has changed the scope of our national and global marketplace. Many people have cruised the globalization steering wheel down the information superhighway. Many organizations have sped this journey up through the development and changes of corporate compatibility. Some people have placed their vehicle on cruise control, making sure to stay on the path that leads through each valley, canyon, and causeway.

What is their purpose? Who will be the one behind the wheel establishing the new face of international expansion? The spirit of international entrepreneurship is a major contributing factor that has affected the way people expand their horizons. No longer does one feel that the road to entrepreneurism stops within the borders of their own country. The key elements of entrepreneurial drive and the economic, political, technological, and social changes that have occurred over the last decade have dramatically created business opportunities for global business.

International entrepreneurship has led pioneers and others down the paths of entrepreneurship freedom, stopping at every nook, corner, and valley to find the opportunities that will unfold in today's emerging international markets.

Knowing You Have Entrepreneurial Compatibility

Entrepreneurial drive is a society that is unlike other organization's existence in today's global economies of scale. The entrepreneur's passion is to conquer and seize opportunities that most individuals would not tackle and do not have the emotions to stomach. Their motivation is to be a steward for change through innovative products or services. They have a creative mind that can think independently about ideas of success and failure. Most entrepreneurs are known for their hard work and their dedication to their respective businesses. Entrepreneurs have established themselves as risk-takers and leaders of optimism. These unique men and women make up a strong percentage of today's innovators as the leaders of global expansion in the twenty-first century.

Keys of Entrepreneurial Drive

Entrepreneurs have a unique form of identity from their inception as leaders in our business forefront. These keen attributes lead highly talented individuals to be less resistant to change and provides them with a burning desire of resiliency to succeed. The entrepreneurial drive sets the table for everyone to have the business savvy or opportunity to succeed.

The key ingredients to entrepreneurial drive are:

- Ability to *seize opportunities* for personal and professional benefit
- *Creative* ability to develop business opportunities
- *Independent thinker*

- *Hard worker* and so is their environment
- *Optimistic*—uncertainty does not bother these types of individuals
- *Innovator*—the strongest quality of an entrepreneur
- *Risk taker*
- *Visionary*
- *Leader*

The entrepreneurial drive seizes opportunities that will benefit them both personally and professionally. Entrepreneurs have a tendency to be hard workers and they carry these same expectations into their environment. Optimism drives their spirit and the uncertainty does not bother these type of individuals. The entrepreneurial spirit establishes one's ability to be a risk taker and have a vision for the success of their idea. They have to be innovators to the products and services they sell and a leader that reflects the environment of their strategic vision.

Multinational Corporations and Global Markets

From the late 1940s through the late 1960s, multinational corporations (MNCs) from the United States had little competition in global markets.[1] In fact, MNCs were the only forms of organizations allowed to eat in the lion's den of China for several years. Today, smaller firms have the ability to develop business opportunities through smaller companies who take less resources and operational cost to secure an opportunity in the global marketspace.

More and more American entrepreneurs are embarking on the road to China and many have found their fortunes. Over the past two decades, as China has liberalized its economy, several large companies have prospered by moving manufacturing into China or, more rarely, by producing goods for the Chinese market.[2] Investments by major organizations like GM, Volkswagon, and other major automobile manufacturers are drastically expanding their operations in China. The behemoths have faced several roads that are hard to overcome because of their intensive size and labor costs. The corporate streamline of a major multinational organization only absorbs the ideas of a loose idea thinker.

Global Opportunities for Small Businesses

Yet, more than often not, major multinationals have found making money in China considerably harder than expected.[2] With intensive operational cost, small entrepreneurs and businesses have been able to seize the opportunity in the international markets of China.

Entrepreneurs and Second Chances

In 1990, Tommy Hodinh founded his own logistic company. Hodinh was a Vietnamese refugee who arrived in the United States in 1972. At the tender age of eighteen, with limited English skills, Hodinh managed to put himself through college. He then worked for IBM for fifteen years, first as an engineer and later as a member of the IBM management team. The whole time he worked for "Big Blue" he knew he wanted to do something else. "I always wished I had the money to start my own company. I had the experience, but I didn't have the capital."

By the 1990s, the barriers to starting a small technology company had dropped considerably. Hodinh realized it did not cost that much to start a company anymore. Since small office space was reasonably priced and the cost to become incorporated was a few thousand dollars, he was able to embark on starting his new venture with his savings. In 1990, Hodinh co-founded MagRabbit Incorporated, which is a software duplication and logistics company based out of Austin, Texas. The first six years were considered the growing years of slow and steady growth, which led to securing a commercial bank loan for MagRabbit. Today, MagRabbit now has more than one hundred employees, nearly $10 million in annual sales, and clients around the world.

Hodinh proved to himself to seek an opportunity for his personal and professional benefit. Not only did he overcome the obstacles of cofounding MagRabbit Incorporated, Hodinh was the first person of Asian American descent in the software business in Austin, Texas.

Key Ingredient for Success

Hodinh was concerned about *seizing* opportunities to start his own business and knew he had the talent from management experience with a Fortune 500 company like IBM. In 1990, Hodinh seized the opportunities to develop technology and proved that his strategic window would lead him to entrepreneur success in the southwest region of the United States, which would later be known as "The Silicon Valley of the South."

(Adapted from Kurlantzic, J. About face—the face of entrepreneurship. *Entrepreneur Magazine.* January 2004: 62. See also http://www.magrabbit.com/current/Press_Entrepreneur.htm.)

Many corporations have faced the difficulties of working with multinational corporations and the powers of strategic alliances in the Chinese markets. Small businesses like Robert Kushner's Pacific China Industries, Ltd. have been able to open the gates of China and have been well received in the Chinese market. One contributing factor to their success as small business entrepreneurs is the research and study time placed in the international markets with a smaller team focus and a smaller scales strategy that has captured the short-term audience of the Chinese market.[2] Robert's personal savvy led him to China. His professional drive helped him to understand the cultural differences that would lead to the expansion of his company's products and services.

Pacific China Industries, Ltd.

Robert Kushner is the founder and managing director of Pacific China Industries, Ltd. PCI is a fifteen-person company that develops and manufactures novelties in China. PCI is full of tchotchke products from dancing rock stars to dashboard mounts.

(Adapted from Kurlantzic J. Promised land. *Entrepreneur Magazine.* January 2004: 66–69.)

The Entrepreneurial Test

Entrepreneurial compatibility is influenced by people who think *independently*. The people who are "outside the box" and have difficulty conforming to structure remove themselves from the foundation of a corporation. Some major corporations embrace this spirit and formulate the ideas to be incorporated with their strategic plans and vision. If they are unsuccessful in their environment, the entrepreneurial tendency is to take the optimistic approach and leave the corporate structure and develop a flat structure with the correct environment for business.

Intrapreneurial or Entrepreneurial? That Is the Question

The intrapreneurial or entrepreneurial culture is more prevalent today as the world economy becomes more globalized. An *intrapreneurial culture* has formulated strategies with a positive outlook toward global expansion for many MNCs.

A Kindred Intrapreneurial Spirit

The Tokyo Disneyland Success

Multinational organizations that embrace the intrapreneurial spirit have been successful in market globalization in international markets. These tales account for detailed marketing mistakes and successes. Walt Disney has let optimism blind their initiative for value, research, and intrapreneurial cultural stewardship.

Tokyo Disneyland opened in 1983 on 201 acres in the Eastern suburb of Urazasu. The Orientland ownership group would build, own, and operate the theme park while Disney would advise and consult the Orientland group. Orientland borrowed approximately $650 million that would be needed to bring the project to fruition. Disney invested no money but received 10% of the revenues from admission and rides and 5% of sales on food, drink, and souvenirs.

While the Japanese took some time to respond, by 1990 they began flocking to Tokyo Disneyland by the millions. By 1990, some 16 million a year passed through the turnstiles, about one-fourth more than visited Disneyland in California. In the fiscal year of 1990, revenues reached $988 million with profits of over $150 million. Indicative of the Japanese preoccupation with things "American," the parks serve almost no Japanese food and the live entertainers are mostly American.

As success heightened in Tokyo, Disneyland executives were soon to realize they had been successful in expanding into global markets, but could have gained a significant portion of revenue generation by taking a substantial amount of ownership in Tokyo Disneyland.

Optimism

The intrapreneurial culture directed by Michael Eisner and the Disney executive team provides a close relationship between the executive management team and the board of directors of Walt Disney. These similar qualities or interests led the intrapreneurial culture that established significant strategic initiatives for Walt Disney from the early eighties through the end of the 1990s with Euro Disney.

(Adapted from Sterngold, J. Cinderella hits her stride in Tokyo. *New York Times* 17 February 1991: 6.)

If intrapreneurial opportunities decline within the strategic vision of a corporation, many bright minds either become an extension or leave the organization to build their own organization of leadership and vision. This spirit is defined as *intrapreneurial culture* and the environment will develop a strategic vision.

These two types of culture lead to positive organizational communities in small and major business opportunities.[3] MNCs have expanded the spirit of the intrapreneurial vision, which has led to global expansion in their respective industries. The entrepreneurial leader undertakes the mission of defending their vision, which, in return, leads to opportunities that major organizations have not researched and developed. That is why the entrepreneur is able to overcome big business and, more importantly, able to understand the entrepreneurial process at an international level in emerging markets in the United States, Europe, and Asia.

The Economic Challenges of International Entrepreneurship

The economic compatibility that will lead the wave of international expansion through hearts of compassionate and new ventured entrepreneurs will have to adapt and change to the constant economic filters of geographic economics. The issues of foreign trade have produced barriers for entry for all opportunists who would like to expand their business into global markets.

The United States has seen a rise in debt over the past few years. From mid-2000, the U.S. and global economy has weakened significantly following one of the largest stock market declines in the postwar period, the terrorist attacks of September 11, 2001, major internal combustion in major corporations leading to corporate failure, and the wars in Iraq.[4]

These economic events have had a significant impact on the judgment of idealists to produce opportunities in the national and global markets. The economic picture in the United States has played a major role in the impact on the emerging markets in Eastern Europe, Asia, and Latin America. The U.S. budget deficit, global interest rates, and the U.S. dollar have been exposed by the debt linked to the U.S. government and policy.[4] It has developed adverse effects on short- and long-term interest rates. The traditional distribution structures in Japan, Europe, and other countries have seen rapid changes to barriers into key markets for small businesses that offer products and services.

The United States has been a major player to the world economic outlook. The high levels of foreign currency denominated debt, as such countries have become extremely sensitive to global real interest rates.[4] The outcome has left the opportunity for global markets to accelerate. This phase will withdraw the fiscal stimulus over the next decade, leading to economic global expansion, in a manner that pays due attention to incentives to work and invest in the United States. Many corporations now seek nonintensive labor markets to secure employment to reduce overhead costs and make their organization more profitable for their short- and long-term economic goals.

Entrepreneurs understand that countries will have to increase the flexibility of their economies through structural reforms and speed up their economies through their own integration into the global economy.

Global Market Integration

The economic picture today is one of several bundled hot buttons. Each geographic region of the world has now been integrated to the advancement in technology and services. This threshold has developed several key communication channels that have broken down the environment of semantics and sparked the interest for organizations to consider global integration.

Though many U.S. consumers associate globalization with leading multinationals like Coca-Cola or GE that have huge operations in many countries, small businesses have actually been one of the main drivers of global integration. According to the U.S. Department of Commerce, between 1987 and 1999, the number of small and mid-sized U.S. exporters more than tripled to 224,000.[5] By 1999, 97% of American exporters were small businesses, though smaller exporters still only accounted for one-third of total U.S. export sales.[5]

Entrepreneur's Venture

It is apparent that venture capitalist may worry that too much cash is chasing too few good deals. Entrepreneurs in key sectors are realizing the opportunity is changing seasons. The springtime for funding by venture capitalists would support this statement since there have been significant contributions to specific industry sectors over the last seven years.

Entrepreneurs who have focused in these industry sectors have seen the cash come their way from venture capitalist organizations. Based on numbers listed by 2003 amount invested, these are the key areas that venture capitalists have been far from bean counting:

1. **Connectivity/Communication Tools**—Accel Partners, Intel Capital, and Microsoft are sharing this round of funding with some $38 million for Groove Networks, Beverly, Massachusetts, whose peer-to-peer technology creates secure, virtual workspaces that can be used by widely dispersed people.

2. **Biotechnology**—Favrille, a four-year-old San Diego-based biotech that has developed personalized cancer treatment made from a patient's own tumors, secured $44 million in funding in April. Two days later, the company registered with the SEC for an initial public offering.

3. **Non-Financial Business Services**—Menlo Ventures, NEA, Alloy Ventures, and Deutsche Post Ventures handed over $20 million plus in funding to an organization called Open Harbor. The San Carlos, California based company's software helps global businesses deal with the ever-changing worldwide trade regulations. DHL is standardizing its custom processes with Open Harbor's software.

(Adapted from Florian, E. The venture rebound. *Fortune Magazine* 3 May 2004: 115–116.)

Global Inflation

According to *Grolier's* online encyclopedia, *inflation* is a process in which the average level of prices increases at a substantial rate over a considerable period of time. In short, more money is required to buy a given amount of goods and services. An understanding of *global inflation* is key to building opportunities in international entrepreneurship simply because it is a foothold to your revenue stream in your international venture(s) of business. For the first time in the history of the world, inflation is a universal phenomenon with all currencies tied together. Global inflation outlines the environment for which you formulate certain strategies as they affect different segments of the global marketspace.

Emerging Global Markets

Emerging markets in Eastern Europe, Asia, and Latin America are where more than 75% of the growth in world trade over the next twenty years is expected to occur.[1] The *reunification* of Hong Kong, Macau, and China has placed all Asians under the control of the same Asian leaders for the first time in over a century.

After more than four centuries, the final remnant of European occupation of Chinese territory was repatriated. The handover of Macau was an event of great importance to the Chinese leadership in what is viewed as the major struggle of this century. The outcome has restored the Chinese territory and sovereignty from outside occupation and exploitation. The country has been a hot spot for the last five years since the Chinese systems have wanted to integrate the key economic financial systems from the one country.[6] The significant importance for international entrepreneurship is that the value of their monetary system holds limited complexity in the pursuit of valuations toward currency, which could develop a critical thinking system toward your organization's entrance into the marketplace.

The *European Monetary Union* and the switch from local country currencies to one monetary unit for Europe illustrate the global integration movement of the twenty-first century. In 1978 the community decided to re-launch monetary integration at the Brussels European Council by creating a *European Monetary System* (EMS), with the objectives of stabilizing exchange rates, reducing inflation, and preparing for monetary integration.[7] *Euro* is the currency of twenty-seven European Union countries, stretching from the Mediterranean to the Arctic Circle. Euro banknotes and coins have been in circulation since January 1, 2002, and are now a part of daily life for over 300 million Europeans living in the euro area.[7]

China as the Engine of the Global Economy

It has been speculated that, because of accumulated debts, the United States is losing its ability to provide a strong source of demand that supports the growth of the global economy. This is considered structural incompatibility putting global growth at risk, which goes further and concludes that an unsustainable potential deficit in global demand now exists as a consequence of the way in which the monetary and financial systems of major East Asian econo-mies are managed—a deficit which the United States has temporarily filled by creation of credit.

The United States has compensated for the East Asian demand deficit by providing the main source of global demand growth for a decade, but the United States has also experienced fi-nancial imbalances as a result (a large current account deficit and accumulated debts). And this has only been able to continue because changes to the global financial system in the early 1970s permitted sustained trade deficits to be financed by creating money (rather than balanced with gold reserves).

At the same time, high levels of public spending have been needed to sustain demand in other major economies (i.e., China, France, Germany, Italy, Japan), resulting in some cases of public debt levels that are also becoming critical considering the costs and benefits of common cur-rencies and, by implication, the relative desirability of fixed versus flexible exchange rates

Economic Outlook for Global Markets

In 2003, strong global economic growth has been anticipated, with an initial expectation that growth would be sustained by U.S. demand.

However, the U.S. economy suffers fiscal imbalances (namely large current account deficits and foreign debts), which many observers have seen as a threat to the sustainability of U.S. and global growth.

(From Center for Policy and Development China's Development: Assessing the Implications, Queensland and Australia. September 2002–October 2003.)

The *International Monetary Fund* (IMF) and the World Bank Group are two global institutions created to assist nations in becoming and remaining economi-cally viable.[1]

To balance the inadequate monetary reserves and unstable currencies, the IMF was formed to resolve these issues. So long as these conditions exist, world markets cannot develop and function as effectively as they should. The IMF helps overcome these particular market barriers, which plagued international trading before World War II.[1] Originally, the IMF was an agreement signed by twenty-nine countries. Today, over 181 countries are members of the IMF.

Entrepreneurs must understand the importance of this economic environ-ment because it plays an important role in international trade by helping main-tain the stability in the financial markets and by assisting countries that are seek-ing economic development and restructuring.

Microsoft Evaluates the International Price Challenges

Gartner, Inc., Market Research Reports Microsoft Dealings in Emerging Asian Markets

The Microsoft Corporation recently lowered the cost of a package that includes its Windows operating system and Office suite of software in Thailand to $40, according to a report from market research firm Gartner, Inc. The move, according to Gartner, is in response to the increasing use of the Linux operating system. Gartner indicates that the company may take similar price cuts in China as well. The cost of the same package in the United States starts at about $380.

1.   Will the cost differentiation change Microsoft's market share in the Thailand environment?
2.   Was this a good decision on Microsoft's entry into the Thailand software market?
3.   Explain why you feel Microsoft made the cut back in the international region?
4.   Do you feel Microsoft's decision was right in making this move in Thailand?
5.   How do you feel it will affect their revenue in China versus the United States?

(Adapted from Technology and Newsbytes, *Biz Education*, November–December 2003 and complete history and description from Gartner, Inc., http://www. http://www3.gartner.com/Init.)

The International Entrepreneur Political Perspective

The emerging global economy brings together unity and global nations, which provides outlets of competition. Worldwide competition gives an opportunity for entrepreneurs as well as the buying consumer population. The roadways that open also creates a market capitalization which endorses free enterprise in new markets and small markets that are considered large enough to become viable opportunities.

The main concern of the twenty-first century will be the geopolitical forces that monitor and issue policy for the exchange of goods and services in the global markets. As competition develops in certain markets, the contingency for *protectionism* will become the hot button in most respective markets. The passions for trade will grow, which has already been established in the last decade of the twentieth century. The economies of the industrialized world have entered their mature state of the product life cycle and will be more than modest over the next twenty years.

Protectionism

Protectionism helps nations utilize legal barriers, exchange barriers, and psychological barriers to restrain entry of unwanted goods.

Protectionism on trade maintains these rules for barriers to entry for government restrictions on trade to:

1. protect infant industries
2. protect home markets
3. keep money in home country
4. encourage capital accumulation
5. maintain the standard of living and real wages
6. conserve natural resources

7. industrialize a low wage nation
8. maintain employment and reduction of unemployment
9. increase national defense
10. increase business size for respective industry
11. increase retaliation, bargaining, and negotiation power.

Protectionism is established to make global markets conscious of their worldwide shortage on raw materials and natural resources.

(Adapted from Woellert L. Why do nations tariff? *The World and I* July 1997: 64.)

The Organization for Economic Cooperation and Development (OECD) estimates that the economies of the OECD member countries will expand about 3% annually for the next twenty-five years, the same rate as the past twenty-five years.[8] Organizations like the World Trade Organization (WTO) were formed to help the social, political, and economic changes that will lead the global economy to the future victories in international trade and policy.

The World Trade Organization (WTO)

The United States was a catalyst in the expansion of the definition of trade issues. At the signing of the Uruguay Round trade agreement in Marrakech, Morocco, in April 1994, U.S. representatives pushed for an enormous expansion on trade which resulted in the creation of the WTO, which encompasses the General Agreement on Trades and Tariffs (GATT) structure and extends to new areas not adequately covered in the past few policies for trade.

The WTO is an institution that sets the rules for trade between its 132 members, provides a panel of experts to hear the rule on trade, and disputes between members, leading to binding decisions on trade policy.

(Adapted complete history and description of WTO visit http://wto.org/.)

The European Union (EU)

The European Union is a unique, treaty-based, institutional framework that defines and manages economic and political cooperation among its twenty-seven European member countries. The Union is the latest stage in a process of integration begun in the 1950s by six countries—Belgium, France, Germany, Italy, Luxembourg, and the Netherlands—whose leaders signed the original treaties establishing various forms of European integration.

These treaties gave life to the novel concept that, by creating communities of shared sovereignty in matters of coal and steel production, trade, and nuclear energy, another war in Europe would be unthinkable. While common EU policies have evolved in a number of other sectors since then, the fundamental goal of the Union remains the same: to create an ever-closer union among the peoples of Europe.

(Adapted from http://www.eurunion.org/infores/euguide/Chapter1.htm.)

General Agreement on Tariffs and Trade

The United States and twenty-two countries signed the General Agreement on Tariffs and Trade (GATT) shortly after World War II. This agreement paved the way for the first effective worldwide trade agreements to be conducted into policy. The agreement provides a process to reduce tariffs and created an agency to serve as a watchdog over world trade.

(Adapted from Complete description and history of GATT visit http://www.wto.org/wto/about/about.htm.)

When an entrepreneur is formulating a strategic decision to enter a global market you should keep in mind the different geopolitical challenges. You should know your state of controllable and uncontrollable initiatives when entering a market. With the continued strengthening for opportunities in international entrepreneurship one must focus on the continued strengthening and creation of regional market groups:

European Union (EU)	North American Free Trade Agreement (NAFTA)
ASEAN Free Trade Area (AFTA)	Free Trade Area of America (FTAA)
Southern Cone Free Trade Area (Mercosur)	Asia-Pacific Economic Cooperation (APEC)

The market groups have enabled entrepreneurs in emerging markets and helped to protect policy and practices of business worldwide. Entrepreneurs will constantly have to examine the way they conduct business and remain flexible enough to react to the rapidly changing global trends to be competitive.

When an entrepreneur seizes an opportunity in global markets there are several factors he or she should consider to entering an emerging market for global business. Key areas for an entrepreneur to understand when researching opportunities in global markets include:

1. Understanding the balance of trade relationship between merchandise imports and exports in prospective target markets.
2. Extensively researching the political forces of the global environment to have alternative outlines for strategy and implementation for barriers to enter market(s).
3. Understanding the development of domestic industry and how countries will protect existing industry: establishing tariffs, quotas, boycotts, monetary barriers, non-tariff barrier, and market barriers.[1]

The market groups and research techniques will be explored in later chapters of experimental exercises and the areas of study chapters of this book. The political and legal issues for an entrepreneur will be a challenging process for one to win in their quest for international emergence for global markets.

◎ Social and Cultural Differences in International Markets

Social policy covers a great number of issues which do not stand on their own but, as is increasingly recognized, are both diverse and interlinked. For example, tackling social exclusion involves simultaneously addressing barriers to labor market re-integration, health care issues, and educational aspects and their perception by different countries. Entrepreneurs must evaluate social indicators to provide the broad perspective needed for any international comparison and assessment of social trends and policies.

Social culture is very valuable in our professional and personal cultures. These indicators help set standards and practices that we implement in our daily activities, whether we are in a professional or personal environment.

Corporate Culture and Entrepreneurship

Since the 1990s, the need to pursue corporate entrepreneurship has arisen from a variety of pressing problems including technological changes, innovations, and improvements in the marketplace.[9]

The corporate culture has also formed a relative deprivation toward many entrepreneurial spirits that exist in this organizational culture. The spirit of the entrepreneur has perceived weakness in the traditional methods of corporate management.[10] Most of this is caused by power and influence from top-level management and corporate streamlining. The chain of command takes control and the end result is the loss of entrepreneurial-minded employees who are disenchanted with bureaucratic organizations.[11]

The bureaucracy enables other organizations to find opportunities and opens the door for organizations that possess a flatter structure. The world globalization has helped open doors that used to be closed. New technologies and the pursuit for core competencies has led to growing levels of international competition

The pursuit of corporate entrepreneurship as a strategy to counter these problems, however, creates a newer and potentially more complex set of challenges on both a practical and a theoretical level. On a practical level, organizations need guidelines to direct or redirect resources toward establishing effective entrepreneurial strategies. On a theoretical level, researchers need to continually reassess the components or dimensions that explain and shape the environment in which corporate entrepreneurship flourishes.

Workforce Diversity and Globalization

Organizations understand that they are no longer constrained to their natural national borders. A British firm owns Burger King, and McDonald's sells burgers in many different eastern countries. American companies receive almost 75% of their revenues from sales outside the United States.[12] These examples illustrate that the world has become a global outlet and community. In return, entrepreneurs have become capable of working with people from different cultures. *Glo-*

balization has led many organizations to *adapt* to working with people of different ethnic descent and understanding the opportunities to work with managers in different markets representing different cultures. To work effectively in different cultures, entrepreneurs must understand the significance of the cultures they wish to build relationship and customer rapport with as well as adapt their management style to their differences.

Workforce diversity must be addressed among people within given countries. Workforce diversity means that organizations are becoming more heterogeneous in terms of gender, race, and ethnicity. Workforce diversity is an issue in Canada, Australia, South Africa, Japan, and Europe as well as the United States. Managers in the United States and Canada are no longer in work groups that represent their country population.[12] Today, many of these countries have offices established in eastern parts of Asia and Europe, which develops an integration of different cultures working for the same purpose and mission.

Cultural Orientation and Integration

The increasing diversity of American society only enhanced small businesses' willingness to look abroad. As rising numbers of immigrants came to the United States in the 1990s from Latin America and South Asia and started businesses; a large number of those foreign-born entrepreneurs naturally looked to their homelands for export markets. In 2000, studies found that nearly one-third of all start-ups in Silicon Valley were led by a person of South Asian descent, many of whom outsourced a percentage of their companies' work to India or Pakistan.[13]

Accelerated Vision to Value—An International Entrepreneurship Passion

i2 Technologies

i2 was founded in the late eighties by Sanjiv Sidhu and Ken Sharma, two visionaries in what was later to be known as supply chain management. Sanjiv and Ken's passion was to apply technology and best practices to eliminating inefficiencies in business. From humble beginnings in a two-bedroom Dallas apartment where the first program was created, i2 has grown today to over $1 billion in revenues with more than 1,000 customers and 500 deployments in the last year alone.

i2 recognizes the vast potential waiting to be unleashed in the value chain through value chain management, allowing collaboration across functions in a company as well as across companies in the value chain. This is the next frontier for increasing productivity, and the philosophy to which i2 is applying its expertise, passion, and technology.

i2 Technologies has stuck by this mission since it's inception. The i2 philosophy basically believes if you take care of your customers, they will take care of themselves, which will lead to relationship development between i2 and the organization.

Sanjiv Sidhu founded i2 Technologies, Inc. in 1988 with the vision of helping businesses make more intelligent decisions by using information resources.

Under his leadership, i2 has grown to become a market leader, serving such powerhouse clients as Texas Instruments, 3M, IBM, Johnson & Johnson, Lipton, Ford Motor Company, Dell Computer, Toshiba, Warnaco, and Coca-Cola. In March 2000, he led the company through a merger with Aspect Development, the largest software industry merger to date. His multinational team of nearly 5,000 employees is one of the most experienced and highly educated workforces in the business.

Sidhu's overriding concern and the central tenet of his business philosophy is providing optimum value for i2's customers through value chain management. To that end, i2 goes beyond just pioneering and establishing e-business process optimization technology, to tie the technology directly to the value that customers will receive in savings and efficiencies in running their business.

Before starting i2, Sidhu was an engineer working in the world-renowned artificial intelligence laboratory at Texas Instruments in Dallas. Based on his observation that even the smartest people can juggle no more than nine variables when making decisions, he proposed a design for computer software based on artificial intelligence and advanced simulation techniques. The software he proposed enabled planners at Texas Instruments to dramatically improve the management of the production process by taking real-life constraints and variables into account when making planning decisions.

(Adapted from i2 Technologies Website http://www.i2.com/Home/Services/index.html.)

Elements for entrepreneur analysis on culture global markets focus on:[14]

1. Material culture—technology and economics
2. Social institutions—social organization, education, and political structures
3. Humans—their belief systems and values
4. Aesthetics—graphic and plastic arts, folklore, music, drama, and dance
5. Language—language barrier(s) and semantics

Understanding culture deals with a certain individual, group, or country's design in living. This is one of the most crucial research elements for opportunities in international entrepreneurship. One must analyze certain factors when evaluating cultural compatibility to meet the expectations of consumer needs for maximum profitability.

The Technological Effect on International Entrepreneurship

Technology has been a key to help move products from manufacturer to end-user, providing local inventory, technical product support, sales, and service. Technology moves at a record pace and sometimes, once obtained, is already obsolete. In today's world, technology is a challenging and ever evolving field. New computer technologies, increased competition, and continued growth in global markets make today's opportunities for entrepreneurism remarkably different from what they were only a few years ago.

How It Affects Global Competition

The global competition challenge for entrepreneurs requires them to adapt with broad skills and an incredible ability to learn at faster paces than in previous decades of the technology workforce. The range for technology helps in the automating tasks for manufacturing, plant maintenance, construction operations, accounting, sales and marketing, purchasing, inventory, and profit management. The computer systems that are designed to carry the logistics of pinpoint tracking for packages have definitely helped cultivate the direction in distribution services. E-logistics and system integration make an attractive force that will present an accurate tracking system in a distribution delivery environment.

The Information Superhighway

Since the mid 1990s, the Internet has become a technology phenomenon where there has been a strong beginning; however, there are no predictions on where it will end. It is a full-force market tool that has helped innovate the way we work, how we think, and how we deliver products and services. The Internet has also created extra value to our value chain. It helps us have direct access to goods and services, while also providing us updated current information on where the company's vision will be tomorrow.

With the growth in the use of the Internet, businesses more and more become e-businesses handling many transactions on the Web. Electronic mail and communication barriers are now more accessible than ever. New business ventures can communicate domestically as well as internationally. This has led to increased production and less expense to a company portfolio for small, medium, and major corporations. It has also led to more home-based businesses and a new way of how we view entrepreneurship.

The knowledge and software have been an intangible benefit to how entrepreneurs can conduct business. The Java programming language is one of the main drivers that have led to this e-commerce expansion. For an entrepreneur to understand that Extensible Markup Language (XML) and trans-coding are among the technologies supporting the infrastructure for e-business can be an essential advantage to their competition. From "bricks and mortar" companies to online e-commerce services, no one can get ahead without having the Internet in their market strategies for how they conduct business worldwide.

E-commerce: The Entrepreneur Tool of Technology and Production

E-commerce helps you compete in an increasingly demanding marketplace with a wide scope of domestic and international exposure. E-commerce has helped provide support to many of the major elite corporations that are publicly and privately traded. It has also been a major contributor to many small businesses and their business venture foundation. The production levels and expectations have helped balance the data analysis and implementation efforts that many organizations have had to commit to in order to landscape their e-commerce and Internet infrastructure.

Integrating e-commerce into your company means improved operations, decreased costs, increased sales, and facilitated communication with customers, partners, and employees. The recommendations are high and the demand from consumers is to make sure that you have a gateway via the Internet. This helps create confidence to products and services that already have traditional value and help keep a relationship with efficient channels of production that establishes a legacy between business-to-consumer (B2C) and business-to-business (B2B) companies.

The Rate of Technological Change

In the early 1990s, Congress passed laws that helped enable the benchmarking in e-commerce. Technology has played a major role in all opportunities for entrepreneurism. The effects of e-commerce helped entrepreneurs exchange information plus provide products and services to local, national, and global markets.

Companies like Cisco Systems helped create a value chain to make networking products that could handle an enormous amount of data and route it from one computer to thousands of other locations within an intranet and Internet infrastructure. The company sits atop a $12 billion Web-enabled value chain. Cisco sits as the front-runner in providing core technologies that help build the network infrastructure.[11]

Most companies today need these transmission facilities to exchange information and goods on the Wide Access Networks (WAN). Broadband systems generally are fiberoptic. Telephone companies are retrofitting their toll and exchange fibers to tie their networks into one synchronous optical network. The main challenge that all participants have experienced in placing this architecture is making the network capable of flowing freely and synchronously. It will take time because of how much money is involved. The telecom cannot keep spending at the rate they have been in years past because of the incredible amount of funding that is needed and the scarcity of resources. Broadband will arrive, but personally even two years is much too optimistic.

The roadmap for extending direct fiber connections to smaller business and residential customers will tie networks and communities together. This same architecture has potential application for residential customers. The industry is in the deployment of new technologies that make it economical for the first time to provide the virtually unlimited bandwidth of fiber to smaller customers, supporting new broadband service applications targeted to small businesses and all consumers. Consider this analysis:

In 1990, people discovered the capability of Windows and personal computers became a phenomenon. The value chain extended these links with the introduction to pathways and channels that have connected an estimated 200 million people in only ten years. Food for thought: it took television three times that long just to have 50 million in market penetration. This is one of the most effective management tools for aspiring entrepreneurs for global expansion.

Rate of New Product Introductions

The rate of new product introductions has moved faster than the rate of the Internet and e-commerce combined. This chain links all highly integrated companies to form alliances to see who can help innovate and re-innovate the technological products the fastest.

Companies are pouring millions of dollars to provide each link that connect these pieces of technology. The old technology phrase that comes to mind, "we are only two years from failure," that has definitely sent a message across the globe to all companies who want to contribute in new business innovations in technology.

Effect of the Internet on International Entrepreneurship

The Internet has changed the way the industry distributes goods and services. A major effect is how distribution companies evaluate their services for allocating and distributing goods. The customer today has much more emphasis on how their roles will affect the distribution industry. An efficient network that will facilitate the exchange and delivery for goods and services has had distribution companies. Distribution companies have had to create network optimization to obtain and control the flow process between the whereabouts and exact location of their goods and services through information. They have also had to implement and enhance logistics on their technology for product tracking. These are key elements that help keep their network alive and mobile for service production.

What Can Brown Do for You?

United Parcel Services

The UPS e-Logistics solution enables these online enterprises to leverage core UPS strengths—global delivery network, extensive IT systems, and supply chain management experience—to outsource the difficult "back-end" processes of running an e-business. It's a quick and cost-effective supply chain solution for small- and medium-sized B2B and B2C companies.

In an interview with UPS chairman James Kelly, he discusses how information technology has helped create new businesses from its delivery service. The company invested $1 billion a year, ten years ago. The focus of this investment was to try to make UPS available to receive and exchange information with customers.

Kelly's executive team wanted to re-engineer a company objective to meet the needs of the customer worldwide. In this way, he could exchange information with the customer and maintain fluent continuity with the transportation and logistics system networks. The average packages that are delivered from the industry are 13.5 million. The upgrade in their logistics system provided top-notch services that in return gave UPS the ability to tell their customers where their packages were and to use this information to provide broader services across the supply chain.

(Adapted from www.usps.com/archives/newsreleases/, United Parcel Services. June 2001.)

◎ What Can Be Learned

Successful Business Opportunities in International Entrepreneurship

Most people understand the challenges they face when they opt to go into business for themselves. Everyone knows the road of having success in the corporate environment of small, medium, and large corporations. *Free enterprise* has been an incredible advantage to Americans in our national democracy. The freedom of private business to organize and operate for profit in a competitive system without interference by government beyond regulation necessary to protect public interest and keep the national economy in balance only exists in democratic forms similar to the United States. So how does that affect pursuing opportunities in our global society? Our assumption must take us back to the most important questions that anyone pursuing or seeking a business opportunity must face. Do you know if you are entrepreneurial compatible?

Entrepreneurial Savvy

The professional benefit of being successful with an international business opportunity will depend on one's self, as well as enabling others to act and share in the creating of the organization's mission. The entrepreneurial drive must lead others to understand the importance of ownership and empowerment in the organization. They must act as stewards who understand the organizational culture and environment. The organization as a whole must be optimistic and look for the opportunity to produce results. The entrepreneurial leader must model the way for the organizational community to understand their vision and purpose. A lot of soul searching will transpire for the entrepreneurial drive to catch on as a fever that is burning hot through their entire organizational community. Encouraging others and building an organizational environment that shares the optimistic uncertainty with a vision in mind will lead to a successful organization in today and tomorrow's global society.

Alternative Approaches of International Entrepreneurship

The international entrepreneur must know that he or she will place a lot of emphasis on the work ethic through the power of a vision or growth image, even if it is only an illusion. This is perhaps the most crucial strategy that must be set in motion early for a business opportunity to be successful from its embryonic beginnings.

The opportunities for business opportunities in the international market place for an entrepreneur are not as challenging as they were just one decade ago. There are several alternative approaches that can be utilized as a competitive advantage for the emergence into global markets.

- The Internet and its expanding role in international markets.
- The political and social integration of big emerging markets (Asia, Eastern Europe, Japan, and China).

- The economic spurt evolving in global middle-income households.
- The collaborative qualitative and quantitative research conducted by organizations through strategic alliances and corporate and functional development in major corporations and small businesses.
- Trends in channel structures in Europe, Japan, and developing structures.
- Ethics and social responsibility in today's global environment.[15]

These different areas need to be evaluated by an idealist to formulate strategies for a successful road in breaking the international ground barriers. Many have attempted to examine particular factors associated with success in entrepreneurship such as the following:

- Financial Factors that Provide Opportunities for Entrepreneurs
  Lack of records is a main major contributor to the failure of a small business in the first ten years. Records are a major component and a major asset to the financial agenda. One must also remember the value of exchange rates as they are implementing strategies in the global environment.

- Incentive and Control Systems
  Understanding the five P's,
  1. *The purpose behind the opportunity*—This includes the leader's vision, mission, goals, and objectives, as well as strategies for achieving the mission and vision in a global market.

  2. *The principles behind entering the market*—The principles, assumptions, philosophy, and attitude that the entrepreneur embraces through their organizational community.

  3. *The processes for succession*—The organizational structure and procedures to make the products or services compatible in the organizational infrastructure to support the system and international structure.

  4. *The outcome or performance that is expected*—If the leaders of the organizations have enabled all members of their organizations to buy into their mission and vision, the organizations' results will maximize profitability, which will lead to additional incentives and rewards based on performance.

  5. *The people behind the idea*[16]—The people are the most crucial foundation to the channels of your road to international embryonic success. These people are committed to believing in the purpose, the principles, and the process for the organization to succeed in the twenty-first century as we enter the globalization era.

- Market and Entry Approaches
  Examine cases of success and failure utilizing different marketing strategies to introduce products, services, and ideas into the market place. The entrepreneurial drive will lead to research in the areas which are barriers to enter in a global emerging market. The high barriers and/or expectations of swift retaliation from existing competitors lead to seven major barriers that develop the strategic windows for an entrepreneur to enter an emerging market.

Economies of scale—For which the decline of unit costs of a product or service that occurs as the absolute volume of production in a given time period increases.

Product differentiation—Established organizations may enjoy strong brand identification and customer loyalties that are based on actual or perceived product and service differences.

Capital requirements—The need to invest large financial resources at the outset. This could become an important factor to your organization entering the emerging global market space.

Switching costs—Referring to the one-time cost that buyers of the industry's outputs incur as they switch from one company's product or service to another. These are uncontrollable barriers that must be reviewed by an entrepreneur entering a major market that is uncharted by business outside the respective country(ies).

Access to distribution channels—In some countries, entering existing distribution channels or country structures requires a new firm to entice distributors through price incentives (breaks), cooperative advertising allowances, or sales promotions.

Cost disadvantage independent of scale—Established organizations in globalization may possess cost advantages that cannot be replicated by new ventures and the threat of competition.

Government policy—The governing bodies of the respective countries will help control entry to certain types of industries that could affect the internal structures of cultures of business in the respective countries. Countries must pay close attention to policy and government regulations for aspiring entrepreneurship.[17]

Summary

An entrepreneur must understand all of the facts and assumptions for entering their idea into the global marketspace. Once this steward has assessed their organizational core competencies, they must evaluate the alternative approaches to make a successful launch into the twenty-first century with their newfound business product or services. These strategies will be discussed in later chapters of this book. The macroenvironments, economic, political, social, and market driven/technology demands need to be examined as possible causal factors in the success or failure of international entrepreneurship. The right drive, the right passion, and the right strategic window will lead unique men and women to be the revolutionary business leaders of global expansion in the twenty-first century.

Discussion Questions

1. What role do organizations like the International Monetary Fund, World Bank, and European Monetary System play in international trade?
2. What are some reasons a country would employ protectionist measures? What types of groups or organizations are in place in the global arena to mediate issues between countries with regard to protectionism?
3. Give an example of each of the three key areas that an entrepreneur should understand while researching global market opportunities: (1) balance of trade relationships; (2) political forces that affect entry to market; and (3) domestic industry development and how countries will protect their own existing industry.
4. Describe the five elements for analysis on culture that entrepreneurs should focus on when considering global markets according to Herskovits.
5. What effects has the Internet had on international entrepreneurship and how does it relate to its future?

Endnotes

1. Cateora, P., and J. Graham. 1999. *International Marketing*, 10th ed. Boston, MA: McGraw-Hill.
2. Kurlantzic, J. Promised land. *Entrepreneur Magazine*. January 2004: 66–69.
3. Kuratko, D. F., Montagno, R. V., and J. S. Hornsby. 1990. Developing an intrapreneurial assessment instrument for an effective corporate entrepreneurial environment. *Strategic Management Journal* 11:49–58.
4. Lee, C. The global implications of the U.S. fiscal deficit and of China's growth. *World Economic Outlook* April 2004: 63–66.
5. Kurlantzic, J. International success in today's world economy. *Entrepreneur Magazine* February 2003.
6. Layman, J. Macau's handover to mainland China. CSIS Hong Kong Update August–September 1999.
7. European Communities, 1995–2003. Legal notice. http://europa.eu.int/geninfo/disclaimer_en.htm.
8. Robbins, S. P. 2003. Challenges and opportunities of organizational behavior. In *Organizational Behavior*, 10th ed. New Jersey: Prentice Hall: 14.
9. Miller, D., and P. Friesen. 1985. Innovation in conservative and entrepreneurial firms: two models of strategic management. *Strategic Management Journal* 3:1–25.
10. Hayes, R. H., and W. J. Abernathy. 1980. Managing our way to economic decline. *Harvard Business Review* July–August: 67–77.
11. Cisco Systems, June 2001. www.cisco.com/archives/newsreleases/.
12. Kanter, R. M. 1985. Supporting innovation and venture development in established companies. *Journal of Business Venturing* 1:47–60.
13. Kurlantzic, J. Stay Home? *Entrepreneur Magazine* February 2003: 66–69.
14. Herskovits, M. 1952. *Man and His Works*. New York: Alfred A. Knopf: 634.
15. Pride, W., and O. C. 2000. Ferrell. *Marketing and its Environment. Marketing Concepts and Strategies*. Boston: Houghton Mifflin Company: 79–107.
16. Pryor, M., White, J., and L. Toombs. 1998. Organizational variable and the five P's. *Strategic Quality Management*. Houston, TX: Dame Publications: 1–3.
17. Parnell, J. A. 2001. *Industry Competition. Strategic Management Concepts*. Texas A&M University Commerce: 23–26.

Part Two

Specialized Topics

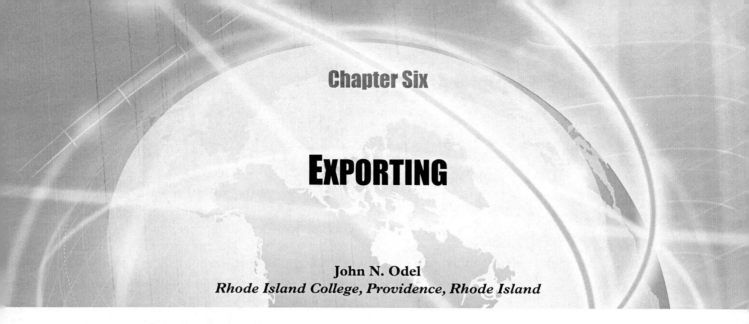

Chapter Six

EXPORTING

John N. Odel
Rhode Island College, Providence, Rhode Island

Learning Objectives

Upon completion of this chapter, students should be able to:

- Better grasp the large potential for success for the entrepreneur through exporting.
- Identify sources of information for international market analysis.
- Be aware of the financing options available to the entrepreneur who exports.
- Determine advantages and disadvantages of direct exporting and indirect exporting, as well as the role of freight forwarders.
- Strengthen knowledge of resources, government and private, to assist the entrepreneur in exporting efforts.
- Better comprehend utilization of e-commerce by the entrepreneur who exports.
- Understand various payment options used in export.
- Be aware of changing export controls/regulations.

Key Terms

ATLAS database	financing options
ELAN/SBIs	freight forwarders
entrepreneurial support organizations	INCO terms
export costs	OPIC/USAID
export management companies	proactive and reactive efforts in exporting
exporting mindset	SCORE/SBDC
export trading companies	trade intermediaries

◎ Introduction

Exporting involves the sale of products manufactured in the one country (often the home or domestic country of the company) to consumers in another (foreign) country.[1] Exports support over 11 million jobs in the United States. In recent years, international sales have contributed to nearly 30% of domestic growth. With 96% of the world's population and 67% of the world's purchasing power living outside of the United States, it is not surprising that there is great potential for growth for U.S. businesses.[2] This participation in international trade is not limited to large companies; while the number of U.S. firms that send products and services to international markets has tripled since 1990, fully two-thirds of that substantial growth results from firms having less than twenty employees.[3] The U.S. Small Business Administration reports that small businesses represent 97% of American exporters.[4]

Given the incredible growth of the world market, the falling of trade barriers, and the advances in communication and transportation, exporting is no longer the venue of large multinational corporations. Exporting has become a vital aspect of the operations of U.S. businesses, regardless of size. The globalization of the economy has created enormous opportunities for many small businesses. While there are a number of avenues an entrepreneur may pursue to go international, such as alliances with foreign firms or investing in the ownership of assets in a foreign market, this chapter will focus on exporting, as this is commonly the initial foray into international trade.[5,6]

There are many reasons why an entrepreneur or a small business should consider exporting as a viable option for his or her enterprise. As has often been said, the world is shrinking and this can be an advantage for the entrepreneur or small business. Advances in communication and in transportation have substantially reduced many of the barriers to entry for smaller ventures into international trade. Costs and complexities associated with cross border business, although they still exist, have largely been reduced in intensity. It has been argued that the size of the enterprise, while it may impact certain activities, may no longer be as pivotal a factor as it once was in an enterprises' decision to enter, or its degree of operations in, international trade, particularly for firms with more than twenty employees.[7-9]

Benefits Associated with Exporting

Exporting can offer many opportunities to the entrepreneur. Exporting can make the world the market, product, or service of the entrepreneur. It can expand sales by opening new markets for the entrepreneur. Increasing sales is a prime reason for the entrepreneur to consider exporting. Entrepreneurs are now opening businesses with the intention to become global at the very start of the venture.[10] Foreign demand for the entrepreneur's product or service is also a viable reason for exporting. Given improved capacity for communications, it is entirely possible that a nondomestic potential customer may see or learn about the entrepreneur's product and contact the entrepreneur to attempt to purchase the product or service, and then have it sent to them in the customer's home country.

Also, the weak value of the U.S. dollar can actually serve as a stimulus for increased purchase of U.S. goods by foreign consumers, as the decrease in value reduces the price(s) of U.S. goods, making them more attractive. Exporters can profit from increased sales, and U.S. exporters may retain workers. The exporters may also find that they can augment diminishing domestic sales and income by sales of products overseas.

Exporting also allows the entrepreneur to have access to another (foreign) market without having the associated expenses of establishing and maintaining local operational facilities. Using export as a tool to tap the foreign markets, the entrepreneur has access to expanded markets without encountering the expense and potential risk of placing assets in another country.

Another reason for exporting is to increase the life of the product or service. Another market could be found for a product or service that has matured in another market where demand for that item may now be falling as a result. Similarly, exporting could be explored when the entrepreneur identifies an unmet need or niche in an international context. If the entrepreneur believes that he or she could respond to that need, such an event could seem appealing, even if it is in an international setting.

Other considerations may include that the entrepreneur's exporting activity is in response to the fact that significant domestic customers of the entrepreneur's product or service may have international operations (and/or may have moved to an international location entirely) and the entrepreneur seeks to maintain a commercial relationship with that customer so the entrepreneur now follows the customer. Also, the principle of diversification may prompt the entrepreneur to give serious thought to cross-border sales.

As economic conditions vary across the world, the entrepreneur may find it advantageous to pursue sales internationally when the domestic economy may be soft or stagnant. Exporting may be motivated by the entrepreneur having strong family or heritage ties to another country or region. The entrepreneur may choose to sell his or her product or service to that locale even though it is made in another country.

The same advances in technology, transportation, and communication that reduce some of the barriers to exporting may in fact be vehicles to promote the product or service of the entrepreneur and facilitate international demand and sales. As will be explored in more detail later in this chapter, the Internet opens new doors for the entrepreneur in terms of having an active export program.

Exporting Mindset

In order to benefit from exporting, there are a number of initial considerations that the entrepreneur must become aware of and familiar with:

- commitment
- analyzing your firm's capabilities
- export potential of your product or service

- locating foreign markets
- market entry strategies
- learning export procedures
- processing an export order[11]

The decision to pursue exporting as a viable option for your entrepreneurial firm should not be taken lightly. Rather than being an afterthought, exporting should be thought of as a component of the small firm's overall strategic plan.[12] It should involve an assessment of the enterprise and of the entrepreneur to determine the export readiness and what skills/abilities of the firm and the entrepreneur and how they could benefit from training and/or assistance from export specialists.[13] It will require an investment of your time and effort in order to yield successful outcomes. To be successful, the entrepreneur should devote time to foreign markets as well as domestic markets, even during periods of successful domestic business (not just looking internationally when the domestic market is soft). Your firm is no longer operating only in the domestic market when you choose to export your product or service.

Advancing beyond domestic borders will require some adjustments and the adjustments will be in operational aspects but also in the way of thinking, or the outlook, of you and your enterprise.[14] Entering the international arena is at once exciting and concerning. It is exciting because it opens new doors and potential new markets for your product or service, reaching more and different customers. It can lead to expansion or growth if that is what you desire, bringing a sense of difference and change.

But the very sense of change that it brings can also be perceived as threatening or at least troubling. The newness it can bring can be concerning as it is likely to involve tasks and activities that you may not be familiar with. The unknown quality of what to do and how to do it—perhaps even where to start—can be a stumbling block that may even prevent the entrepreneur from doing little more than just consider exporting. It has been suggested, however, that if the entrepreneur sees exporting as more than just a means of increasing economic strength of the enterprise, but also as a vehicle for learning (and thereby strengthening the enterprise), it may positively impact the decision of the entrepreneur to engage in exporting.[15,16]

It is very important that you, the entrepreneur, be firmly committed to reaching out to markets. Viewing foreign markets and international trade as a potentially valuable source of business activity will assist you in your efforts to develop a successful exporting operation.[17] You must realize the investments in time and effort as well as the adjustments it is likely to require in your enterprise. The potential for return, though, can be considerable and worthwhile.

Changing Perspectives/Changing Markets

A new generation of internationally minded entrepreneurs is aware of markets beyond domestic borders.[10,18] These individuals are aware of growing markets in developing and developed nations. Entrepreneurs of various heritages may choose to sell their products/services to consumers in the country/region of their cultural or ethnic background. Some of these regions boast enormous numbers of potential consumers. The combined populations of the nations of the Indian subcontinent nearly rival China's 1.2 billion. Entrepreneurs and their businesses can take advantage of the North American Free Trade Agreement to expand the markets for their products/services by selling to our closest neighbors Mexico and Canada. The nations of South/Central America are also a growing market for the products/services of U.S. businesses. The proposals for the Free Trade Agreement of the Americas (FTAA) may increase the access to this region, heightening its attractiveness for U.S. enterprises.

Of course, the nations of Western Europe have always been a market for the products/services of American businesses. With its expansion to increased numbers of member nations, and the introduction of a common currency, the European Union will yield a very attractive market of nearly 500 million consumers (more than twice the size of the population of the United States).

Brief Summary of Benefits of Exporting

- Increased profits
- Increased market share
- Extending the life cycle of the product or service
- Offsetting the seasonality of products
- Increased productivity
- Better utilization of company personnel[11]

These and other reasons have made exporting a very attractive option for U.S. entrepreneurs. Exporting provides a number of very attractive options for the entrepreneur especially given the increased competition in the U.S. market, from U.S. competitors, and from companies outside of the United States.

Proactive Efforts to Engage in Exporting

Being proactive suggests that the entrepreneur has decided on active engagement in international trade via exporting. The entrepreneur makes a concerted effort to search, identify, and explore a foreign market(s). This is a planned activity with a recognized commitment of the resources of the entrepreneur and his or her firm. Such international activity becomes part of the overall plan of the entrepreneurial venture, in terms of operations and as a venue for future growth. As discussed elsewhere in this text, in pursuing such a course of action the entrepreneur is well served by developing an international business plan. This document assists the entrepreneur with comprehensively addressing the international dimension of the enterprise. Allocations of time, money, personnel, and additional resources of the enterprise can be detailed within this document. Costs and benefits can be formulated; an analysis of all the enterprises' activities as well as the overall goals of the entrepreneur can be represented in this plan. The international business plan is a highly valuable document for the entrepreneur considering any kind of international operation, but can be of particular use in, and for, exporting. Based on this information the entrepreneur can better match the enterprises' abilities and the resources which are available to the entrepreneur (examples of which may be found at the end of this chapter) with the opportunities presented internationally.[19]

Reactive Efforts to Engage in Exporting

Reactive exporting occurs when a firm responds to product inquiries from foreign consumers. In such cases the entrepreneur does not employ an active search for (new) foreign markets or demand for the entrepreneur's goods. Similarly, the entrepreneur may respond to demand for products/services from past domestic customers who have located their facilities in another nation(s).

The entrepreneur who engages in online marketing may find that the Internet (given its global nature) may yield contacts with/from consumers outside of the country of the entrepreneur. The entrepreneur may choose to follow through with such contacts and find that this passive approach to sales generation may yield a foreign market that may be served via export.

Costs Associated with Exporting

Some considering adding an international dimension to their small business may hesitate due to the added costs often associated with exporting.[20] Licenses, fees, insurance, overseas shipping, customs agents, and bills of lading are all examples of potential costs. The entrepreneur may also consider opportunity costs, as exporting is a process that is likely to require a large investment of time (especially when initiating an export activity.) The entrepreneur may consider that this time could be better spent on his or her domestic market.[19]

International trade does have costs beyond those of a purely domestic trade, yet the costs may not be as arduous as the entrepreneur examining exporting may initially anticipate. An additional cost may be that the entrepreneur has no knowledge of international markets and no prior experience in international trade; this may make the entrepreneur feel that exporting is beyond his or her skill or ability. This perceived cost may make the entrepreneur much less likely to pursue exporting as a viable option for the growth and development of his/her business.

Advantages of the Entrepreneur/Small Firm in International Trade

Small firms have a number of advantages that large firms may not have; for example, being able to more rapidly respond to changing demands from the marketplace. This flexibility of being able to respond and adapt to changing market conditions in a relatively short amount of time is often a key asset of an entrepreneurial venture. This can be of significant importance in the international trade arena.

Yet, large firms have the advantage of size. A large firm is more likely to be able to have personnel and resources it can dedicate to exploring international markets and running its export operations. The smaller firm may not be able to draw on such internal resources. This may be a factor which limits the participation of smaller firms in international trade/export.

However, small- and medium-sized firms can work cooperatively to facilitate export success and assist each other in achieving their goals. State, local, and regional entrepreneurial support organizations often sponsor programs available to small businesses to ease their entry into international markets. These organizations can be government or private and can provide substantial pathways and ways to work together. Such networking can aid not only in entering a foreign market, but it may also be a resource for members of the network over the long term.[21]

Resources to Support the Entrepreneur in Exporting and Market Assessment

There are numerous resources the entrepreneur may call on to assist him or her in the entire export process, particularly in the analysis of foreign markets. This section will highlight government and private organizations that can assist the entrepreneur in market analysis, financing, and further exploration of the exporting option.

As attractive as international trade may appear for the entrepreneur, and it may be very beneficial, it is very important that the entrepreneur carefully assess whether or not a market exists for his or her product or service and if there is potential for market growth and determine if the product or service will be competitively priced.

If this sounds similar to what was done in the creation of a domestic-based business plan for the enterprise, it is. The variable(s) here are the international market, the factors affecting transportation and distribution, and access to information. Assessing an international marketplace may not be as easy as investigating a market in your own city, state, or nation, but it is not as difficult as it may seem as a result of the large number of assets the American small business/entrepreneur has when looking into a foreign market.

The U.S. Small Business Association (SBA) and U.S. Department of Commerce have many resources available to assist in market determination from online items and databases to the face-to-face assistance provided by Export Assistance Centers (EACs) and local/regional organizations comprised of U.S. Department of Commerce Trade Specialists and others who concentrate in international trade.

EACs are located across the United States (a list is provided in the appendix of this chapter.) These agencies pull together various federal resources and other initiatives designed to provide support to the entrepreneur/small business. They work with the small businesses individually on topics ranging from identification of foreign markets, to developing marketing approaches for the targeted markets, and assistance in linking small firms/entrepreneurs with financing mechanisms focused on exporting.

To assist the entrepreneur in the myriad legal matters that he or she may encounter, the SBA, in conjunction with the Federal Bar Association, has the Export Legal Assistance Network (ELAN). This program connects the entrepreneur with experienced international trade attorneys to address issues such as contracts, agreements between the parties involved in the various aspects of exporting, and payment resolution matters. Under this program the initial consultation with the attorney is free of charge.[22]

Many entrepreneurs can receive skilled managerial and trade assistance from the Service Corps of Retired Executives (SCORE) and Small Business Development Centers (SBDCs). Small Business Institutes (SBIs) affiliated with colleges and universities can work with the entrepreneur to perform market assessments and analyses. Private entrepreneurial support organizations or exporting organizations can also provide information for the entrepreneur and may augment the material available from government sources.

Using these resources will help the entrepreneur better identify a foreign market and determine whether or not it will be a viable market for that entrepreneur. In order to make this determination the entrepreneur needs to do the following:

- Classify his/her product;
- Find countries with the largest and fastest growing markets for his/her product;
- Determine which foreign markets will be the most penetrable;
- Define and narrow those markets he or she intends to pursue;
- Talk to U.S. customers doing business internationally; and
- Research export efforts of U.S. competitors.[23]

Classification is done through the use of the Standard Industrial Classification (SIC) code; other systems include the North American Industry Classification System (NAICS), the Standard International Trade Classification system (SITC), and the Harmonized System (HS). Knowing the classification codes of your product or service is important in the gathering and interpretation of data that may be available and in obtaining tariff information. (The U.S. Bureau of the Census—USB—can be of help in identifying the HS number of the entrepreneur's product.)

The utilization of the databases, such as the National Trade Data Bank, and support organizations will be of great value for the entrepreneur in securing appropriate data and properly analyzing the information to be able to make informed decisions about where to market his or her product or service as well as which markets are likely to be more receptive to the product or service. Seeking the advice of various agencies/departments (in person and online) can also help in determining levels of competition in the target markets. The counsel of current traders and other sources may add color or detail or supply a richness of information to augment the analysis of statistical data.

Use of Automated Trade Locator Assistance System (ATLAS), also referred to as Export Access, through the SBA's Office of International Trade can greatly assist the entrepreneur considering exporting. ATLAS can help identify the largest potential markets for the entrepreneur's product/service using a variety of criteria (including sales and dollar volume). This system works best if the entrepreneur has already done some preliminary investigation and has indicated certain target markets (supplying more specific information assists in getting the best results from the database). ATLAS is accessible, at no cost, at SBA regional offices.[22]

Export Options

The following will be examined in this section:

- Direct exporting
  - The enterprise engages in the complete export process by itself. Often it will utilize a representative to sell product/service to distributors, retailers, or end-use consumers.
- Indirect exporting
  - The enterprise utilizes the services of a third party, trade intermediary to arrange for sale and shipment of goods/services.
- The use of third party trade intermediaries and trading companies in exporting
- Export trading company
- Export management company
- International distributors
- Freight forwarders
- E-exporting

After the market analysis and the analysis of his or her own firm, the entrepreneur can choose between two approaches to export of a product/service. The entrepreneur may decide to handle the entire export operation him or herself. Direct exporting involves the use of independent distributors or the entrepreneur's own international sales office or (increasingly common) via the Internet and the business' own Web site.[24] The Internet substantially expands the entrepreneur's potential for being closely involved in the marketing and sales of his/her product or service. The use of the Internet and/or e-commerce also makes it much easier and more efficient for such operational aspects to be handled by the entrepreneur.[25]

Indirect exporting involves the use of a third party or trade intermediaries to conduct the distribution and sale of the entrepreneur's product/service in an international market. There are variations in the types of services the intermediaries may provide and whether or not they may specialize (and if so, how? For example, by product, market, region).

The major types of trade intermediaries are an export management company and an export trading company. Other trade intermediaries include export agents, remarketers, or merchants. Attention will be directed to the export management company, the export trading company, and international distributors.

The export management company (EMC) is an organization that assists in the export of the product/service of the business that is seeking to export its items to an international market. Usually operating on a contract basis, the EMC will function as the department of the business that handles the exporting operation for their client. The EMC will contact foreign sales representatives and/or distributors on behalf of their client. The EMC generally will provide foreign market research, select international distributors, and conduct marketing, sales, ordering, and transportation activities involved in the export of the product or service. The documentation required in the export process may even be completed by the EMC.

Another feature is that the EMC may obtain and review credit information as well as be a source of advice on foreign accounts and payment terms. Services such as these may make the EMC an attractive option for the small firm entering the export waters. However, there is a concern that, as the EMC is an independent agent, the firm working with the EMC may lose control over its product or service and may not be actively involved in the item's promotion or sales. Therefore, the business considering using the EMC must weigh the benefits as well as the costs.[26]

An export trading company (ETC) is another trade intermediary that the entrepreneur may choose as a means of indirect exporting. The ETC usually purchases the product or service from the entrepreneur's business and then proceeds to transport and sell the item in an international market(s). Often the ETC will obtain orders from international consumers for the product or service prior to its purchase of those items. While this does present another venue for exporting of the product or service, the entrepreneur must again consider whether the loss of control of its product or service, and its international distribution, is balanced by the savings of the labor and involvement in direct export. The services an ETC can provide for smaller enterprises that export are assistance with making personal connections with interested buyers in foreign markets and the expertise of the ETC regarding the competitive situation in foreign markets.[27] Trading companies can vary in size with the United States having a large number of smaller trading companies. Non-U.S. trading companies are some of the largest in the world.[28]

International distributors are another trade agent that can be utilized by the entrepreneur who exports. International distributors already have relationships with overseas stores and consumers. The international distributor will purchase the entrepreneur's product, make use of the sales team of the distributor, and identify foreign buyers. This can facilitate the entrepreneur's goal of getting his or her product in the hands of foreign consumers and can be very helpful in the export process. However, as with all intermediaries, the entrepreneur is best served by carefully examining potential international distributors before making a final choice. Researchers have identified a number of rules to be followed when selecting an overseas distributor for your goods.[29]

Rules to Be Followed When Selecting an Overseas Distributor

1. Examine potential distributor's ability to provide the service/support needed.
2. Prior to signing an agreement, learn about and become familiar with the distributor and the professional relationship you will establish. Involve an attorney in the formation of the contract/review of documents.
3. Examine cultural differences.
4. Review/be aware of local laws in the country(ies).[29]

Freight Forwarders

Once the decision has been made to commit the organization to international trade, the issue of transporting the product must be addressed. Moving goods internationally is more involved than moving goods from one part of a city to another, from one part of the state to another, or, for that matter, moving items from state to state. The entrepreneur is now moving items across national boundaries, not mention across large distances, which may involve transport across oceans.

The shipment of goods from one nation to another involves many concerns not typically seen in domestic travel; for example, the packaging of an item to withstand long ocean trips or the efficient use of space to reduce costs in air freight. The documentation and government regulations (from the exporter's home nation to those of the foreign destination) and even the choice of transport, sea, air, or land are points the entrepreneur engaged in international trade must contend with. Especially, as the choices made may influence the ultimate cost of the item to the end consumer as well as the speed of its delivery to that consumer. The entrepreneur must weigh all the costs associated with the different forms of transportation with the time it will take to have the items reach the consumer and, subsequently, the amount of time it will take for the entrepreneur to be paid.

The freight forwarder is an organization that will transport the items of the exporting organization to the international destination. Such organizations are knowledgeable of the documentation and regulations (U.S. and foreign) associated with export as well as being familiar with various methods of shipping items cargo to international locations. Freight forwarders can be good sources of information, especially when the entrepreneur is new to export because they can supply information on the various procedures and costs associated with moving products internationally.[23]

The freight forwarder may also assist in working with the customs broker to make certain that all documents and customs documentation and regulations are complied with. If arrangements have not been made by the entrepreneur to transport the product(s) he or she is exporting to the cargo carrier (for example, ship or plane), the freight forwarder may assist the entrepreneur in this regard by moving the product(s) for export to the carrier to the loaded on the vessel.[23]

E-exporting

The advances in communication and in technology that have served to decrease the costs(s) and time of traditional exporting (whether direct exporting or via a trade intermediary), have also brought about a new mechanism for the entrepreneur who exports. In fact, many of the concerns of the traditional export process, such as communications and the marketing of the product or service, are not the obstacles they once were when the entrepreneur employs the Internet as the vehicle for trade.

The low cost of the Internet, its relative ease of use (for the exporter and the buyer), and its global reach have made it an attractive alternative to aspects of the more traditional export process. This low cost access to global markets is especially enticing for smaller firms which have been severely limited from participating in foreign markets largely due to the excessive costs that were involved.

The worldwide reach of the Internet and the huge number of people connected by it (more than 600 million, and the growth rate is astounding) identify strengths of this medium. Also, the range of trade categories presents opportunities for the entrepreneur who exports. In addition to sales to the consumer (business to consumer or B2C), options include business-to-business (B2B), government-to-business (G2B), as well as peer-to-peer (P2P) (so called e-marketplaces).

As the potential markets for e-exporting vary, so do the types of Web sites the enterprise can have to serve these markets. The costs of Web site construction and the various features which the site may have can vary widely, and the site may be customized to meet the specific demands of the target market and the exporting objective(s) of the enterprise. The variations in the sites have three general characteristics. The *transactional site* offers a full range of services to the potential client: searching, ordering, payment, even after sales service contacts are all done online. Some systems can tie in with other systems such as accounting and inventory management. The *information delivery site* functions more to increase market awareness of the entrepreneur's product or service rather than act as a venue for handling purchases. In many ways, this is an electronic brochure highlighting aspects of the enterprise's product or service. *E-marketplaces* are "market makers"; sites that bring together buyers and sellers to make exchanges possible. Sites such as these include online auctions and business matching services.

Of course, e-exporting does not eliminate all of the hurdles often associated with exporting, such as transoceanic shipping, but several significant impediments no longer have the influence they once had. As a result of low cost worldwide access and information dissemination, a barrier to international trade that was largely driven by "deep pockets" has been greatly diminished. However, there are still other steps involved in exporting and these steps have expenses, and these expenses must be met. The next section examines the possibilities for financing export efforts of the entrepreneur.[25]

Financing for Small Business Export Initiatives

Although international trade is an exciting and potentially very lucrative area for many entrepreneurs, obtaining funding to help this become a functional reality is not always easy. Many local financial institutions may work well in domestic situations; however, they just may not have the international expertise from which they can draw when an entrepreneur seeks assistance from them in an international endeavor. In response to this, the U.S. Small Business Administration has three loan packages for entrepreneurs participating in export: SBA Export*Express*, The Export Working Capital Loan, and the International Trade Loan.

SBA Export*Express* is a potentially useful program that combines lending assistance with technical assistance in an effort to help the entrepreneur secure adequate financing. Technical assistance comes from the involvement of a representative from a U.S. EAC who will contact the borrower to offer aid. According to the SBA, this is its most flexible financing program yet. Among the uses of the proceeds of this loan package are supporting participation in trade shows, translating product literature, revolving letters of credit, and constructing or renovating facilities in the U.S. to produce products/services for export.

The Export Working Capital Loan Program (EWCP) is another vehicle to help the entrepreneur secure sufficient capital for an export transaction. This particular package can be useful in situations when the entrepreneur has developed export leads but needs additional capital to complete the transaction. The proceeds from this instrument can be applied to the acquisition of inventory for export, financing costs of U.S. labor and overhead for service company exports, and financing foreign accounts receivable, among other uses.

The International Trade Loan can provide assistance to small businesses already involved in exporting, those becoming ready to engage in export, as well as those negatively impacted by import-based competition. Uses of this package include the building of new facilities, the purchase of new or refurbishing machinery, as well as making other improvements that will stay in the United States for the production of goods or services.[2]

The Export–Import Bank of the United States (the Ex-Im bank) is also a potential source of financing for the small business. The Ex-Im Bank is an independent federal government agency that is responsible for supporting the export of U.S. products and services. The Ex-Im Bank offers loan and guarantee programs, but also information services and insurance programs to reduce the financial risk of the exporter. Some of the products the Ex-Im Bank offers are direct and intermediary loans, loan guarantees, and pre-export loans.

In addition to the Working Capital Guarantee Program (WCGP) highlighted above, the Ex-Im Bank also provides short-term export credit insurance. This program can be useful to the entrepreneur as it can serve to limit the entrepreneur's exposure in terms of international risk; it may also assist in offering credit to international buyers as well as providing funds for working capital. Both programs have certain restrictions including "local content" requirements and length of operation. Other bank insurance initiatives such as the Small Business and Umbrella insurance programs are focused on small firms who are new to exporting.[30] The Ex-Im Bank is located in Washington, DC, but has regional offices in New York; Chicago; Long Beach, California; San Jose, California; Miami; and Houston. The hotline number for the Ex-Im Bank is 800-565-EXIM.

Concerns about risk(s) in international trade have been listed as a barrier to engaging in export by some entrepreneurs.[20] To address this issue, as noted above, the Ex-Im Bank offers some insurance for the entrepreneur. A more extensive approach is taken by the Overseas Private Investment Corporation (OPIC). This U.S. government development agency works to encourage economic growth and development in emerging markets principally by issuing insurance programs designed to mitigate the risk a business may encounter in international trade especially as related to political instability and market reforms.

OPIC has recently begun programs designed to assist small businesses particularly in working with emerging markets. OPIC now has the Small and Medium Enterprise Department to focus on the needs/concerns of small- and medium-sized (U.S.) firms looking to enter new emerging foreign markets. OPIC is a self sustaining entity, which charges (market-based) fees for its products.[31]

There may be other financial support programs the entrepreneur can take advantage of. Other U.S. federal departments or agencies may have their own focused international trade incentives and these may be available to the entrepreneur. Some may be focused on certain economic sectors and may be options the entrepreneur may consider only if the exported product/service is aligned with the various government department or agency. For instance, a U.S. Department of Agriculture international trade initiative may be available only to enterprises that have an agriculturally focused product/service.[32]

Similarly, the U.S. Agency for International Development (USAID) is the federal agency that focused on the delivery of the U.S. Foreign Economic Assistance Program. The USAID's Center for Trade and Investment Services assists in promoting business activity between U.S. businesses and foreign entrepreneurs in developing/emerging nations. Likewise, the U.S. Trade Development Agency is a federal institution that provides grants for feasibility studies or other planning approaches for major projects that are economic development proprieties in certain countries.[32]

Payment Options

The payment for the product or service of the entrepreneur becomes somewhat more complicated when considering international trade (primarily export). The entrepreneur has a number of payment options available and each has advantages and disadvantages, although these are not always readily apparent or determined by numerical figures alone.

One option is to demand payment in advance. While this will eliminate the risk of the entrepreneur sending the product or delivering the service and not receiving payment and may be the most practical option, it may also result in lost business as many potential buyers may not have, or be willing to commit, the resources prior to receiving the item(s).

Another alternative is a line of credit (LC). This is a financial instrument issued by a bank that is meant to reduce the risk of the exporter not receiving payment for the product or service transported to the international customer. The letter of credit is opened by the importer, or buyer. An irrevocable letter of credit cannot be changed without the express permission of the exporter. The letter of credit is confirmed by a U.S. bank (usually a bank that is familiar with international trade; often it may have its own international trade/finance department or specialized personnel). Once confirmed, the foreign credit risk to the exporter is nearly eliminated. The letter of credit also offers some protection to the buyer since payment is not authorized until the exporter supplies proof (documentation) that the terms and conditions of the letter of credit have been met.

Documentary collection (draft) is another method of payment in international trade. As the name implies, payment for the items is not made until various documents are produced and received (this payment system, payment on collection, is similar to cash on delivery). With this format of payment, the buyer of the items shipped by the exporter will need to pay, or agree to pay, the exporter before securing the documents needed to take charge of the shipment. A benefit of this format for the buyer is that it gives the buyer extra time (the time needed for the shipment to arrive) to pay. During this time, the exporter still retains the title to the shipment until payment is received. Documentary collection may take different forms.

The utilization of the documents against payment form of this payment alternative requires that the buyer cannot receive the shipping or other documents until payment is made. The form using the term "documents against acceptance" indicates that the buyer is allowed to take title of the shipment after the shipment arrives and the buyer signs a note promising to pay (time draft) after a certain amount of time after documents have been received. This payment method carries risk that the exporter may not receive payment if the buyer does not acknowledge presentation or accept the documents.

Utilizing the open account method of payment generally carries a significant amount of risk for the exporter, but is more commonly being demanded by competitive conditions in the marketplace.

Terms of Trade

In 1936, the International Chamber of Commerce (ICC) established a common set of rules (and terms to describe them) of international trade. These International Commercial Terms (Incoterms) have since undergone several revisions and updating, but the entrepreneur who exports should be aware of these terms and be familiar with their use. It is important that these terms be understood as they are commonly used in international trade contracts. The objective of Incoterms is to mitigate the confusion over the control and insurance of products at the various stages of the shipping process. These terms also govern what is expected of the exporter and importer in terms of packaging for international shipment and clearance. It would be in the exporter's best interest to employ the correct Incoterm when crafting a formal contractual relationship. The ICC has several documents/charts which detail the correct usage/latest version of Incoterms (ICC Publishing 212-206-1150 or www.iccbooks.com).[33,34]

As international sales are different from domestic sales, the exporter should be aware of a number of factors that may impact the terms of the sale/terms of payment. These factors include (but are not limited to) the following:

- price and payment terms, including the currency of the transaction and when payment will be made
- competitive pressures
- forwarder and carrier options
- opportunities for loss and damage
- previous experience with buyer
- city and country of destination
- customs' clearance in buyer's country
- formalities in seller's country, if appropriate
- current economic and political situation in buyer's country[35]

Examples of Incoterms[36]

Cost and Freight (CFR): The seller is responsible for the costs/freight of transporting the product to the named destination. However the risks of product damage/loss are transferred to the buyer when the products pass over the ship's rail. The buyer is responsible for insurance.

Cost, Insurance, and Freight (CIF): CIF is essentially CFR with the seller also having the additional responsibility to provide insurance against damage/loss of products.

Delivered at Frontier (DAF): More commonly used in rail/truck transport. The seller fulfills his or her obligations when the products have arrived at the frontier but before the customs border of the country of destination as identified in the contract. The seller is responsible for the costs and risks up to this point, but the buyer must arrange for the products clearing customs and the associated costs.

Ex works (EXW): The buyer takes charge of the products at the seller's dock and is responsible for carriage and insurance.

Free on Board (FOB): In relation to shipment by sea, the seller of the products is responsible for getting the product to the ship at the exit port; the buyer assumes risks and cost of transporting the products once they "pass the ship's rail" in the home port of the seller.

Free Alongside Ship (FAS): The seller is required to deliver the products alongside the ship at the port. At this point the buyer then assumes all risk and costs for the products. FAS requires the product buyer to be responsible for the products being cleared for export and to pay the loading costs.

Sources of Assistance to Entrepreneurs Who Export

As has been discussed, the international trade arena is vast and can be confusing to even the most seasoned exporter, let alone the entrepreneur who may be considering venturing beyond domestic borders. There exists a large array of resources that are available to assist the entrepreneur in navigating a successful course from idea inception to closing the deal and receiving payment. This chapter highlights resources available to U.S. entrepreneurs, however, similar support mechanisms may exist in other countries as well. The concerned entrepreneur is encouraged to investigate the presence of such organizations/programs in his/her individual country. Unfortunately, many entrepreneurs/small businesses may not be aware of the aid and assistance in exporting that currently exists.[37]

Given that exporting can generate new or additional sales for an entrepreneur, and that the entrepreneur is likely to maintain or expand his/her workforce to meet the demand for the product or service being exported, it is not surprising that many organizations are available to assist the entrepreneur in getting involved in export and even expanding his or her participation. In the United States and other countries there are a wide range of organizations, government and private, some that are low or no cost and others that charge a fee, to support the entrepreneur in exporting.

The United States federal government has many programs the entrepreneur can make use of to begin the export quest or to sharpen skills or answer questions that may be encountered. These include the agencies of the U.S. Small

Business Administration, the U.S. Department of Commerce, and its International Trade Administration.[38] But certainly these are not the only agencies; for instance, if your product/service is in the agriculture industry, the U.S. Department of Agriculture's Foreign Agricultural Service can be of great value. A list of some of the U.S. federal agencies/departments which may be of interest to the entrepreneur who is exploring exporting may be found in the appendix at the end of the chapter.

In addition to federal departments and programs promoting exporting, in just about every state there are state and local export-trade organizations or initiatives. Many of these organizations provide similar types of support programs as those of the federal government, yet these may offer more focus to the specific needs/problems of enterprises in that state.[39] The entrepreneur who is interested in finding such information should contact his or her state or local international trade office, secretary of state, and/or local or regional business development agency.

Export assistance is also available from the private sector. Many organizations and associations will work with local enterprises to support their exporting efforts. Often these associations have manufacturers, bankers, law firms, freight forwarders, and others involved in international trade as members. It may be that companies from across a geographic region will combine their efforts to better enable entrepreneurs to take part in exporting activities. Such organizations can be of value to the entrepreneur as they respond to the exporting questions with a common geographic perspective and they may be knowledgeable of other, more regionally or locally focused, opportunities or mechanisms to support the entrepreneur's exporting. Examples of such organizations are included in the appendix at the end of the chapter.

Trade Missions (State, Regional, Federal)

Trade missions may be another source of assistance and support for the entrepreneur seeking to enter foreign markets. Trade missions are organized tours of foreign markets during which time meetings with potential consumers are usually arranged. These trade missions also allow the entrepreneur to learn how to navigate the various cultural and regulatory matters which may be obstacles or even present opportunities for the entrepreneur who exports. Trade missions are coordinated by state, regional, or even federal officials/agencies and commonly involve a number of businesses, trade, or government officials from the originating locale. Often trade missions are part of a more encompassing effort of economic development in the originating locale. To learn more about upcoming trade missions in your area, contact your local SBA office, your local SBDC, or the EAC that serves your area. (Contact information for some of these organizations may be found in the appendix at the end of this chapter.)

Export Licenses/Controls

According to the U.S. SBA, the majority of export transactions do not require specific approval from a U.S. government agency, so they do not need a license. Technically, however, the most exported items are exported under a general license. This license does not require an application. Generally, export licenses (or special permissions or validated licenses) are needed in situations involving national security, foreign policy, crime control, or items of potential threat or harm (for more information, contact the U.S. Trade Information Center). The entrepreneur who exports would be well advised to verify that the product or service that is being exported does, indeed, not require a special license. This helps to avoid any unexpected difficulties.[23,40]

There is, however, increased attention to preventing certain U.S.-origin items/technology from being acquired by rogue states/organizations/individuals. The current administration seeks legislation to strengthen export controls as well as streamline the process to promote economic growth and ensure national security.[41] According to the U.S. government, a small number of exports do require a license. In situations involving items related to national security; foreign policy; nuclear nonproliferation; nuclear, biological, or chemical (NBC) weaponry/technology; weapons of mass destruction (WMD); or items that may have dual-use require licenses, as do situations involving regional stability, crime control, and terrorist concerns. The requirements for licenses depend on the end use/end user of an item, the destination, and the item's technical characteristics. In order to verify if a license is required, the entrepreneur who exports should contact the U.S. Trade Information Center (TIC), especially as licensing requirements may change.

The reporting regulations, governing the identification of items exported from the United States, have been updated. In 2005 many of the changes and reporting mechanisms reflected the increased attention to national security and general increased oversight. Exporters will no longer be filing the shipping export declaration (SED) as this will be passed out. Exporters will file electronic export information via the automated export system (AES). This system allows for enhanced scrutiny by the various agencies which monitor U.S. exports. "Perhaps the most significant change [of the updating of the reporting regulations] will be the broadening of enforcement authority, which will expand beyond the Census Bureau to include the Office of Export Enforcement (Bureau of Industry and Security) and US Immigration and Customs Enforcement (Department of Homeland Security)." The new regulations also carry stiffer penalties for failure to comply with them.[42]

In order to maintain compliance with the AES, the exporter should pay close attention to the classification of the products being exported (using the appropriate Export Commerce Control Number); the valuation of the products should be fair—not undervalued—(as U.S. government authorities will be closely monitoring this); licensing should be consistent with the description of the product; ultimate consignee information (the end user of the product), authorities will be giving this close attention so the exporter should also carefully review this and is required to inform the authorities of this information.[42]

The U.S. government also makes available a list of illegal exports. The entrepreneur who exports is strongly urged to check updated versions of this list online.[43]

Illegal Exports: Lists to Check[43]

Check these lists to insure your products are not being illegally sold to barred persons or entities.

- **Denied Persons List**—list of persons to whom export privileges are denied by written order of the Department of Commerce.
- **Unverified List**—includes names and countries of foreign persons who in the past were parties to a transaction with respect to which BIS could not conduct a prelicense check (PLC) or a post-shipment verification (PSV) for reasons outside of the U.S. government's control.
- **Entity List**—these end users have been determined to present an unacceptable risk of diversion to developing weapons of mass destruction or the missiles used to deliver those weapons.
- **Specially Designated Nationals List**—alphabetic master list of specially designated nationals and blocked persons.
- **Debarred List**—defense trade controls list.

Summary

As discussed, exporting provides a viable option for engaging in international business. Also, as highlighted, one need not be a large firm to be involved in exporting. The exploration of markets in nations beyond their home point is an activity that more businesses are taking advantage of. This opportunity is not just for large multinational corporations: indeed, ventures of all sizes are successfully operating in markets outside of their home nations.

Often, an initial consideration for the entrepreneur is the lack of knowledge about other countries/markets which may be appropriate for them. Other important issues may include financing, both to support the export of the product/service as well as receiving payment, and learning about/complying with various regulations. The information in this chapter is intended to respond to these, and other, concerns of the entrepreneur regarding exporting.

The path to the export of products/services may not be as arduous as some may think. In fact, there are a large number of resources to assist the entrepreneur with becoming an exporter. The resources are for first-time exporters as well as for the entrepreneur who may have some experience with this opportunity. Many agencies and organizations are available to help promote the export of U.S. products and services. In the appendix to this chapter, the entrepreneur will find a listing of export assistance centers, Web sites, and organizations that provide information exploring exporting (both for the beginner and the seasoned professional). Also the entrepreneur should look into local or regional initiatives that encourage/support exporting, such as the local Chamber of Commerce, the local or regional SBA office, SBDC, as well as the Secretary of State of the entrepreneur's home state (or its Development Agency or equivalent) to learn about trade missions or such events that may be sponsored by that office. By contacting these agencies, the entrepreneur will be in a better position to become involved in the international arena and expand his or her market and opportunities.

Discussion Questions

1. List, and briefly describe, three sources of assistance that the entrepreneur who is new to exporting could make use of to assist him or her in entering the international market.
2. Identify the various sources of financing that may be available to the entrepreneur who exports.
3. Your department head is concerned about exporting. Prepare a list of potential difficulties associated with exporting and indicate how you would respond to and overcome these difficulties.
4. What is direct exporting? What is indirect exporting?
5. What is the difference between proactive and reactive efforts to engage in exporting?

Suggested Reading

Abdnor, J. 1988. The spirit of entrepreneurship *Journal Of Small Business Management* 26(1).

Baird, I. S., Lyles, M. A., and J. B. Orris. 1994. The choice of international strategies for small business. *Journal of Small Business Management* 1994;32(1).

Bonaccorsi, A. 1992. On the relationship between firm size and export intensity. *Journal Of International Business Studies* 23(4).

Carrier, C. 1999. The training and development needs of owner-managers of small businesses with export potential. *Journal Of Small Business Management* 37(4):30–41.

Coalition of New England Companies for Trade (CONECT).

De Noble, A. F., Castaldi, R. M., and D. M. Moliver. 1989. Export intermediaries: Small business perceptions of services and performance. *Journal Of Small Business Management* 27(2):9.

Julien, P-A., and C. Ramagalahy. 2003. Competitive strategy and performance of exporting SMEs: An empirical investigation of the impact of their export information search and competencies *Entrepreneurship Theory And Practice* 27(3):227–245.

Kawas, R. B. 1997. Export financing. *Economic Development Review* 15(2):61–62.

Louter, P. J., Ouwerkerk, C., and B. A. Bakker. 1991. An inquiry into successful exporting. *European Journal Of Marketing* 25(6).

Mittelstadt, J. D., Harben, G. N., and W. A. Ward. 2003. How small is too small? Firm size as a barrier to exporting from the United States. *Journal Of Small Business Management* 41(1):68–84.

Moini, A. H. 1998. Small firms exporting: How effective are government export assistance programs? *Journal Of Small Business Management* 36(1):1–15.

Northeast Export, Louanne, Lemieux, Commerce Publishing Company, Inc.

Oystein, M. 2002. The Born Globals: A new generation of small European exporters. *International Marketing Review London* 19(2/3):156.

Philp, N. E. 1998. The export propensity of the very small enterprise (VSE). *International Small Business Journal* 16(4):79–93.

Westhead, P., Wright, M., and D. Ucbasaran. 2001. The internationalization of new and small firms: A resource-based view. *Journal of Business Venturing* 16(4):333–358.

Wilson, C. D. 1990. Delaware exporter assistance program for small and medium sized companies. *Economic Development Review* 8(3).

Wolf, J. A., and T. L. Pett. 2000. Internationalization of small firms: An examination of export competitive patterns, firm size, and export performance. *Journal of Small Business Management* 38(2):34–47.

Wright, P. C., and W. Nasierowski. 1994. The expatriate family firm and cross-cultural management training: A conceptual framework. *Human Resource Development Quarterly* 5(2).

U.S. Department of Commerce, International Trade Administration.

U.S. Department of Commerce, U.S. Commercial Service. 2000. *The Small Business Financial Resource Guide.*

U.S. Small Business Administration. *Bankable Deals: A Question and Answer Guide to Trade Finance for US Small Business.*

U.S. Small Business Administration. 2003. *Breaking Into the Trade Game: A Small Business Guide.*

U.S. Small Business Administration, Office of International Trade.

Weiss, K. D. 1997. *Building an Import/Export Business*, 2nd ed. New York: John Wiley & Sons, Inc.

Zodl, J. A. 1995. *Export Import: Everything You and Your Company Need to Know to Compete in World Markets.* Cincinnati, OH: Better Way Books.

Endnotes

1. Longnecker, J. G., Moore, C. W., Petty, J., Palich, W., and E. Leslie. 2005. *Small Business Management: An Entrepreneurial Emphasis*, 13th ed. New York: Thomson.

2. U.S. Small Business Administration. Export Financing for Small Business.

3. International Trade Administration. www.export.gov/ explore exporting/whatsinitforme.html.

4. SBA Office of Advocacy. Economics Statistics and Research. *Small Business Frequently Asked Questions.* http://appl.sba.gov/faqs/faqindex. cfm?arealD=24.

5. Baird, I., Lyles, S., Majorie, A., and J. B. Orris. 1994. The choice of international strategies by small businesses. *Journal of Small Business Management* 32(1).

6. Mittelstadt, J. D., Harben, G. N., and W. Ward. 2003. How small is too small? Firm size as a barrier to exporting from the United States. *Journal of Small Business Management* 41(1):68–84.

7. Westhead, P., Wright, M., and D. Ucbasaran. 2001. The internationalization of new and small firms: A resource-based view. *Journal of Business Venturing* 16(4):333–358.

8. Bonaccorsi, A. 1992. On the relationship between firm size and export intensity. *Journal of International Business Studies* 23(4).

9. Wolff, J. A., and T. L. Pett. 2000. Internationalization of small firms: An examination of export competitive patterns, firm size, and export performance. *Journal of Small Business Management* 38(2):34–47.

10. Oystein, M. 2002. The born globals: A new generation of small European exporters. *International Marketing Review* 19(2/3):156–175.

11. U.S. SBA Office of International Trade. 2004. *Is Exporting For You?* 2004. http://www.sba.gov/oit/ export/IsExforYou.htm.

12. Kalantaridis, C. 2004. Internationalization, strategic behavior, and the small firm: A comparative investigation. *Journal of Small Business Management* 42(3):245–262.

13. Carrier, C. 1999. The training and development needs of owner-managers of small businesses with export potential *Journal of Small Business Management* 37(4):30–41.

14. Wright, P. C. 1993. The personal and the personnel adjustments and costs to small businesses entering the international marketplace. *Journal of International Small Business Management* 31(1).

15. Burpitt, W. J., and D. Rondinelli. 2000. Small firms' motivations for exporting: To earn and learn? *Journal of Small Business Management* 38(10):2–13.

16. Burpitt, W. J., and D. Rondinelli. 1998. Export decision-making in small firms. The role of organizational learning. *Journal of World Business* 33(1):51–68.

17. Louter, P. J., Ouwerk, C., and B. A. Bakker. 1991. An inquiry into successful exporting. *European Journal of Marketing* 25(6).

18. Oystein, M., and P. Servais. 2002. Born global or gradual global? Examining the export behavior of small and medium-sized enterprises. *Journal of International Marketing* 10(3):49–72.

19. Palmetto Consulting, Inc., for SBA Office of Advocacy. 2004. *Costs of Developing a Foreign Market for a Small Business: The Market & Non-Market Barriers to Exporting by Small Firms.* Palmetto Consulting, Inc.: Dahlonega, GA.

20. Leonidou, L. C. 2004. An analysis of the barriers hindering small business export development. *Journal of Small Business Management* 42(3):279–302.
21. Welch, D. E., Welch, L. W., Wilkinson, I. F., and L. C. Young. 1998. The importance of networks in export promotion: policy issues. *Journal of International Marketing* 6(4).
22. Gatewood, E. J. External assistance for startups and small businesses. 2004. In: Bygrave, W. D., and A. Zacharakis, eds. *The Portable MBA in Entrepreneurship*. New Jersey: John Wiley and Sons.
23. U.S. Small Business Administration. 2003. *Breaking into the Trade Game: A Small Business Guide.* Washington, DC: U.S. SBA.
24. Hisrich, R. D., and M. P. Peters. 1998. *Entrepreneurship*, 4th ed. New York: Irwin/McGraw-Hill.
25. Saadet, L., and D. Greer. Going online: E-exporting, Office of Information Technology and Electronic Commerce, Trade Development. *Export America/* Internet Marketing Articles Archive.
26. Basic question: To export yourself or to hire someone to do it for you? *Business America* April 1987:14–17.
27. DeNoble, A. F., Castaldi, R. M., and D. M. Moliver. 1989. Export intermediaries: Small business perceptions of services and performance. *Journal of Small Business Management* 27(2).
28. *Fortune*, July 22, 2002.
29. Lucash, R., Geisman, J., and W. Contente. 1991. Choosing an overseas distributor. *Small Business Reports* 16(8):68–71.
30. Lesonky, R., and staff of Entrepreneur Magazine. 2001. *Entrepreneur Magazine's Start Your Own Business: The only Start-Up Book You'll Ever Need*, 2nd ed. New York: Entrepreneur Media.
31. Overseas Private Investment Corporation: http://www.opic.gov/.
32. U.S. Small Business Administration. *Bankable Deals*. Washington, DC: U.S. SBA.
33. Brown, P. 2001. *Export America*.
34. Incoterms 2000: www.iccwbo.org/incoterms/understanding.asp.
35. Cook, T. 2001. Controlling the terms of sale. *Export America*.
36. www.transways.com.au/terms-conditions/inco.aspx.
37. Brush, C., Mbaku, J. M., Curley, M. D., and J. H. Park. 1992. Assessment of Export market awareness and export capabilities of small firms: Evidence from metropolitan Atlanta. *Arkansas Business and Economic Review* 25(4).
38. Abdnor, J. 1988. The spirit of entrepreneurship. *Journal Of Small Business Management* 26(1).
39. Wilson, C. D. 1990. Delaware Exporter Assistance Program for Small and Medium Sized Companies. *Economic Development Review* 8(3).
40. Export Controls. *Export America*. July 2000.
41. U.S. Bureau of Industry and Security, Export Administration Act. 2005. http://www.bxa.doc.gov/eaa.html.
42. Murphy, P. 2004. Get ready for the new reporting. *Northeast Export* 8:10.
43. http://export.gov/shipping_documentation_and_requirements/exp_control_licenses.asp.

APPENDIX

Export Assistance Centers

ATLANTA
Territory: Georgia, Alabama, Kentucky,
   Tennessee, Mississippi
U.S. Export Assistance Center
285 Peachtree Center Avenue, NE, 9th Floor
Atlanta, Georgia 30303
Tel: 404-657-1961
Fax: 404-657-1970

BALTIMORE
Territory: Maryland, Virginia, West Virginia,
   District of Columbia
U.S. Export Assistance Center
World Trade Center
401 East Pratt Street, Suite 2432
Baltimore, Maryland 21202
Tel: 410-962-4539
Fax: unavailable at this time

BOSTON
Territory: Maine, Vermont, New Hampshire,
   Massachusetts, Connecticut, Rhode Island
U.S. Export Assistance Center
World Trade Center, Suite 307
Boston, Massachusetts 02210
Tel: 617-424-5953
Fax: 617-424-5992

CHARLOTTE
Territory: North Carolina, South Carolina
U.S. Export Assistance Center
521 East Morehead Street, Suite 435
Charlotte, North Carolina 28202
Tel: 704-333-2130
Fax: 704-332-2681

CHICAGO
Territory: Wisconsin, Illinois, Indiana
U.S. Export Assistance Center
Xerox Center
55 West Monroe Street, Suite 2440
Chicago, Illinois 60603
Tel: 312-353-8065
Fax: 312-353-8098

CLEVELAND
Territory: Ohio, Western New York, Western
   Pennsylvania
U.S. Export Assistance Center
600 Superior Avenue, Suite 700
Cleveland, Ohio 44114
Tel: 216-522-4731
Fax: 216-522-2235

DALLAS
Territory: Oklahoma, Texas, Louisiana
North Texas U.S. Export Assistance Center
2000 East Lamar Boulevard, Suite 430
Arlington, Texas 76006
Tel: 817-277-0767
Fax: 817-299-9601

DENVER
Territory: Wyoming, Utah, Colorado,
   New Mexico
U.S. Export Assistance Center
1625 Broadway Avenue, Suite 680
Denver, Colorado 80202
Tel: 303-844-6622 ext. 18
Fax: 303-844-5651

DETROIT
Territory: Michigan
U.S. Export Assistance Center
211 West Fort Street, Suite 2220
Detroit, Michigan 48226
Tel: 313-226-3670
Fax: 313-226-3657

LOS ANGELES

Territory: Southern California, Nevada, Arizona, Hawaii

U.S. Export Assistance Center
11150 West Olympic Boulevard, Suite 975
Los Angeles, California 90064
Tel: 310-235-7203
Fax: 310-235-7220

NEWPORT BEACH

Territory: Southern California, Nevada, Arizona, Hawaii

U.S. Export Assistance Center
3300 Irvine Avenue, #307
Newport Beach, California 92660-3198
Tel: 949-660-1688 ext. 307
Fax: 949-660-1338

MIAMI

Territory: Florida, Puerto Rico
U.S. Export Assistance Center
100 South Biscayne Boulevard, 7th Floor
Miami, Florida 33131
Tel: 305-536-5521 ext. 183
Fax: 305-536-6740

MINNEAPOLIS

Territory: Minnesota, North Dakota
U.S. Export Assistance Center
U.S. Small Business Administration
Plaza VII Tower
45 South 7th Street, Suite 2240
Minneapolis, Minnesota 55403
Tel: 612-348-1642
Fax: 612-348-1650

NEW ORLEANS

Territory:
Delta U.S. Export Assistance Center
One Canal Place
365 Canal Street, Suite 1170
New Orleans, Louisiana 70130

NEW YORK CITY

Territory:
U.S. Courthouse
40 Foley Square, Room 3004
New York, New York 10007

PHILADELPHIA

Territory: Eastern Pennsylvania, Delaware, New Jersey

U.S. Export Assistance Center
The Curtis Center
601 Walnut Street, Suite 580 West
Philadelphia, Pennsylvania 19106
Tel: 215-597-6101
Fax: 215-597-6123

PORTLAND

Territory: Southern Washington, Oregon, Southern Idaho, Montana

U.S. Export Assistance Center
One World Trade Center
121 SW Salmon Street, Suite 242
Portland, Oregon 97204
Tel: 503-326-5498
Fax: 503-326-6351

RHODE ISLAND

US SBA SBDC/EAC
Bryant University
North Smithfield, Rhode Island

SAN JOSE

Territory: Northern California
San Francisco District Office
U.S. Small Business Administration
455 Market Street, 6th Floor
San Francisco, California 94105-2420
Tel: 415-744-8474
Fax: 415-744-6812

SEATTLE

Territory: Northern Washington, Alaska, Northern Idaho

U.S. Export Assistance Center

4th & Vine Building

2601 4th Avenue, Suite 320

Seattle, Washington 98121

Tel: 206-553-0051

Fax: 206-553-7253

ST. LOUIS

Territory: South Dakota, Nebraska, Iowa, Kansas, Missouri

U.S. Export Assistance Center

8182 Maryland Avenue, Suite 303

St. Louis, Missouri 63105

Tel: 314-425-3304 ext.228

Fax: 314-425-3381

**Also, look into local SBDC offices to verify if there may be a local EAC in your State/city.

Sources of Export Financing

1. **The United States Export–Import Bank:** This U.S. government run entity exists to support export initiatives through the provision of financing for such endeavors. It also is a source of valuable information on matters related to insurance, guarantees, and the availability (and various forms) of export-related credit/financing.

2. **The U.S. Small Business Administration:** Particularly through its Export Revolving Line of Credit guarantee loan program and a number of other initiatives through its Office of International Trade and in cooperation with various other Federal agencies/organizations. Contact your regional/district/state SBA office to learn of the current list of programs.

3. **State/Regional/Federal Trade Development Agencies:** As noted earlier, various agencies at state, local, regional, and the federal level may have dedicated funds or initiatives to support trade/export development to support the businesses and economies of their constituent population.

4. **Trade Finance Bankers/the International Trade/Finance department(s) of commercial banks:** Various private/local financial instruments may be available to lend support to export efforts of small businesses.

Web Sites

As the World Wide Web changes, organizations and their sites may be added, adjusted, or eliminated. Therefore the accuracy of these lists may vary.

U.S. Government-Sponsored Sites

1. Bureau of Export Administration: www.bxa.doc.gov
2. Census Bureau: www.census.gov
3. Census Bureau Foreign Trade Division
4. Department of Agriculture—Foreign Agricultural Service (FAS): http://www.fas.usda.gov/
5. Department of Commerce: www.commerce.gov
6. www.BuyUSA.com (includes matchmaking service offered by U.S. Commercial Service)
7. Export Assistance Center: www.e-expousa.doc.gov
8. Export portal of U.S. government: www.export.gov
9. Bureau of Industry and Security: Trade Information Center, Trade Compliance Center, Office of Export Trading Company Affairs
10. Federal Maritime Commission: www.fmc.gov
11. International Trade Administration: www.ita.doc.gov
12. International Trade Commission: www.usitc.gov
13. Market Development Cooperator Program: http://www.ita.doc.gov/td/mdcp/ (a program of the International Trade Administration)
14. Oversea Private Investment Corporation: www.opic.gov
15. Tariff and Tax Information - Export.gov. Trade Information Center 1-800-USA-TRADE Home. Export Questions. Country Info. Trade Offices. Tariffs & Taxes. Resources. Export Programs . . . http://www.trade.gov/td/tic/tariff/
16. U.S. Commercial Service Portugal: http://www.buyusa.gov/portugal/en/1. html. The U.S. Commercial Service in Lisbon, Portugal offers valuable assistance to help U.S. business export goods and services to the Portuguese market and markets.
17. U.S. Customs Service: www.customs.ustreas.gov
18. U.S. Trade Development Agency: www.tda.gov

Examples of Information Sources

1. Northeast Export Magazine: www.northeast-export.com
2. Central and Eastern Europe Business Information Center: http://www.mac.doc.gov/ceebic/
3. Coalition of New England Companies for Trade (CONECT): www.conect.org
4. Economist Magazine—Country Briefings: www.economist.com

U.S. Federal Departments or Agencies or Sources of Information for the Entrepreneur Exporter

1. U.S. Small Business Administration (SBA); SBA's Office of International Trade
2. Small Business Development Centers (SBDCs)
3. Small Business Institutes (SBIs)
4. Export Assistance Centers (EACs)
5. Export Legal Assistance Network (ELAN)
6. Export.gov (Web portal for export information): http://www.export.gov
7. U.S. Department of Commerce: U.S. International Trade Administration; District Export Councils
8. Trade Information Center
9. U.S. Foreign Commercial Service (U.S. & FCS)
10. U.S. Bureau of the Census: trade data/statistics
11. Automated Trade Locator Assistance System (ATLAS)
12. National Trade Data Bank: database of U.S. publications on export and international economic information.
13. The World Factbook: geographic and demographic statistical information from the CIA.
14. *ExportAmerica:* a U.S. publication available online as well concerning export related matters.

_____

(List adapted from Breaking into the Trade Game: A Small Business Guide, US SBA)

Examples of Private Sector Associations to Support Exporting

1. American Association of Exporters and Importers
2. Small Business Exporter's Association
3. National Federation of International Trade Associations
4. (Local) Chambers of Commerce
5. The Coalition of New England Companies for Trade (CONECT)

In addition to making use of the resources described in this chapter, the entrepreneur who is looking to export should also get to know others in their industry or various entrepreneur support organizations (such as the local chamber of commerce, the state, regional, federal trade organizations), the entrepreneur may find it useful to participate in networking events. Such events are opportunities for entrepreneurs to gather with and meet other individuals and organizations who are also exploring international trade/exporting. U.S. Customs officials, U.S. Foreign Commercial Service officers, more experienced entrepreneurial exporters, attorneys, trade intermediaries, bankers, and insurance representatives are all individuals the entrepreneur who is looking to export should become familiar with. Networking events for exporting are often organized by local trade and development offices or by trade associations such as the North East Exporters Association.

Cautions for New Exporters:
The 12 Most Common Mistakes

1. Failure to obtain qualified export counseling and to develop a master international strategy and marketing plan prior to starting export operations of your business.
2. Insufficient commitment by top management to overcome the initial difficulties and financial (and time) requirements of exporting.
3. Insufficient care in selecting overseas sales representatives or distributors.
4. Lack of focus: Reliance on orders from around the world rather than concentrating on one or two geographical areas and establishing a basis for profitable operations and orderly growth.
5. Neglect of export business when the domestic market booms.
6. Failure to treat international distributors and customers on an equal basis with domestic counterparts.
7. An assumption that a given market technique and product will automatically be successful in all countries.
8. Unwillingness to modify products to meet regulations or cultural preferences of other countries.
9. Failure to print service, sales and warranty messages in foreign languages.
10. Failure to consider use of an export management company when the firm cannot afford its own export department or has tried one unsuccessfully.
11. Failure to consider licensing or joint venture agreements when import restrictions, insufficient resources or a limited product line cause companies to dismiss international marketing as unfeasible.
12. Failure to provide readily available servicing for the product.

(Adapted from http://www.sba.gov/aboutsba/sbaprograms/internationaltrade/index.html. Most Common Mistakes of New-To-Export Ventures. *Business America* 1984:9.)

Chapter Seven

GLOBAL ECONOMICS AND FINANCE

Dale R. Funderburk
Texas A&M University, Commerce, Texas

Learning Objectives

Upon completion of this chapter, students should be able to:

- Understand trade between countries as it relates to economic specialization and resource utilization.
- Understand comparative advantage as a basis for trade between nations.
- Identify the differences between absolute advantage and comparative advantage.
- Identify the major theories attempting to explain patterns of cross-border exchange.
- Understand the relationship between expanding markets, economic efficiency, and the impact on consumers and producers.
- Understand the microeconomic principles of exchange rate determination.
- Understand the nature and advantages of common currency regimes.
- Understand the various types and sources of risks involved in trade between nations.
- Understand the major instruments and techniques available for financing international trade.
- Identify agencies devoted to the promotion of international trade.

Key Terms

absolute advantage
banker's acceptance
bill of exchange
comparative advantage
country risk premium
currency board
derived demand
dollarization

factor endowment
factoring
industrial policy
law of one price
Leontief's paradox
Mercantilism
Porter's Diamond

⊘ Introduction

Two of the most often discussed and written about topics in business over the past half-dozen years have been entrepreneurship and globalization. While the term "entrepreneurship" once tended to be associated primarily with small business activity, and "globalization" was more often associated with giant corporate entities, both phenomena are now recognized as highly relevant, even critical, issues for business entities of all sizes. Today's entrepreneur can ill afford to be ignorant of the forces driving, the opportunities afforded by, or the threats imposed by markets that are rapidly expanding on a global scale. These general topics comprise the focus of the present chapter. Specifically, the chapter is divided into two parts: real analysis or trade theory and monetary analysis and international finance. Trade theory is addressed first, focusing on the basis for international trade and the microeconomic implications of expanding markets and trade. The second part of the chapter focuses on finance issues related to international trade, especially exchange rate determination, risks peculiar to international trade, methods and instruments used to finance international trade, and agencies and institutions that promote international trade.

⊘ Trade Theory: The Basic Economics of International Trade

It is a bit ironic and more than a bit disturbing that even in the twenty-first century, economists and policy-makers still find it necessary to educate the public on the advantages of specialization, increasing productivity, and free trade. There is scarcely a scheduled meeting of a major trade institution or organization but what it must contend with the disruptive efforts of large, well-organized protests. From Seattle to Washington to Prague to Genoa, meetings involving the World Trade Organization (WTO), the International Monetary Fund (IMF), World Bank, North American Free Trade Agreement (NAFTA), and the proposed Central American Free Trade Association (CAFTA) have all been targets of "anti-globalization" protesters. Terms such as "globalization," "offshoring," and "outsourcing" have become the derisive rallying mantra of those fearing the effects of rapidly globalizing markets. And, unfortunately, elective office seekers all too often find it politically advantageous to capitalize on the insecurities and fears of those threatened by the specter of expanding markets and increased competition. In some respects it is as though much of the world has turned back the calendar two centuries and entered an era that we might call the *New Mercantilism*.

The Basis for Trade

In almost every important respect, globalization is very much like most other facets of basic international economics and finance that have existed and been studied and written about for literally centuries. It is ironic that in the effort to educate today's critics regarding the benefits of free trade, modern economists inevitably turn to the works of two economists of much earlier eras who faced similar tasks, Adam Smith and David Ricardo. Smith, in the late eighteenth century, and Ricardo, in the early nineteenth century, struggled to convince their fellow Britons of the virtues of free trade. In explaining the concept that has come to be known as *absolute advantage*, Smith ridiculed the fear of trade by comparing nations to households. He also refuted the widely held assumption that trade is a zero sum game, demonstrating that trade is a positive sum game. Smith's argument was that since every household finds it worthwhile to produce only some of the goods it needs and buy others with products that it can sell, the same logic must apply to nations. "It is the maxim of every prudent master of a family, never to attempt to make at home what it will cost him more to make than to buy. What is prudent in the conduct of every private family can scarce be folly in that of a great kingdom. If a foreign country can supply us with a commodity cheaper than we ourselves can make it, better buy it of them with some part of the product of our own industry, employed in a way in which we have some advantage."[1] In short, it simply makes good economic sense to allow Brazil to grow Brazil nuts and Iceland to grow Eskimo Pies, and then trade, rather than have each country waste resources in trying to produce goods for which they have no advantage.

David Ricardo[2] refined and extended the analysis of Smith, developing a theory of *comparative advantage*. Ricardo demonstrated that nations can gain from specialization even if they lack an absolute advantage—that trade, including cross-border trade, does not require absolute advantage. In explaining the basis for trade between two countries, such as England and Portugal, Ricardo showed that if a country is relatively better at making wine than wool, then it makes good economic sense for that country to put more resources into wine, and to export some of the wine to pay for imports of wool. This is true even if that country is the world's best wool producer, since with specialization and trade it would have more of both wool and wine than it would have without trade. Thus, a country does not have to be the best (the most efficient, or low-cost, producer) at anything to gain from trade. The gains follow from specializing in those activities, which, at world prices, the country is relatively better at, even though it may not have an absolute advantage in them. Because it is relative advantage that matters, it is inaccurate to say that a country has a comparative advantage in nothing.

While there have been newer, more sophisticated theories developed to explain trade patterns between nations, the theory of comparative advantage still constitutes the base on which these theories are constructed and, even today, may be considered the key theoretical underpinning of trade theory. Consider, for example, the theory developed by two Swedish economists, Eli Heckscher[3] and Bertil Ohlin[4] (and later refined, expanded, and formalized by MIT economist Paul Samuelson[5,6]), aimed at explaining trade patterns between nations. Noting how prices differed quite substantially between various countries before they opened trade, Heckscher and Ohlin expressed doubt that demand or technological considerations (emphasized by Ricardo) accounted for most of the international price differences existing in the real world. This theory, often referred to as a *factor endowment model*, hypothesizes that countries export the products that use their abundant factors intensively, and import the products using their scarce factors intensively. Thus, as a simple example, a nation with large oil reserves will have a comparative advantage in oil production over another nation with fertile soil, which will have a comparative advantage in agricultural production.

Economists note that while the Heckscher–Ohlin theory is intuitively appealing and was once widely accepted on the basis of mere casual empiricism, it has not held up so well empirically. When the first serious attempt to test the theory was made by Professor Wassily Leontief[7,8] in 1954, the results were surprising. Using the 1947 input-output table of the U.S. economy, Leontief reached the counter-intuitive conclusion that the U.S., the most capital abundant country in the world, exported labor-intensive commodities and imported capital-intensive commodities. This result, which came to be known as the *Leontief Paradox*, took the economics profession by surprise and stimulated an enormous amount of empirical and theoretical research on the subject.

Perhaps of greater interest to students of business strategy is the theory of national competitive advantage developed by Harvard business professor Michael E. Porter.[9] Whereas classical theories propose that comparative advantage resides in technological differences and/or the factor endowments (land, natural resources, labor, and size of the local population) that a country may be fortunate enough to inherit, Porter argues that these theories are inadequate or even wrong. He contends that a nation can create new advanced factor endowments such as skilled labor, a strong technology and knowledge base, government support, and culture. After conducting a detailed study of ten nations to learn what leads to success, he developed the concept that has become known as *Porter's Diamond*. According to Porter, a nation attains a competitive advantage if its firms are competitive. Firms become competitive through innovation. These innovations may include technical improvements to the product or to the production process. He differentiates his theory from the traditional trade theories by arguing that national prosperity is not inherited, but created by choices. Thus he contends that national wealth is not set by factor endowments, but created by strategic choices.

According to Porter, four attributes comprise the basis for a country's diamond of national competitive advantage. He uses a diamond shaped diagram as the pivotal graphic of a framework to illustrate the determinants of national advantage. This diamond then represents the national playing field that countries establish for their industries. These four attributes include (1) factor conditions—the nation's position in terms of factors of production, such as skilled labor and infrastructure; (2) demand conditions—including the degree of sophistication of consumers in the domestic market; (3) related and supporting industries—which includes suppliers and complementary industries; and (4) firm strategy, structure and rivalry—conditions for organization of companies, and the nature of domestic rivalry.

While Porter's theory, much like that of Heckscher–Ohlin, may be intuitively appealing and is supported by considerable anecdotal evidence, Harfield[10] points out that Porter is not without critics. "His lack of clear definitions for his 'models' is a matter of agreement rather than debate." Harfield further notes, ". . . there is a similar large scale concern with his lack of empirical data." Thus, to what degree can a nation influence, or even engineer, a national competitive advantage? The extensive literature on the concept of *industrial policy* would seem to cast considerable doubt on the prospects of a country's developing a national competitive advantage through strategic planning and public policy.

Expanding Markets and Economic Efficiency

At root, globalization is merely a manifestation of improving market efficiency. Economists have long understood that improving communication and transportation lead to market expansion and, ultimately, to greater market efficiency. By the term market efficiency, we refer simply to the effects of forces (such as the improving quality and speed of transfer of information and greater mobility) that tend to reduce transaction costs and thus make exchange more efficient. And as markets become more efficient, producers also must respond by becoming more efficient. It is a basic axiom of economics that competition in the marketplace provides the impetus for greater productive efficiency. As more and better information becomes available and as mobility—both of resources and output—improves, participants in the marketplace are pressed to become more efficient. They must become more sensitive to the state of technology and to least-cost combinations of resources. As larger numbers of buyers and sellers come to interact in the market, overall economic efficiency improves.

Thus, it may be concluded that international trade and globalization are not only the results of increasing economic efficiency, they are causative forces as well. However, it is critical to note that while improved economic efficiency increases overall material well-being, markets do not necessarily ensure that the benefits of increased efficiency are shared by all. There is no assurance that expanding markets, increasing competition, and greater market and productive efficiency will lead to what we may consider a more equitable distribution of income. Consequently, some argue that carefully crafted government policies are necessary in order to correct some of the injurious effects of the impersonal marketplace.

The Microeconomic Impact of Expanding Markets

While economic globalization presents a plethora of new managerial challenges and marketing opportunities and threats, the basic microeconomic implications of the trend are relatively straightforward. As transportation and communications improve, the process impacts the nature and scope of competition. As markets expand, there is invariably an impact on producers and sellers, resource suppliers, and consumers. In the text that follows, we consider the effects of expanding markets and globalization on each of these groups.

Producer/Seller Impact

For producers and sellers the added competition associated with new, expanding markets invariably brings about new pressures for ingenuity and efficiency. Less innovative, less efficient producers whither and vanish in the face of added competition while more innovative, more efficient producers and sellers prosper and expand. This happens whether the expanding marketplace occurs within the context of a small, local, village economy or in the context of an increasingly integrated and competitive "global village." It must be kept in mind, however, that a firm may be inefficient through no fault of its own. The roots of the problem may be entirely external. A firm may be inefficient because of its own ineptitude or because of factors (both microeconomic and macroeconomic in scope) outside its control. While a particular producer/seller may be able to be the low cost provider in a small, restricted market, that same firm may be unable to compete effectively in an expanded market setting. As markets expand, some producers find themselves without access to the best sources of essential raw materials. Also, a firm may not have access to low-cost resources—especially labor. Government-mandated cost increasing measures such as minimum wage legislation, detailed safety regulations, paid leave requirements, and payroll taxes imposed to fund any number of entitlement programs may place a producer at a distinct competitive disadvantage, especially when posited against competitors whose governments impose no such cost-raising requirements.

Finally, it must be kept in mind that producers themselves are also consumers. They must acquire the resources, technology, and raw materials used in producing the output they sell. Consequently, globalization and increasing competition may benefit the producer by allowing the firm to buy inputs at lower prices. Along this line, it is interesting to note that when President Bush imposed tariffs on imported steel in March 2002, he did win favor (for a time) with U.S. steel producers, but he also incurred considerable wrath from firms in steel-consuming industries. Thus, while he may have helped himself politically in steel-producing states like Pennsylvania and West Virginia, he did not help himself in steel-consuming states like Tennessee, where auto producers suffered from (and complained bitterly about) the higher steel prices.

Resource Suppliers: Labor

As is the case with sellers of goods, broadening markets entail both new opportunities and new threats for sellers of labor services. As transportation and communications improve, labor markets also broaden and become more competitive. Consequently, marketable skills become the watchword for labor. It is significant to note that historically, most foreign competition was in the manufacturing sector. Thus the domestic workers who felt most threatened by foreign trade tended to be blue-collar production workers. Today, however, as we are seeing that more and more services are also tradable, many more highly-specialized, technically-educated, and skilled workers are experiencing the threat of job loss and dislocation.

For many years workers have crossed national borders to work. The United States has used foreign, migrant workers to supply needed manual labor for decades.[i] Construction workers have for years traversed the globe to provide the expertise and skilled labor necessary for both private and public projects. This is a trend that continues to expand in terms both of geographic area covered and skills and occupations involved. For example, under a special program instituted in 1999, the United States Department of Labor allows certain hospitals in "disadvantaged" areas to employ temporary foreign, nonimmigrant workers as registered nurses for periods up to three years. And increasingly, highly-skilled, technical workers are able to cross national borders to supply critical labor needs in advanced, as well as less developed, countries. Under another program, called H1-B, the United States allows employers to employ foreign workers temporarily (on a nonimmigrant basis) in specialty occupations. Participants in this program must hold a bachelor's degree or the equivalent in a specific specialty (e.g., engineering, mathematics, physical sciences, computer sciences, medicine and health care, education, biotechnology, and business specialties). When initially established, the H1-B program contained a limit of 65,000 workers. The program continues to expand, however, with many U.S. firms involved in computer/information technology (e.g., Google, Microsoft, Intel) regularly lobbying for increases in the ceiling, arguing that they cannot compete in the global marketplace without the services of increasing numbers of foreign workers.

An additional point should be made with regard to labor in a global market setting with rapidly advancing technology. Historically, the physical location of the worker vis-à-vis the employer or "job site" was critical. It was necessary either for the worker to be mobile and go to the job site, or else for capital to migrate to the workers. Increasingly, however, there are more and more jobs for which the physical location of the worker is inconsequential. Because of advances in computers and information technology, first some workers were able to work at home and to go into the office only occasionally. The natural progression is that more and more jobs require the physical presence of the worker rarely if at all. Thus a worker in Dallas may be bidding against others in Dublin, Delhi, Dubrovnik, or even Dhaka. And while many jobs will continue to require the physical presence of the worker—if a custodian is to wax a floor, he or she must be in that specific room—more and more jobs will not. This is merely another dimension of a globalizing labor market.

Finally, it must be acknowledged that there are invariably significant short-run costs associated with increased specialization and/or increasing productivity stemming from globalizing labor markets. Those who are displaced and who must shift jobs will inevitably experience costs. In addition to direct retraining and/or relocation costs, there may well be spells of unemployment and reduced wages. However, the same may be said of any improvement in productivity, whether related to international trade or not. By its very nature, productivity im-

---

i. The government's H2-A temporary agricultural certification program establishes a means for agricultural employers who anticipate a shortage of domestic workers to bring nonimmigrant foreign workers to the United States to perform agricultural work or services of a temporary or seasonal nature.

provement entails being able to produce more (or better) output with the same, or lesser, units of labor input. The introduction of the roller and pan, and later the spray gun, instead of a brush to paint buildings was clearly an increase in productivity, but was resisted mightily by painters and their craft unions. Invariably, improvements in productivity involve some labor displacement or dislocation. It is an unfortunate but unavoidable byproduct of progress.

Given that there are costs (and losses) resulting from the expanding volume of international trade (and the accompanying economic realignment and restructuring), governments at times find it necessary to devise ways of mitigating the harm accruing to the short-run losers. For example, in the United States, Trade Adjustment Assistance (TAA) has been developed in order to help those harmed by international trade by providing extended unemployment benefits, worker retraining, and temporary taxes on imports. As a case in point, the government created a special program (NAFTA-TAA) for workers laid off because of NAFTA. In 1994, 17,000 workers qualified for this program. However, it has always been widely and loudly argued by organized labor that many more workers have been negatively impacted by cross-border trade than these program numbers suggest, and that many more workers should be certified eligible for such assistance. It is noteworthy that President Barack Obama supports extension and expansion of the program, including the extension of such assistance to service industry and high-tech workers.

Resource Suppliers: Capital

A major determinant of factor market efficiency is mobility. Because funds are much more mobile than is labor, money and capital markets exhibit a higher degree of efficiency than do labor markets and, consequently, can and will globalize much more rapidly. While physical capital migration may continue to be a relatively slow and expensive process, the process of funding capital accumulation is becoming much more competitive and efficient. Bryan and Farrell[11] were noting by 1994 that the *law of one price* was beginning to operate in global capital markets. They pointed out that in the new global markets, participants are increasingly able to price financial instruments more precisely across markets in multiple currencies. They further argued that the global capital market will play an ever greater role in determining the rate of return on capital investments, while the actions of central banks will matter ever less. This has important public policy implications. Perhaps the most important of these is that the global capital market is integrating to the point where the price of government debt is market-determined. Increasingly, debt will be priced according to its specific risks and return, independent of the efforts of governments to control their own interest rates. Consequently, governments that issue debt for the purpose of funding entitlements and/or who pursue inflationary policies will pay ever-increasing costs for such policies. Conversely, it is likely that funds will flow to the developing nations which will then grow and modernize faster as a result. Likewise, private investment in the developed world is likely to be greater.

Consumers

Consumers are the one group that almost universally benefits from the added competition associated with expanding markets. Even during the Middle Ages, as transportation and communication advances moved markets beyond the bounds of small, rural villages, it was the consumer who inevitably reaped the benefits of new and improved products, new and better choices, and lower prices. As international trade has grown and widened, consumers have benefited. In those economies where governments have erected barriers against expanding trade, consumers have suffered from fewer product choices, higher prices, and a stagnant or declining standard of living. Countries such as Myanmar, Romania, Cuba, Zimbabwe and North Korea are cases in point.[ii]

ⓒ Currency Issues and International Finance

The primary function of money is to provide an alternative to barter. By serving as a medium of exchange, money reduces transactions costs and makes exchange more efficient. Differences in the currencies or monetary units used by countries engaging in international trade all too often lead, unfortunately, to the introduction of new risks and other inefficiencies. In order for markets to function with maximum efficiency, the framework within which international trade is carried out must be such that all mutually beneficial trade can occur with a minimum of effort. Instead, we permit financial arrangements to become so tangled that some trade that would have benefited trading parties is not carried out at all. Thus, a major challenge is to find and institute a set of arrangements that will promote a free flow of trade.

What determines the rate at which the money of one country can be converted into that of another? In this section of the chapter, we examine first the mechanism by which exchange rates are determined in uncontrolled or free markets. Next, we examine some of the risks associated with international trade and investment, some of the methods and instruments used in making payment as well as financing international trade, and finally, some of the agencies that serve to promote international trade.

Exchange Rate Determination

When we consider the rate at which the currency of one country can be converted into that of another country, the first principle to keep in mind is that we are dealing with a price. For example, the exchange rate between the U.S. dollar

---

ii. Organizations such as the Hoover Institution, the Heritage Foundation, and the Frazier Institute rank countries in terms of economic freedom. Each of the countries listed here rates very poor in terms of international commerce—having very high levels of protectionism, high barriers to capital flows and foreign investment, and/or little protection for property rights. These rankings demonstrate that countries with higher levels of economic (market) freedom enjoy higher levels of per capita income.

and the British pound sterling should be viewed simply as the dollar price of the pound (viewed from the vantage point of the American), or the pound price of the dollar (viewed through the eyes of the British trader). Thus, while we use the specialized term "exchange rate" to describe the price of a foreign currency, it is nonetheless a price.[iii] Given that exchange rates are merely prices, the understanding of how such rates are determined in a free market becomes a straightforward exercise in basic microeconomics. In any free market, prices are determined by the forces of demand and supply, representing the interaction of buyers and sellers. In any given country, supplies of foreign currencies come into the market from the export of goods and services, from unilateral transfers into the country, and from capital movements into the country. Demands for foreign currencies arise from import activities, from unilateral transfers out of the country, and from capital movements out of the country. These form the basis for the determination of relative currency prices, or exchange rates.

To establish a home country's demand function for a foreign currency, one could think of that currency as though it were a commodity. Alternatively, the concept of *derived demand* is useful. Normally, one does not acquire a foreign currency for the sake of merely owning or holding that currency. The desire to acquire a foreign currency derives from the desire to acquire foreign produced goods. Thus, the demanders should be thought of as those who want to make payments to parties in the other country. Using a simple two country example for illustrative purposes, assume that the U.S. is the home country and Mexico the foreign country. The demand for the peso would merely be expressed in terms of the quantities of pesos that people in the U.S. would be willing to buy at various alternative prices of the peso, other things being equal. A demand curve for the peso would slope downward to the right, reflecting the fact that the lower the dollar price of the peso, the less expensive are Mexican goods in terms of dollar prices (see Figure 7.1A).

Given that the U.S. demand for pesos stems from the importation of Mexican goods, transfers to that country, and capital movements from the U.S. to Mexico, it follows then that a change involving any of those variables will have the effect of shifting the peso demand curve. Thus, if Americans develop a stronger taste for Mexican produced goods, the demand curve for the peso will shift outward to the right. Similarly, say that real interest rates in Mexico rise relative to U.S. real rates.[iv] Other things remaining unchanged, this will produce a rightward shift of the demand curve for pesos. Increased direct investment in Mexico by U.S. enterprises also may be expected to shift the curve to the right. The re-

---

iii. As a matter of custom, certain prices are referred to by special names. Thus, while the price of a car or an ice cream cone is called a price, the price of loanable funds is referred to as an interest rate, the price of a unit of labor is called a wage rate, and the price charged for the use of real property is called rent. Nonetheless, all are prices and as such are determined in a market economy through the forces of supply and demand.

iv. Real interest rates, like other real (as opposed to nominal) values in economics, have been adjusted for price level effects. A real interest rate would be measured as the nominal (unadjusted) rate of interest minus the rate of inflation.

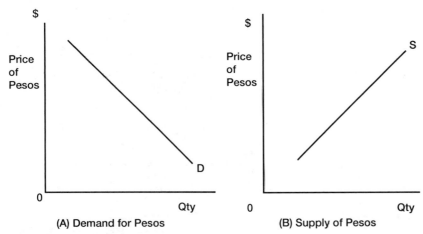

FIGURE 7.1 Supply and demand of pesos.

moval of trade barriers between the two countries (such as those targeted by NAFTA) also should result in an increase in the demand for pesos, again resulting in a rightward shift of the demand curve for pesos.

The supply schedule of a foreign currency, in this case the Mexican peso, can be established in a similar fashion. Suppliers of pesos are the Mexicans who purchase goods and services from the United States. They supply (or place on the market) pesos through the act of acquiring dollars needed to pay for U.S. produced goods. The peso supply curve then represents the quantities of pesos that will be placed on the market at alternative dollar prices of the peso, other things remaining unchanged (see Figure 7.1B). Thus, as incomes rise in Mexico and Mexicans begin to import more U.S. goods, the effect will be to increase to supply of pesos entering the exchange market—shifting the peso supply curve outward to the right. If the price level in the U.S. rises relative to the price level in Mexico, American goods become less attractive vis-à-vis Mexican produced goods, thus decreasing the supply of Mexican pesos placed on exchange markets. This would, of course, be depicted as a leftward shift of the peso supply curve.

As is the case with all market-determined prices, the exchange rate is determined in the market (in this case currency markets) through the interaction of buyers and sellers. Given that the demand curve reflects the preferences of buyers and the supply curve reflects the preferences of sellers, then it follows that the intersection of the demand curve and the supply curve represents that price (exchange rate) at which the number of pesos placed on the market by suppliers just matches the quantity that buyers are willing and able to take off the market (see Figure 7.2C). Thus, point e in Figure 7.2C could be thought of as the market-determined dollar price of the peso.[v] Alternatively, it could be considered the equilibrium exchange rate between the peso and the dollar.

v. Since an exchange rate represents the value or price of one currency in terms of another, the U.S. dollar price of the Mexican peso and the peso price of the dollar are, mathematically, reciprocals. That is, if the dollar price of the peso is $0.08642 per peso, then the peso price of the dollar is 1\0.08642, or 11.572 pesos per dollar. Similarly, if the dollar price of the pound sterling is $1.7881 per£1, the pound price of the dollar must be 1\1.7881, or £0.5593 per $1.00.

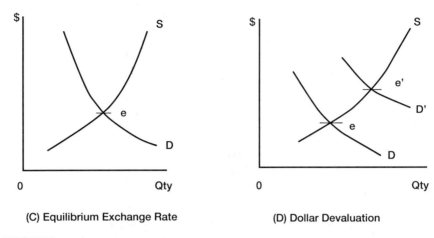

(C) Equilibrium Exchange Rate   (D) Dollar Devaluation

FIGURE 7.2   Equilibrium exchange rate between the peso and the dollar.

An exchange rate that is freely determined in international currency markets varies or fluctuates according to changes in international demand and supply conditions. Using our earlier example, assume that Americans begin to import more Mexican products, invest more in Mexico, and take more vacations in Mexico. The combined effect of these changes would be to increase the demand for pesos, meaning that the demand curve for the peso shifts to the right (see Figure 7.2D). As the dollar price of the peso rises, the exchange rate would correspondingly adjust, moving from e to e'. This movement could be described as a rise in the dollar price of the peso, or alternatively, as a decline (or devaluation) of the dollar versus the peso.

As another example, assume that a political and economic crisis hits Mexico (such as the so-called "Tequila crisis" of 1994–1995), sending that country's economy into a severe slump. One would expect this to decrease the demand for the peso and, at the same time, increase the supply of pesos coming onto the market. Why? Because of the increased uncertainty and instability associated with doing business in Mexico, Americans (and other internationals) would be less apt to invest in Mexico. That would shift the peso demand curve to the left. At the same time, many of those holding pesos might decide to flee that currency, fearing its loss of value, and move into dollars. This would shift the peso supply curve to the right. The effect? The dollar price of the peso would fall. This could be described either as a decline in the dollar price of the peso, or a peso devaluation vis-à-vis the dollar. From the viewpoint of the U.S., it would be seen as an appreciation of the dollar relative to the peso.

Control of Exchange Rates

In the previous section, our analysis of international currency markets assumed a floating, or flexible, system of exchange in which relative currency values were determined by private demand and supply forces in the market. A floating, flexible, or freely fluctuating exchange rate system is one in which the prices of currencies are determined by competitive market forces. Until around 1971, however, international exchange rates were controlled by governments. Rates were not permitted to move in response to changes in demand and supply. Because rates were fixed for a long period of time by government policy, this system is generally referred to as a fixed exchange rate system. A fixed or pegged exchange rate system is one in which the prices of currencies are established and maintained by government intervention. Although the fixed rate system is no longer in use among the major trading nations, there are some advantages to such a system.

Hoping to gain a trade advantage over their trading partners, one nation after another devalued its currency during the Great Depression of the 1930s. This process of competitive devaluation, referred to as "beggar thy neighbor," has a devastating effect on world trade. Following the depression, the U.S. and other major trading nations sought to reestablish a fixed exchange rate system in order to rebuild international trade and finance. Under the Bretton Woods agreements of 1945, a new system was devised that would have as its key feature the free convertibility of the U.S. dollar into gold. The U.S. agreed to buy or sell gold as necessary in order to maintain the $35 per ounce price that had been established by President Roosevelt in 1933. The other signatory nations agreed to buy and sell dollars to maintain their exchange rates at agreed-upon levels. This new system was called the "gold-exchange system" or the Bretton Woods system. The IMF was established to police and manage the new system. The primary function of the IMF was to be to offer temporary assistance (loans) to countries that experienced severe balance-of-payments difficulties, thus enabling them to maintain the agreed-upon exchange rate. Only in extreme cases involving "fundamental disequilibrium" in a nation's balance-of-payments were changes in exchange rates to be permitted. Devaluation was viewed only as a last resort. In general, the Bretton Woods agreements were grounded in the belief that only relatively fixed exchange rates could provide the stability necessary to restore world trade to pre-depression levels.

Two of the major benefits of a fixed exchange rate regime are that it eliminates most exchange rate risk (discussed later) and reduces transactions costs associated with trading in different currencies. The development and spread of the euro, as well as attempts by various countries to peg their national currencies to some anchor currency through the use of *currency boards* are reflections of the benefits of adoption of a common currency and/or elimination of exchange rate instability. *Dollarization* is but another example of the attempt to gain the advantages of a common currency—elimination of exchange rate fluctuations and reduction of transactions costs.

Country Risk

While all business transactions involve some degree of risk, those involving trade across international borders carry additional risks not present in domestic transactions. These additional risks, collectively called country risk, typically include risks arising from a variety of national differences in economic structures, policies, socio-political institutions, geography, and currency. When doing business across international boundaries, and especially when investing in foreign countries, it is critical that one understand the nature and extent of such risks and develop strategies and techniques to mitigate against potential losses stemming from such factors. However, those doing business internationally generally lack the specialized knowledge and/or the data gathering and analyzing ability required to obtain the needed information. Their resources are better utilized attending core business activities. This, of course, gives rise to another market—the market for another type of specialized information. Any number of entities analyze and attempt to quantify country risk. Among those entities that measure country risk are the following providers: Bank of America World Information Services, Business Environment Risk Intelligence, Euromoney, Institutional Investor, Standard and Poor's Rating Group, and Moody's Investor Services. Country risk analysis is commercially available from a very extensive group of services.

Those who analyze country risk normally decompose the composite risk into several components, identifying certain variables for use in measuring and quantifying the various elements of risk. While the definitions and measurement of the components are not completely standardized, and while the different components sometimes overlap as to measurement criteria, some of the more widely used divisions include the following.

Economic Risk

This element of risk arises from the potential for detrimental changes in fundamental economic goals of the country, or a significant change in the country's comparative advantage. Analysts examine traditional measures of monetary and fiscal policy (inflation/deflation trends, soundness of the financial system, tax policy, government expenditures and transfers relative to income, the government's debt situation), and, for longer-term investments, other real growth factors.

Sovereign Risk

This element of risk is associated with a government's becoming unwilling or unable to meet its loan obligations. Sovereign risk stems from the fact that a private lender faces a unique risk when dealing with a sovereign government. In the event that a government decides not to meet its obligations, the private lender has little or no realistic recourse in the court system—in that it normally requires the permission of the government in order to sue it. A government's debt repayment history, any repudiation of such obligations in the past, and variables reflecting the government's ability to pay are factors used in assessing sovereign risk.

Political Risk

This is the risk arising from a change in political institutions stemming from a change in government control, social fabric, or other noneconomic factors. It covers the potential for internal and external conflicts, plus expropriation risk.

Since there exist few reliable, quantitative measures to help assess political risk, analysts must examine qualitative factors such as relationships of various groups in a country, the decision-making processes of the government, and the history of the country.

Transfer Risk

This element of risk is that arising from a decision by a foreign government to restrict capital movements. Government-imposed restrictions can make it difficult or impossible to repatriate profits, dividends, or capital. Given that a government can change capital movement rules at any time, transfer risk applies to all types of investments. Quantifying the risk is difficult because the decision to restrict capital movement may be a purely political response to another problem. However, in economic terms, there are some variables that exhibit predictive value concerning if and when a country might find it necessary and/or advantageous to restrict capital movements. For example, a growing current account deficit as a percent of gross domestic product (GDP) might signal a more pressing need for foreign exchange to cover that deficit. The risk of a transfer problem increases if no offsetting changes develop in the capital account.

Exchange Rate Risk

This is the risk associated with any unexpected adverse movement in the exchange rate. Exchange rates fluctuate on a continuous basis as a result of short-run factors such as currency speculation activities, changes in a country's import/export position, fluctuations in interest rates, and normal funds flows. Economic fundamentals determine and bring about adjustments in exchange rates over the longer run. And while it is often possible to eliminate or at least minimize exchange rate risk through various hedging mechanisms, that strategy normally is impractical over the life of a plant or similar direct investment. Factors that reflect the degree of over- or under-valuation of a currency can help isolate and quantity exchange rate risk.

Neighborhood Risk

This element of risk, also called location risk, may be associated with spillover effects caused by problems in a region, or even by problems with a country's significant trading partners. When Brazil devalued its real in January 1999, that action had a devastating effect on the Argentine economy, effectively spelling the ultimate doom of that country's "convertibility" regime. The concept of "contagion" is at the core of this element of risk. Factors such as membership in international trading alliances, distance from economically or politically important countries, and other aspects of geography provide key indicators of neighborhood risk.

The effects of differences in country risk show up in any number of venues relative to business and economic activity. One clear reflection of the impact of country risk is found in international differences in interest rates. Keeping in mind the law of one price, which suggests that international interest rates will converge until the observed differences reflect only differences in maturities and risks, the concept of *country risk premium* becomes of interest. This concept refers to the increment in interest rates that would have to be paid for loans and investment projects in a particular country compared to some standard. One way of establishing the risk premium of a country is to compare the interest rate that the market establishes for a standard security in the country (e.g., treasury debt) to the comparable security in the benchmark country (e.g., U.S. treasury bills, notes or bonds). If the debt issues involve payment in the same currency (e.g., U.S. dollars) and have the same maturities, then the difference must be attributable to country risk. There are a number of agencies and institutions that calculate and make available data relative to country risk premiums.

The existence of country risk affects virtually all aspects of international trade. Whether it is the payment terms for international trade, the financing methods and instruments, or necessary inducements and rewards associated with such trade, country risk and differences in risks are paramount considerations. Some of those areas are discussed in very brief terms in the following section.

Payment Terms for International Trade

Every shipment abroad requires some form of financing while in transit. Additionally, the supplier (exporter) needs financing, either internally generally or externally acquired, to buy or manufacture its goods. The buyer (importer) must carry these goods in inventory until they are sold. In some cases, the supplier will have sufficient cash flow to finance the entire trade cycle out of its own funds and, thus, be willing to extend credit until the importer has converted the goods into cash. Alternatively, the buyer may be able to finance the entire cycle by paying cash in advance. Usually, however, some in-between approach is chosen, involving a combination of financing by buyer, seller, and third parties. Thus, in any international trade transaction, credit is inevitably provided by the supplier/exporter, buyer/importer, one or more financial institutions, or some combination of these.

There are five principal means of payment in international trade. Associated with each is a different degree of risk to the exporter and the importer. As a general rule, the greater the protection afforded the exporter, the less convenient are the payment terms for the importer. Thus, when choosing among payment methods to require, the supplier must weigh the benefits in risk reduction against the cost in terms of lost sales. The five basic means of payment used to settle international transactions are briefly discussed here—ranked in order of increasing risk to the exporter.

Cash in Advance

Under the prepayment or cash in advance method, the exporter will not ship the goods until the buyer has remitted payment to the exporter. This method affords the exporter the greatest protection and allows it to avoid tying up its own funds.

Prepayment is often required of first-time buyers whose creditworthiness is unknown, or where there is political instability in the importing country. Most buyers, however, are unable and/or unwilling to bear all the risk by prepaying the order. Additionally, due to competitive pressures, requiring payment in advance is not something that generally works for exporters unless they have a unique product or market niche. When this method of payment is used, the payments are most often made in the form of an international wire transfer to the exporter's bank account, or foreign bank draft.

Letter of Credit

This is an instrument issued by a bank on behalf of the importer promising to pay the exporter upon presentation of shipping documents in compliance with a set of stipulated terms. In effect, the bank is substituting its credit for that of the buyer. This method may be viewed as a compromise between the seller and the buyer because it affords certain advantages to each party. The exporter is assured of receiving payment as long as it presents documents in accordance with the agreement. When credit is extended, this method of financing offers the exporter the greatest degree of safety. The advantage to the importer is that it does not have to pay for the goods until shipment has been made and documents are presented in good order.

Drafts

This instrument, also known as a *bill of exchange*, is an unconditional written order—usually drawn by the exporter and addressed to the importer—ordering the buyer to pay on demand (or at a specified future date) the face amount of the draft. The draft represents the exporter's formal demand for payment from the buyer. Inasmuch as banks are not obligated to honor payments on the buyer's behalf, the draft affords the exporter less protection than does the letter of credit. However, the draft does enable the exporter to use its bank as a collection agent. The bank forwards the draft or bill of exchange to the foreign buyer (either directly or through a branch or correspondent bank), collects on the draft, and then remits the proceeds to the exporter.

Drafts may be either sight drafts or time drafts. Sight drafts must be paid on presentation. Time drafts are payable at some specified future date and as such become a useful financing technique. A *banker's acceptance*, discussed below, is a time draft that has been accepted by the drawee, the bank to which the draft is addressed.

Consignment

Under this arrangement, goods are only shipped, but not sold, to the importer. The exporter ships the goods to the importer while still retaining actual title to the merchandise. The importer has access to the goods but does not have to pay for them until they have been sold to a third party. The exporter is thus placed in a position of having to trust the buyer to pay once the goods are sold, with very limited recourse in case of default. Because of the high risk, consignments are infrequently used except in special cases such as affiliated or subsidiary companies trading with the parent company.

Open Account

Functionally, open account selling is the opposite of cash in advance, or prepayment. The exporter ships the merchandise and expects the buyer to remit payment according to the agreed-upon terms. The seller is relying completely on the creditworthiness, integrity, and reputation of the buyer, meaning obviously that open account terms carry the highest risk of nonpayment. Adding to the risk is the fact that any subsequent collection activities that may be necessary will be guided by the laws and customs of the buyer's country. Historically, this method of financing normally has been used only when the buyer and seller have mutual trust and considerable experience in dealing with each other. However, as world markets become more competitive, open account terms are gaining in usage and are sometimes the only means of entry. Thus, despite the risks, open account transactions today are widely used, especially among industrialized countries in North America and Europe where the overall volume of trade is very high and credit information is readily available.

Financing Techniques in International Trade

Due to the additional risks and complications involved in international transactions, banks today play a critical role in financing such trade. As the volume of trade has grown in recent years and financing has become such an integral part of international transactions, banks have progressed from financing individual trade deals to providing comprehensive solutions to trade needs. This is especially true of large U.S. banks located in major money centers. These services may include combining bank lending with funds from government export agencies, international leasing, and even risk insurance. However, in addition to straight bank financing, there are a number of other techniques available for trade financing. Some of the more important ones are discussed here.

Bankers' Acceptances

A banker's acceptance is an order to pay a specified amount of money to the bearer on a given date. Bankers' acceptances have been in use since the twelfth century, though they were not a major money market security until the volume of international trade ballooned in the 1960s. They are used primarily in international trade with the purpose of financing goods that have not yet been transferred from the seller to the buyer. The great strength of the banker's acceptance is that it can allow an exporter to receive funds immediately, yet allow an importer to delay its payment until a future date. Keeping in mind that the banker's acceptance is a time draft drawn on a bank, it follows that whenever the bank "accepts" the draft (by stamping "accepted" across the instrument), it makes an unconditional promise to pay the holder of the draft the stated amount on the specified date. Thus, the bank effectively has substituted its own credit for that of the borrower. In the process, it has created a negotiable instrument that is traded freely in money markets. Typical maturities on bankers' acceptances are thirty to 180 days, with the average being ninety days. Maturities can be tailored, however, to cover the entire period needed to ship and dispose of the goods financed.

Accounts Receivable Financing: Factoring

Factoring, which involves the sale of the seller's accounts receivable to a third party, is becoming increasingly popular as a trade financing vehicle. The third party, or factor, buys a company's receivables at a discount from face value, thereby accelerating their conversion to cash. As with any debt-like claim, there will be charges for the time value of money and the credit risk associated with the receivables. Most factoring is done on a non-recourse basis, meaning that the factor assumes all the credit and political risks (except those involving disputes between the transacting parties). The factor performs its own credit approval process on the foreign buyer before purchasing the receivable. For providing this service—which can be relatively expensive—the factor purchases the receivable at a discount and also receives a flat processing fee.

Though becoming more widely used in international trade, factoring of foreign accounts receivable is less common than factoring of domestic receivables. Most international factors or factoring houses are subsidiaries of a major bank or commercial finance company, having the knowledge and expertise to collect in their own country. Factors often utilize export credit insurance to mitigate the additional risk of a foreign receivable.

Forfaiting

Because capital goods tend to be quite expensive, meaning that importers may not be able to make payment for the goods within a short time period, longer-term financing becomes necessary. To deal with this problem a special of factoring called "forfaiting" is sometimes used. Forfaiting is the discounting, without recourse to the original holder, of medium-term export receivables (such as a promissory note or bill of exchange). These are normally very large transactions (in excess of $500,000) with the receivables being denominated in fully convertible currencies such as the U.S. dollar, the euro, or the British pound sterling. The technique is most often used in cases of capital goods exports with a five to seven year maturity involving semiannual installment payments. Since the forfaiting institution (usually a subsidiary of a large international bank) assumes the risk of nonpayment, it must assess the credit worthiness of the importer just if it were extending a medium-term loan. As is the case with many international transactions, the critical nature of country risk analysis is readily apparent.

Agencies That Promote International Trade

Due to the inherent risks associated with international trade, government institutions as well as the private sector offer various forms of export credit, export finance, and guarantee programs to reduce risk and stimulate foreign trade. Three prominent agencies that provide these services in the United States include the Export–Import Bank of the United States (Ex-Im Bank), the Private Export Funding Corporation (PEFCO), and the Overseas Private Investment Corporation (OPIC). These institutions are briefly described in turn.

Export-Import Bank of the United States

The Ex-Im Bank is the only U.S. government agency dedicated solely to financing and facilitating U.S. exports. Established in 1934 with the original goal of facilitating Soviet-American trade, its current mission is to finance and facilitate the export of American goods and services and maintain the competitiveness of American companies in overseas markets. Operating as an independent agency of the U.S. government, it has financed, guaranteed, or insured over $400 billion in U.S. exports. Ex-Im Bank's programs are generally designed to encourage the private sector to finance export trade by assuming some of the underlying credit risk and providing direct financing to foreign importers when private lenders are unwilling to do so. Pursuant to these objectives, the Ex-Im Bank offers programs that are classified as guarantees (the two most widely used of which are the Working Capital Guarantee Program and the Medium-Term Guarantee Program), loans (two of the most popular being the Direct Loan Program and the Project Finance Loan Program), and insurance (the most widely used of which is the Bank Letter of Credit Policy).

Private Export Funding Corporation

PEFCO, a private corporation, is owned by a consortium of commercial and industrial companies. It was created in 1970 by the Bankers' Association for Foreign Trade to mobilize private capital for financing the export of big-ticket items (such as aircraft or power generation equipment) by U.S. firms. It purchases the medium- to long-term debt obligations (usually five to twenty-five years) of importers of U.S. products at fixed interest rates. PEFCO finances its portfolio of foreign importer loans through the sale of its own securities. These bonds are readily marketable since they are in effect secured by Eximbank-guaranteed loans.

Overseas Private Investment Corporation

OPIC, formed in 1971, is a self-sustaining federal agency that provides U.S. investors with insurance against loss due to the specific political risks of expropriation, currency inconvertibility, and political violence (i.e., war, revolution, or insurrection). Since 1971, OPIC has supported over $145 billion in U.S. investment overseas. To qualify, the investment must be a new one or a substantial expansion of an existing facility, and must be approved by the host government. Coverage is generally restricted to a maximum of 90% of equity participation. OPIC also provides business income coverage, which protects a U.S. investor's income flow if political violence causes damage that interrupts operation of the foreign enterprise. While the cost of the coverage varies by industry and risk insured, these costs are not based solely on objective criteria. They also reflect subsidies geared to achieve certain political gains, such as fostering development of additional energy supplies.

Summary

This chapter was divided into two major focuses—the microeconomic foundations and principles explaining and surrounding the development, expansions, and patterns of international trade, and the financial considerations associated with carrying out trade between nations. The first portion of the chapter deals with the various microeconomic explanations of cross-border trade. Adam Smith's attention to the concept of absolute advantage was reviewed and assessed as representing merely an extension of the basic economic principles of specialization and efficient resource allocation. Next, David Ricardo's theory of comparative advantage was presented as a more generally applicable explanation of the development and expansion of cross-border trade. Even today, the principle of comparative advantage is the most widely accepted explanation for specialization and trade. Additionally, some of the newer, more sophisticated theories aimed at explaining trade patterns between nations were examined. Among these was the factor endowment theory, which hypothesizes that countries tend to export the products that use more intensively their abundant resources, and import goods that call for more intensive use of their scarce resources. Finally, consideration was turned toward Michael Porter's theory in which he argues that national competitive advantage is not necessarily a condition that merely stems from the bundle of land, natural resources, land, labor, and entrepreneurial ability that a country may be fortunate enough to inherit, but rather is something that can be created and developed by strategic choices.

Also in the microeconomic portion of the chapter, we focused on the impact of expanding cross-border trade as it affects different groups in an economy. Consumers constitute the largest group in this regard and is perhaps the one group that almost universally benefits from expanding markets and intensifying competition. They reap the benefits of wider product choice and lower prices. Producers, on the other hand, may benefit or suffer as a result of expanding markets and increased competition. Some thrive in the climate of expanding markets and competitive challenges, while others wither under the sting of increased competition and the associated need to improve efficiency and control costs. Labor, and especially organized labor, often resists trade expansion on the grounds that it costs jobs. Generally that "job loss" is actually "job displacement" as opposed to a net loss of employment, but the impact on the displaced worker (or even an industry, business or region) can be devastating all the same.

The second portion of the chapter examines how exchange rates are determined in a free market environment. Factors affecting the demand for and supply of national currencies were examined and used to illustrate how relative currency values respond to market conditions. Next, certain of the regimes and strategies for dealing with fluctuating currency values as well as other elements of risk peculiar to cross-border trade were identified and examined. The impetus for and advantages of common currency regimes, such as Europe's adoption of the euro as a common currency and the Americas' experimentation with "dollarization," were also examined.

Particular attention was paid to the fact that international trade presents special difficulties and involves significantly greater (and different) challenges than does trade within national boundaries. Specifically, the means and instruments required to provide for a climate of confidence and to ensure timely payment between parties that do not have long, established trading histories, and who may operate under different trading customs and laws, are not insignificant.

Finally, for any business interested in availing itself of many of the numerous opportunities provided by globalizing markets, it was noted that there are private entities as well as federal agencies devoted to the promotion of international trade and which offer programs and assistance specifically targeted at these endeavors. These include the Export-Import Bank, the Private Export Funding Corporation, and the Overseas Private Investment Corporation.

Discussion Question

1. Explain the various types and sources of risks involved in trade between nations.

Endnotes

1. Smith, A. 1937. *Wealth of Nations*. New York: Random House, Modern Library Edition, Book IV: 2.
2. Ricardo, D. 1966. *Principles of Political Economy and Taxation*. London: Cambridge University Press.
3. Heckscher, E. 1919. The effect of foreign trade on the distribution of income. *Ekonomisk Tidskrift* 21:1–32.
4. Ohlin, B. 1933. *Interregional and International Trade*. Cambridge, MA: Harvard University Press.
5. Samuelson, P. 1949. International factor price equalization once again. *Economic Journal* 59: 181–197.
6. Samuelson, P. 1953. Prices of factors and goods in general equilibrium. *Review of Economic Studies* 21:1–22.
7. Leontief, W. 1954. Domestic production and foreign trade: The American capital position reexamined. *Economica Internazionale* Feb:3–32.
8. Leontief, W. 1956. Factor proportions and the structure of American trade: Further theoretical and empirical analysis. *Review of Economics and Statistics* 386–407.
9. Porter, M. *The Competitive Advantage of Nations*. London: Macmillan;1990.
10. Harfield, T. 1998. Strategic management and Michael Porter: A postmodern reading. *Electronic Journal of Radical Organization Theory* 4(1).
11. Bryan, L., and D. Farrell. The savings surge. *The Wall Street Journal* November 7, 1994.

Chapter Eight

CROSS-CULTURAL CUSTOMS AND COMMUNICATION STYLES

Anatoly Zhuplev
Loyola Marymount University, Los Angeles, California

Learning Objectives

Upon completion of this chapter, students should be able to:

- Understand the essence of culture, cultural customs, and their role and key applications in three areas of international entrepreneurship: international marketing, international negotiations, and international management.
- Comprehend cultural dimensions and their impacts on international entrepreneurship.
- Explore cross-cultural aspects of communications, negotiations, and marketing in international entrepreneurship.
- Develop cross-cultural awareness through self-assessment.
- Gain cross-cultural knowledge and skills in international negotiations.

Key Terms

achievement vs. ascription
body language
communication
context vs. context in communication
cross-cultural management
cross-cultural/inter-cultural communication
cultural dimensions/variables
cultural values and norms
culture
culture shock
direct vs. indirect communication
ethnic culture
ethnocentric vs. polycentric cultural orientation
formal vs. informal communication
global managers

individualistic vs. collectivistic cultural orientation
international management
international negotiations
long-term vs. short-term cultural orientation
masculine vs. feminine cultural orientation
national culture
negotiations
neutral vs. emotional cultures
nonverbal communication
organizational culture
power distance (high vs. low)
uncertainty avoidance (high vs. low)
universalism vs. particularism
work/organizational culture

⊙ Introduction

Globalization unleashes business opportunities and, at the same, intensifies entrepreneurial competition on unprecedented scale. Often, business enterprises are attracted to go international through unplanned events and unexpected encounters resulting from personal travel or business meetings. Sometimes, contemplating and initiating an international business venture is triggered by personal experiences, cross-border ethnic connections, or through conscious pursuit of marketing opportunities offered by globalization. Increasingly, many enterprises are being pressed to go international in order for business survival to stay competitive through outsourcing or strategic alliances overseas. Innovations in transportation bring about greater ease, efficiency, and affordability in international shipping, travel, and tourism on a massive scale, thus facilitating international commerce and investment. Crucial improvements in information technologies (computers, the Internet, e-mail, Skype, Web-based bilingual translation, or video imaging, to name a few) facilitate personal, business, and political communications; cross-cultural interactions; travel; and other exchanges in truly global fashion. Intensified political–economic dialog among nations on bilateral, multilateral, regional, and global basis as well as diminishing barriers for international commerce and investment amplify these processes. Under these dynamics, going international is paramount for small and large companies. These forces expose big and small companies internationally and bring international competition upon them even if their intended primary strategy is domestic.

Whatever the entrepreneurial motivation or situation, international entrepreneurial enterprises face vast diversity and interdependence in political, economic, socio-cultural, technological, and other conditions. Understanding, interpreting, and transforming these conditions into entrepreneurial success requires cross-cultural awareness and acumen.

The foundations and driving forces of entrepreneurism are similar around the world, but cultural values and norms shaping organizational forms, business customs, and patterns of communication vary. In some cultures it takes a major focus, effort, time, and skills to develop the personal relations and trust that are considered prerequisites for business. In other cultures entrepreneurs take care of business first by getting right to the point and focusing on "hard" variables—product/service offering, pricing, customer value proposition, or financials. In the latter, "soft variables," personal relationships are treated as a by-product of business. In fact, those relationships may or may not be an integral part of business. In some cultures, a person's age, gender, ethnic origins, affiliation with a social class, or religious orientation are key priorities in this person's organizational status and role in business decision making and therefore should be paid close attention to in negotiations, marketing, or management. In other cultures, while these characteristics should be given consideration, other factors—formal educational qualifications, professional competence, business efficiency, or technical expertise—are of critical importance in defining a person's status, role, and career advancement and have different priorities and implications for negotiations, marketing, and management.

Cultural diversity and cross-cultural variations in international entrepreneurship stem from differences within and between nations in geography, climate, religion, historical patterns, language, family traditions, government, law, economics, technology, and other conditions. In turn, culture affects individuals, groups, organizations, and nations. Cross-cultural customs and communications are the medium connecting (sometimes integrating, sometimes dividing) various aspects of the entrepreneurial process.

Culture, a fluid and multifaceted phenomenon, is hard to rationalize and express in a rigid linear fashion. Mastering cross-cultural customs and communications styles is an art that, being applied under different business situations, may suggest different practical forms and solutions. Apart from knowledge, it requires skill development. Over the past few decades Hofstede, Troompenaars, and other researchers and practitioners have advanced understanding of cultures around the world through crystallizing cultural dimensions or variables that explain general patterns of business thinking and behavior in the national, ethnic, or organizational cross-cultural setting. The work of Philip Harris, Robert Moran and Sarah Moran, Richard Lewis, Jeffrey Curry, Kamal Fatehi, and others bring together theoretical and practical perspectives rationalizing cross-cultural approach to international management, negotiations, and other applications. In this chapter, we focus on cross-cultural characteristics and impacts of culture on international entrepreneurship.

Culture and Its Role in International Entrepreneurship

The processes and outcomes of international entrepreneurship are affected by many interdependent factors, conditions, and situational circumstances. While "hard" factors and variables—product characteristics, financial ratios, business strategy, law, or regulations—are at the core of the entrepreneurial process, culture plays a crucial but often "soft," intangible role in driving or hampering this process.

Culture is the collective programming of the mind that distinguishes the members of one human group from another. Culture, in this sense, includes systems of values and values are among the building blocks of culture. Culture is also viewed as a system of ideas and norms that are shared among a group of people and that, when taken together, constitute a design for living.[1] Culture, cultural values, and norms encompass and permeate our life and work and the way we behave, think, and conduct day-to-day business although, normally, we do not specifically attribute our thinking and behavior to specific cultural forces in a rational way. At any given time and place, a multitude of natural, economic, legal, technological, social, and other forces interacting with each other result in certain cultural effects, outcomes, and changing patterns on various levels, from individual to global. Likewise, a multitude of cultural forces, forms, and manifestations affect natural environment, economic dynamics, legal system, technological developments, social fabric, and other aspects of our being. As a basis and outcome of interactions and interdependent transactions in business, culture takes place on international, national, subnational, regional, industry, and corporate levels.

Conducting business in some cultures (e.g., Japanese or Arabic) becomes possible only after establishing reasonably close personal relationships where securing trust and other "intangible" factors precede business. On the contrary, in other cultures (e.g., the United States or UK) it is customary to pick up a phone and start discussing and doing business right away without first establishing strong personal bonds, trust, and mutual empathy.

Among numerous practical cultural applications in international entrepreneurship three key areas stand out: international marketing, international negotiations, and international management. Technological advances in communication and transportation make international entrepreneurship more cost affordable and easier for a broad range of small- and medium-sized companies. Falling trade barriers and proliferation of freedom in exchange of information and people make many products and marketing strategies more homogeneous on a global scale. However, *international marketing* continues to be different across countries, depending on regional and local cultural patterns.[i] *International negotiations*, particularly crucial at initial stages of the international entrepreneurial venture initiation process, are also strongly affected by culture. And, finally, *managing international* joint business ventures, maintaining various kinds of business alliances, or simply managing domestic company comprised of multicultural workforce requires complex multicultural understanding.

It is common in international entrepreneurship for two or more parties from different national cultures to interact in cross-border business transactions. With a certain degree of generalization this form can be categorized as *inter-national culture* where business behavior over time tends to blend into a more homogeneous patter mitigating inter-national differences.

A participant in a business transaction may be representing a certain nation, but his or her individual cultural profile may deviate from this nation's general cultural profile based on this person's religious affiliation, ethnic behavioral norms, position in the national social stratification, and other cultural traits. *National culture* is a convenient operational term, although sometimes it distorts reality: in multiethnic countries national culture is often comprised of different subcultures existing in this nation along the lines of its ethnic groups, regions, industries, firms, social/interest groups, business firms, and individuals. Thus, the categories of national character and national culture reflect this level in integrated form.

Ethnic culture can characterize distinctive ethnic groups populating a nation; many nations comprise different ethnic groups, often quite distinctive in their language, religion, beliefs, values, and other cultural characteristics. For instance, there are three major ethnic groups in Canada (English speaking, French speaking, and native Canadians), two major ethnic groups in Turkey (Turks and

---

i. Despite remaining national differences in consumer demand and government regulations on a wide variety of consumer products, food, clothing, and other culturally bound items; many commodities (e.g., oil, agricultural products); industrial products (aircraft, equipment); technological gadgets (cell phone, MP3 player); and other products and services tend to be increasingly global.

Kurds), several dozen relatively sizeable ethnic groups in Russia, and a "melting pot" in the ethnically diverse United States.

Regional culture often corresponds with the boundaries of ethnic culture but can be a mix of several ethnic cultures populating the region and differentiating themselves on the basis of local climate, geographic landscape, historical events (wars, political unions), or an industry dominant in the area. A good example would be regional cultural differences that exist between northern and southern regions in many large countries (e.g., the United States, Italy, or Germany).

Culture specific to a particular *industry* or economic sector may also have its unique impact on business. Sometimes industries within national borders have very distinctive differences in business culture. For example, informality and personal relations play an important role in the Hollywood film production and decision-making or in the "dot.com" industry. On the other hand, business procedures and etiquette in the banking industry are much more formal, transparent, and strictly regulated. Due to strategic importance for a national economy or other reasons, some industries operate with preferential treatment, financial support, and administrative control from government under the nation's industrial policy. For instance, industrial policy affects agriculture, railroads, and aircraft production in the European Union (EU), oil industry in Russia and Venezuela, or some export-oriented "national champions" in Japan and South Korea.

Organizational or corporate *culture* resulting from a juxtaposition of many previous types comprises a culture of specific organization. The dynamics of corporate culture include: routine behavior when people interact, such as organizational rituals and ceremonies and the commonly used language; norms that are shared by work groups throughout the organization, such as "a casual Friday"; dominant values held by the organization, such as "commitment to quality" or a "customers come first" attitude; certain philosophy as a driving force behind organizational policies toward employees, customers, shareholders, and other groups of stakeholders; patterns in "organizational politics," and the perception of organizational climate by its major stakeholders through the physical layout; the way employees interact, resolve their conflicts, and so on. Often, organizational culture reflects personalities of its founders (Disney, Ben & Jerry's, Google, or Dell Computer Corporation in the United States; Li & Fung in Hong Kong; Richard Branson's Virgin Group in the UK; or Toyota in Japan), a type of industry and product, evolution of business, and other factors. Corporate size also has strong impact on business culture suggesting significant differences between large and small business organizations.

In a broad sense, entrepreneurial culture in a nation is a contributing factor and an outcome of the business macro environment comprised of religious effects, political forces, legal systems, economic conditions, socio-demographic structures, and technological environments. Under this framework, the individual's cultural profile and behavior are shaped by the family, educational systems and institutions (schools, universities), profession, gender, age, race, community, friends, personal networks, and other conditions.

Geert Hofstede, in his well-known cross-cultural study from 1967 to 1973, surveyed 116,000 respondents from over seventy different countries around the world working in IBM's local subsidiaries in fifty countries and three regions.

TABLE 8.1 Dimensions of National Culture (Hofstede and Trompenaars)

CULTURAL DIMENSIONS AND COUNTRIES	DESCRIPTION OF THINKING AND BEHAVIOR
Power Distance *Countries with highest power distance:* Malaysia, Guatemala, Panama, Philippines, Venezuela *Countries with lowest power distance:* Austria, Israel, Denmark, New Zealand, Ireland	The extent to which people accept unequal distribution of power. In higher power distance cultures, there is a wider gap between the powerful and the powerless.
Individualism vs. Collectivism *Individualistic countries:* U.S., Australia, Great Britain, Canada, the Netherlands *Collectivistic countries:* Guatemala, Panama, Colombia, Venezuela, Pakistan	Individualism leads to reliance on self and focus on individual achievement; the extent to which individuals or closely knit social structures such as the extended family (collectivism) are the basis for social systems.
Masculinity vs. Femininity *Countries with highest masculinity:* Japan, Austria, Switzerland, Ireland, Mexico *Countries with lowest masculinity:* Sweden, Norway, Denmark, Costa Rica, Finland	The extent to which assertiveness and independence from others is valued. High masculinity leads to high sex-role differentiation, ambition, and material goods.
Uncertainty Avoidance *High uncertainty avoidance countries:* Greece, Portugal, Guatemala, Uruguay, Belgium *Low uncertainty avoidance countries:* Singapore, Jamaica, Denmark, Costa Rica, Sweden	The extent to which the culture tolerates ambiguity and uncertainty. High uncertainty avoidance leads to low tolerance for uncertainty and to a search for absolute truth and predictability.
Long-Term Orientation (based on limited data) *Countries with long-term orientation:* Mainland China, Hong-Kong, Taiwan, S. Korea *Countries with short-term orientation:* West Africa, Philippines, Canada, UK, U.S.	The extent to which people focus on past, present, or future. Present orientation leads to a focus on short-term performance achievements.
Universalism vs. Particularism *Universal cultures:* U.S., Switzerland, Germany, Sweden *Particular cultures:* France, Italy, Spain, the Middle East	Universalistic cultures develop rules that apply to all relationships and situations. Particularistic cultures focus on the uniqueness of each situation.
Neutral vs. Emotional *Neutral cultures:* Japan, UK, Indonesia *Emotional cultures:* Italy, France	Interactions are based on objectivity and neutrality, or they are based on emotional bonds.
Specific vs. Diffuse *Specific cultures:* U.S., Australia, the Netherlands *Diffuse cultures:* France, Italy, Japan, Mexico	Relationships are specific to situations or generalize to different situations.
Achievement vs. Ascription *Achievement-based cultures:* U.S., Canada, Norway, Sweden, UK *Ascription-based cultures:* Middle East, Eastern Europe, France	People's worth is judged by their recent performance and achievement, or by an ascribed status based on other factors such as birth or social class.

TABLE 8.1 Dimensions of National Culture (Hofstede and Trompenaars) (continued)

CULTURAL DIMENSIONS AND COUNTRIES	DESCRIPTION OF THINKING AND BEHAVIOR
Perception and Use of Time *Present-oriented and linear:* U.S., Germany. *Past-oriented:* Mexico	Focus and value are placed on the present, the past, or the future.
Perceptions of Physical Environment *Environment to be used:* Brazil, Portugal, S. Korea *Environment to be respected:* Japan, Egypt, Singapore, Sweden	Either the individual or the environment is seen as dominant; the environment is either used or respected.

(Adopted from Hofstede, G. 1980. *Culture's Consequences: International Differences in Work-Related Values.* Beverly Hills, CA: Sage Publications; Trompenaars, F. 1994. *Riding the Waves of Culture: Understanding Culture and Diversity in Business.* London: Nicholas Brealey.

Subsequent studies validating the earlier results have included commercial airline pilots and students in twenty-three countries, civil service managers in fourteen countries, "up-market" consumers in fifteen countries, and "elites" in nineteen countries.[2] The Hofstede study reduced the world's vast cultural variety to five universal dimensions allowing for international comparisons in managerial patterns: *power distance, individualism, masculinity, uncertainty avoidance,* and *long-term orientation.* In the 1980s, F. Trompenaars studied over 15,000 people in organizations in forty-seven countries and came up with seven cultural dimensions: *universalism vs. particularism, individualism vs. collectivism, neutral vs. emotional, specific vs. diffuse, achievement vs. ascription, perception and use of time,* and *perception of physical environment.*

Although Hofstede and Trompenaars' studies have methodological and practical limitations, they give the international entrepreneur a good framework for cross-cultural generalization and practical guidance. An integrated summary of Hofstede and Trompenaars' findings and their cross-cultural impact on business are presented in Table 8.1 and Figure 8.1.

Cross-Cultural Aspects of International Communication

Communication is the heart of business. It involves transmitting and sharing meaning by messages through media such as words, behavior, or material artifacts. Unlike research and development or engineering that heavily rely on technology (computers, manuals, experiments, etc.) business is well grounded in human behavior-based interactions. International entrepreneurs engage in communications in many ways. Initiation of international business venture requires complex research of products, markets, technologies, financing, cost analysis, legal issues, global positioning, entry strategy, and other issues. These activities involve reading, listening, speaking, writing, interacting with other people, and

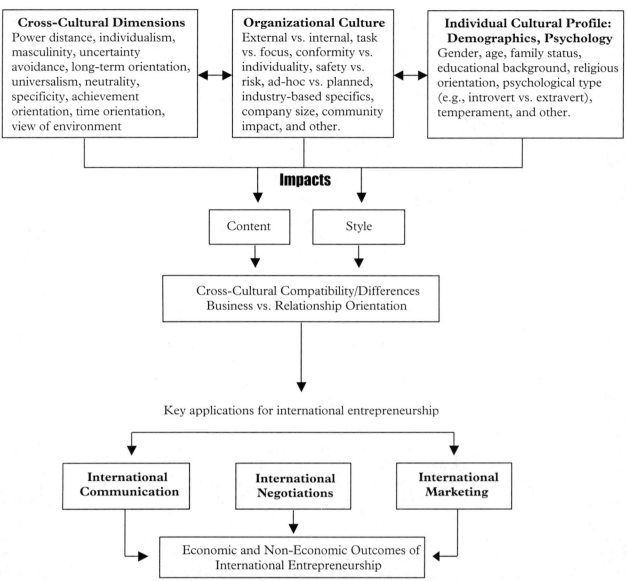

FIGURE 8.1 Cross-Cultural Impact on International Entrepreneurship
(Adapted from Ghauri, P., and J-C. Usunier. 1996. *International Business Negotiations.* 28.)

eventually traveling and negotiating internationally. International marketing includes collecting information on products, prices, promotion, and channels of distribution networks where personal connections and other informal aspects are paramount. Finding a reliable international distributor or a client by building trust requires strong motivational, communication, and other human skills. Managing a foreign subsidiary, a joint venture, or maintaining an international business alliance requires complex cross-cultural knowledge and applications in international management where human communication is a key.

Communication in a cross-cultural entrepreneurial environment is graphically presented in Figure 8.2.

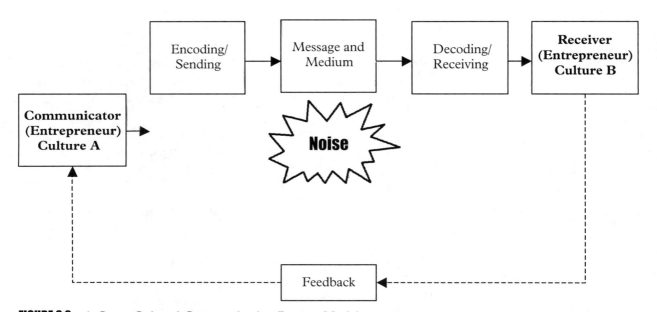

FIGURE 8.2 A Cross-Cultural Communication Process Model
(Adapted from Deresky, H. 2003. *International Management: Managing Across Borders and Cultures.* New Jersey: Pearson Education, Inc.: 126–127.)

Communicator: In the global business environment an entrepreneur from culture A (for example, the United States) may initiate his/her international business venture by sending ideas, inquiries, intentions, proposals, descriptions, samples, etc. to an individual from culture B, for example Japan.

Encoding/sending: The U.S. entrepreneur transforms his/her business ideas, inquiries, etc., into a certain transmittable format (verbal, written, graphic, nonverbal, etc.) that the Japanese counterpart should understand.

Message: The U.S. entrepreneur sends a verbal or nonverbal message with a definite intended content (e.g., a business proposal or pro-forma invoice). A purpose of the message may be to have the Japanese counterpart understand an idea, accept a product for distribution, or verify some regulatory requirements related to importing this product to Japan. However, this intended content is transmitted in a certain environment that also includes unintended components: a tone of voice (in case of a verbal communication), facial expression, body language (in case of a face-to-face communication), a writing style, or some business circumstances relevant to the situation.

Medium: This is a channel through which the message is sent. The U.S. entrepreneur can choose from a variety of options: e-mail, fax, telephone, face-to-face meeting, videoconference, Skype, Web site, etc. Each communication channel has its own pros and cons, including those grounded in a cross-cultural acceptance. For example, making an unsolicited ("cold") call is a common practice in the United States. However, in many Asian cultures, including Japan, this practice is less acceptable, and, instead, using an intermediary is a common way of initiating business communication.

Decoding/receiving: Using his or her own cultural frame of reference, level of education, professional knowledge, and previous business experience, the Japanese counterpart receives, interprets, and understands the message in the cultural and situational business context. The receiver then may decide to provide feedback to the communicator that is often used to confirm that the message was received and had the intended effect on the receiver. Again, maintaining a two-way communication is very common in U.S. business culture and often much less common in other cultures, frustrating American entrepreneurs who are waiting in vain to receive feedback from their overseas counterparts.

Noise: At every stage, the communication process is distorted by the environmental impact. In addition to noises typical for mono-cultural communications in a domestic business, there are numerous kinds of noises/distortions related to international communications. It can be a language barrier in translation and interpretation of message from English into Japanese. Or it can be technological incompatibility between the transmitting and receiving fax machines because of the differences in electric voltage and frequency, or outdated telephone lines. Sometimes, communication breakdowns happen for economic reasons: a receiver in a poor country may be hesitant to respond to a message sent by a sender from a wealthy country because of the high international telephone/fax/Internet rates. Numerous problems and breakdowns in international communication happen due to the cultural misinterpretation and misunderstanding.

One of the major cross-cultural differences in international entrepreneurship depends on the balance between content and context in communication between individuals affiliated with different national cultures.

Cultures with *high content/low context* stress straightforward exchange in facts in communication. Information is given primarily in words, and the meaning is expressed explicitly, often in writing: the entrepreneur says what is meant and means what is said. In other words, the entrepreneur in the high content culture tends to emphasize an intended content and put it in a structured, straightforward format. Typical examples of national cultures with high communication content are the United States or Germany. On the contrary, many other national cultures, like Japan, China, or some Arab nations, have a tendency toward *high context/low content* in communication style. Under this type of communication shared experience and established personal relations make certain things well understood without them needing to be stated explicitly (people can "read between the lines" and understand each other's "body language"). Rules for speaking, keeping silence, and behaving are implicit in the context. For example, the relationship-based Japanese culture tends to avoid "losing face." In this context, to sidestep embarrassment and for other cultural reasons, the Japanese counterpart in his or her negotiation with the U.S. counterpart is not likely to say "no," should there be a need. He or she is more likely to say: "It will be difficult," or "I will think about your proposal." The Japanese use of language is particularly unique and very different from other cultures. What is actually said has no meaning or significance whatsoever. Japanese use their language as a tool of communication, but the words and sentences themselves give no indication of what they are saying. What they want and how they feel are indicated by the way they address their conversational partner. Smiles, pauses, sighs, grunts, nods, and eye movements convey everything. The Japanese leave their fellow Japanese perfectly well what has been agreed, no matter what was said. Foreigners leave the Japanese with a completely different idea. Usually they think that everything has gone swimmingly, as the Japanese would never offend them by saying anything negative or unpleasant.[3] In dealing with high context cultures, the U.S. entrepreneur should pay much more attention to the body language, surrounding events and circumstance, facial expression, and other unintended and informal communication aspects beyond the message itself.

Other important cross-cultural characteristics in international communication include: *direct* (preference for explicit one- or two-way communication, primarily in words, including identification, diagnosis, and management of a conflict) *vs. indirect* (preference for implicit communication and conflict avoidance); *expressive* (emotive and personal communication style with high degree of subjectivity, stress on relationships) *vs. instrumental* (unemotional, impersonal, high degree of objectivity); *formal* (high emphasis on following protocol and social order) *vs. informal* (stress on dispensing with ceremony and rigid protocol).[4] Solid knowledge and operational skills in using these cross-cultural characteristics in international entrepreneurship may help in avoiding blunders in communication, negotiations, and marketing. It may also facilitate greater effectiveness and efficiency in these areas of international business.

Cross-Cultural Aspects of International Negotiations

International business negotiations take place at every stage of the entrepreneurial process, from venture initiation to termination of business relationships. Culture is an important component in international business as a whole, but it is particularly vital during the initial stages of a business venture where parties learn about the venture itself, the surrounding business environment, and, of utmost importance, building trust while trying to strategically protect themselves. On a very general level, the key steps in the international negotiation process include but are not limited to: (1) preparation (collecting task-related information, forming the negotiating team, preparing the agenda); (2) building the relationship (establishing rapport, entertaining an international counterpart's team, learning about personalities, gaining trust); (3) first round of task-related information exchange; (4) persuasion (applying strategies, tactics, and arguments to strive in achieving the set goals); (5) concessions (making and discussing counterproposals resulting from the first round of information exchange); (6) reaching and legitimizing agreement, and (7) post-agreement activities, including verification of progress towards achievement of the set goals, as well as resolution of disagreements and conflicts. As seen from this simple list of negotiation activities, all of them are strongly immersed in culture, and culturally bound communication style.

Cultural impacts on negotiation may vary depending on a managerial perspective (see Table 8.2).

TABLE 8.2 Negotiation Factors and Cultural Responses: a Managerial Perspective

NEGOTIATION FACTORS	RANGE OF CULTURAL RESPONSES		
Definition of negotiation	contract	← →	relationship
Negotiation opportunity	distributive	← →	integrative
Selection of negotiators	experts	← →	trusted associates
Protocol	informal	← →	formal
Communication	direct	← →	indirect
Time sensitivity	high	← →	low
Risk propensity	high	← →	low
Groups versus individuals	collectivism	← →	individualism
Nature of agreements	specific	← →	general
Emotionalism	high	← →	low

(Adapted from Lewicki, R. J., Saunders, D. M., and B. Barry. 2006. *Negotiation*, 5th ed. New York: McGraw-Hill/Irwin: 420.)

Although it is difficult to categorize the world's rich cross-cultural mosaic into specific boxes related to the entrepreneurial process or the international negotiation process, certain useful generalizations can be made (see Table 8.3) on the basis of the above cultural variables. Due to a limited space, cultural impacts on negotiations are discussed only on the high end of the cultural dichotomies.

What characteristics distinguish successful negotiators from average negotiators? While the specific answer to this question depends on the context and assessment criteria that are culturally driven, one study of British negotiators offers some insights. According to this study both average and successful negotiators spend the same amount of time planning. The difference is *what* was planned.

- Good negotiators develop twice as many alternatives as less effective negotiators. This leaves them with more options when negotiations deviate into uncharted waters.
- While the main objective of negotiations is to reduce and reconcile different interests, experienced negotiators spend much more time on areas where there is common ground and agreements are possible, rather than devoting excessive time to topics where obvious differences exist. Experienced negotiators also "nibble away" at differences rather than tackling head on.
- Skilled negotiators spend more time exploring long-term issues and their effects than do average negotiators. This practice puts companies emphasizing short-term objectives at a negotiating disadvantage.
- Good negotiators are flexible in setting goals. They define goals within ranges (for example, a return on investment of 10% to 20%) rather than as definite targets ("We must get a minimum 14% return").
- Unskilled negotiators have definite sequences of points to cover, ranked usually by their order of importance. Skilled negotiators go into meetings with a

TABLE 8.3 Cultural Impacts on International Negotiations

CULTURAL VARIABLES	KEY POTENTIAL IMPACTS ON NEGOTIATING WITH REPRESENTATIVES OF THIS CULTURE
High Power Distance	Reliance on intermediaries, at least at initial stages. Negotiating teams are split into participants with high decision-making power and those with no power. Several initial rounds of negotiations with low power negotiators may be required before final decision involving high-ranked negotiators can be reached. Establishing personal rapport is extremely important. Situations causing the other side to "lose face" should be avoided.
High Individualism	Expression of independent judgments, opinions in negotiation, and decision making. An advance study of strong and weak points in negotiators' background (personal, educational, professional, business), as well as their positions in the decision making process is advised. Business (task-related) aspects vs. relationships are emphasized. Using individual negotiators and small teams as opposed to large teams. Preference for structure and priorities in presenting information according to negotiators' individual profiles and roles in negotiations. Taking into account individual motivations and responsibilities for the outcome of negotiations in developing your negotiation strategy and conflict resolution can increase leverage in negotiation.
High Masculinity	High priority is placed on effectiveness and efficiency of the business under negotiations, lesser emphasis on issues beyond the bottom line. Explicit presentation of information and high assertiveness on all stages of negotiations. Lesser likelihood for female negotiators to be involved in key decision making roles. Situations causing the other side to "lose face" should be avoided. The opposite party's "macho" propensity can be exploited.
High Uncertainty Avoidance	Restraint toward entrepreneurial business ideas and bold projects that are not backed up by information and/or resources. Risk avoidance. Abundance of supporting information, feasibility studies, and references required in order to back up the major points under negotiations. Slower pace of negotiations and decision making, possibility of several rounds of negotiations. High reliance on formal rules and procedures in dealing with complex and uncertain matters.
High Long-Term Orientation	Be prepared to deal with adherence to traditional, forward-oriented priorities. Reservations toward product, technological, and business innovations. Certain role played by nonbusiness considerations (e.g., community, nationwide issues) beyond the bottom line.
Universalism vs. Particularism	Universalism presumes the reliance on formal rules and procedures universally applied toward various situations. Merit-based promotion and remuneration. Egalitarianism. Particularistic types entail reliance on personal relationships, taking into account specific cases and individual circumstances rather than general categories. Inclination toward revising conditions that have been already agreed upon.
Neutral vs. Emotional	Neutral types tend to operate with and appeal to the logic, methods, facts, statistics, structures, and priorities in negotiations. They lean toward putting business aspects first. On the contrary, emotional types emphasize personalities and interpersonal relationships on various stages of the negotiation process.

TABLE 8.3 Cultural Impacts on International Negotiations (continued)

CULTURAL VARIABLES	KEY POTENTIAL IMPACTS ON NEGOTIATING WITH REPRESENTATIVES OF THIS CULTURE
Achievement vs. Ascription	Achievement-oriented type in negotiations tends to have characteristics similar to those associated with high individualism, masculinity, and short-term orientation. Greater likelihood for young negotiators with professional knowledge and skills to be included in a team. On the contrary, ascriptive cultures are likely to be associated with the characteristics of collectivism, femininity, and long-term orientation. Team composition and negotiating power may be based on age, hierarchical status, or the length of tenure in the firm. Nepotism, versus professionalism, may also play a role.
Cooperation vs. Competition	Negotiation is a give and take game, and there is always something to gain and something to lose. Cultures with high propensity for cooperation are more likely to pursue nonconfrontational strategies in lieu of the long-term mutual benefits with a "win-win" outcome. On the opposite, cultures oriented toward competition often emphasize a "go it alone" strategy and short-term "the winner takes all" orientation.

series of issues to tackle but do not have a predetermined sequence. The second method makes it more difficult for the other side to determine what the opposite negotiating team considers as the critical issues. This method also maintains a balance among the issues, thereby minimizing the chances that either side will hurt the negotiations by applying pressure on sensitive issues.

- Successful negotiators generally go through four phases: (1) building up rapport; (2) learning about the proposed agreement, including its technical, legal, and business aspects; (3) bridging differences through reason, persuasion, and, occasionally, argument; and (4) making concessions and drawing up agreements.[5]

Cross-Cultural Aspects of International Marketing

International marketing involves a number of cultural considerations. *Product* decisions, including brand name, quality, scope of the product line, warranties, and packaging are often culturally bound either directly or indirectly. For example, a beautiful gift packaging in Japan sometimes means more to the customer than the gift itself. *Pricing*, although an economic component of marketing, also varies depending on culture in such aspects as list price, discounts, bundling, payment terms, and financing alternatives. In an anecdotal example a pair of "new Russians" flash and cash nouveau riches discusses their new neckwear. One of them asks another: "How much did you pay for your tie?" "Fifty dollars," goes the answer. "I've got a much better deal for a similar tie in a store across the street," responds the other Russian, "I bought mine for a hundred dollars." *Place* (distribution) is intertwined with culture through such components as distribution channels (fragmented or concentrated), motivating the channel (long-term vs. short-term, monetary vs. intangible), and criteria for evaluating distributors, locations, and logistics (transportation, warehousing, and order fulfillment). *Promotion*/advertising includes such culturally anchored items as choosing the right media, public relations, promotional programs, budget, or the projected results of promotional programs. Compared with other components of the entrepreneurial process (e.g., creativity, product development, technological innovation, or financing), culture is relatively more conservative and unreceptive to change. Globalization tends to make entrepreneurship and marketing more international, whether the company expands overseas or stays domestically, competing with both domestic and foreign firms on its home turf.

Other things being equal, a standard, uniform promotional message on international scale tends to be more attractive to businesses because it does not require expensive country-by-country modifications and because the uniform promotional strategy is easier to design and manage. However, in the majority of real circumstances, localization in product attributes and marketing are dictated by technical standards, import-related government regulatory requirements in a local country, or simply by a limited spending power among the local population. Along with that a need for localization may often be a cultural part of the cultural differences in consumer behavior. In the international marketing context, countries differ in a multitude of ways along a range of dimensions including social structure, language, religion, education, role of the family, and government in shaping and modifying consumer behavior.

In highly stratified societies (India with its caste system is an extreme example of social stratification) market segmentation and other elements of marketing can follow the lines dividing societal layers. Members of society affiliated with specific strata commit themselves to abiding certain life styles, norms, and rituals that stay relatively stable making marketing strategies and methods more uniform and consistent within the same strata.

Among many characteristics of the cultural impact of language on international marketing the "content vs. context" dyad deserves particular attention. In high content/low context cultures, such as the United States or Germany, marketing should emphasize rational approach, logic, facts, numbers, etc., focusing on cost vs. functionality and quality. On the contrary, low content/high context countries, such as Japan, require more emotional, "irrational" appeal by referring images, family, friendships, group relationships, or even nationalistic appeal. Many countries, based on their cultural traditions, restrict marketing of alcohol, tobacco, and weapons, but are relatively more flexible on pornography, nudity in advertising, or using substances (e.g., the Netherlands). Some countries restrict hostile and comparative advertising or using children in advertising.

Islamic religion strictly forbids charging and receiving interest in conducting business. In Hinduism, the cow is a sacred animal and devout religious Indians do not eat beef.

There are numerous striking examples of cultural blunders committed in international marketing by U.S. firms with strong international reputation that cost them dearly. For example, S.C. Johnson Wax, a manufacturer of waxes and polishes, has encountered resistance to its lemon scented Pledge furniture polish among older consumers in Japan. More careful market research revealed that the polish smelled similar to a latrine disinfectant used widely in Japan in the 1940s. Cheetos, a bright orange and cheesy-tasting snack from PepsiCo's Frito Lay unit, do not have a cheese taste in China. Chinese consumers generally do not like the taste of cheese because it has never been a part of traditional cuisine and because many Chinese are lactose-intolerant. One of the famous examples was Disney's 1992 expansion to Paris, France, where the famous entertainment firm committed a litany of cultural blunders, from trying to restrict the use of alcohol in the theme park to serving croissants and coffee, a typical French breakfast, while patrons wanted bacon and eggs, U.S. style.[1]

Due to historical, political–economic, and other reasons, different countries have different structure in the distribution systems depending on the industry. For instance, in Asian countries, where family connections and personal relations come first, distribution systems can be fragmented or concentrated, with long or short channels; a U.S. exporter will have a difficult time trying to penetrate distribution networks on his or her own. At initial strategic stages, an attempt should be made to form an alliance with a local company and time and effort should be invested in long-term relationships to develop personal trust, a precondition to business success.

Cross-Cultural Aspects of International Management

As the entrepreneurial venture grows, expands internationally, and matures, sound management as opposed to purely entrepreneurial drive becomes increasingly important. Along with many advantages of operating internationally comes cross-cultural organizational complexity. Whether taken in a more traditional perspective, as a set of managerial functions (planning, organizing, influencing, and controlling), or looked upon as a set of roles that managers play in organizations (interpersonal, informational, and decisional), international management experiences have strong cultural impacts.

Under different situational circumstances, U.S.-based international entrepreneurs face cross-cultural managerial challenges in two typical settings: (1) when international business venture is being initiated/managed on U.S. soil by a foreign company in partnership with a U.S. firm; (2) when a U.S. firm initiates/manages its fully owned subsidiary or a joint venture overseas. Although not an international business venture in a strict sense, purely domestic business venture in the United States employing culturally diverse labor force also requires strong cross-cultural acumen and managerial savvy.

With wide breadth and significant complexity of managerial issues in the cross-cultural context, some of the major managerial applications in abbreviated format are presented in Table 8.4. For obvious reason, an attempt to reduce the complex and fluid entrepreneurial reality to an academic scheme reflecting this reality is incomplete and static.

 TABLE 8.4 **Cross-Cultural Implications for International Management**

IMPLICATIONS OF POWER DISTANCE		
MANAGEMENT PROCESSES	LOW POWER DISTANCE	HIGH POWER DISTANCE
Human resource management		
Personnel selection	Educational achievement	Social class; elite education
Training	For autonomy	For conformity/obedience
Evaluation/promotion	Performance	Compliance; trustworthiness
Remuneration	Small wage difference between management and worker	Large wage difference between management and worker
Leadership styles	Participative; less direct supervision	Theory X; authoritarian, with close supervision
Motivational assumptions	People like work; extrinsic and intrinsic rewards	Assume people dislike work; coercion
Decision making/organizational design	Decentralized; flat pyramids; small proportion of supervisors	Tall pyramids; large proportion of supervisors
Strategy issues	Varied	Crafted to support the power elite or government

IMPLICATIONS OF UNCERTAINTY AVOIDANCE		
MANAGEMENT PROCESSES	LOW UNCERTAINTY AVOIDANCE	HIGH UNCERTAINTY AVOIDANCE
Human resource management		
Personnel selection	Past job performance; education	Seniority; expected loyalty
Training	Training to adapt	Specialized
Evaluation/promotion	Objective individual performance data; job switching for promotion	Seniority; expertise; loyalty
Remuneration	Based on performance	Based on seniority or expertise
Leadership styles	Nondirective; person-oriented; flexible	Task oriented
Motivational assumptions	People are self-motivated, competitive	People seek security, avoid competition

TABLE 8.4 Cross-Cultural Implications for International Management (continued)

IMPLICATIONS OF UNCERTAINTY AVOIDANCE

MANAGEMENT PROCESSES	LOW UNCERTAINTY AVOIDANCE	HIGH UNCERTAINTY AVOIDANCE
Decision making/organizational design	Smaller organizations; flat hierarchy; less formalized, with fewer written rules and standardized procedures	Larger organization; tall hierarchy; formalized; many standardized procedures
Strategy issues	Risk taking	Averse to risk

IMPLICATIONS OF INDIVIDUALISM

MANAGEMENT PROCESSES	LOW INDIVIDUALISM	HIGH INDIVIDUALISM
Human resource management		
Personnel selection	Group membership; school or university	Universalistic, based on individual traits
Training	Focus on company-based skills	General skills for individual achievement
Evaluations/promotion	Slow, with group; seniority	Based on individual performance
Remuneration	Based on group membership/organizational paternalism	Extrinsic rewards (money, promotion) based on market value
Leadership styles	Appeals to duty and commitment	Individual rewards and punishments based on performance
Motivational assumptions	Moral involvement	Calculative; individual cost/benefit
Decision making/organizational design	Group; slow; preference for larger organizations	Individual responsibility; preference for smaller organizations

IMPLICATIONS OF MASCULINITY

MANAGEMENT PROCESSES	LOW MASCULINITY	HIGH MASCULINITY
Human resource management		
Personnel selection	Independent of gender, school ties less important; androgyny	Jobs gender identified; school, performance, and ties important
Training	Job oriented	Career oriented
Evaluation/promotion	Job performance, with less gender-based assignments	Continues gender tracking
Remuneration	Less salary difference between levels; more time off	More salary preferred to fewer hours

TABLE 8.4 Cross-Cultural Implications for International Management (continued)

IMPLICATIONS OF MASCULINITY

MANAGEMENT PROCESSES	LOW MASCULINITY	HIGH MASCULINITY
Leadership styles	More participative	More Theory X; authoritarian
Motivational assumptions	Emphasis on quality of life, time off, vacations; work not central	Emphasis on performance and growth; excelling to be best; work central to life; job recognition important
Decision making/organizational design	Intuitive/group; smaller organizations	Decisive/individual; larger organization preferred

IMPLICATIONS OF LONG-TERM ORIENTATION

MANAGEMENT PROCESSES	SHORT-TERM ORIENTATION	LONG-TERM ORIENTATION
Human resource management		
Personnel selection	Objective skill assessment for immediate use to company	Fit of personal and background characteristics
Training	Limited to immediate company needs	Investment in long-term employment skills
Evaluation/promotion	Fast; based on skill contributions	Slow; develop skills and loyalty
Remuneration	Pay, promotions	Security
Leadership styles	Use incentives for economic advancement	Build social obligations
Motivational assumptions	Immediate rewards necessary	Subordinate immediate gratification for long-term individual and company goals
Decision making/organizational design	Logical analysis of problems; design for logic of company situation	Synthesis to reach consensus; design for social relationships
Strategy issues	Fast; measurable payback	Long-term profits and growth; incrementalism

(From Hofstede (1980, 1991). Adapted from Cullen, J. 1999. *Multinational Management. A Strategic Approach.* Cincinnati, OH: South-West College Publishing: 64,67,69,71.)

Summary

The cultural categories in Table 8.4, however academically pure and practically convenient, are always intertwined and have blurred borders. Additionally, all kinds of these cultural categories across the world, from national to organizational, are subject to various degrees of change under advances in technology, communication, transportation, falling trade barriers, and proliferation of freedom in exchange for information and people. The former, seemingly monolithic Soviet Union with its almost 300 million people is no longer; Eastern European countries are being integrated into the EU; China and India are opening up to become formidable global players; and even traditional Japan is shifting its distinctive cultural patterns as generational cultural norms and values evolve.

Business ventures, cases, and actors in international entrepreneurship are in many ways unique, requiring situational approach. And, finally, a great deal of practical experience and common sense are needed in addressing international entrepreneurship in cross-cultural context.

Discussion Questions

1. Define culture, its role, and key practical applications for international entrepreneurship in terms of international marketing, international negotiations, and international management.
2. Explain national and corporate culture and discuss main points in their relationship.
3. Explain the meaning of cultural dimensions identified by Hofstede and Trompenaars in their studies.
4. American business communication style is commonly characterized as high content/low context; in contrast, Japanese business communication style has high context and low content. Explain this difference and possible cross-cultural implications for the U.S.–Japanese international business negotiations.
5. According to Hofstede, American culture is characterized by the highest level of individualism in the world. On the other hand, Latin American countries such as Ecuador, Guatemala, and Venezuela have the lowest level of individualism and, respectively, highest level collectivism. What cultural impacts is such a contrast in cultures likely to have on business negotiations between Americans and their counterparts from these Latin American countries?
6. What are the major impacts of high power distance and high social stratification on market segmentation?

Case 8.1

A large Baltimore manufacturer of cabinet hardware had been working for months to locate a suitable distributor for its products in Europe. Finally invited to present a demonstration to a reputable distributing company in Frankfurt, it sent one of its most promising young executives, Fred Wagner, to make the presentation. Fred not only spoke fluent German but also felt a special interest in this assignment because his paternal grandparents had immigrated to the United States from the Frankfurt area during the 1920s. When Fred arrived at the conference room where he would be making his presentation he shook hands firmly, greeted everyone with a friendly *guten tag*, and even remembered to bow his head slightly as is the German custom.

Fred, a very effective speaker and past president of the Baltimore Toastmasters Club, prefaced his presentation with a few humorous anecdotes to set a relaxed and receptive atmosphere. However, he felt that his presentation was not very well received by the company executives. In fact, his instincts were correct, for the German company chose not to distribute Fred's hardware products.

- What went wrong?
- How would you approach this problem?
- Study Germany's cultural profile online at http://www.geert-hofstede.com/hofstede_germany.shtml as well as Germany's business culture guide at http://www.executiveplanet.com/index.php?title=Germany. Formulate for recommendations for Fred's presentation.

(From Hill, 2006).

Suggested Reading

Brake, T., Walker, D. M., and T. Walker. 1995. *Doing Business Internationally. The Guide to Cross-Cultural Success*. New York: Irwin.

Chang, L-C. 2003. An examination of cross-cultural negotiation: Using Hofstede framework. Journal of American Academy of Business 2(2):567–570.

Chang, L-C. 2002. Cross-cultural differences in styles of negotiation between North Americans (U.S.) and Chinese. Journal of American Academy of Business 1(2):179–187.

Curry, J. E. 1999. *International Negotiating. Planning and Conducting International Commercial Negotiations*. San Rafael, CA: World Trade Press.

Derecky, H. 2008. *International Management. Text and Cases*, 6th ed. Upper Saddle River, NJ: Pearson/Prentice Hall.

Dumoulin, D. 2006. Cultural marketing: Culture versus country. *Brand Strategy* July:34.

Ehanee, M. N., Kirby, S. L., and D. Nasif. 2002. National culture, trust, and perceptions about ethical behavior in intra- and cross-cultural negotiations: an analysis of NAFTA countries. *Thunderbird International Business Review* 44(6):799.

Faure, G. O. 1999. The cultural dimension of negotiation: The Chinese case. *Group Decision and Negotiation* 8(3):187–215.

Francrsco, A. M., and B. A. Gold. 1998. *International Organizational Behavior. Text, Readings, Cases, and Skills*. Upper Saddle River, NJ: Prentice Hall: 187–215.

Fraser, C., and Z. Frazer. 2002. An exploratory investigation into cultural awareness and approach to negotiation of Greek, Russian and British managers. *European Business Review* 14(2):111–127.

Geert Hofstede Analysis. http://www.cyborlink.com/besite/hofstede.htm. Accessed October 28, 2008.

Gestenland, R. R. 2002. *Cross-Cultural Business Behavior: Marketing, Negotiating, Sourcing and Managing Across Cultures*. Herndon, VA: Copenhagen Business School Press.

Harris, P. R., Moran, R. T., and S. V. Moran. 2004. *Managing Cultural Differences: Global Strategies for the Twenty-First Century*, 6th ed. Burlington, MA: Elsevier Butterworth-Heinemann.

Hill, C. 2008. *Global Business Today*, 5th ed. New York: McGraw-Hill/Irwin.

Hofstede, G. 1980. *Culture's Consequences: International Differences in Work-Related Values*. Beverly Hills, CA: Sage Publications.

Lee, K. G. Y., and J. L. Graham. 2006. Tension and trust in international business negotiations: American executives negotiating with Chinese executives. *Journal of International Business Studies* 37:623–641.

Lewicki, R. J., Saunders, D. M., and B. Barry. 2006. *Negotiation*, 5th ed. New York: McGraw-Hill/Irwin.

Lewis, R. 2006. *When Cultures Collide. Leading Across Cultures*, 3rd ed. Boston, MA: Nicholas Brealey International.

Marks, R. H. 2005. Launching a consumer product in China. *Multinational Business Review* 3(3):107–122.

Mattock, J. 2003. *Cross-Cultural Communication: the Essential Guide to International Business*, 3rd ed. Sterling, VA: Kogan Page.

Metcalf, L. E., Bird, A., Peterson, M. F., et al. 2007. Cultural differences in negotiations: A four country comparative analysis. *International Journal of Cross-Cultural Management* 7(2):147–168.

Mintu-Wimsalt, A. 2002. Personality and negotiation style: The moderating effects of cultural context. *Thunderbird International Business Review* 44(6):729.

Rackham, N. *The Behavior of Successful Negotiators*. Reston, VA: Huthwaite Research Group. In: Hill, J. 2005. *World of Business. Globalization, Strategy, and Analysis*. Florence, KY: Thompson/South-Western.

Salacuse, J. W. 2003. *The Global Negotiator: Making, Managing and Mending Deals Around the World in the Twenty-First Century*. New York: Palgrave/McMillan.

Salacuse, J. W. 1999. Intercultural negotiation in international business. *Group Decision and Negotiation* 8(3):217–236.

Song, Y-J., Hale, C. L., and N. Rao. 2004. Success and failure of business negotiations for South Koreans. *Journal of International and Area Studies* 11(2):45–65.

Wade, J. 2004. The pitfall of cross-cultural business. *Risk Management* 51(3):38–42.

Wigley, C. 2006. Asian marketing: East meets West. *Brand Strategy* July:38.

Zhu, Y., Pieter, N., and R. Bhat. 2006. A cross-cultural study of communication strategies for building business relationships. *International Journal of Cross-Cultural Management* 6(3):319–341.

Endnotes

1. Hill, C. 2008. *Global Business Today*, 5th ed. New York: McGraw-Hill/Irwin: 89–90.

2. Hofstede, G. *Culture's Consequences: International Differences in Work-Related Values*. Sage Publications. Beverly Hills; Geert Hofstede Analysis (2004) http://globaledge.msu.edu/ibrd/offsite.asp?URL=http%3A%2F%2Fwww%2Ecyborlink%2Ecom&ResourceCategoryID=17&CategoryTitleText=Reference%3A+Culture&ResourceLinkText=Business+Etiquette+Around+the+World&GRPage=GR%5FCulture%2Easp, accessed April 16, 2004; http://spectrum.troyst.edu/~vorism/hofstede.htm, accessed April 17, 2004.

3. Lewis, R. 2006. *When Cultures Collide. Leading Across Cultures*, 3rd ed. Boston: Nicholas Brealey International: 513–514.

4. Brake, T., Walker, D. M., and W. Thomas. 1995. *Doing Business Internationally. The Guide to Cross-Cultural Success*. New York: Irwin Professional Publishing: 54–59.

5. Rackham, N. 1976. The Behavior of Successful Negotiators. Reston Va: Huthwaite Research Group. Adopted from Hill, J. 2005. *World of Business. Globalization, Strategy, and Analysis*. Florence, KY: Thompson/South-Western: 477–478.

Chapter Nine

PROVIDING STUDENTS WITH A WORLDVIEW:

A COMPETENCY-BASED SYSTEM FOR INTERNATIONAL ENTREPRENEURSHIP, EDUCATION, AND DEVELOPMENT*

Sherry E. Sullivan, *Bowling Green State University, Bowling Green, Ohio*
Madeline M. Crocitto, *State University of New York, College at Old Westbury, Old Westbury, New York*

Learning Objectives

Upon completion of this chapter, students should be able to:

- Understand a systematic approach for examining international education that can be used to guide the development or enhancement of international courses and programs in general, and entrepreneurship in particular.
- Understand a competency-based model which will be used as the systematic framework for examining how to develop globally competent students.
- Understand how the framework is used to present various methods and techniques for helping students learn more about managing international ventures and partnerships.
- Understand strategies for the further advancement of international entrepreneurship education.

Key Terms

cultural awareness

expatriate assignments

intelligent career model

knowing competencies

service learning projects

*Special thanks to Howard Tu for his assistance with this project. Thanks also to book editor Shawn M. Carraher for his useful comments and to John R. Gavencak for his helpful feedback.

◎ Introduction

Within the past ten years we have witnessed major shifts in the business world, away from the dominance of large, stable organizations to smaller, adaptive, global entities. There is a confluence of a changed set of work cohorts with different attitudes about work, seemingly endless opportunities for business and communication offered by new technology, and undreamed of ease of travel and communication across borders. This is hardly news to business educators who have anticipated, participated, and educated students for a business environment vastly changed from the one in which they worked and studied.

As the newer generations move into and through the workforce, their work expectations, ethics, and behaviors indicate a strong penchant for technological-mediated communication, individualism, and work–non-work balance.[1] These preferences must be considered, given that the combined percentage of the workforce of Generation X (people born between 1961–1976) and Generation M "Millennials" (born between 1977–1992) is now equivalent to that of the baby boomers. The newer generations admire the growth of independent business owners such as Google founders Larry Page and Sergey Brin; Facebook's Mark Zuckerberg; ECKO Clothing start-up by Marc Ecko, Seth Gerszberg, and Marci Tapper; and Roc-a-fella recording mogul Jay-Z. At the same time, we increasingly recognize the opportunities of entrepreneurship for those with a unique vision of potential products and services as well as those who are not comfortable with, constrained by, or disenchanted with corporate life.[2] People from all parts of the world have migrated to other countries for better opportunities. For example, in the United States, Hispanics comprise 14% of the population with buying power that has quadrupled from 1990 to 2007. This engenders business opportunities to meet the needs of this growing market[3] for those we can consider "cultural entrepreneurs."

We are entering a new age of "entrepreneurshipism" in which entrepreneurial activity is rising worldwide. There is evidence that overall interest in the self-determination of founding one's own business is steadily increasing. In response to this, more colleges and universities are offering courses and centers to help students create and develop their own entrepreneurship and intrapreneurship abilities, with some recognizing the necessary global nature of small business.[4]

Thus, we are obligated to help our students develop a greater level of international awareness of distinct markets and knowledge transfer in order to start, gain, and maintain a competitive advantage.[5,6] An entrepreneurial perspective, whether inside or outside of an organization, is the key to competitiveness in contemporary business. Small businesses create 60% to 80% of all new jobs, employ approximately half the percentage of workers, and comprise 45% of the payroll of the private sector. Although small, these entrepreneurial firms constitute 97.3% of exporters, with 28.9% of the value of all exports.[7]

Despite these wide-reaching changes, many university professors struggle to effectively prepare future entrepreneurs to succeed in a rapidly changing, global environment. There have been changes in international business that are not yet explained and the costs of internationalizing a small business are not well defined.[8] Reasons for this may be attributable to one or more conditions. Entrepreneurship as a course of study is relatively new and often considered a subset of general management. As such, it does not have a distinguishing conceptual framework.[9,10] There is a lag in the availability of course materials which reflect the global reality of entrepreneurship. Textbooks may have, at most, one chapter, if any, on global aspects of business. Similarly, international business texts seldom contain a chapter heading about entrepreneurship.

Also, despite general awareness of the globalization of business, the role of entrepreneurs in the global economy has received less attention from management scholars. It is difficult to find a professor teaching entrepreneurship with academic training in the area as well as an international and entrepreneurial background. In addition to teaching the conceptual nature of entrepreneurship, this particular course material requires a specific set of skills which many academics may lack, especially within the additional complexity of global markets. For example, one study produced for the Small Business Administration (SBA) found small businesses lacked planning for doing business internationally and were intimidated by the details of exporting.[11]

As a result, U.S. educators have lagged in developing a curriculum focused on international entrepreneurship and the types of program which would help students accurately determine international business opportunities. Students leave without practical skills.[12] This is important, because educated people are more likely to become entrepreneurs and, when they do so, employ more people. Two-thirds of college students express an interest in becoming entrepreneurs. These students are a resource of innovation which should be identified and nurtured.[13] University faculty have an obligation to prepare future entrepreneurs by increasing their awareness of the international aspects of doing business, not only within the United States, but across the globe.

The purpose of this chapter is to present educators with a systematic approach to guide the development or enhancement of international courses and programs with an emphasis on international entrepreneurship. The chapter begins by presenting a competency-based model which will be used as the systematic framework for examining how to develop globally competent students. Next, this framework is used to present various methods and techniques for helping students learn more about managing international ventures and partnerships. Finally, we conclude by recommending strategies for the further advancement of international entrepreneurship education.

A Competency-Based View of International Entrepreneurship Education

The field of entrepreneurship, and even the definition of it, has defied characterization. Perhaps the most valid approach is offered by Shane who describes the context of entrepreneurship as uncovering, appraising, and seizing opportunities by individuals.[9] Thus, rather than viewing international education as a hodgepodge of activities or organized by functional areas (e.g., human resources, strategy, organizational theory), we suggest faculty focus on developing students' competencies so that they may identify and act upon entrepreneurial opportunities. One such framework that focuses on individual competencies is DeFillippi and Arthur's[14] intelligent career model.

Well-known scholars Robert DeFillippi and Michael Arthur[14] posit that knowledge—and its accumulation—changes in response to shifting environmental, employment, and personal variables; it is not dependent on or subordinate to a single organization—or country. They advocate a learning-centered approach that reflects the shift from employees' assumed long-term commitment to a firm, in which competencies were built according to organizational needs, to a model of occupational excellence, wherein employees seek to continually upgrade the skills valuable to the global marketplace. We think DeFillippi and Arthur's[14] framework may be effectively used as a guide to teaching entrepreneurship. Their forms of knowledge are especially relevant to educating students, who may already possess awareness that their interests and preferences are not conducive to organizational employment, as well as for challenging the naïve view that if someone starts a small business locally, then international issues are less relevant.

Knowing Competencies

DeFillippi and Arthur[14] identified three forms of knowing competencies as manifested in people's beliefs and identities (knowing why), knowledge and skills (knowing how), and network or relationships (knowing whom). The knowing why competency reflects a person's values and motivation. Knowing why relates to the person's identity and the fit between this identity and choices made relative to tasks, projects, and organizations and countries. Knowing how refers to the skills and knowledge needed for performance on the job. It is the person's level of expertise. Individuals may use their various employment settings and experiences on different projects to both apply and expand the skills and knowledge they possess. Knowing whom refers to the relationships or links which contribute to an individual's networking activities. The friends, colleagues, and professional associations with whom individuals network can help build a reputation, provide needed visibility and access to opportunities, as well as present new sources for learning outside of the person's organization and country. Table 9.1 provides a summary of the knowing competencies of university students.

DeFillippi and Arthur's[14] ideas on knowing competencies have been applied to the study of such topics as mentoring,[15] leadership,[16] and networking.[15] As depicted in Table 9.2 on pages 164–165, drawing from the ideas of intelligent careers,[14,16–19] we will examine how developmental experiences and exercises can be used to enrich students' knowing why, how, and whom competencies, thus suggesting a systematic approach to international education.

Developing Knowing Why Competencies

Students' international education can be examined on both cognitive and behavioral levels. Assessment on a cognitive level may be accomplished by a self-test or

TABLE 9.1 The Knowing Competencies of Students

Knowing Why	Individuals have different career goals and will seek situations that support their preferences and identity. Early in their academic career, students are exposed to different fields of study and from this exposure they begin to learn what they enjoy, are good at, and identify with. Their identity is then translated into choices about their college major and what types of organizations they wish to work in. Once in their first job after college graduation, the knowing why competency continues to be tested and developed. Was the right organizational and career path chosen? Is the work satisfying?
Knowing How	Upon completion of their college programs, these newly-minted graduates are sometimes placed in job situations that are more trials by fire than an application of their educational experiences. Their organizations may be more diverse and spread across many countries, being much different than the individuals they interacted with at university. Moreover, even as proficiencies are developed, requirements shift, requiring a need for continuous learning.
Knowing Whom	The need to develop the knowing whom competency becomes readily apparent to students seeking jobs. Students network with more senior students and alumni to learn more about job openings and organizational cultures. They also learn to join professional associations to make contacts with others doing similar work or who might have job positions available.

classroom test of the factual and cultural aspects of doing business globally. Assessment on a behavioral level would occur when a student is placed in another culture or actually engages in international commerce. However, many students are unable to participate in international exchange or internship programs which increase students' knowing why (individual's beliefs and identities), knowing how (knowledge and skills), and knowing whom (network or relationships) competencies. Thus, the behavioral and networking features of students' knowing competencies may provide the biggest challenge to university professors, especially when students have not traveled or worked internationally, and the university has few international exchange programs.

Self-Assessment

Faculty should emphasize to students that intelligence, motivation, adaptability, and entrepreneurship are characteristics of successful managers, regardless of country context.[20] One method to attune students to their entrepreneurial potential and develop their knowing why competency is to have faculty administer a measure of entrepreneurial orientation such as Grant's[21] personality scale (for other measures, see Lyon, Lumpkin, and Dess[22]). Students with a proclivity to-

TABLE 9.2 Competency-Based System for International Education

TECHNIQUES	KNOWING WHY	KNOWING HOW	KNOWING WHOM
Self Assessment Simulated Business Experience: Visiting microcultures Creating own cultures Understanding others' created cultures Self examination after acting as consultants to fellow students in other courses	Learning about one's preferences and possibilities. The creation and examination of constructed cultures act like a mirror in which students gain a better understanding of their own identity based upon the culture in which they were reared. Visiting microcultures provide a comparison between student's culture and other cultures again highlight aspects of their own cultural identity.		
Cultural Awareness Activities including: 1. Service learning consulting to small businesses in the community 2. Country research 3. Reading other countries' fiction 4. TV programs, news reports, and movies on and from other countries 5. Strange facts exercises 6. Playing games of other countries	Learn from entrepreneurs from other countries. Learn about what environments you prefer to work in; learn about own identity and values by studying the values of other cultures.	Learn about doing business across borders irrespective of company size. Learn specific knowledge about countries and cultures.	
Preparation and Actual Travel to Other Countries: International internships Travel abroad programs International team assignments	Learn about oneself and one's identity by completing career assessment and planning exercises. Learn about oneself by the actual experience of living and working with those of different cultures and backgrounds.	Learn specific knowledge about countries and cultures by actually living and adapting to that culture. Learn by interacting with host country nationals. Develop an awareness of another language and its nuances.	Develop an international network of contracts. Building networks of friends and colleagues from other countries.

TABLE 9.2 Competency-Based System for International Education (continued)

TECHNIQUES	KNOWING WHY	KNOWING HOW	KNOWING WHOM
Pedagogical Approaches Service learning projects for international students Service learning projects for non-U.S. aid organizations interviewing expatriates	Build globally relevant skills while helping those from other countries. Learn about social issues in other countries via organizational involvement.	Social learning from helping international students. One on one interaction to building self-awareness and knowledge of another culture.	
Career Assessment and Planning Interview HR managers	Self-examination of values and beliefs about others' understanding of the role of business and the human condition. Learning about oneself by career assessment and planning.		

ward entrepreneurial activity may have had little opportunity to express or try out their interests. Although parents or other family members who are entrepreneurs can serve as important role models for interested students,[21] not all students have such role models. Some students, especially minorities, have not considered entrepreneurship as a career option because they have not had sufficient exposure to entrepreneurial activities and are unaware that they possess the aptitude for such activities.[23] This self-assessment process is similar to the first stage in preparing oneself for an international assignment (i.e., self-evaluation and awareness[24]), which is necessary before any action is taken.

Simulated Business Experiences

Simulations can help overcome the lack of actual international experiences and provide students with greater awareness of their own beliefs and identity (knowing why) in comparison to other cultures. For example, Harrison and Hopkins[25] suggest student teams live and work in "microcultures" in order to stimulate international travel. Microcultures may include involvement with groups, organizations, or individuals in a neighborhood dominated by a particular racial or ethnic group and/or with ties to other countries; for example, rushing a fraternity/sorority or attending a Star Trek convention. Other cross-cultural experiences may be developed based on religion (e.g., visiting an Amish family, attending religious services other than those of one's own religion), racial or ethnic diversity (e.g., visiting restaurants, shops, museums and festivals in various ethnic neighborhoods), or differences associated with age (e.g., visiting a senior citizens center, retirement complex, or day care center).

Similarly, cultural lessons gained by international travel could be simulated by permitting student teams to create their own cultures. For example, following a ten week training approach developed for Peace Corps volunteers, students also become responsible for creating a community. The development of norms in this uncertain environment simulated the experiences the Peace Corps volunteers could actually experience in their assigned countries. As the community evolved, trainees were encouraged to evaluate the emergent organization and interpersonal relations.[26]

Another exercise that permits the simulation of international experiences requires that the class be divided into two groups, with each group developing its own, unique culture. After the groups have practiced their new culture, representatives from each group are sent to the other group to learn about its culture. The groups then meet as a whole for a debriefing session. Each group presents what it learned about the other culture; the accuracy of their findings is checked by the other group.[27] This exercise provides students with the opportunity of trying to decipher another culture. It emphasizes the value of observation and thoughtful interaction for understanding cultural diversity. Just as openness is linked to the knowledge transfer necessary for organizational learning, it is salient to the environmental scanning necessary for successful entrepreneurship. Students will discover that intercultural sensitivity, in terms of both sending and receiving messages among different cultures, is necessary for understanding another culture.[28]

Faculty should be vigilant in seeking opportunities to internationalize business education. They may not be difficult to find. For example, some colleagues have students in various functional business courses (e.g., finance, human resources, economics) act as consultants to their fellow students in an international business course. In these circumstances, students can understand the contribution of each functional area to a successful business and how functional knowledge can be used to conduct business in various international settings.[29]

In sum, faculty may be especially challenged when teaching future entrepreneurs who lack international experience. One means of overcoming this obstacle is the use of high quality simulation experiences. The use of simulation exercises can increase students' knowing why competencies by providing opportunities for them to examine their own ideas and beliefs in comparison and contrast to the beliefs and norms of other cultures. These exercises may also demonstrate the value of liberal arts courses and various business disciplines in understanding global business.

Cultural Awareness: Developing Knowing Why and How Competencies

Students' knowing why competency will become more salient as they develop their knowing how competency. This may be especially true for U.S.-born students whose families have been in the United States for several generations.

These students have grown up unfamiliar with a non-U.S. culture and without hearing a foreign language spoken at home. Further, the U.S. education system often does not require foreign language until the upper grades and, in some cases, not at all. So the nuances of another culture gained by living with relatives and friends from another country as well as by long-term study of another language which includes its literature and history are missed.

However, there are a number of activities which can be used to increase students' awareness of the cultures and business environments of other countries. Such activities help students build their knowing why competencies (their beliefs and identities) as they gain greater awareness of who they are in terms of the types of environments in which they would prefer to work. By comparing their own cultures to other cultures, students learn not only about similarities and differences, but also about whom they are in comparison to others. Similarly, such activities help build students' knowing how competencies (skills and knowledge) as they gain specific knowledge about working and living in other countries and how to manage cultural differences.

Experience through Service Learning

Even the most astute person with an entrepreneurial bent may still be stymied by how to begin. One way to build students' confidence is to have them apply the skills they have developed in college to service learning projects. Service learning is a form of experiential learning in which students, often working in teams, use their business skills to benefit the community.[30] Although the usual context is a nonprofit organization or an identifiable community need, we extend this notion to small businesses in the community. We have found that small businesses are often founded by people from other countries and/or different racioethnic groups. Our students must immediately communicate effectively and become familiar with different ways of doing things. Students also better understand how their skills are useful to themselves and others as well as the role of entrepreneurship in upward mobility. For example, one of our student teams had a member from another country. The team acted as consultants to a small clothing store owned by a fellow countrywoman of that team member. The team suggested an updated computer check-out system and did some research into locations for an additional store which resulted in a written analysis delivered to the store owner. Another team conducted a customer survey, suggested business cards with appointments, promotional items, and gift certificates for a small beauty salon. The salon was owned by a woman from Eastern Europe, where she had no experience with free markets and marketing. Students remarked that at first they found their projects ambiguous, were not sure how to proceed, and felt they didn't have enough experience to provide advice. However, they enjoyed making and implementing recommendations. Their presentations revealed that they learned a great deal and it was clear to us that they developed confidence in their judgments. Besides gaining interpersonal, team-building, and communication skills, our students sharpened their business acumen and realized the contribution of entrepreneurs to economic activity and an improved quality of life. We know that some students maintain contact with their "clients," viewing them as role models of entrepreneurial action as well as sources of information about how to do business across national borders.

Activities to Enhance Cultural Awareness

One relatively simple exercise to create cultural awareness is to permit each student or student team to choose a country to research. Student research should capture the rapidly changing global environment and myriad sources of information available.[31] Students investigate and report back to the class about the country's business environment, ethical standards, and culture. For example, although it is common knowledge that service activities such as customer service call centers are exported to India, research will show that India's economy was not always forward-reaching.[32] Attitudes toward entrepreneurial activities and work in general should also be included in these types of assignments. Faculty can save these reports for later use, permitting students in subsequent terms to examine past and current reports to see how rapidly some countries, such as China, change from one year to the next. Such research experiences can be further improved by the use of virtual tours, interviews with entrepreneurs or government officials about doing business in that country, and examining entrepreneurial opportunities in that environment. Students may team up with students from the countries examined, sharing digital pictures, knowledge, and personal experiences. Enhancing country research through contact with entrepreneurs, government officials, and students from another country would also increase a student's networking skills (knowing why competencies). Using technology for this type of communication should also help students realize the increasing ease in entering new international markets and running a business,[33] thereby further supporting their entrepreneurial interests. In fact, some colleagues report success with hands-on projects for graduate students which require them to consult to small businesses and their small business development agency. Students interact continuously with the business owner and use the resources of the agency. Having students interact with government officials and agencies is especially important because it helps students to realize that many international efforts would not be operational without extensive government support.[34] A similar project can be used for undergraduate students and relies on technology and secondary information.[35]

Another highly useful technique for enhancing students' awareness of other cultures is to have them read the fiction of other countries. Students are provided with a list of the cultural values of the country of interest and assigned a story to read in which they search for evidence of these values. With more mature students, this process may be reversed; that is, a story is assigned and then students are asked to evaluate the country's values based on the story. This process usually causes students to react to the values of the countries more intensely than they normally would when reading a textbook description of the country's culture.[36] For even greater student involvement and development of the knowing why competency, students can be asked to find a story, novel, or book representative of a country of special interest to them. Each student then makes a short, oral presentation about the content of his or her reading and how it reflects the values and customs of the chosen country. Students often choose stories from countries of their ancestry and report insights from parents or grandparents about life in that country. Similarly, recent immigrants and exchange students often choose stories from their home countries and provide a much richer description of their countries beyond what would be available in any textbook. These students are in a position to share their comparisons of the cultures of their own countries and the culture of the United States.

In addition to using fiction to learn about other cultures, television news programs like *20/20*, *Nightline*, *Primetime Live*, and *60 Minutes* often feature interesting reports on life in other countries. Cable channels (e.g., A&E, History, Discovery) often run documentaries about the history and culture of other countries, which may be assigned or shown in class. These professional productions capture students' attention and provide a comprehensive amount of information.

Likewise, watching news reports from other countries can also help U.S. students realize that such agencies as the BBC, unlike U.S. news agencies, tend to emphasize world news rather than news of their own country. This same pattern of reporting can be noted by comparing a U.S. broadcast of a current event and how other countries cover the same event. U.S. students are also often surprised by the differences in humor in television programs produced by other English-speaking countries. Often U.S. students cannot understand jokes that focus on the country's politics or use English terms that they are unfamiliar with (e.g., WC or water closet for toilet, tube or underground for subway). Major motion pictures and films made in other countries often shown on cable television networks can also be used to illustrate cultural differences and similarities as well as provoke examination of one's own stereotypical views of other cultures. Similarly, foreign-made films (e.g., "Monsoon Wedding") may bring to life what students have studied,[37] offering cultural and political allegories, with enlightening views of values, customs, and attitudes while challenging common stereotypes.

In addition to television programs and movies, specific exercises can be used to better understand common stereotypes of other countries while increasing knowledge about those countries. For example, faculty can present the class with "strange facts" about a certain country. These facts are used to provide students with a very mild sense of culture shock. Students are presented with a list of statements that indicate the "strangeness" of another culture. For example, statements about Japan could include: "Dependency is a sign of health; independence is considered a kind of sickness," and "Bosses often introduce their subordinates to prospective marriage partners." Items listed are discussed and students are asked to describe what it would be like to be a manager in a company in which workers held these attitudes.[38] Such exercises usually produce much discussion, especially about differences in ethical standards or the impact of business policies on workers' personal lives. Sullivan and Tu[39] reported that when conducting the exercise, international students criticized the Western students for implying that the Japanese culture was wrong. They detailed idiosyncrasies about Western cultures that, from their perspectives, were strange or illogical. This exercise helps students learn more about themselves (knowing why) and about other countries.

Similar exercises include "number superstitions" or "directional differences." The number superstitions exercises translates English numbers into a Chinese dialect (e.g., four = death[38]). The directional differences exercise asks students to point to the future and past. Students will learn that Westerners tend to view the future as being in front of them and past behind them, whereas Asians believe the past is in front of them as it has been lived and is known whereas the future is behind them as it is unknown and yet unseen. These are simple but useful ways to increase cultural awareness. Another interesting exercise that increases both knowing why and how competencies is "Japanese group dynamics."[38] The professor asks five to seven students to volunteer for a fishbowl experiment. After the volunteers leave the room, the professor asks the remaining students to look for the following themes in the upcoming interaction: membership, status, communication, and leadership. When the group returns, they are asked to "Find your rightful place in this group." The purpose of this exercise is to study the differences between U.S. and Japanese group dynamics. Students are directed to pay attention to why the group had so much difficulty with the task. Usually, individuals will conclude that the assigned task was too vague. Professors may then lead the class in a discussion of how group structure in Western societies is typically "task dependent" whereas Japanese groups are built on "frames." The idea that gender, age, seniority, city of origin, schools attended, company prestige, and one's rank serve as frames for Japanese group structure is emphasized.

An important, but overlooked, aspect of gaining awareness of cultural differences is examining the influence of nonverbal communications. In Western countries, individuals tend to rely heavily on the spoken word, whereas in countries like Japan, China, and in the Middle East the external environment, situation, and nonverbal behavior are crucial elements in communication. A failure to understand the importance of nonverbal and environmental cues can dramatically reduce an international manager's effectiveness. There are a number of exercises that focus on communication. One interesting role-playing exercise that illustrates the importance of the context of communications is called "outside expert."[40] Students pretend that their companies have sent them overseas. Their task is to ask host country nationals questions in order to develop future business plans. However, unbeknownst to the students, their questions are answered according to the following rules: (a) if the student is smiling when he/she asks a question, the question is answered "yes," and (b) if the student is not smiling, the question is answered "no." Thus, most students will find the responses to their questions confusing. Although these rules may seem odd to U.S. students, Asians and many Arabians place a higher value on the context of the question than on the content.

A useful technique that challenges student to think about their own cultural identity, as well as the thinking patterns of those of other cultures, is having students play the games of other countries. For example, the ancient Chinese board game called "Go" is especially useful, as it requires students to think in nontraditional, non-Western ways. The strategy of Go is to move around your opponent's weak spots and gain control of territories. This strategy of Go is much different from the strategy of chess, which is the game most Westerners learn, in which one confronts opponents head on and captures playing pieces.[41]

Likewise, a simulation that can be used to illustrate the differences in cultural values is the Model United Nations program, which is hosted on many university campuses. For the Model UN, students act as ambassadors to discuss current issues actually being discussed in the real United Nations. Students studying entrepreneurship should be encouraged to participate in such programs as they inform students about current international issues, especially in business, and build the skills necessary to function effectively in global business.[42] Sessions of the student UN could be observed, taped, or downloaded to be used as the basis for class discussions.

In sum, exercises as well as TV programs and movies can be used to increase students' knowing how and why competencies as they challenge stereotypes and examine situations from different perspectives. These types of culturally laden activities can also provide information and insights about how entrepreneurship is viewed in a society and help students gain a better understanding of the global business environment.

International Internships and Travel: Developing Knowing Why, How, and Whom Competencies

Academic internships and travel, study abroad, and student exchange programs have the greatest impact in developing all three of a student's knowing competencies. There is no better method to learn about another culture than to experience it "in person." Exchange programs can help students learn more about who they are (knowing why), specific skills about living and adapting to different cultures (knowing how) and interacting with host country nationals, and developing an international network (knowing whom). Despite the popularity of technology, perhaps nothing may replace the social capital developed with face-to-face contact. Although technology may nurture and sustain social relationships, many cultures rely on personal face-to-face relationships in order to do business. Social capital helps the entrepreneur develop a network and build a reputation, provides access to more information, and has been linked to higher levels of performance.[43]

There has been explosive growth in the percentage of students studying abroad and the areas of the world in which they study. Over a ten-year period from 1997 to 2007, the percentage of students studying in other countries increased 150%, with the most recent yearly growth of 8%. More students are studying in Asia, Africa, Latin America, and the Middle East, with 55% of students involved in short-term programs.[44] One excellent example of a program that increases all three knowing competencies is the Global Leadership Program at the University of Michigan. This program creates an environment in which individuals learned to simultaneously work with, and learn from, individuals from multiple cultures (see http://www.execed.bus.umich.edu/programs/ for more details). Sharon Lobel[45] described her experiences as consultant to the program when she traveled to Brazil with a culturally diverse team of executives. The team was composed of seven students from three countries. They were to write a report and develop a video that assessed business opportunities in Brazil. The program was built upon the team-building paradigm and its goals were to: (a) provide a culturally diverse team with a challenging and meaningful task; (b) establish a unique team identity; (c) expose the team to moderately risky situations so that team members could learn to rely on one another; and (d) create opportunities for reflection on styles of interaction. These goals were achieved by the assignment in Brazil and the pre-trip weekend participation in an Outward Bound program. Such international experiences as the Global Leadership program provide students with a "realistic job preview" of what a longer-term international assignment might entail and what issues are particular to doing business in another country. Because most universities sponsor some form of these programs, we will not discuss them in detail but will instead focus on methods and techniques that faculty members can introduce in their own classrooms. (For more information on international programs, see Sullivan & Tu.[39])

As more U.S. universities develop exchange programs with universities in other countries, greater opportunities exist now than in the past. However, it appears that non-U.S. students may be the greater beneficiaries of such programs because they are usually fluent in English and can more readily study in U.S. universities. U.S. students with minimal foreign language skills may be limited to studying in schools abroad where instruction is solely in English. This language deficiency, along with the growth in the nontraditional student population in the United States (which often means older students with more family responsibilities), suggests that the possibility of studying in another country for an extended period of time is less likely for U.S. students.

These obstacles, however, can be overcome with university support. For example, the Old Westbury Foundation of the State University of New York College at Old Westbury offers scholarships which cover the costs for students participating in exchange programs with universities in a number of other countries. These courses are offered during the compressed summer or winter sessions and last two to three weeks. Although these shorter periods of study are no substitute for living in another culture for an extended period of time, such innovative programs permit individuals employed full-time and/or with other obligations to gain exposure to another country. Because these programs are for a limited time, careful planning is needed. For example, a successful study trip may have students visiting a different company each day coupled with university instruction, and staying with host families.[46] This type of multifaceted exposure encourages business students to develop an awareness of the complexity of global business and the role of entrepreneurship in a particular society.

It is important that networking with entrepreneurs be included in these types of study abroad arrangements. For example, the State University of New York at Old Westbury has hosted groups of graduate students from Korea who asked specifically about touring local government agencies. Professors followed-up on their suggestion and requests and discovered that the group was composed primarily of entrepreneurs in a wide range of small businesses. Value was added to the limited time the students had in the U.S. by arranging for tours to businesses in the same industry as those of the visiting students (e.g., a small, specialized toy store and a hardware store). Because the big box retailers had started international expansion, faculty arranged tours of two of them in the local area. Some of the students were alternately amazed and frightened about the potential threat to their businesses. These adult learners were busy running their businesses and were unaware of the impact on their business of companies headquartered in other countries. In the same way, when U.S. students are abroad, faculty should arrange tours to relevant businesses and encourage the host university to consider arranging international teams of student consultants to work on small business issues.

International Team Assignments and Service Learning Projects

In perhaps the most entrepreneurial aspect of business education, students visiting another country may work in teams, perhaps with students of the host country, to develop business plans.[47] An interesting alternative or supplemental project to study abroad would be a team-based global research project using the Internet. Such projects have been used to successfully increase students' information about an international target market and how to conduct business in their chosen country.[35,48] Unlike simulations, such projects permit students to interact with fellow students around the world. For example, a high school teacher set up a project in which his students purchased goods from another country and also sold them to their international counterparts, providing a first-hand entrepreneurial experience with doing business in another country without travel and the related costs.[37]

Additionally, service learning projects could be developed to include international students or address the needs of international students. For example, one of the author's students developed a club for exchange students. Exchange students often study in small groups and, depending in their culture, may have limited interaction with native-born students. The students designed a system that encouraged the U.S. and visiting students to meet to discuss ways to promote greater interaction and plan a range of activities from which both groups might learn from one another. Students registered this international student exchange club with student government, which provided a budget to underwrite activities that promoted mutual cultural exchange and learning. The club provides exchange students with the opportunity to correspond with U.S. students before their arrival. The U.S. students show them around campus, help them get settled, and serve as "cultural mentors" for the duration of their visit. Faculty can be involved in such clubs, encouraging cross-cultural mentoring beyond club membership.

For increased recognition of the international aspects of entrepreneurship, students can be involved in international service learning projects. This type of assignment often requires students to encourage entrepreneurial ventures as a means of economic and personal development by supplying helpful information and using their business expertise outside their native country. As an added learning experience, students learn about the culture and particular issues related to entrepreneurial activity and economic growth in other parts of the world. Following this idea, students may work with an organization (see www.USAid.gov) that provides support for women and disadvantaged groups in all parts of the world. In one service learning project, students contacted libraries and distributed books which compiled human rights abuses by country. They recognized the extent of the role of government and quality of life issues as components in entrepreneurial activity and business decisions.

Self-Awareness for an Expatriate Assignment

The first step in determining student readiness for an international career is self-assessment. Some students may complete one or two assessment exercises and decide that international assignments do not currently match their personality or needs. Other students may struggle for a longer period of time before they reach their decisions. Because of differences in the timing of decision-making, students should be provided with self-awareness and evaluation techniques throughout their college education. Students may work in organizations as expatriates and after that experience, use their learning to turn to entrepreneurship later in their lives as a means to self-development and economic progress.

An important but often neglected aspect of an international education is helping students carefully evaluate long-term expatriate assignments, international relocations, and the impact of short- and long-term international assignments on careers. Gaining international experience may be especially important to future entrepreneurs, who will not have the support of an international management department that some employees of large firms often rely on. One way for budding entrepreneurs to learn about global business opportunities is to gain experience by working for a multinational corporation. Because most organizations do not provide international training and career planning, it is especially important that faculty help students determine what kind of international focus best matches their career goals.

One useful self-awareness exercise is to provide students with a checklist of factors to consider regarding expatriate assignments. An example of such a checklist is presented in Table 9.3. Students may have difficulty answering the questions and it may be useful to suggest that they consider an incident in their past when they were faced with a new and demanding challenge. More probing questions may follow, including: How did you handle this specific challenge? Did you quickly become frustrated? Did you seek information from others? Did you learn new skills? How did you manage the stress associated with the situation? An alternative to the checklist method is to take the "Overseas Assignment Inventory" by Tucker and Baier.[49] This instrument measures an individual's potential for effectiveness during an overseas assignment using fourteen predictors of success. After the checklist has been completed, a discussion of the common characteristics of effective expatriate managers should follow.

Besides encouraging students to answer self-awareness checklists and complete a cost/benefit analysis of expatriate assignments, faculty can use a number of other exercises to help students determine their interest in international job opportunities. For example, Sullivan and Tu[39] used Adler's survey[50] to identify

TABLE 9.3	International Assignment Readiness Checklist

- Are you flexible?
- Can you easily adjust to change?
- Are you willing to put the time and energy into learning a new language and about a new culture?
- Do you easily become frustrated by things that are not done the way you are accustomed to having them done?
- Do you currently work well with minorities and people of other cultures?
- Do you perceive that an international assignment will have a positive effect upon your career?
- Are your spouse and family supportive of your decision to pursue an international assignment?

students' interest in, and preparation for, international careers. The survey takes approximately twenty minutes to complete and students' results can be compared to Adler's findings.

Another practical exercise for helping students make decisions about international opportunities is to have them interview an expatriate and present their findings to the class. Often, expatriates from other countries live among us and represent an untapped resource for perspectives about our culture and information about theirs. After students conduct interviews, they may present their findings to the class. By speaking with expatriates, students increase their knowing whom competencies and learn first-hand about the possible costs and benefits of an international job opportunity. Moreover, the presentation of their findings increase knowing how competencies, enabling others in the class to learn about a variety of expatriate experiences and about facts related to increased globalization. In a related approach, students should be encouraged to speak with human resource managers or managers in international divisions to learn more about international job opportunities and requirements. These managers could also be asked to speak to student organizations (e.g., Society for Human Resource Management, Society for the Advancement of Management) because developing students' skills and knowledge related to globalization need not be limited to formal class activities.

Overall, study abroad and international assignments help today's workers gain career competencies. Building competencies increases marketability in our contemporary business environment, a worthwhile approach with workers often moving across industry, organizational, occupational, and country boundaries.[51,52] This is necessary for individual learning which cumulatively creates organizational knowledge. Future entrepreneurs should be exposed to international experiences as another means of gaining a competitive advantage and building social and intellectual capital.[53]

Summary

The area of entrepreneurship is receiving increasing attention as a valid area of study, and deservedly so, given its impact on the economic and social well-being of our society. In the past, the study of international business has tended to focus on expatriate managers and the structures of multi-national organizations, which is reflected in international business education. Likewise, there has been little consideration of the need for global skills in entrepreneurship education.

Increased knowing why, how, and whom international competencies are important not only for the highest level executives and expatriate managers, but also for managers and employees who may interact frequently with individuals from other countries via e-mail, teleconferencing, and other virtual office technologies. Workers in today's global environment will need competencies that go beyond those expected of a typical expatriate manager. Those with entrepreneurial inclinations to start a business will have less in the way of resources to learn about the complexities of doing business with firms in other countries unless our pedagogy emphasizes the international aspects of entrepreneurship. Whether individuals are organizationally employed or become entrepreneurs, they all will be working with diverse groups or individuals. Students (and faculty) need to continuously learn the cultural nuances of a society, as culture is imbedded in how business is conducted.

All students should be equipped to function in a multicultural and global world.[54] Research indicates that women and minorities often find entrepreneurship as a means around the glass ceiling and towards upward mobility, with women and minorities owning their own businesses increasing at a rate faster than the national average.[55] Approximately 15% of U.S. firms are owned by minorities with approximately $600 billion in receipts; women in small businesses owned 7.1 million businesses with $951 billion in revenues.[55] As educators, we have an obligation to raise awareness about entrepreneurial enterprise and to prepare students to develop and grow their global entrepreneurial ventures. In order to successfully accomplish this, we need to be vigilant in keeping ourselves aware of and current in international issues. This should be a multi-pronged effort supported by the community and our academic institutions.

Thus, universities must not only offer an international management specialization but must provide students, regardless of major, a broader knowledge base (e.g., focus beyond concerns of single country, the ability to integrate cultural diversity into a worldwide organization), and a greater awareness of cultural differences.[56] As global workers, faculty and students must all embrace continuous learning and the ability to adapt to changing circumstances and cultures.

The purpose of this chapter was to provide a framework for systematically examining intentional education and techniques for developing students' global competencies to improve their career success and entrepreneurial endeavors. We hope that by considering how teaching methods and tools can be used to develop students' knowing why, how, and whom capabilities, business educators can be better prepared to help all students become more culturally aware and ready to participate and contribute to the global market.

Discussion Questions

1. Describe the three main reasons why the education of business students in entrepreneurship often does not reflect the fact that many entrepreneurial start-ups and small businesses derive a substantial portion of their profits from doing business globally.
2. Describe DeFillippi and Arthur's intelligent career model. How can it be applied as a guide to teaching international entrepreneurship?
3. Describe examples of service learning projects and how they could benefit a prospective international entrepreneur.
4. Describe some useful techniques for enhancing students' awareness of other world cultures.
5. What are some ways that a student can determine his/her readiness for an expatriate assignment? What type of firm would a budding entrepreneur most benefit from working for?

Endnotes

1. Glass, A. 2007. Understanding generational differences for competitive success. *Industrial and Commercial Training* 39(2):98–103.
2. Mainiero, L. A., and S. E. Sullivan. 2006. *The Opt-Out Revolt: Why People are Leaving Companies to Create Kaleidoscope Careers*. Mountain View, CA: Davies-Black Publishing.
3. DeBaise, C. September 22, 2006. Retrieved November 14, 2008. www.smsmallbiz.com/marketing/Hispanic_Entrepreneurs_Succeed_in_Fertile_Latino_Markets.
4. Gwynne, P. 2008. More schools teaching entrepreneurship. *Research Technology Management* March-April:6–8.
5. Friedman, T. L. 2005. *The World is Flat: A Brief History of the Twenty-first Century*. New York: Farrar, Straus and Giroux.
6. Gupta, A. K., and V. Govindarajan. 2001. Converting global presence into global competitive advantage. *Academy of Management Executive* 15(2):45–56.
7. http://web.sba.gov/faqs/faqindex.cfm?areaid=24
8. SBA Small Business Research Report #241. *Costs of Developing a Foreign Market for a Small Business*. Palmetto Consulting; 2004.
9. Shane, S., and S. Ventkataraman. 2000. The promise of entrepreneurship as a field of research. *Academy of Management Review* 25(1):217–227.
10. Leitch, C. M., and R. T. Harrison. 1999. A process model for entrepreneurship education and development. *International Journal of Entrepreneurial Behaviour & Research* 3:83–102.
11. Office of Advocacy. Small business research summary #241. *Costs of Developing a Foreign Market for a Small Business: The Market & Non-Market Barriers to Exporting by Small Firms*. Palmetto Consulting; November 2004. http://www.sba.gov/
12. Edwards, R., Crosling, G., Petrovic-Lazarovic, S., and P. O'Neill. 2003. Internationalisation of business education: Meaning and implementation. *Higher Education Research and Development* 22(2):183–193.
13. Small Business Administration: Office of Advocacy. Small business resources for faculty, students, and researchers: Answers to frequently asked questions. October 2005. http://www.sba.gov/stats/arsbfaq.pdf
14. DeFillippi, R. J., and M. B. Arthur. 1996. Boundaryless contexts and careers: A competency-based perspective. In: Arthur, M. B., and D. M. Rousseau DM, eds. *The Boundaryless Career*. New York: Oxford University Press: 116–131.
15. deJanasz, S. C., and S. E. Sullivan. 2004. Multiple mentoring in academe: Developing the professorial network. *Journal of Vocational Behavior* 64(2):263–283.
16. Scandura, T. A., and E. A. Williams. 2002. Formal mentoring: The promise and precipice. In: Burke, R., and C. Cooper, eds. *The New World of Work*. London: Blackwell: 241–257.
17. Arthur, M. B., Claman, P. H., DeFillippi, R. J., and J. Adams. 1995. Intelligent enterprise, intelligent careers. *Academy of Management Executive* 9(4):7–22.
18. Baker, T., and H. E. Aldrich. 1996. Prometheus stretches: Building identity and cumulative knowledge in multi-employer careers. In: Arthur, M. G., and D. M. Rousseau, eds. *The Boundaryless*

Career. New York: Oxford University Press: 132–149.

19. Bird, A. 1996. Careers as repositories of knowledge: Considerations for boundaryless careers. In: Arthur, M. G., and D. M. Rousseau, eds. *The Boundaryless Career*. New York: Oxford University Press: 150–168.

20. Baruch, Y. 2002. No such thing as a global manager. *Business Horizons* January/February:36–42.

21. Grant, J. M. 1996. The proactive personality scale as a predictor of entrepreneurial intentions. *Journal of Small Business Management* 34(3):42–50.

22. Lyon, D. W., Lumpkin, G. T., and G. G. Dess. 2000. Enhancing entrepreneurial orientation research: Operationalizing and measuring a key strategic decision making process. *Journal of Management* 26(5):1055–1085.

23. Ede, F. O., Panigrahi, B., and S. Calcich. 1998. African American students' attitudes toward entrepreneurship education. *Journal of Education for Business* 73(5):291–297.

24. Tu, H., and S. E. Sullivan. 1994. Preparing yourself for an international assignment. *Business Horizons* Jan/Feb:67–70.

25. Harrison, R., and R. Hopkins. 1972. Training for cultural understanding. *Training and Development Journal* 8–10.

26. Harrison, R., and R. Hopkins. 1967. The design of cross-cultural training: An alternative to the university model. *Journal of Applied Behavioral Science* 3:431–460.

27. Zacur, S., and W. Randolph. 1993. Traveling to foreign cultures: An exercise in developing awareness of cultural diversity. *Journal of Management Education* 17(4):510–516.

28. Taylor, S., and S. Osland. 2003. The impact of intercultural communication on global organizational learning. In: Easterby-Smith, M., and M. A. Lyles, eds. *Handbook of Organizational Learning and Knowledge Management*. Malden, MA: Blackwell Publishing.

29. Palocsay, S. W., White, M. M., and D. K. Zimmerman. 2004. Interdisciplinary collaborative learning: Using decision analysts to enhance undergraduate international management education. *Journal of Management Education* 28(2):250–260.

30. Kolenko, T. A., Porter, G., Wheatley, W., and M. Colby. 1996. A critique of service learning projects in management education: Pedagogical foundations, barriers, and guidelines. *Journal of Business Ethics* 15:133–142.

31. Haynes, T. 1998. Learning activities for international business. *Business Education Forum* 54(4):31–33.

32. Javalgi, R. G., and V. S. Talluri. 1996. The emerging role of India in international business. *Business Horizons* September October:79–86.

33. Jagersma, P. K., and D. M. van Gorp. 2003. Spin-out management: Theory and practice. *Business Horizons* March April:15–24.

34. Dlabay, L. R. 1998. Integrated curriculum planning for international business education: Analysis of global business trends. *Delta Pi Epsilon Journal* 158–165.

35. Bell, J., Callaghan, I., Demick, D., and F. Scharf. 2004. Internationalising entrepreneurship education. *Journal of International Entrepreneurship* 2:109–124.

36. Harris, C. 1991. Using short stories to teach international management. *Journal of Management Education* 15:374–378.

37. Glenn, J. M. 2002. Beyond our doorstep: Preparing students for an international business environment. *Business Education Forum* 56(3):9–12.

38. Van Buskirk, B. 1991. Five classroom exercises for sensitizing students to aspects of Japanese culture and business practice. *Journal of Management Education* 15(1):96–112.

39. Sullivan, S. E., and H. S. Tu. 1995. Developing globally competent students: A review and recommendations. *Journal of Management Education* 19(4):473–493.

40. McGarvey, R. 1992. Foreign exchange. *USAir Magazine* June:58–65.

41. Byrne, J. 1992. The best B schools. *BusinessWeek* Oct:60–70.

42. Phillips, M. J., and J. P. Muldoon. 1996. The Model United National: A strategy for enhancing global business education. *Journal of Education for Business* 71(3):142–147.

43. Baron, R. A., and G. D. Markman. Beyond social capital: How social skills can enhance entrepreneurs' success. *Academy of Management Executive* 14(1):106–117.

44 Open Doors. U.S. Study abroad up 8%, continuing decade-long growth. Retrieved November 22, 2008 from http://opendoors.iienetwork.org/?p=131592.

45. Lobel, S. 1999. Global leadership competencies: Managing to a different drumbeat. *Human Resource Management* 29:39–47.

46. Lewis, M. W. 2002. The paradox of "The Box." *BizEd* 2(1):56–58.

47. Kish, V. 2003. Passports to education. *BizEd* 2(2):38–43.

48. Greene, C. S., and R. Zimmer. 2003. An international internet research assignment-Assessment of value added. *Journal of Education for Business* 78(3):158–164.

49. Marquardt, M., and D. Engel. 1993. *Global Human Resource Development.* New Jersey: Prentice Hall.

50. Adler, N. 1984. Women in international management: Where are they? *California Management Review* 26:78–89.

51. Arthur, M. B., and D. M. Rousseau. 1996. The boundaryless career as a new employment principle. In: Arthur, M. B., and D. M. Rousseau, eds. *The Boundaryless Career.* New York: Oxford University Press: 3–20.

52. Sullivan, S. E., and M. Arthur. 2006. The evolution of the boundaryless career concept: Examining physical and psychological mobility. *Journal of Vocational Behavior* 69(1):19–29.

53. Crocitto, M., Sullivan, S. E., and S. M. Carraher. 2005. Global mentoring as a means of career development and knowledge creation: A learning based framework and agenda for future research. *Career Development International* 10(6/7):522–535.

54. Haigh, M. J. 2002. Internationalisation of the curriculum: Designing inclusive education for a small world. *Journal of Geography in Higher Education* 26(1):49–67.

55. U.S. Census Bureau (July 28, 2005). Newsroom U.S. Census Bureau News. Press Release. http://www./releases/archives/business

56. Adler, N., and S. Bartholomew. 1992. Managing globally competent people. *Academy of Management Executive* 6:52–65.

Chapter Ten

GLOBAL FRANCHISING AND OTHER FORMS OF ENTREPRENEURSHIP

Dianne H. B. Welsh, *University of North Carolina Greensboro, Greensboro, North Carolina*
Ilan Alon, *Rollins College, Winter Park, Florida*

Learning Objectives

Upon completion of this chapter, students should be able to:

- Appraise the extent to which emerging markets account for worldwide business growth.
- Determine the characteristics of an emerging market and how they are measured.
- Evaluate why franchising has had such an impact internationally.
- Analyze what forms franchising has taken in different parts of the world.
- Differentiate between emerging and industrialized markets.
- Appraise the extent of franchising worldwide.
- Describe new franchise industry segments and forms that have emerged.
- Differentiate between industrialized and emerging countries and how franchising has developed in these countries.

Key Terms

emerging markets
industrialized markets
international franchising

⊙ Introduction

Franchising has experienced phenomenal growth both in the United States and abroad in recent years. Figures vary, but it is estimated that U.S. franchising generates $800 billion worth of business in gross sales and represents 40% of the retail trade.[1] This chapter examines franchising first in emerging markets around the world, then in industrialized markets. First, we define what an emerging market is, characteristics of emerging markets, why franchising has had such an impact internationally, and research in emerging markets by area of the world market. Central and Eastern Europe, Mexico and South America, Singapore, Malaysia and Hong Kong, China, India, and the Middle East. Then, we look at industrialized markets, beginning with North America. We follow with an examination of Japan, Australia, New Zealand, South Africa, and Europe, including Austria, Denmark, Finland, France, Germany, Greece, Italy, and Norway. Next, the United Kingdom is studied.

⊙ Emerging Markets

While in the United States, Canada, and parts of Western Europe franchising has reached domestic market saturation, emerging markets remain relatively untapped. Emerging markets, accounting for 80% of the world's population and 60% of the world's natural resources, present the most dynamic potential for long-term growth to businesses, in general, and to franchisors, specifically. The U.S. Department of Commerce estimated that over 75% of the expected growth in world trade over the next two decades will come from emerging countries, particularly Big Emerging Countries, which account for over half the world's population but only 25% of its gross domestic product (GDP).

Emerging markets are among the fastest growing markets for international franchisors. Several surveys conducted by Arthur Anderson showed that more and more franchisors are seeking opportunities in emerging markets. An article in *Franchising World* stated, "franchises are springing up in the most unlikely, and for many of us unheard-of, places . . . Those franchisors who can establish a beach-head on these wilder shores could do very well, but the risks are great."[2]

The research that has been conducted in emerging economies helps us better understand international franchising opportunities and threats in emerging economies.

⊙ Background

What Is An Emerging Market?

While there is no consensus definition of the term "emerging market," Czinkota and Ronkainen[3] identified three characteristics associated with an emerging economy:

- Level of economic development
- Economic growth
- Market governance

TABLE 10.1 Summary of U.S. Published Articles in Franchising Research: An International Journal and the Proceedings of the International Society of Franchising Pertaining to Franchising in Emerging Markets*

YEAR	TITLE	AUTHOR(S)
1988	Franchising in Asia	Neilson & Yo
1988	International Business Format . . .	Kaufmann & Leibenstein
1990	Franchise . . . East Asia	Chan & Justis
1991	Opportunities . . . U.S.S.R.	Welsh & Swerdlow
1992	The Future . . . U.S.S.R . . . Students	Swerdlow & Welsh
1992	Franchising Opportunities in the Free . . .	Grimaldi
1992	Pizzas in Mexico . . .	Willems, English, & Ito
1992	Franchising . . . Former Soviet Union	Christy & Haftel
1993	Pizza Hut in Moscow . . .	Christy & Haftel
1993	A Cross Cultural . . . Russian Hotel	Welsh & Swerdlow
1994	A Survey of Franchising in Singapore	Chan, Foo, Quek, & Justis
1994	Franchising in China	English & Xau
1994	Does Business Format . . . Russia	Swerdlow & Bushmarin
1995	Franchising in Brazil	Josias & McIntryre
1995	Franchising in India . . .	Paswan & Dant
1995	Franchising in Indonesia	Chan & Justis
1996	Franchising in South Africa	Scholtz
1996	Franchising into Asia . . .	McCosker
1996	Local Franchising . . . Singapore	Goh & Lee
1996	The . . . Elegant Shoplifter, . . . Kuwait	Welsh, Raven, & Al-Bisher
1997	Franchising as a Tool for SME . . .	Sanghavi
1997	An Overview . . . South African . . .	Scholtz
1998	NAFTA and Franchising . . .	Falbe & Welsh
1998	Franchising in Slovenia . . .	Pavlin
1998	Case Study . . . Mexico	Hadjimarcou & Barnes
2000	New Trends in Slovenian Franchising	Pavlin
2000	Franchising in Mexico	Lafontaine
2001	Int'l Franchising in China . . .	Alon
2001	Int'l Franchising in Emerging Markets . . .	Welsh
2001	The Emerging Patterns of Franchising . . .	Dant & Kaufmann
2001	Publication Opinion About Franchising . . .	Paswan, Young & Kantamneni
2002	An Exploratory Study of Encroaching . . .	du Toit
2002	A Comparative Analysis of Franchise . . .	Terry
2002	Brand-Country of Origin Association . . .	Paswan & Sharma
2003	How Do Franchisors with Int'l . . .	Elango
2003	A Survey of Franchising in China	Bian & Alon
2003	Retail Franchising As An Entry Mode . . .	Picot-Coupey & Cliquet
2003	The Role of Franchising in African . . .	Siggel, Maisonneuve & Fortin
2003	The Franchise Baseline 2002 . . .	du Toit

*The authors do not intend for this list to be comprehensive
Note: For a complete citation, see the Reference list.

Level of Economic Development

The level of economic development is typically measured in terms of GDP per capita. GDP per capita is a useful measure of economic development because it is related to the population's wealth, extent of middle class, and level of industrial and service sector development.[4]

The use of the level of economic development as a demarcation criterion for distinguishing emerging markets equates with the anachronisms of the World Bank and the United Nations, which include terms such as less-developed countries (LDCs), third-world countries, and developing countries. The World Bank divides countries on the basis of GDP per capita into four classes. Three of the big emerging countries (India, China, and Vietnam) fall into the lowest income class. According to the United Nations, only about 15% of the world's population resides in developed market economy countries.[3]

Economic Growth

When dealing with emerging markets, it is important to adjust GDP per capita to purchasing power parity in order to gauge income in relation to the "real" cost of living.[5]

Economic growth is usually measured in terms of the country's GDP growth rate. The usage of economic growth is consistent with the concept of "emerging." Most of the countries referred to as emerging markets have enjoyed GDP growth rates exceeding 5% from 1990 to 1997, with some markets, particularly in East Asia, displaying double-digit growth rates.[3] In 1997, 1998, and 1999, East Asia, Brazil, and Russia encountered financial crises that set back their economies' growth. Such crises demonstrate that the often-touted high growth rates of emerging markets may not be sustainable over a long period of time.

The level of economic growth is among the most important considerations for international franchising expansion.[4] When examining an emerging market's GDP growth, one must contrast it to the growth in the population. If population growth rates exceed GDP growth rates, then the standard of living in those countries will actually drop over time. One useful measure that captures both growth rates is GDP per capita growth rate.

Market Governance

The third criteria for judging emerging markets is the country's market governance. Market governance includes the extent of free market, government control of key resources, stability of the market system, and the regulatory environment. Countries that are liberalizing their economic institutions and democratizing their political structures are often referred to as transitional economies/countries. These transitions have been welcomed by the western economies and regarded as opportunities for international franchising expansion.

Among the most important of the elements of transition, with respect to international investors, are the political and economic risks that are introduced by the reorganization of economic and political units in the emerging marketplace.[3]

Such risks are systematically evaluated by western institutions such as the Economist Intelligence Unit, Institutional Investor, and International Country Risk Guide (ICRG).

Market governance influences a wide range of country risk elements such as government regulation and red tape, political stability, bribery, ownership restrictions, controls of capital flows, and import restrictions, all of which are important to international franchisors' evaluations of foreign market potential.[4]

A number of authors, both industry analysts and academics, have identified emerging markets as a topic that needs further research for the franchise industry. In 1988, Kaufmann and Leibenstein wrote an article for the United Nations when franchising in developing countries was just beginning. In 1990, Welsh conducted the first survey on Russian soil on franchising, at a time when the word franchising had no meaning to the population except when it was coupled with McDonald's. That was the same year the franchise opened in Moscow to a tremendous welcoming by the Russian people and the press.[6] Since that time, franchising in emerging markets has grown dramatically. For example, by 1995, there were twenty-six more franchisors in Brazil alone than there were in all of South America in 1985.[7]

Academics and practitioners have answered the call for more research and evaluation of franchising in these new markets around the globe. Young, McIntyre, & Green examined the content of articles that had been published in the International Society of Franchising Proceedings.[8] Of almost seventy articles between 1987 and 1999, nine dealt with economies in transition and fourteen others dealt with developing economies. Practitioners have also published articles on the topic. For example, Leonard Swartz of Arthur Anderson examined the state of franchising in Asia (China, Indonesia, Singapore, and Malaysia), Eastern Europe (Russia, Poland, Hungary, and Greece), as well as the Middle East (United Arab Emirates, Israel, Saudi Arabia, Kuwait, Egypt), and South America (Chile, Uruguay, Brazil, Argentina, Colombia, and Peru).[1]

Practice and Theory Development

Why has franchising had such an impact internationally? What forms has franchising taken in different parts of the world? A number of authors have addressed these questions. Grimaldi analyzed the opportunities for franchising in free trade zones.[9] Kaufmann looked at the issues of cultural and legal differences in the age of the Internet and the impact of franchising on host country development.[10] Specifically, he examined the modes of entry, cultural differences and proven concepts, cultural differences and technology, legal differences, and host country development. Stanworth and Purdy looked at franchising as a means of technology-transfer for developing economies.[11] Their article explored the background to the internationalization of franchising, favorable factors to the growth of franchising, benefits to developing economies, other consequences to developing economies, advantages and risks to franchisors, as well as government action to encourage franchising. The authors gave special insight into Indonesia, China, and Brazil.

Models are beginning to be developed in international franchising. Thompson and Merrilees examined marketing through a modular approach to branding and operations for international retail franchising systems.[12] Examples of Australian firms extending their franchise systems into Eastern Europe, Asia, and Latin America demonstrate the applicability of this approach to branding in their article. Other authors cite that new symbiotic relationships are created when franchising expands into developing countries. Franchising allows firms to achieve the expanded reach and efficiencies associated with internationalization more rapidly and effectively than the firms could achieve on their own. Dana, Etemad, and Wright developed an Interdependence Paradigm to explain these franchise marketing networks using examples of firms in South Korea and the Philippines.[13]

◎ Research by Areas of the World Market

Central and Eastern Europe

Nitin Sanghavi's article gave his personal perspective on the use of franchising as an economic development tool from his numerous experiences with those countries.[14] He summarized the current state of franchising in Eastern Europe as compared to 1997 when he first looked at the topic.[15]

Swerdlow, Roehl, and Welsh and Alon and Banai, in their respective articles, gave us a historical review of franchise development in Russia as well as a current and future look at the prospects for franchise development in an area of the world that is barely realizing its full potential as an economic power.[16,17] Both articles examined the post-communist economy with a focus on environmental factors associated with international franchise development and entry strategies those potential franchisors would find successful. The articles included some practical suggestions for those entering and maneuvering through this huge market. Skip Swerdlow and Dianne Welsh, along with co-authors, published a number of articles in the early 1990s examining franchising in the former U.S.S.R.[6,18,19] Christy and Haftel published the only case study on franchising in Russia in the early era, Pizza Hut entering the Moscow market.[20]

Aneta Nedialkova specifically examined franchising opportunities in Bulgaria, with a focus on the macroeconomic factors of the Bulgarian economy associated with franchising.[21] While international investors have been developing franchises in Bulgaria for over twenty-five years, the market has remained sluggish, given the government system and bureaucracy. However, a number of positive developments have come about and recent success stories that give reasons to be optimistic concerning the future of franchise development in Bulgaria. Ljiljana Viducic described the two types of franchise arrangements that are prevalent in Croatia, using the examples of McDonald's and Diner's Club.[22] Primarily, franchising has taken the form of several corporate facilities in operation, where local interaction with the store is limited to employment not ownership, and the second form where an entrepreneur is taken on as a franchise holder with the understanding that their capital involvement will increase over time as well as their ownership interest as a full franchisee. Additionally, the article elaborates on the current state of Croatian franchise activity and other forms of market expansion that have been successful in Croatia.

Current conditions, features, and trends in Slovenian franchising are analyzed empirically in an article by Pavlin.[23] Using the definition of franchising adopted by the European Franchise Federation (EFF), there are over forty operating franchise systems in Slovenia currently. He compares these results to studies he conducted on Slovenian franchising that were published in 1998 and 2000. In 1998, there were forty franchises operating in his country, of which twenty participated in his survey on the current state of franchising. The article includes results from a recent survey of prospective Slovenian franchisees identifying their core attributes that include: a willingness to follow the franchise manual and guidelines, creativity and ability to cope with a variety of situations, experience with earlier self-employment, and technical experience; and offers a framework for profitable future development of the industry in Slovenia that might be useful for franchisors and franchisees.

Kazakhstan has approximately 35,000 franchised outlets. Akhmetov and Raiskhanova described franchising from an institutional context and a development perspective, then discussed the economic condition of the country and the reforms that have been established by the government that will enhance business development.[24] Finally, the authors gave their viewpoint on particular franchise industries that they believe would thrive and ended with a discussion of future research that needs to be conducted.

Mexico and South America

Three articles focused on different aspects of Mexican franchising. Teegan examined foreign expansion and market entry from three different perspectives.[25] The first perspective is that of the Mexican franchisee that might purchase the rights to a U.S.-based franchise. The second perspective is that of the U.S. franchisor that might sell the rights to their business format. The third perspective is that of the host government, namely Mexico, in terms of the economic impact and development within their country. The author shared the results of a survey of over seventy Mexican franchisees of U.S.-based franchise systems. Results showed that the commonly held beliefs within both the United States and Mexico concerning the desirability of franchising as a mode of market entry, and caution on the part of franchisees, franchisors, and the host governments is warranted. The article painted a realistic view of the risks and rewards of franchising and a bountiful amount of information for those contemplating franchising in Mexico.

Hadjimarcou and Barnes explained the expansion process of a relatively new and small franchisor, Silver Streak Restaurant Corporation, into Mexico as a case study.[26] The authors detailed the cultural challenges of entering Mexico, the company's efforts to identify a suitable partner in the host country, the adaptation of the concept to address differences in the new market, and the multitude of crucial decisions that need to be made when going international. The authors discussed the recent changes in the law that favor franchising, as well as the role that strategic alliances played in the success of their international franchise efforts. Implications for both research and practitioners are explicated. Silver Streak Restaurant Corporation originally opened their first franchised restaurant in 1996 in Juarez, a city of 1.5 million on the border of the United States.[27]

Falbe and Welsh updated their study that was the first to examine the effect, if any, of the North American Free Trade Agreement (NAFTA) on franchisor perceptions of characteristics associated with franchisee success and failure in Canada, Mexico, and the United States.[28,29] The original research addressed two key issues in franchising. The first was the extent the study of franchisee success and failure by analyzing franchise executives' perceptions of the importance of a number of characteristics associated with franchisee success and failure. Second was to examine differences among the executives' perceptions of these characteristics based on the location of the franchisor—Canada, Mexico, or the United States. Their study found that the respondents' perceptions of the importance of system quality, brand name, local environment and communication, and other scales of franchisor and franchisee activities differed by country of origin. Additionally, results of the study showed that neither business type or franchise size had any effect on perceptions of success or failure. The authors examined the research that has been conducted since the study appeared in 1998 and what we know in 2001.

Josias and McIntyre published the first article examining franchising in Brazil in 1995.[30] In 2001, McIntyre gave us an update on what is now the third largest franchising market in the world.[31] Only the United States and Canada have more franchises than Brazil. The author covered the history of franchising in Brazil, described what is unique about Brazilian franchising, and gave her view of the country's prospects for the future franchise market. McIntyre views Brazilian franchising as ripe for development, as evidenced by the size of the domestic franchise industry, demographics of the population, and current economic conditions.

Singapore, Malaysia, and Hong Kong

Researchers began publishing articles on franchising in Asia in 1995. Mark Goh assessed Singapore's franchise industry by presenting the results from two surveys, one conducted in 1995 and another in 1999.[32] The first survey was mailed to sixty-two franchisors and found that most were engaged in mass market franchising. A second survey of 140 existing and potential franchisors was conducted in 1999 by the Singapore government. At least half of those responding already had franchises operating in other countries, particularly Southeast Asia, but also in the Middle East and Africa. The author summarized the opportunities and difficulties a franchisor may face when entering Singapore.

McCosker reported on a survey of foreign franchises that desired to enter into the Asian markets of Singapore, Malaysia, Hong Kong, and Indonesia.[33] He gathered information from the existing literature as well as franchisors that had already entered these markets and interviews during visits to those countries.

Chan, Foo, Quek, and Justis published an article that reported on a survey that identified the major franchises that existed, the different types of franchises, and the nature and characteristics of franchise agreements in Singapore.[34]

English and Xau explored franchising in China by reporting on the entrance and subsequent experiences of two U.S.-based franchises into that country: Kentucky Fried Chicken (KFC) and McDonald's.[35] They updated the report in a 2001 article.[36] They found that the primary difference that will be experienced by franchisors entering the Chinese market is that the government will be the franchisee. They still believe that the rewards for franchising in China are there, and that patience will be rewarded. In 1995, Chan and Justis looked at franchising in Indonesia by investigating the climate for franchising and the perceptions of the Indonesian people toward franchising.[37]

China

China has the most potential for growth of all markets. Three authors from the Department of Hotel and Tourism Management at the Hong Kong Polytechnic University discussed the rapid expansion of the franchised hotel industry in China and the opportunities that exist for further development.[38] Additionally, they expanded on the creation and growth of indigenous hotel chains. From 1979 to 1999, the number of hotels in China has grown from the ground up, so to speak. There are now 7,035 hotels where there previously were none. The authors related their understanding of China's cultural, economic, and political background that are essential for success in this market. Wilke English, from the United States, teamed up with one of his Chinese students to look at two prominent franchises that entered China early on: KFC and McDonald's.[35,36] The authors have an update from the early beginning of franchising in 1994, when these franchises were in a joint venture arrangement with the Chinese government basically as the "franchisee." The articles covered the challenges faced by these early franchising pioneers and the quick fire success they have experienced. His "Y2K Update" looked at these two systems, which now have about 300 outlets in China. Particularly interesting is the lack of competition these two chains have encountered in China. The author also covered the recent legislation that has been passed in China that contains a similar legal structure to franchising in the United States. This makes franchising much more inviting for potential franchisors to enter this vast and expansive market. With the help of Ilan Alon, Rollins University, who collected the Y2K data, Wilke English compiled price comparisons in U.S. dollars and in yuan of the McDonald's menu items as of 1993 and 2000 compared to Belton, Texas (the author's residence).

Anna Han expanded on these legal issues affecting franchising in China.[39] She pointed out the many market segments and diverse populations that are in China that makes the market interesting as well as challenging for the franchisor. She examined China's franchising measures, how they are defined, and what must be included in franchise agreements to be in full compliance with China's contract law. Intellectual property rights and how they should be protected are also covered. She related that particular care must be given to the selection of

Chinese trade names and marks that accompany patents, trademarks, trade names, copyrights, trade secrets, and domain names. She also examined, in detail, all the laws that franchisors must comply with including labor laws, land use regulations, and tax laws that are in addition to specific laws governing franchising. Dispute resolution, arbitration, and litigation alternatives in franchise agreements and how they are enforced in the Chinese Court of Law are explicated. Ilan Alon interviewed a Chinese beauty parlor franchisor in Shanghai that took place in July of 2000.[40] He uses a standardized interview instrument that consisted of twenty-three questions concerning ownership, franchising, and strategic marketing. Six major findings that are helpful to understanding the state of franchising and business development in China emerged and are summarized in the article: 38% of the franchisor's outlets are in Shanghai, all of the parent stores are in downtown Shanghai, 56% of the outlets in Shanghai are owned by the franchisor, the start-up costs are around $20,000, the franchisor relies on tie-in sales instead of royalties for ongoing income, and the company prefers to own the most profitable locations. S. R. Nair, who owns a U.S.-based company engaged in joint ventures in China, gave us an overview of franchising in China from the perspective of a franchisee.[41] The author painted a picture of the country as it exists today and how it has transformed. He also explored the advantages and disadvantages of franchising in China, the pros and cons of direct and indirect franchising, and the types of opportunities available for foreign firms to invest and establish a foothold in this gigantic market. Richard Hoon, who is responsible for seventeen countries in Asia with Management Recruiters International (MRI), discussed the history of business development since 1992, when the Chinese government announced the decision to reform the economy through decentralization efforts.[42] This was the beginning of many reforms aimed at privatizing state enterprises. Mr. Hoon examined the problems these early franchise pioneers encountered, the state of business today, and his personal experiences opening professional service franchises in this new marketplace.

India

India is a country with a huge potential for franchising growth. It is estimated that the current market in India is approximately $1 billion, and has a growth rate per annum of 30%. The United States government has designated India as a Big Emerging Market (BEM). While many franchises have already begun in India, the country is still in the beginning stage of franchising. Paswan and Dant's 1995 study looked at the definitions of franchising by native Indians and compared it to the American concepts of franchising.[43] They offered the first framework for franchising in India. Paswan, Dant, and Young covered some prospects and caveats for entering this market as a franchisor.[44] Dant and Kaufmann gave a descriptive account that is given from a 2000 survey of franchisors in the Delhi area.[45] The data is divided into six major categories of findings that include the distribution by sectors, scope and ownership patterns, system age and size, franchisee selection, financial arrangements, and operating procedures. The authors compared and contrasted these findings to the technology-based franchise systems that are prevalent in the Delhi area and are considered by some as the future of franchising in India. Paswan, Young, and Kantamneni contrasted the other articles by concentrating on the Indian people's opinions of franchising.[46] The results indicated that there are six major dimensions potential customers use to evaluate a franchise, which are: macro- and socio-economic concerns, social well-being, individual well-being, consumer benefits, quality improvement, and localized development. Paswan, Young, and Kantamneni urged further research in emerging markets to also look at the customer side, as well as the franchisor and franchisee sides of the equation, when evaluating potential markets.

Other Asian Markets

The Middle East

Khan and Khan specifically analyzed the restaurant industry in the Middle East, concentrating on the major trends and success factors related to franchising.[47] The authors emphasized the political and legal considerations, language, culture and traditions, menu items and service, demographic and economic changes, and availability of resources that must be taken into consideration when entering this market. The authors included a table of twenty-two countries that is differentiated by area, population, annual population growth, and GDP. Additionally, handy assessment checklists are included that can be utilized by franchisors considering entering a new market. Raven, two former students, and Welsh presented cases on Starbucks Coffee International and Mercedes Benz in Kuwait.[48] The latter is a real event that transcribed while the Kuwaiti student worked at his family's dealership. The Starbucks article was written in 1996 before Starbucks actually entered this market and is quite forward thinking. Interestingly, as predicted in the original article, Starbucks opened its first outlet in Sharq, Kuwait in 1999, and it has become one of its most profitable stores in the entire region. Both articles give excellent insights into the country, the region, the culture, and its people due to the collaboration between the academic authors and the native Kuwaitis.

Industrialized Markets

North America

Franchising began in the United States in the 1850s with the Singer Sewing Machine Company. One of the most famous beginning franchisors was Henry Ford, who figured out the value of franchise systems to distribute cars quickly to yearning first-time car buyers while not being encumbered with the cost of inventory. Today, franchising encompasses a system that is used around the world to sell over $1 trillion worth of goods and services from Tokyo to New York.[49] Franchising is powerful. Franchising is here to stay.

Currently, franchising is 40% of retail trade in the United States and 25% in Canada.[50,51] In the article, Welsh covered the definitions of franchising, regulations, survival rates, recent developments, and future trends. One trend identified is the focus on self-reliance. Young people want a higher income, job security, and the self-satisfaction that comes with owning their own business or franchise. This will affect franchising growth positively, especially for women and minorities internationally.

John Clarkin examined the differences in expansion strategies among more than 1,200 North American franchises.[52] International market development is continuing to be increasingly important. The study examines two major issues: the differences in size, age, and other characteristics between those pursuing international expansion and those not, and the possible motivations for international expansion. The study found similar results to a study done twenty-seven years earlier that found opportunity recognition as more important motivator for international expansion than market saturation. He explained the reasons for the findings and their implications.

Multi-Unit and Master Franchising

Marko Grunhagen and Robert Mittelstaedt, one of the founders of the International Society of Franchising, gave us a historical synopsis of franchising and a look at the state of the franchise industry and recent developments that have spurred its growth and expansion.[53] They described new industry segments that have emerged, including franchisees' mini-chains that cross states and regions. They also discussed the reasons behind the astronomical growth of multi-unit franchising from the franchisor as well as the franchisee perspectives. The major advantages usually cited to franchise are explicated, with the authors giving some new reasons not previously considered. Grunhagen and Mittelstaedt also looked at the motivations of multi-unit franchisees, which may be different than the usual explanations given for franchising. The literature gave three reasons why individuals franchise: single unit franchisees are so eager to get into business for themselves that they become risk indifferent, multi-unit operators believe they can "beat the system" by the advantages of a larger and more geographically dispersed locations, and franchisees aren't entrepreneurs so they need the system franchising has built-in. The authors argued that entrepreneurship is an important motivator for multi-unit franchisee ownership. The article adds to the body of literature by addressing franchisee motivations and that entrepreneurship is a reasonable explanation for the growth of multi-unit franchising.

Ilan Alon first defined and explained why master franchising is such a popular form for global expansion.[54] He then goes on to develop a group of propositions as to the impact of certain organizational variables on the use of master franchise agreements overseas. These types of agreements are primarily used for business format franchisors. He divides the factors into three explanations: resource-based, knowledge-based, and strategy-based. The resource-based explanation looks at size, age, and brand name asset specificity. The knowledge-based explanations include know-how and experience in managing global operations. Price, product, and strategies are given as strategy-based reasons. These explanations should be examined before a franchisor enters a host country and decides the level of risk that he or she is able to tolerate. Ilan Alon gave a theoretical framework for global expansion that can be added to that is sorely needed in the field.

Somchanok Coompanthu and Kendall Roth's 2002 study focused on international services and explored the various organizational forms that are possible and their impact on profitability.[55] In particular, the article focused on the use of plural management. Plural management can be defined as using a combination of company-owned or company-operated and franchised forms. Unit growth, uniformity, local responsiveness, and system-wide adaptation are all affected by the use of plural management. It was found that when there is high performance ambiguity, or when it is difficult to determine employee job performance, firms are more likely to use franchised forms for international expansion. When there is a great deal of outcome uncertainty, company-owned/operated forms are more likely. The authors urged franchisors to look at the nature of the industry and the organizational forms that have worked best to achieve a higher performance level in the future. Plural management is offered as a strategic solution to the problems of achieving tight control if there is high performance ambiguity and the need to respond effectively to local markets.

M. Krishna Erramilli, Sanjeev Agarwal, and Chekitan Dev (2002) also looked at global entry modes in the service industry.[56] However, the article focused on nonequity modes of entry that feature minimal or no investment requirements. In particular, these nonequity modes are popular among consumer-services firms, such as hotels and restaurants. Professional-services firms, for example, consulting businesses, rarely use this form. The study looks at the reasons for choosing between two nonequity modes: franchising and management service contracts. The article took the perspective that the form that most effectively transfers organizational capabilities is the form that should be adopted rather than the one that provides the most effective control over the subsidiary. The latter is most recommended by international business theories. An international sample of hotel firms was used to find that capabilities that are difficult to imitate cannot be effectively transferred through franchising. In such cases, a management-service contract was preferable. Infrastructure was found to be critical to the type of mode chosen and the success of the franchise. Additionally, the level of development of the country had an effect. In countries where customers are more service conscious, and there is an ample supply of talented managers and investors, franchising worked better. The authors warned that firms focus mostly on the transfer characteristics of their business when making these modal decisions. If they are not perfectly imitable, there will be problems with franchising, and more calling for management-service contracts.

Global Franchise Relationships

Jorg Sydow examined the service sector also, but looked at network leadership.[57] He argued that, strategically, franchise systems need to link to inter-organizational networks and be more relationship oriented. He also covered the management practices that are necessary for this to happen and anchors his recommendations in the theories that have been developed on structure. He illustrated the application of this theory with six business format franchise networks in Germany: McDonald's (fast food restaurants), OBI (retail superstores), Aufina (real estate agencies), Schulerhilfe (tutoring providers), ComputerLand (retail sales and computer services), and Hyper Services (service providers). Jorg Sydow offered concrete suggestions for the industry to follow, as well as implications for management that have global applications.

Charles Keith Hawkes and Soumava Bandyopadhyay built a framework that examined the cultural and legal barriers that American franchisors could face as they globally expand.[58] Their framework is built on two dimensions: the cultural distance of the market from the United States, and the extent of legal barriers in the market. Strategies that should be taken by the franchisor given these barriers are explicated. For example, Italy and Spain have many legal barriers but are culturally close so the business format needs to be adapted more. In Japan, there are fewer legal barriers but are culturally distant so more product adaptation should occur. In the Gulf Region (Middle East), a great deal of adaptation of the product and the business format would be necessary because many legal barriers exist in these countries and they are culturally distant. In all, this article offered practical advice that is easily understood and implemented.

The United States

Fred DeLuca created the second largest franchise operation in the world when he created Subway.[59] In North America, they just surpassed McDonald's with the most number of locations. With Annie Smith and Les Winograd, Fred told his story of how Subway conquered America and then spread worldwide. It all began in 1965 with the help of a family friend who loaned him $1,000 to help pay for college tuition. In 2002, it has more than 16,000 franchised restaurants in seventy-four countries. The article covered the management challenges facing the franchise as it has expanded globally, as well as a summary of its growth in certain countries, including Australia, Venezuela, India, and China. The article concludes with a summary of future endeavors on the horizon.

Ilan Alon analyzed how these industries have expanded globally through the number of outlets, including size and scale, the growth rate, the pricing strategy, and the geographical dispersion.[60] These factors aid in explaining why franchisors have gone global. However, there are differences between the three industries that are discussed. For instance, the age of the franchise was insignificant for the hotel and professional business service categories, and had a negative relationship on internationalizing in the retailing sector. One of the most interesting findings of the study involved the fact that younger franchisors in the retail sector were more likely to franchise. Ilan Alon provided clear evidence that the decision to go international should be studied at the industry level. This study cleared the way for the development of a complete model of internationalization that is sorely needed by the franchise industry to make better decisions on where, when, and why to go global.

Canada

With a population of thirty million and its close proximity and culture, Canada oftentimes is the first stop for U.S. franchisors to expand internationally. Paul Jones and Michelle Wong described the current state of the Canadian market, including currency, banking, legislation at the federal and province levels, and regulations.[61] Additionally, the authors discussed the numerous factors to consider in adapting franchise agreements to the Canadian market, in particular, the enforcement of contracts from one province to the next. Two provinces have their own franchise legislation: Alberta and Ontario. Canada has followed the lead of the European Union and enacted the Personal Information Protection and Electronic Documents Act which protects all personal information in the private sector collected in the course of commercial activities by companies. Quebec has had such legislation in place since 1994, while Ontario has prepared a draft of its own privacy legislation and two other provinces are in the process of doing the same. In 2004, the federal legislation will extend to the provinces that have not passed their own legislation concerning privacy. In all, Jones and Wong's article comprehensively covered all basic aspects of what a franchisor needs to know to enter the market. It would benefit potential and existing franchisees to read the article as well to get a total understanding of the entire franchise system in Canada.

The Pacific Rim

This vast area of the world is an open door to franchisors looking for densely populated consumer markets that are receptive to new opportunities. Despite the critics' misgivings, Western fast food chains first entered East Asian markets with a great deal of success. KFC average sales per store in Asia are $1.2 million, compared to per store revenues in the United States of $750,000. Stephen Choo chose three franchisors with different capabilities and levels of internationalization to illustrate the critical success factors needed to enter the East Asian market.[62] Dome Coffees from Australia, The Coffee Bean & Tea Leaf Company from the United States, and Royal Copenhagen Ice Cream from Australia are qualitatively analyzed using the techniques of Yin[63] and Miles and Huberman.[64] Results showed that there were six main key success factors in the East Asian market: distance management, contract enforcement, cultural adaptability, host country risk management, marketing approach, and partnership management. The greater the cultural differences between the franchisor and franchisees in East Asia, the more important these success factors become in transferring a profitable franchise system. Choo made a significant contribution in providing any potential or current franchisor a useful insight into approaching and competing successfully in this market.

Japan

Nitin Sanghavi reviewed the opportunities and challenges for companies to use franchising as a growth strategy in the Japanese market.[65] He covered the recent developments in the Japanese and retail consumer markets, the effect of the stock market, and what it will take to be profitable in this densely populated country. Compared to other industries, franchising has done relatively well, maintaining a growth rate of 6% to 8%. In terms of number of stores, service-related franchises showed the most growth, although sales per store were not as significant as food services or retail commerce franchises. Of the total increase in sale of the franchise industry as a whole, 70% was in retail commerce franchises. The author engaged the reader to understand the effect of various business customs and life-style trends on franchise success in Japan and how the franchise should include these factors in its overall business strategy and structure to be successful.

Australia

Lorelle Frazer explained the franchise market on this unique continent that is regarded as a leader in franchise practices.[66] The current legislation on franchising dates back to 1998. Overall, their Franchising Code of Conduct has been declared effective in making franchising more professional and growth in franchising has occurred since it was passed. There are approximately 700 business format franchisors in Australia. In fact, Australia has more franchisors per capita than the United States. There are about 51,100 franchise units in the country, which has expanded steadily despite much industry consolidation. There are a median of twenty-four franchise units per system so there is still the potential for expansion in this country. Frazer gives us an optimistic view of the future of franchising in Australia.

New Zealand

Franchising in New Zealand has grown exponentially in the past five years. John Paynter summarized the history of franchising and the results of the annual survey of the Franchise Association of New Zealand.[67] A total of 111 systems are analyzed in terms of the number currently operating in the country, the number of people employed, the number of franchised and company-owned units, the percentage increase in sales growth, the industry groupings by percentage, the number of native franchise operations, and the median start-up costs, among other statistics. Of particular interest are his results of the number of systems that have Web sites (84%) and the failure rate data. Over a three-year period, only 6% failed and a miniscule 16% of franchisors (6% of franchisees) considered franchising to not be a good return on their investment. A hardy 77% rated their system excellent or above average. These results are good news for the industry.

Leo Paul Dana encapsulated the New Zealand franchise market, which has the highest number of franchises per capita.[68] Additionally, three-quarters of these are New Zealand-based franchisors. Foreign franchisors are primarily from Australia. Dana gave us a detailed description of both as well as possible legislation that may be enacted in the future. New Zealand currently does not have any franchise legislation, but may enact similar legislation in the future that mirrors the one passed in July of 1998 in Australia.

He also discusses initiatives that the government should consider to aid in franchise development as well as future challenges to the industry. In particular, Dana identified that future research should explore why New Zealand franchisors tend not to expand globally.

Israel

Leo Paul Dana analyzed the current state of franchising in Israel, explains why franchising has gained popularity quickly, and the reasons for its accelerated growth.[69] He gave two basic reasons for this phenomenon. First, Israel is a country composed of many immigrants. In the 1990s, there were a million new immigrants. Secondly, thousands of defense military personnel retired in their early forties with a lump sum payment from the government of $250,000 and were looking for investment opportunities. Many bought franchises. That has fueled the growth of home-grown franchises in banking, financial services, fashion, and fast food. Interestingly enough, Israeli franchisors have not ventured abroad to a great extent with a couple of notable exceptions. Burger Ranch has done well entering the Hungarian and Romanian markets, while Reliable Rent a Car has done well expanding into the Mediterranean region of Cyprus, Egypt, Italy, Malta, Portugal, Spain, and Turkey. He also summarized the legal environment in Israel and what he sees as possible franchise legislation and protection in the future.

South Africa

Scholtz in his 1996 and subsequent 1997 articles, described the state and penetration of franchising as a form of business in South Africa.[70,71] He included an overview of the environment for franchising, the population, and the legal regulations concerning franchising. In 1997, he reported that there were 170 franchise systems and 6,000 outlets operating in the country and that the market was ripe for more entry of international franchises.

Anita du Toit's study of franchising in South Africa focused on the issue of encroachment in multi-brand franchises with the use of in-depth interviews of franchisors who had operated a business format franchise and had two or more franchised brands.[72] About 10% of the franchisors in South Africa met the criteria. Qualitative analysis with the use of themes to give a larger, consolidated picture was utilized following the suggestions of Creswell.[73] Eight themes emerged and are described in detail in the article: brand management systems, achieving economies of scale, brand positioning, cultural divergence, conflict between stakeholders, policies on geographical proximity, failure of acquisitions, and separation of brands. Du Toit concluded by making recommendations for future research based on her results and theorized that perhaps multi-brand franchises may not be able to be managed successfully to avoid encroachment. She also included some great recommendations that, if incorporated, would improve brand management of multi-brand franchises and assist in avoiding encroachment problems, good suggestions wherever the franchise is located world-wide.

◎ Europe

Most of the world's international business, trade, and investment occur among three regional markets, Europe, North America, and Asia, also known as the Triad. Rugman advanced the thesis that globalism—the existence of a single market unified by economic and political forces—is a myth; triad-based international business is the past, present, and future reality of international trade.[74] More profound is the fact that most trade occurs within the triad. For example: 90% of all cars produced in Europe are sold in Europe and over 60% of EU countries' exports go to other EU countries. Rugman's research also suggests that national governments regulate most service sectors, limiting market forces, and that business needs to: *think regional, act local, and forget global.*[74]

In Europe, the EU is the central economic organization that drives the region, the world's largest economic superpower, a huge consumer market of 370 million people, and a union of twenty-seven nations that continues to attract prospective members. The EU is the world's leading exporter—with a total value of $814 billion, 20% of the world's trade volume—and the second largest importer.[75] The euro, the official currency of the EU, has so far shown to be stable, convertible, and has increasingly become an internationally viable alternative to the U.S. dollar for business transactions and central bank operations.

While economically many of the European countries are integrated, the history, language, and culture of individual countries are unique. The plurality of cultures and languages in Europe makes complete standardization more difficult, if not impossible, for franchising systems. For example, a consistent image and a single brand formula can fail abroad as Eddie Bauer, Marks and Spencer, and Wal-Mart can attest.

A study of more than 1,500 consumers and forty retail grocery and clothing brands in France, Germany, and the UK found appreciable differences in buyers' motivations. The French wanted service and quality, the British wanted affinity, and the Germans desired price/value. As such, in Germany discount-food market accounts for 32% of franchises, compared with 8% in France. Thus, companies need to adjust their product offering, pricing, brand image, or service and tailor their image at the national level.[76] The European market is much more heterogeneous than the U.S., and a careful strategy of adjusting the franchising concept to national differences is advisable.

In the section that follows, the franchising conditions in twelve European countries are reviewed. Table 10.2 provides some descriptive statistics for these countries taken from the International Franchise Association's Web site. According to the statistics, these countries account for over 347 million consumers with an average GDP per capita exceeding $24,500 with a combined market of about $7.8 trillion. Additionally, franchising in Belgium, Ireland, Netherlands, and Sweden is covered.

Overview of Franchising in Europe

Stanworth and Purdy gave a review of the European markets from the perspective of UK franchisors and discussed the expansion plans of British franchisors

TABLE 10.2 European Countries Examined

COUNTRY	LANGUAGE	CAPITAL CITY	POPULATION	PER CAPITA GDP
Austria	German	Vienna	8,078,000	$25,655
Denmark	Danish	Copenhagen	5,300,000	$32,000
Finland	Finnish	Helsinki	5,130,000	$16,000
France	French	Paris	58,000,000	$23,000
Germany	German	Berlin	82,000,000	$25,000
Greece	Greek	Athens	11,500,000	$11,305
Italy	Italian	Rome	56,900,000	$20,000
Norway	Norwegian	Oslo	4,400,000	$33,300
Portugal	Portuguese	Lisbon	9,900,000	$10,901
Spain	Spanish	Madrid	40,000,000	$13,200
Switzerland	German	Bern	7,110,000	$35,614
United Kingdom	English	London	59,100,000	$24,300

(From International Franchising Association, www.franchise.org. Retrieved Aug, 29, 2002.)

to penetrate the markets of the EU.[77] Forty-one percent of their sample claimed to either operate in another European country or plan to become active in the EU shortly. Stanworth and Purdy suggested that companies aspiring for international expansion may underestimate the real cost of expansion, need to develop linguistic skills, and plan to develop some company-owned outlets, if they want to emulate what the UK international franchisors are already doing. The EU markets can be ranked by the number of franchisors in descending order: Spain, Germany, UK, France, Italy, Portugal, Netherlands, Sweden, Austria, Greece, Belgium, Ireland, Denmark, and Finland. Mendelsohn reviewed the comparative legal environment for franchising in Europe, discussing the European Commission regulations relating to franchising and a number of key franchising cases heard before the European Court of Justice—including Yves Rocher, Computerland, Pronuptia, ServiceMaster, and Chales Jourdan.[78] The assertion in these cases is that the market sharing arrangements inherent in franchising may violate EC competition law. The legal environments of franchising are examined in ten countries: Austria, Belgium, Finland, Germany, Italy, Netherlands, Portugal, Spain, Switzerland, and the United Kingdom.

Sherman offered final suggestions to European franchisors wishing to internationalize their operations by discussing key trends.[79] While international franchising has been mostly U.S. led, European franchisors are expanding overseas in increasing numbers. Sherman advised European franchisors wishing to expand into the United States to thoroughly understand their strengths and weaknesses, potential target markets, partners, trademarks, products and services, company resources, and rationale for expansion.

Two international franchising lawyers, Mazero and Martyn, provided an analysis and a checklist for due diligence in international franchising.[80,81] This topic is increasing in importance because of new requirements and renewed focus on money laundering, corruption, and terrorism internationally. The authors advised franchisors to investigate prospective franchisees thoroughly by reviewing prospective franchisees publicity, credit history, corporate affiliations, civil and criminal reports, real property, bankruptcy records, liens and judgments, and regulatory authorities.

Unlike the U.S., Europe is much more cosmopolitan, consisting of a variety of nations and cultures with differing and often conflicting histories. The European franchisors have one distinct advantage over American franchisors in Europe. They are often multi-lingual and they understand the cultural variations within their markets better than Americans. American franchisors' transaction costs can be high in terms of translating materials, adapting manuals, brochures and advertising, overcoming cultural and geographical distance, and controlling local operations.

American franchisors should ask themselves the following questions. Can the company's core competency and brand travel? Are the company's abilities and know-how valued in foreign cultures? Are there economies-of-scale or first-to-market advantages in entering the European market? Are there entrenched competitors with more acceptable brand recognition? What adjustments do they need to make to the standard formula? The answers to these questions lie in franchisors' ability to recognize opportunities and threats in the environment and strengths and weaknesses in their organization.

The implications of cultural and environmental diversity to franchisors wishing to do business in Europe is twofold: (1) franchisors need to adapt their franchising concept and management style to local cultures, and (2) franchisors need to find ways to cooperate with local partners and governments to promote entry into a variety of service sectors that are sometimes restricted or regulated. Such cooperation can happen if the two sides understand the benefits and limitations of franchising as they relate to the host market economic and social goals and needs.

Austria

No special franchising law exists in Austria and franchise agreements typically fall under the civil law which regulates contracts, consumer protection, competition, and intellectual property. Austrian and European antitrust regulations are important determinants of case law. Details on applicable laws of franchising in Austria are given by Marco Hero.[82]

Denmark

Sanghavi discussed retail franchising in Denmark.[14] Denmark is one of the most affluent members of the EU, and franchising has much potential there. His chapter on Denmark reviewed the franchising development in the country, the infrastructure and legal environment, the franchising market, the financial environment, and the marketing environment. As an appendix to the article and as a reference to the reader, Sanghavi attaches the European Code of Ethics for Franchising to which Denmark subscribes. The paper concluded that opportunities for retail franchising in Denmark are abundant.

Finland

Tuunanen presented and analyzed data on franchisors in Finland from 1999 to 2002.[83] His research indicated that there are 164 franchisors in Finland, employing 38,000 people, and generating gross annual sales of about $3.25 billion. Tuunanen reviewed the key definitions of franchising, created a framework for identifying business format franchising in Finland, and collected and analyzed the data with a variety of methods.

While Tuunanen's analysis provided a franchisor perspective, Torikka and Tuunanen examined franchisee-training programs.[84] In Finland, the government participates in the education of franchisees through economic development centers. In recent years, a number of programs have emerged to train current and prospective franchisees. Torikka and Tuunanen evaluated the effectiveness of these programs by describing career shifts of the trainees. They report the results from a sample of one hundred graduates of the first five programs and found that one-sixth bought a franchise. These results showed that government agencies can promote franchising and economic development through focused educational programs. These programs had a major effect on the success rate of the trainees.

France

Penard, Raynaud, and Saussier presented an overview of franchising in France, with detailed statistics and discussed the current legal environment.[85] The authors found that franchisors in France attempt to establish a balance between company-owned stores and franchisee-owned stores, and that this balance is sector specific. Furthermore, domestic franchisors charge higher royalties as compared to foreign franchisors, which often require fixed fees.

Cliquet and Rozenn answered the call of Penard, Raynaud, and Saussier for industry-specific franchising research.[86] They examined variations to franchising in French hotel chains. Half of the chains have at least 15% franchisee ownership. Dual distribution, using both company-owned and franchisee-owned outlets, simultaneously has accelerated the growth of the French hotel sector, ensured territories are adequately covered, lowered the financial burdens of expansion, and maintained control over operations and renovations. Plural forms of organization stimulated competition among members of the organization (multi-unit franchisees, franchisees, and company-operated units), and provided operational flexibility to adjust to economic cycles and changing client behavior or legislative guidelines. Drawbacks to this system included most notably the possibility of network conflict, particularly between the company-owned outlets and the franchisee-owned outlets, which sometime compete directly with one another. Multiple-unit franchising is growing rapidly in France.

Rozenn and Cliquet further investigated the French hotel sector in relation to the franchising sector.[87] This sector is motivated in part by increases in travel and tourism into France. The authors examined the survival, growth and stability of French hotels for the period 1995 to 1998 and argued that franchisors using a dual distribution strategy or a franchising strategy are more competitive than totally company-owned hotels in the long run; and predicted that national companies will outlast foreign companies in the French hotel sector.

Germany

Germany is the largest economy in Europe. Flohr examined the legal environment to franchising in Germany by outlining relevant laws concerning contracts, consumer protection, antitrust and competition, intellectual property, and labor.[88] On a higher level, the EEC Block Exemption for Vertical Restraints of 1999 is discussed in the context of German franchising.

Schlamp described franchising as it applies to women in Germany.[89] General conditions for women in Germany, startup businesses by women, and women-based businesses and their role in the economy are discussed. Franchising is seen as a way for women to mobilize their business ventures and a solution to some of the problems they face.

Greece

Dimou and Ikkos presented the climate for franchising in Greece, the economy, business environment, and the overall profile of Greek franchising.[90] Greece is a member of the European Monetary Union and its economy improved appreciably in the 1990s. The retail sector was significantly restructured in the 1990s due to changes in real incomes, a substantial urbanization, and an inflow of capital from the European community. According to the authors, Greece has 400 franchisors with over 4,000 outlets. Greek franchisors recently have expanded into the Cyprus and the Balkan countries because of physical and cultural proximity. The authors provided a detailed analysis of the environmental and industry factors affecting franchising in Greece.

Italy

Luca, Majocchi, and Pavione examined the Italian economy from a franchising perspective in detail.[91] The authors provided a history of franchising, present conditions for growth statistics, as well as offer their thoughts on prospects for different industries.

Vianelli's article complements Luca et al. by examining Italian franchising as a mode of entry into international markets.[92] While Italian franchisors have limited experience with internationalization, a few have achieved considerable success, most notably the Benetton group. Positive country-of-origin effects of the *made in Italy* image has helped the Italian fashion industry gain recognition and acceptance internationally. This is evident by the presence of Italian high fashion outlets in the most exclusive streets of European capitals. About eighty Italian franchisors are presently franchising abroad. Half of the Italian franchisors overseas operate in the personal items category, which includes clothing, intimate wear, footwear, and accessory type products, followed by the hotel, restoration, and household article sectors. Benetton, for example, sells most of its clothes through its international franchised outlets. Franchising has paved the way to export Italian made products. The ten largest destinations of Italian exports are Germany, France, United States, UK, Spain, Switzerland, Belgium, Netherlands, Austria, and Greece. Italy mostly trades with European countries.

Norway

Singh described the franchising environment in Norway.[93] Norway is an industrial, oil-rich country, with a high standard of living. Norway is not part of the EU. As of 2002, there were 184 franchisors with a network of over 7,253 outlets. Franchising is relatively new to Norway, but the country is making strides in developing the sector and franchising is poised for growth. The political environment in Norway is stable, labor laws and taxes are demanding on employers, and franchising enjoys no specific restrictions. Singh explained the social, economic, legal, and consumer environments of franchising. She then examined franchising from the standpoint of price, promotion, and place considerations.

Portugal

Dahab, Cunha, and Cardim discussed international franchising in Portugal.[94] By looking into the process of McDonald's entry into the country, the authors attempted to shed light on the need for adaptation to local circumstances. They analyzed the factors leading to international franchising in Portugal, addressed the organizational structure of franchising, and present empirical evidence from the McDonald's case, which is discussed in detail.

⊚ United Kingdom

The United Kingdom is an important international market for international franchisors. The retailing and service sectors are highly developed and about one-third of British retailing is franchised.

Cross, Burton, and Rhodes employed the transaction cost approach to franchising to explain the use of intermediaries—such as a master sub-franchisor—in international franchising development.[95] These intermediaries are more likely to be used when the market is geographically and culturally distant, when smaller, less experienced franchisors internationalize, when markets are less developed, when larger number of foreign markets are served, and when more extensive host country operations are established. Direct franchising is more likely to occur with franchisors that have more resources and more experience in international markets. Diseconomies of scale, associated with managing the franchisor-intermediary relations, discourages franchisors from using intermediaries in international expansion.

Stanworth, Brodie, Wotruba, and Purdy utilized a sample of 673 independent contractors in direct sales franchising to examine this low-cost, low-entry barrier business which attracts mostly women who are interested in part-time and self-employment opportunities.[96] Their study looked at changes in self employment in a variety of countries (mostly European), presented a typology of direct sales franchising based on two dimensions: product/service and home-based/external premises, and compared and contrasted franchising to direct selling.

Unlike Cross et al.[95] and Stanworth et al.[96] who utilized survey methodology, Quinn examined international franchising using a qualitative, ethnographic approach.[97] This approach provided an in-depth explanation for the internationalization of one UK franchising firm from 1987 to 1995. The author explained the company's initial market entry, patterns of internationalization, and the changing nature of expansion efforts. Keys to successful international franchise expansion were new product development and aggressiveness in obtaining qualified franchisees.

Summary

The advent of franchising is a worldwide phenomenon, and the importance of franchising cannot be overlooked. In countries around the globe, franchising affects the economy substantially and is becoming a larger percentage of the retail trade daily. It accounts for $1 trillion in retail spending per year and employs one of every sixteen workers in the United States. In some countries, franchising is approaching half their total retail sales. Although franchising has its critics, and there are franchises to definitely avoid, it is here to stay. The more we know about franchising, the better off the public and the industry will be. Franchisors, franchisees, those studying franchising, the governments of countries interested in furthering economic development and employment, and the massive populations who desire the opportunity to try franchising themselves through purchasing a franchising, starting their own franchise or tasting its fare, all need this information.

Areas ripe for future research include the various forms of franchising that exist and the ability to adapt to the ever-changing global marketplace. Franchising is becoming more complex in order to adapt to a world marketplace that is increasingly becoming more accessible with technological advances. There are more forms of franchising, and there is an increasing symbiotic relationship among the various stakeholders of franchising: franchisors, franchisees, host markets, and consumers. What hasn't been addressed is the addition of franchisee associations in these symbiotic relationships and that they are becoming at least as powerful, if not more powerful in some spheres, as associations worldwide that have been traditionally composed of franchisors. These influential organizations will continue to wield an increasing share of power in the future. Furthermore, it is likely that such franchisor and franchisee organizations respectively will join in associations of their counterparts by region or to mirror political associations, such as the European Franchise Federation (EFF) has formed as the EU has become a reality. In a larger part, these organizations will eventually exert a major influence on supplier networks, legislation, regulatory standards and safeguards, and shared technology and communication. They will transcend language and cultural barriers to create networks that are user-friendly. John Naisbitt, author of *Megatrends*, predicted that the future of franchising would benefit from an increasingly service-based economy, an increasingly convenience-oriented society, a more specialized workforce, more participation by women and minorities, and an increasingly globally-based marketing strategy.[98] His future trend analysis is coming true sooner than originally predicted. Research will only make us understand where these trends are and where the industry is going.

Family business franchises are now entering their second generation, and a small number are even third generation franchises. This is particularly true of franchises in the United States, as it has the longest history of franchising. However, other parts of the world that particular franchises first developed, such as hotel and restaurant industries, are also experiencing "trans-generational franchising." Trans-generational franchising, as defined by Welsh, is the "on-going operation of a franchise or franchises that have gone from the original franchisee(s) to another generation of franchisee(s) that are connected either by family membership or ownership."[99] When the international component is added to a trans-generational franchise or network of franchises, a more complex form of franchising emerges. This has major implications for the franchisor who is trying to maintain positive relationships with franchisees. Additionally, the franchisor may be trans-generational. Welsh calls this the "blind date" phenomenon in franchising. The ability of the franchise system to sustain these long term relationships could have a major impact on the future of franchising.

The Raymond Family Institute conducted a survey on U.S. family businesses and family business franchises took part.[100] Understanding the impact of family businesses on franchising and the actual size of this population that is predicted to keep growing in the future is a major research phenomenon. Since franchising accounts for 5% of the 8 million small businesses in the U.S., and two-thirds of these small businesses are considered family businesses, the impact of this combination is profound in real terms today. In some parts of the globe, such as the Pacific Rim, the percentage of family businesses is even higher, up to 90% or more. Tomorrow, the way we do business from a management, marketing, and legal standpoint may be very different based on these changing demographics. This area is ripe for research and methodologically should be studied using longitudinal data analyses.

Franchising, more than any other time in our history is facing many new challenges. That is why leadership, vision, and strategic decision-making applied to the franchise industry is so important.[28,29] If the industry is to continue to grow, it needs to transform itself into a twenty-first century learning organization. Technology can be compared to a moving treadmill, with the speed of information continually ramping up to the next level. Communication is of utmost importance in this age. The environment must be continually scanned for relevant information on the market and its customers. The franchisor and the headquarters staff must provide leadership to communicate their vision to the franchise community. In turn, the franchisees, customers, and associations must communicate their vision of the future to the franchisor. Strategic decision-making must evolve from this interaction. It is important that the vision is clear to all stakeholders. The world marketplace demands it.

Discussion Questions

1. What is an emerging market?
2. What are the two types of franchise arrangements in Croatia?
3. In Mexico, what are the three different ways to enter the market?
4. What is the third largest franchise market in the world?
5. What country has the most potential for growth of all markets?
6. What six major findings were uncovered by Alon with a Chinese beauty parlor franchise that tells us much about franchising in China?
7. Where did franchising begin, what year, and with what company?
8. How big is franchising in Australia?
9. What questions should American franchisees ask themselves?
10. What are the cultural and environmental impacts to franchises wanting to do business in Europe?

Endnotes

1. Swartz, L. N. 2001. Franchising successfully circles the globe. In: Welsh, D. H. B., and I. Alon I, eds. *International Franchising in Industrialized Markets: Central and Eastern Europe and Latin America.* Riverwoods, IL: CCH, Inc.: 43–62.
2. Amies, 1999, Franchising World. 27–28.
3. Czinkota, M. R., and I. A. Ronkainen. 1997. International business and trade in the next decade: Report from a Delphi study. Washington, DC: Georgetown University Working Paper, #1777-25-297.
4. Alon, I., and D. I. McKee. 1999. Towards a macro-environmental model of international franchising. *Multinational Business Review* 7(1):76–82.
5. Arnold, D. J., and J. A. Quelch. 1988. New strategies in emerging markets. *Sloan Management Review* 7–20.
6. Welsh, D. H. B., and S. Swerdlow. 1991. Opportunities and challenges for franchisors in the U.S.S.R.: Preliminary results of a survey of Soviet university students. *Proceedings of the International Society of Franchising,* Miami Beach, FL.
7. International Franchise Research Centre. 2000. World wide franchising statistics. IFRC Web Site, www.wmin.ac.uk/~purdyd/.
8. Young, J. A., McIntryre, F. S., and R. D. Green. 2000. The International Society of Franchising: A thirteen-year review. *Proceedings of the International Society of Franchising.* San Diego, CA; 2000.
9. Grimaldi, A. 1992. Franchising opportunities in the free trade zones of developing countries. *Proceedings of the Society of Franchising.* Palm Springs, CA; February.
10. Kaufmann, P. J. 2001. International business format franchising and retail entrepreneurship: A possible source of retail know-how for developing countries-Post-script. In: Welsh, D. H. B., and I. Alon, eds. *International Franchising in Industrialized Markets: Central and Eastern Europe and Latin America.* Riverwoods, IL: CCH, Inc: 80–86.
11. Stanworth, J., and D. Purdy. 2001. Franchising as a source of technology transfer to developing countries. In: Welsh, D. H. B., and I. Alon, eds. *International Franchising in Industrialized Markets: Central and Eastern Europe and Latin America.* Riverwoods, IL: CCH, Inc.: 87–104.
12. Thompson, M., and B. Merrilees. 2001. A modular approach to branding and operations for international franchising systems in emerging markets. In: Welsh, D. H. B., and I. Alon, eds. *International Franchising in Industrialized Markets: Central and Eastern Europe and Latin America.* Riverwoods, IL: CCH, Inc.: 105–118.
13. Dana, L. P., Etemad, H., and R. W. Wright. 2001. Franchising in emerging markets: Symbiotic interdependence within marketing networks. In: Welsh, D. H. B., and I. Alon, eds. *International Franchising in Industrialized Markets: Central and Eastern Europe.* Riverwoods, IL: CCH, Inc.: 119–130.
14. Sanghavi, N. 2001. Retail franchising in Denmark: Strategic overview. In: Welsh, D. H. B., and I. Alon, eds. *International Franchising in Industrialized Markets: Western and Northern Europe.* Riverwoods, IL: CCH, Inc.: 111–136.
15. Sanghavi, N. 1997. Franchising as a tool for SME development in transitional economies: The case of Central European countries. *Proceedings of the International Society of Franchising.* Orlando, FL; March.

16. Swerdlow, S., Roehl, W. S., and D. H. B. Welsh. 2001. Hospitality franchising in Russia for the 21st century: Issues, strategies, and challenges. In: Welsh, D. H. B., and I. Alon, eds. *International Franchising in Industrialized Markets: Central and Eastern Europe and Latin America*. Riverwoods, IL: CCH, Inc.: 149–170.

17. Alon, I., and M. Banai. 2001. Franchising opportunities and threats in Russia. In: Welsh, D. H. B., and I. Alon, eds. *International Franchising in Emerging Markets: Central and Eastern Europe and Latin America*. Riverwoods, IL: CCH, Inc.: 131–148.

18. Swerdlow, S., and N. Bushmarin. 1994. Does business format management master Marxism in post-coup Russia? Franchise system mentality creeps into the lodging industry. *Proceedings of the International Society of Franchising*. Las Vegas, NV; February.

19. Swerdlow, S., and D. H. B. Welsh. 1992. The future of franchising in the U.S.S.R.: A statistical analysis of the opinions of Soviet university students. *Proceedings of the International Society of Franchising*. Palm Springs, CA; February.

20. Christy, R. L., and S. M. Haftel. 1993. Pizza Hut in Moscow: Post-coup system development and expansion. *Proceedings of the International Society of Franchising*. San Francisco, CA: February.

21. Nedialkova, A. A. 2001. Bulgaria-economic development and franchising. In: Welsh, D. H. B., and I. Alon, eds. *International franchising in emerging markets: Central and Eastern Europe and Latin America*. Riverwoods, IL: CCH, Inc.: 203–214.

22. Viducic, L. 2001. The role of franchising in establishing and internationalization of business with special reference to Croatia. In: Welsh, D. H. B., and I. Alon, eds. *International Franchising in Industrialized Markets: Central and Eastern Europe and Latin America*. Riverwoods, IL: CCH, Inc.: 215–222.

23. Pavlin, I. 2001. New trends in Slovenian franchising. In: Welsh, D. H. B., and I. Alon, eds. *International Franchising in Industrialized Markets: Central and Eastern Europe and Latin America*. Riverwoods, IL: CCH, Inc.: 189–202.

24. Akhmetov and Raiskhanova (2001)

25. Teegan, H. 2001. Franchising in Mexico. In: Welsh, D. H. B., and I. Alon, eds. *International Franchising in Industrialized Markets: Central and Eastern Europe and Latin America*. Riverwoods, IL: CCH, Inc.

26. Hadjimarcou, J., and J. W. Barnes. 2001. Strategic alliances in international franchising-The entry of Silver Streak restaurant corporation into Mexico. In: Welsh, D. H. B., and I. Alon, eds. *International Franchising in Industrialized Markets: Central and Eastern Europe and Latin America*. Riverwoods, IL: CCH, Inc.: 293–306.

27. Hadjimarcou, J., and J. W. Barnes. 1998. Case study: Strategic alliances in international franchising-the entry of Silver Streak Restaurant Corporation into Mexico. *Journal of Consumer Marketing* 15(6):598–607.

28. Welsh, D. H. B., Adler, M. F., Falbe, C. M., Gardner, R. O., and L. A. Rennick. 2001. *Multiple Uses of the Internet in Franchising*. Symposium at the International Society of Franchising. Las Vegas, NV; February.

29. Falbe, C. M., and D. H. B. Welsh. 1998. NAFTA and franchising: A comparison of franchisor perceptions of characteristics associated with franchisee success and failure in Canada, Mexico, and the United States. *Journal of Business Venturing* 13(2):151–171.

30. Josias, A., and F. S. McIntrye. 1995. Franchising in Brazil. *Proceedings of the International Society of Franchising*. San Juan, Puerto Rico; February.

31. McIntyre, F. 2001. Franchising in Brazil. In: Welsh, D. H. B., and I. Alon, eds. *International Franchising in Industrialized Markets: Central and Eastern Europe and Latin America*. Riverwoods, IL: CCH, Inc.: 223–232.

32. Goh, M. 2001. Singapore's local franchise industry: An assessment. In: Welsh, D. H. B., and I. Alon, eds. *International Franchising in Industrialized Markets: China, India, and Other Asian Countries*. Riverwoods, IL: CCH, Inc.: 187–208.

33. McCosker, C. F. 1996. Franchising into Asia: An overview of selected target markets. *Proceedings of the International Society of Franchising*. Honolulu, HI; February.

34. Chan, P. S., Foo, J. K. S., Quek, G., and R. T. Justis. 1994. A survey of franchising in Singapore. *Proceedings of the International Society of Franchising*. Las Vegas, NV; February.

35. English, W., and C. Xau. 1994. Franchising in China: A look at KFC and McDonald's. *Proceedings of the International Society of Franchising*. Las Vegas, NV; February.

36. English, W., and C. Xau. 2001. Franchising in China: Y2K update. In: Welsh, D. H. B., and I. Alon, eds. *International Franchising in Industrialized Markets: China, India, and Other Asian Countries*. Riverwoods, IL: CCH, Inc.: 57–65.

37. Chan, P. S., and R. T. Justis. 1995. Franchising in Indonesia. *Proceedings of the International Society of Franchising*. San Juan, Puerto Rico: February.

38. Pine, R., Zhang, H. Q., and P. Qi. 2001. The challenge and opportunities of franchising in

China's hotel industry. In: Welsh, D. H. B., and I. Alon, eds. *International Franchising in Industrialized Markets: China, India, and Other Asian Countries*. Riverwoods, IL: CCH, Inc.:67–81.

39. Han, A. M. 2001. Legal aspects of franchising in China. In: Welsh, D. H. B., and I. Alon, eds. *International Franchising in Industrialized Markets: China, India, and Other Asian Countries*. Riverwoods, IL: CCH, Inc.: 83–104.

40. Alon, I. 2001. An interview with a Chinese franchisor in Shanghai: XiangXiangShanShouShen—A beautification parlor. In: Welsh, D. H. B., and I. Alon, eds. *International Franchising in Emerging Markets: China, India, and Other Asian Countries*. Riverwoods, IL: CCH, Inc.: 105–108.

41. Nair, S. R. 2001. Franchising opportunities in China from the perspective of a franchisee. In: Welsh, D. H. B., and I. Alon, eds. *International Franchising in Industrialized Markets: China, India, and Other Asian Countries*. Riverwoods, IL: CCH, Inc.: 109–121.

42. Richard Hoon (2001)

43. Paswan, A. K., and R. P. Dant. 1995. Franchising in India: An introduction. *Proceedings of the International Society of Franchising*. San Juan, Puerto Rico; February.

44. Paswan, A. K., Dant, R. P., and J. A. Young. 2001. The evolution of franchising in India: Prospects and caveats. In: Welsh, D. H. B., and I. Alon, eds. *International Franchising in Industrialized Markets: China, India, and Other Asian Countries*. Riverwoods, IL: CCH, Inc.: 131–158.

45. Dant, R. P., and P. J. Kaufmann. 2001. The emerging empirical patterns of franchising in India. In: Welsh, D. H. B., and I. Alon, eds. *International Franchising in Industrialized Markets: China, India, and Other Asian Countries*. Riverwoods, IL: CCH, Inc.: 159–172.

46. Paswan, A. K., Young, J. A., and S. P. Kantamneni. 2001. Public opinion about franchising in an emerging market: An exploratory investigation involving Indian consumers. In: Welsh, D. H. B., and I. Alon, eds. *International Franchising in Industrialized Markets: China, India, and Other Asian Countries*. Riverwoods, IL: CCH, Inc.:173–186.

47. Kahn, M. A., and M. M. Khan. 2001. Emerging markets for restaurant franchising in Middle Eastern countries. In: Welsh, D. H. B., and I. Alon, eds. *International Franchising in Industrialized Markets: China, India, and Other Asian Countries*. Riverwoods, IL: CCH, Inc.: 209–227.

48. Welsh, D. H. B., Raven, P., and F. Al-Bisher. 1996. The case of the elegant shoplifter, Shuwaikh, Kuwait. *Franchising Research: An International Journal* 1(3):43–45.

49. Reynolds, J. 2002. Forward. In: Welsh, D. H. B., and I. Alon, eds. *International Franchising in Industrialized Markets: North America, the Pacific Rim, and Other Countries*. Riverwoods, IL: CCH, Inc.: 9–10.

50. Fenwick, 2001

51. Scrivener, 2001

52. Clarkin, J. E. 2002. Market maturation or opportunity recognition? An examination of international expansion by U.S. and Canadian franchise systems. In: Welsh, D. H. B., and I. Alon, eds. *International Franchising in Industrialized Markets: North America, the Pacific Rim, and Other Countries*. Riverwoods, IL: CCH, Inc.: 65–94.

53. Grunhagen, M., and R. A. Mittelstaedt. 2002. Multi-unit franchising: An opportunity for franchisees globally? In: Welsh, D. H. B., and I. Alon, eds. *International Franchising in Industrialized Markets: North America, the Pacific Rim, and Other Countries*. Riverwoods, IL: CCH, Inc.: 95–116.

54. Alon, I. 2000. The organizational determinants of master international franchising. *Journal of Business & Entrepreneurship* 12(2):1–18.

55. Coompanthu, S., and K. Roth. 2002. International services: The choice of organizational forms and plural management. In: Welsh, D. H. B., and I. Alon, eds. *International Franchising in Industrialized Markets: North America, the Pacific Rim, and Other Countries*. Riverwoods, IL: CCH, Inc.: 137–158.

56. Erramilli, M. K., Agarwal, S., and C. S. Dev. 2002. Choice between non-equity entry modes: An organizational capability perspective. In: Welsh, D. H. B., and I. Alon, eds. *International Franchising in Industrialized Markets: North America, the Pacific Rim, and Other Countries*. Riverwoods, IL: CCH, Inc.: 159–184.

57. Sydow, J. 2002. Franchise systems as strategic networks: Studying network leadership in the service sector. In: Welsh, D. H. B., and I. Alon, eds. *International Franchising in Industrialized Markets: North America, the Pacific Rim, and Other Countries*. Riverwoods, IL: CCH, Inc.: 185–198.

58. Hawkes, C. K., and S. Bandyopadhyay. 2002. International growth of U.S. franchising: Cultural and legal barriers. In: Welsh, D. H. B., and I. Alon, eds. *International Franchising in Industrialized Markets: North America, the Pacific Rim, and Other Countries*. Riverwoods, IL: CCH, Inc.: 199–208.

59. DeLuca, F., Smith, A., and L. Winograd. 2002. The subway story: Making North American franchising history. In: Welsh, D. H. B., and I. Alon, eds. *International Franchising in Industrialized Markets: North America, the Pacific Rim, and Other Countries*. Riverwoods, IL: CCH, Inc.: 209–222.

60. Alon, I. 2002. Organizational factors of U.S. international franchising: A comparative study of retailing, hotels, and professional business services. In: Welsh, D. H. B., and I. Alon, eds. *International Franchising in Emerging Markets: China, India, and Other Asian Countries*. Riverwoods, IL: CCH, Inc.: 223–232.

61. Jones, P., and M. Wong. 2002. Franchising in Canada. In: Welsh, D. H. B., and I. Alon, eds. *International Franchising in Industrialized Markets: North America, the Pacific Rim, and Other Countries*. Riverwoods, IL: CCH, Inc.: 233–248.

62. Choo, S. 2002. Valuable lessons for international franchisors when expanding into East Asia. In: Welsh, D. H. B., and I. Alon, eds. *International Franchising in Industrialized Markets: North America, the Pacific Rim, and Other Countries*. Riverwoods, IL: CCH, Inc.: 249–268.

63. Yin, R. K. 1994. *Case Study Research Design and Methods*, 2nd ed. Beverly Hills, CA: Sage Publications.

64. Miles, M. B., and M. A. Huberman. 1994. *Qualitative Data Analysis*, 2nd ed. Beverly Hills, CA: Sage Publications.

65. Sanghavi, N. 2002. Franchising as a growth strategy in the Japanese retail market. In: Welsh, D. H. B., and I. Alon, eds. *International Franchising in Industrialized Markets: Western and Northern Europe*. Riverwoods, IL: CCH, Inc.: 269–286.

66. Lorelle Frazer (2002)

67. Paynter, J. 2002. Franchising in New Zealand: History and current status. In: Welsh, D. H. B., and I. Alon, eds. *International Franchising in Industrialized Markets: North America, the Pacific Rim, and Other Countries*. Riverwoods, IL: CCH, Inc.: 297–312.

68. Dana, L. P. 2002. Franchising in New Zealand. In: Welsh, D. H. B., and I. Alon, eds. *International Franchising in Industrialized Markets: North America, the Pacific Rim, and Other Countries*. Riverwoods, IL: CCH, Inc.: 313–324.

69. Dana, L. P. 2002. Israel's experience with franchising. In: Welsh, D. H. B., and I. Alon, eds. *International Franchising in Industrialized Markets: North America, the Pacific Rim, and Other Countries*. Riverwoods, IL: CCH, Inc.: 325–332.

70. Scholtz, G. J. 1996. Franchising in South Africa. *Proceedings of the International Society of Franchising*. Honolulu, HI; February.

71. Scholtz, G. J. 1997. An overview of South African franchising. *Franchising Research: An International Journal* 2(4):145–151.

72. du Toit, A. 2002. An exploratory study of encroachment in multi-brand franchise organizations. In: Welsh, D. H. B., and I. Alon, eds. *International Franchising in Industrialized Markets: North America, the Pacific Rim, and Other Countries*. Riverwoods, IL: CCH, Inc.: 333–362.

73. Cresswell, J. W. 1994. *Research Design: Qualitative and Quantitative Approaches*. Thousand Oaks, CA: Sage Publications.

74. Rugman, A. M. 2001. The myth of global strategy. *Insights* 2:11–14.

75. Wright, J. W. 2000. *The New York Times Almanac*. New York, NY: The New York Times.

76. Child, P. N., Heywood, S., and M. Kliger. 2002. Do retail brands travel? *The McKinsey Quarterly* 1:11–13.

77. Stanworth, J., and D. Purdy. 2003. Breaking into the European union using franchising. In: Welsh, D. H. B., and I. Alon, eds. *International Franchising in Industrialized Markets: Western and Northern Europe*. Riverwoods, IL: CCH, Inc.: 55–74.

78. Mendelsohn, M. 2003. Comparative review of legal issues in Europe. In: Welsh, D. H. B., and I. Alon, eds. *International Franchising in Industrialized Markets: Western and Northern Europe*. Riverwoods, IL: CCH, Inc.: 75–92.

79. Sherman, A. 2003. Final reflections: Key trends for European franchisors. In: Welsh, D. H. B., and I. Alon, eds. *International Franchising in Industrialized Markets: Western and Northern Europe*. Riverwoods, IL: CCH, Inc.: 111–136.

80. Mazero, J. G, and I. G. Martyn. 2003. Due diligence for international franchisors: Practical considerations to avoid criminal and civil liabilities. In: Welsh, D. H. B., and I. Alon, eds. *International Franchising in Industrialized Markets: Western and Northern Europe*. Riverwoods, IL: CCH, Inc.: 499–510.

81. Mazero, J. G, and I. G. Martyn. 2003. International franchisors due diligence checklist. In: Welsh, D. H. B., and I. Alon, eds. *International Franchising in Industrialized Markets: Western and Northern Europe*. Riverwoods, IL: CCH, Inc.: 511–516.

82. Hero, M. 2003. Legal aspects of franchising in Austria. In: Welsh, D. H. B., and I. Alon, eds. *International Franchising in Industrialized Markets: Western and Northern Europe*. Riverwoods, IL: CCH, Inc.: 93–110.

83. Tuunanen, M. 2003. Compilation of Finnish franchising statistics. In: Welsh, D. H. B., and I. Alon, eds. *International Franchising in Industrialized Markets: Western and Northern Europe*. Riverwoods, IL: CCH, Inc.: 137–164.

84. Torikka, J., and M. Tuunanen. 2003. Finnish franchisee training program: An exploratory study. In: Welsh, D. H. B., and I. Alon, eds. *International Franchising in Industrialized Markets: Western and Northern Europe*. Riverwoods, IL: CCH, Inc.: 165–188.

85. Penard, T., Raynaud, E., and S. Saussier. 2003. An overview of franchising in France. In: Welsh, D. H. B., and I. Alon, eds. *International Franchising in Industrialized Markets: Western and Northern Europe*. Riverwoods, IL: CCH, Inc.: 189–206.

86. Cliquet, G., and P. Rozenn. 2003. Survival analysis of French hotel franchising. In: Welsh, D. H. B., and I. Alon, eds. *International Franchising in Industrialized Markets: Western and Northern Europe*. Riverwoods, IL: CCH, Inc.: 27–254.

87. Cliquet, G., and P. Rozenn. 2002. Plural form development in the French franchise networks. In: Welsh, D. H. B., and I. Alon, eds. *International Franchising in Industrialized Markets: North America, the Pacific Rim, and Other Countries*. Riverwoods, IL: CCH, Inc.: 207–226.

88. Flohr, E. 2003. The legal environment of franchising in Germany. In: Welsh, D. H. B., and I. Alon, eds. *International Franchising in Industrialized Markets: Western and Northern Europe*. Riverwoods, IL: CCH, Inc.: 255–270.

89. Schlamp, S. 2003. Women and franchising in Germany. In: Welsh, D. H. B., and I. Alon, eds. *International Franchising in Industrialized Markets: Western and Northern Europe*. Riverwoods, IL: CCH, Inc.: 271–278.

90. Dimou, I., and A. Ikkos. 2003. The status quo of Greek franchising opportunities for future growth. In: Welsh, D. H. B., and I. Alon, eds. *International Franchising in Industrialized Markets: Western and Northern Europe*. Riverwoods, IL: CCH, Inc.: 279–298.

91. Luca, P., de Majocchi, A., and E. Pavione. 2003. Franchising in Italy: Trends and development. In: Welsh, D. H. B., and I. Alon, eds. *International Franchising in Industrialized Markets: Western and Northern Europe*. Riverwoods, IL: CCH, Inc.: 299–330.

92. Vianelli, D. 2003. Franchising as a mode of entry for Italian companies in international markets. In: Welsh, D. H. B., and I. Alon, eds. *International Franchising in Industrialized Markets: Western and Northern Europe*. Riverwoods, IL: CCH, Inc.: 331–352.

93. Singh, S. 2003. Understanding Norway for potential franchising. In: Welsh, D. H. B., and I. Alon, eds. *International Franchising in Industrialized Markets: Western and Northern Europe*. Riverwoods, IL: CCH, Inc.: 353–372.

94. Dahab, S. S., Cunha, M. P. E., and R. L. Cardim. 2003. Internationalization of franchising: Juggling local tastes and brand consistency. In: Welsh, D. H. B., and I. Alon, eds. *International Franchising in Industrialized Markets: Western and Northern Europe*. Riverwoods, IL: CCH, Inc.: 373–390.

95. Cross, A. R., Burton, F., and M. Rhodes. 2003. International expansion of UK franchisors: An investigation of organizational form. In: Welsh, D. H. B., and I. Alon, eds. *International Franchising in Industrialized Markets: Western and Northern Europe*. Riverwoods, IL: CCH, Inc.: 419–448.

96. Stanworth, Brodie, Wotruba, and Purdy (2002)

97. Quinn, B. 2003. The internationalization process of a franchise system: An ethnographic study. In: Welsh, D. H. B., and I. Alon, eds. *International Franchising in Industrialized Markets: Western and Northern Europe*. Riverwoods, IL: CCH, Inc.: 471–490.

98. Naisbitt, J. 1982. *Megatrends*. New York: Warner Books.

99. Welsh, D. H. B. 2002. Franchising: A 21st century perspective. In: Welsh, D. H. B., and I. Alon, eds. *International Franchising in Industrialized Markets: North America, the Pacific Rim, and Other Countries*. Riverwoods, IL: CCH, Inc.: 47–64.

100. Markins, C. 2002. Businesses needed for national survey. *IFA Insider* 7(15):4.

Chapter Eleven

GOING INTERNATIONAL? ALTERNATIVE MODES OF ENTRY FOR ENTREPRENEURIAL FIRMS

Nadia Ballard, *Mercado Management Services, LLC, Longwood, Florida*
Ilan Alon, *Rollins College, Winter Park, Florida*

Learning Objectives

Upon completion of this chapter, students should be able to:

- Understand the various modes of entry that are available to small or medium enterprises (SMEs).
- Understand the exporting, licensing, franchising, contract manufacturing, turnkey operations, management contracts, international joint ventures, and fully-owned subsidiaries as they relate to SMEs.
- Understand the factors that motivate the mode of entry decision from the standpoint of the company and the environment in which it operates.
- Understand the advantages and disadvantages of the different modes of entry.
- Understand the approaches that an SME can utilize in expanding its business abroad.

Key Terms

external factors
fully-owned subsidiary
indirect and direct exporting
internal factors
international franchising

international licensing
international joint venture
management contract
turnkey operations

◎ Introduction

Entrepreneurs are used to taking high risks for the potential of high returns on their ventures. Entering foreign markets can be both more risky and more rewarding for many entrepreneurial businesses, but with a well thought-out entry strategy and sound execution, most entrepreneurs can minimize the risks and increase their chances for success in the international marketplace.

This chapter examines the various modes of entry that are available to small or medium enterprises (SMEs). In particular, it discusses the exporting, licensing, franchising, contract manufacturing, turnkey operations, management contracts, international joint ventures, and fully owned subsidiaries as they relate to SMEs.

The entry into foreign markets is very frequently accidental for entrepreneurs.[1] One likely scenario from the last decade is that the first order from abroad came as a result of the company's exposure on the Internet, or a mention of the company's products in a chat room or a blog. If a company is taking a full advantage of its Internet presence, it should virtually expect to gain international cyber clients within months.[i]

Whether a firm takes a more deliberate action to grow its international market share after the first few successful exports is up to the entrepreneur and his or her vision for the company. However, business owners today should not think that just because they are well entrenched in their home market, they are immune to the competitive pressures of globalization. It is likely that, even if a business does not pursue international strategy, international competitors, suppliers, and buyers would eventually pursue it (see "Sharpening Its Focus"). The authors of this chapter are of the opinion that a company that decides to limit itself to a single domestic market is likely to be much less competitive and successful than its internationalized counterparts.

Some of the many reasons for going international include:

- Expand beyond a saturated domestic market
- Find new source of profits
- Add to your firm's competitive edge
- Diversify and grow your markets to hedge against economic crises
- Follow customers who are going abroad.

The remainder of this chapter is divided into three sections. The first discusses the factors that motivate the mode of entry decision from the standpoint of the company and the environment in which it operates. The second section is the heart of the paper, which analyzes the advantages and disadvantages of the different modes of entry. Within this section, several illustrations and SME prac-

---

i. Assuming that the company is conducting an active Internet marketing campaign with emphasis on search engine placement, Web site advertisements, affiliate marketing strategy, and other marketing methods. Also, to be appealing and understandable to international visitors, a Web site should use (at a minimum) common English language, simple navigation signs, and graphics and clear pictures and descriptions of the products/services offered.

tices are provided. Finally, the conclusion reflects on approaches that an SME can utilize in expanding its business abroad.

◎ Factors That Influence the Mode of Entry Decision Process

Once a decision has been made to go international, a deliberate consideration of the mode of entry should ensue. The decision process is influenced by a number of factors that may often pull the decision makers in opposite directions. An SME goes through successive decision-making process that includes answering the following questions:

- Can our product be marketed abroad?
- What the key success factors for our products?
- Is secondary data available for those markets/products?
- What additional data is needed and how can we get it?

Text Box 11.1 International Competition on Domestic Turf: Sharpening Its Focus

Diamond Machining Technology Inc. makes manual sharpening tools that are used by the U.S. Olympic speed skating and luge teams and endorsed by PBS' *American Woodshop* host Scott Phillips.

But even though the Marlborough, Massachusetts, company has been in business twenty-seven years, has revenue between $5 million and $10 million, and has established itself as a leader in its field, the tool-sharpening trade is anything but easy.

The company, started in 1976, didn't take long to reach its first do-or-die decision. A couple of years after DMT launched a line of industrial sharpening products using diamonds, it faced significant competition from lower-priced sharpeners from Israel.

David Powell, an engineer by trade, responded by developing DMT's signature product, the Diamond Whetstone, a small, handheld sharpening tool. "We had to come up with a different product that would keep us alive," Elizabeth Powell said.

DMT introduced the Diamond Whetstone at the Gourmet Product Show in San Francisco in 1979. That same year, the Diamond Whetstone was also featured in the Brookstone catalog.

The company started by marketing directly to consumers, quickly establishing a niche among hunters, cooks, athletes, gardeners, and woodworkers, all of whom wanted tools that wouldn't eat away the metal edges of their blades.

"It was a time when tools were being made with harder metals, and there was a real push to improve strength. It was timely, I guess, to introduce diamond products to the consumer world."

The company is currently facing competition from diamond-based sharpeners from China, which can cost up to 20% less than DMT's products, so the Powells are emphasizing their brand's quality and looking to expand its market to the more casual consumer. Although DMT had no plans to compete in international markets, foreign competition on its own turf forced this thirty-employee company to hone their best product.

(Adapted from Archambeault, B. Sharpening its focus. *Boston Business Journal* [electronic version]. February 19, 2004. Retrieved March 13, 2004 from http://www.bizjournals.com/orlando/entrepreneur/2004/02/19/1.html.)

- Which of our products have the highest potential abroad?
- Which markets have the greatest potential for our products?
- Do we have excess production capacity?
- What are the characteristics of our target market?
- What are the international capabilities of the firm?

Answering these questions is the first step in a preliminary market analysis for market and mode of entry selection.

To discuss all the different forces involved in the entry mode decision process, we categorize these factors into two major groups: internal and external factors. The *internal factors* have to do with the firm's resources, overall strategy, management mindset, time commitment, and, very importantly, types of products or services considered for international markets. For most entrepreneurial firms, the key issues discussed during this initial stage of the decision process revolve around:

- Financial resources—How much can we spend on international market expansion? Should we borrow funds or use accumulated financial assets? Are the potential rewards of this initiative worth the financial risks?
- Human resources—Should we hire new staff or use existing personnel to lead the expansion effort? What would be the compensation for the new position? How would the new management role be defined? Where would the position be located?
- Type of product and/or service—Which of our products/services should we market internationally? How adaptable are they? What is required to make them ready for the target market?
- Time horizons—How much time can we dedicate to the international expansion effort? Are we willing to accommodate longer receivables cycles?
- Risk tolerance—Are we prepared to absorb the higher risks inherent in dealing with currency exchange rates, unfamiliar political, legal and market environments, economic cycles, etc.?

Recent studies have focused on the accelerated timeframe in which SMEs move from domestic to internationalized operations, leading academics to question the stage model for the internationalization process (see Figure 11.1). The question "Are some firms born global?" has been raised. A recent study of 677 small and medium companies in France, Denmark, and Norway finds that "going global" sooner depends in large part on the company's internal makeup, developed at the initial stages of their creation. The most important indicator of how quickly a firm would be ready and willing to export depended on the early development within the firm of resources beneficial to international market competitiveness.[2] These findings further underscore the importance of internal evaluation before moving into international business.

In addition to the internal factors, many external factors also need to be considered before a final decision on the mode of entry can be made. Factors that affect the company's choice to enter a foreign market but are independent of management's decisions are called *external factors*. External factors fall under two categories: target country factors and domestic country factors.

Target country factors that should be considered when choosing a mode of entry include:

- Market—its size, competitive environment, marketing infrastructure, etc.
- Production conditions—everything from the cost, quality, and quantity of local materials and labor to the transportation, communications, energy supply, and other similar economic infrastructure components.
- Environmental conditions—this broad category includes most of the political, economic, geographic, and social factors that make one country more attractive for international commerce than another. Examples include government policies toward foreign trade, the overall rate of foreign investment, the gross national product, the diversification level of the local economy, the country's corruption ratings, and cultural and language barriers.

Some *domestic country factors* also strongly influence the foreign market entry mode. For example, if a company has a large enough domestic market, it can grow to a significant size before it chooses or needs to expand internationally. The choices of market entry methods can differ significantly for small and large companies, depending on their capitalization, production capacity, and marketing resources, among other issues. Conversely, a large domestic market can make some companies disinterested in expanding internationally due to the significant growth opportunities at home, while a small domestic market would spur even small companies to seek international expansion sooner. Other domestic country factors that would spur a company to seek international markets include competitive pressure at home, high domestic production costs, and favorable government policies toward exporting (tax incentives, trade support programs), for example.

Methods of Entry to International Markets

Because most entrepreneurial businesses are small to medium in size, their initial choices for international market entry tend to include low- to moderate-risk strategies, such as exporting, licensing, and franchising. As the companies become bigger and more successful internationally, some may decide to deepen their presence and commitment to particular foreign markets by entering into contract manufacturing, turnkey operations agreements, or management contracts and even forming international joint ventures (IJVs) or investing in fully owned subsidiaries. Figure 11.1 is a graphic of these most common market entry methods, ranked by the increase in risk for the entering firm. Another form of international market entry, the international business alliance, is discussed separately later.

Exporting   The most common and low-risk method of entering overseas markets, exporting is also the one requiring the least investment in financial, marketing, and human resources and time. Because of its low commitment requirements, exporting is the preferred mode of entry of most small and medium entrepreneurial businesses. It is an especially well suited method for initial market

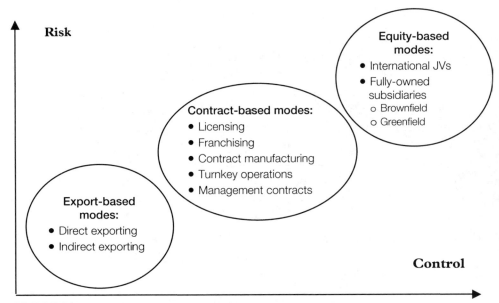

FIGURE 11.1 Risk and control considerations in choosing modes of entry.

tests due to the relative ease of pulling out of a market if it turns out to not be profitable.[3]

The main difference between exporting and the other entry modes is that exporting is limited to actual physical products that are produced outside the target country market. By nature, service companies cannot perform their services domestically and then ship them to another country; thus, they are required to use contractual or investment entry modes. Exported products, on the other hand, can be sold overseas by intermediaries who specialize in this activity from the home base—*indirect exporting*; or they can be distributed directly through agents and/or distributors in the target country—*direct exporting*. An alternative that falls under the direct exporting method is to export products to a direct branch or subsidiary of the company, which assumes that some form of direct investment in the target market has already been made.[1]

One small electronics firm's experience with direct exporting started after the company decided to actively pursue international markets for its specialized products. The management of the company took a deliberate, analytical approach to selecting its first international target markets, while remaining mindful of the limited resources they could dedicate to the expansion. First, with the help of the U.S. Department of Commerce, they researched product exports based on commodity numbers taken directly from the export documentation's schedule B. This is an excellent indicator of market export potential because it is directly related to the company's products.

Next, they analyzed the hits on their Web site to see where most of their visitors were coming from. While this measure can be volatile, over time it can provide a rich source of data on the countries that show most interest in the company's products. Third, management looked at the company's customers and/or competitors to find relevant foreign markets. Since their competitors tend to be other small firms, not publicly traded or known, little information existed on competitors. However, examining the internationalization of the industry as a whole or the internationalization of large multinational companies proved to be helpful. Finding the local buying centers of the multinational companies was the most challenging part of this research. After settling on several potential markets, the company ranked them first by their market potential and next by the ease of entry. The firm evaluated and prioritized the most promising markets before moving on to the decision of the actual mode of entry.

The company decided to use direct exporting as mode of entry due to the specialized nature of its products and the specific industries that held the largest market potential. The next step in the process centered on deciding whether it would be more advantageous to divide their target markets by geographic- or in-dustry-specific criteria and, consequently, whether to look for distributors whose network covers a wide geographic area or for distributors who are well estab-lished in the specific industries chosen as target markets. The company decided industry-specific knowledge and relationships were more important than geo-graphical coverage of the market. Therefore, the following indicators were used to select the appropriate distributor:

- Does the distributor have established connections in the targeted industries?
- Is the distributor familiar with the type of products manufactured by the company?
- Does the distributor have experience working with American companies?
- What are the distributor's size, current product lineup, and revenues?
- Will the distributor allow the company to conduct independent marketing and sales within the country?

The company's search for the right distributor started with a visit to the U.S. Commercial Service's industry specialists located in the target countries. These international trade professionals were instrumental in providing in-depth analy-sis and contact information for the first stage of the selection process.

After several meetings and evaluations of a few potential partners, the com-pany was able to form an agreement with a distributor based on mutual business objectives, interest, and compatibilities.

As with all others forms of market entry, an entrepreneur who is considering exporting should do plenty of research and planning before committing to a market or a distributor. Despite the advance of global free trade, some countries remain hostile to imports and impose many barriers on them such as high tariffs, taxes, or currency exchange restrictions. Learning about the importing environ-ment of one's target country market or hiring a country specialist who knows the local government's import requirements for the specific product(s) is essential. Also a must is researching and hiring a reputable and trusted distributor, whether at home or abroad. Some of the ways to ensure that an exporting partner(s) meets the company's criteria for doing business in the target market is by re-searching the company's market reach and infrastructure, ethic standards, finan-cials, and track record. References and current client interviews are an excellent way to ensure that an intermediary in the international market(s) maintains and enhances the company's good brand by providing an equivalent level of service, pricing, and ethical behavior. Last, to ensure that the importing company's legal rights and privileges are protected, one should review the country's laws and regulations regarding import/export partnerships. The laws and regulations of some countries make it problematic to pull out of a distribution or an agent contract even when that party is not performing its contractual duties.[3]

Licensing Another popular method for market entry is through licensing. *International licensing* is the process of transferring the rights to a firm's products to an overseas company for the purpose of producing or selling it there. For a set royalty fee, the *licensor* allows the *licensee* to use its technology, trademark(s), patent(s), and other intellectual property in order to gain presence in the market(s) covered by the licensee.

Licensing is an attractive mode of entry for many entrepreneurial firms because, like exporting, it involves smaller upfront risks and expenditures. Since most of the costs of developing the licensed products have already been incurred, the royalties received often translate into direct profits for the licensor.[4] This form of market entry is most appropriate for countries that impose barriers to imports such as high tariffs and profit repatriation restrictions, and for mature products with relatively standardized production.[3]

Licensing is not without its drawbacks, however. As with export partners, a firm considering licensing is advised to thoroughly research its potential licensees and their professionalism standards and to devise detailed legal contracts specifying the agreement's constraints, compensation rates, duration, and other similar issues. Such a cautious approach is important especially for countries where the legal protection for intellectual property is weak or not strongly enforced by the government. All too often, licensing companies have found themselves competing against their very licensees who have copied their know-how and entered the markets with little or no research and development expenses. High tech firms considering licensing should be especially wary of the dangers of technology expropriation.

Franchising A form of licensing that eliminates some of the concerns described in the previous section is international franchising. *International franchising* gives more control to the *franchisor* company over the *franchisee* who has licensed the company's trademarks, products and/or services, and production and/or operation processes. Control is exerted through the franchise fee which can be expropriated if contracts are not adhered to and there are elaborate contracts that govern the relationship between the franchisor and the franchisee/s. On the flip side, the franchisor is also required to provide more materials, training, and other forms of support to the franchisee. A well functioning franchise provides a win-win arrangement for both parties: the franchisor gets to expand into new markets with little or no risk and investment and the franchisee gets a proven brand, marketing exposure, established client base, and management expertise to help him or her succeed.

Although franchising in most developed countries of North America and Europe has reached a saturation point, many emerging markets are experiencing

Text Box 11.2 Success Factors in Exporting

A 2001 study published in the *Journal of International Marketing* sought to extract the definitive factors contributing to harmonious or problematic exporting partnerships. Based on their interviews of 201 U.S. exporting manufacturers, the researchers developed the following export management guidelines for other firms looking to excel in international business relationships:

- Treat exporting as a bundle of evolving business relationships that are not defined just by the financial terms of the agreements but are dynamic and evolving. Therefore, each one should be monitored and cared for both individually and as a part of the overall international business portfolio.

- Relationships with people from other countries are most successful when conducted by skilled relationship management managers who have cross-cultural experience and language proficiency. The training in international business skills of the rest of the company's staff is also important for smooth relationships with overseas customers.

- A proactive approach that assigns strategic importance to the firm's international operations and is supported by all departments and staff is essential. It is important for the firm to conduct systematic market analysis and appraisal of the exporting operations and the international customer base.

- Dealing with customers that are thousands of miles away physically and psychologically creates certain barriers to developing proper customer relationships. Exporters should make concerted efforts to reduce the distance by learning about their international clients through specialized literature, economic data, field trips, cross-cultural training, and simulations, etc.

- Continuously building and enhancing the trust between the partners is essential to a sustained and prosperous international relationship. Being a trustworthy business partner is especially important in certain cultures and an exporter should take deliberate steps to gain and retain that trust even through the inevitable problems that arise in the course of any long-term business relationship.

- Reducing the uncertainties inherent in international business is a crucial factor in creating a hospitable environment for a cross border partnership. Establishing communication, organizational, financial, and operational processes that ensure the reliable dissemination and acquisition of long-distance information is critical.

- It is challenging enough to come to a mutual understanding even between domestic partners, but when different cultural, political, environmental, and economic factors come in, the challenge is even greater. Open-mindedness, goodwill, and reciprocity are essential for a long-lasting international partnership.

- Being flexible and willing to accept small sacrifices, costs, restrictions, etc., in an international business relationship fosters commitment and long-term view. When this flexibility and commitment is mutual, the relationship can truly blossom.

- As in any relationship, open and continuous communication is key. To facilitate communication across the national, organizations, and personal differences, both parties should invest in cross-cultural training, onsite visits, and interactive communication technologies.

- Conflict is inevitable and healthy for an international business partnership, when managed properly. Exporters should ensure that conflict is kept functional, overt, and controllable in order to be dealt with and resolved quickly.

- Just as all companies strive for intra-company cooperation, the goal of greater inter-firm cooperation, goal compatibility, and information dissemination should be a priority for any exporter-importer relationship.

(Adapted from Leonidou, L. C., Katsikeas, C. S., and J. Hadjimarcou. Executive insights: Building successful export business relationships: A behavioral perspective. *Journal of International Marketing. 2002;*3:96–115.)

phenomenal growth in international franchising. To succeed in developing countries, an entrepreneur who is considering this mode of market entry should consider several important environmental factors such as the level of economic development, the economic growth rate of the country, and its market governance policies before starting to look for potential franchisees there.[5]

While franchising has been the domain of mostly large, multi-national corporations (MNCs) such as McDonald's, Dunkin' Donuts, and Holiday Inn, the advent of international franchising is opening unprecedented opportunities to smaller companies who are diligent with their contracts, revenue oversight, and quality control to enter new free markets and compete successfully.

Contract Manufacturing   Contract manufacturing, or outsourcing, has garnered much attention recently for its economic and business benefits as well as for its controversial but inherent trend to move production jobs across borders. Contract manufacturing's growing popularity is due to the large savings it can produce in the financial and human resources areas of a business.

The arrangement of using cheaper overseas labor for the production of finished goods or parts by following an established production process is called *contract manufacturing* or *outsourcing*. Companies using this mode of entry benefit not only from lowering their production costs but also from an entry to a new market with small amounts of capital and with no ownership hassles. Some of the drawbacks of using outsourcing methods is the loss of control over the manufacturing process and the working conditions in the facilities, which can potentially lead to lower quality of the goods and/or human rights abuses and result in bad publicity and financial damages to the company's brand. Nike, Timberland, and several other high-profile American firms have served as unintentional examples of this undesirable scenario. In recent years, multiple firms from emerging markets such as China and India have emerged to help SMEs lower their costs by sourcing products, manufacturing, and services abroad. Contract manufacturing can enable future competitors who acquire critical skills in manufacturing your product, learn about your market, and are more likely to vertically integrate forward.

Turnkey Operations   Another contractual entry mode to a new market is participation in a turnkey project. *Turnkey operations typically* involve the design, construction, equipment, and, often, the initial personnel training of a large facility by an overseas company which then turns the key to the ready-to-run facility over to the purchaser.

Most often the province of the largest specialized construction and manufacturing companies, turnkey operations projects are usually contracted out by governments for enormous projects such as the building of dams, oil refineries, airports, energy plants, etc. Nevertheless, opportunities exist for the participation of smaller entrepreneurial firms as subcontractors for turnkey projects.[6]

Because of their extraordinary size and scope, many such projects require long-term commitment of personnel, financial reserves, supplies, and other resources. Before a small company decides to participate in turnkey operations, it should carefully examine whether it is ready to absorb the long-term currency exchange fluctuations, the extended drain on its resources and the other elevated political, economic, and financial risks that are likely to come up in such complex undertakings. Some SMEs providing specialized services can sell their service/product through turnkey operations. One such company in Orlando markets airport development services to developing countries' governments using regional joint venture partners for the construction and financing the project through major international banks. There is always a risk that the last payment for the project upon completion will not be paid as the incentives to pay decrease.

Management Contract   A mode of entry into new markets that is most widely used in the hotel and airline industries is management contracting. Under a *management contract*, a company in one country can utilize the expertise, technology, or specialized services of a company from another country to run its business for a set time and fee or percentage of sales. For example, many owners of hotel buildings contract with well-known hotel management firms such as The Ritz-Carlton Hotel Company, LLC, to develop and manage their properties.

While the management company is responsible for day-to-day operations, it cannot decide on ownership, financial, strategic, or policy issues for the business.[3] Such arrangement is suitable for companies that are interested in earning extra revenues abroad without getting entangled in long-term financial or legal obligations in the foreign market.

International Joint Ventures   As part of the larger category of international business alliances (see Text Box 11.3), IJVs have been one of the most popular methods for entering international markets. A form of foreign direct investment (FDI), *joint ventures* are created when two or more companies share ownership of a third commercial entity and collaborate in the production of its goods or services. IJVs are attractive to businesses because of the relative ease of market entry they offer, their shared risk, shared knowledge and expertise, and the potential for synergy and competitive advantage in the global marketplace.[4]

International joint ventures are formed for different reasons, the four main being to continue the expansion of an existing business, to introduce the company's products to new markets, to introduce foreign products to the company's existing markets, and to branch out into new business.[7] IJVs can also take many different forms (see Figure 11.2):

- Two or more companies from the same country form an alliance to enter another country.
- An overseas company joins a local company to enter its domestic market.
- Firms from two or more countries band together in a JV formed in a third country.
- A foreign private business and a government agree to join forces in a pursuit of mutual interests.
- A foreign private firm enters into a JV with a government-owned firm to enter into a third national market.

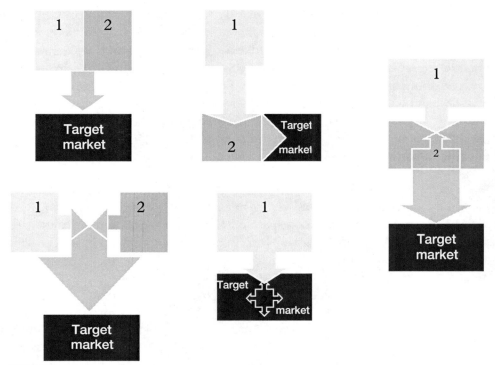

FIGURE 11.2 International joint ventures arrangements.

Much has been written about the factors contributing to the success and (more often) failures of cross-border strategic alliances such as joint ventures. To summarize, the most general issue with such an arrangement is maintaining the delicate balance between the partners' goals and objectives, management requirements, contributions, organizational and national cultures, and the myriad of other factors that make some collaborations successful and others not.

For entrepreneurs, joint ventures are a fitting way of entering into new markets with little or no international business experience, and for entering some specific countries where people tend to value trust as a cultural characteristic and are more open to international collaboration.[6]

Fully Owned Subsidiaries   As the most capital-intensive mode of entry, fully owned subsidiaries are usually considered viable only for large, internationally experienced corporations who can afford the great risks associated with ownership and operation of a business in a foreign country. Entering a market through a *fully owned subsidiary* involves buying an existing business (also called *brownfield strategy*) or building new facilities (also called *greenfield strategy*) in a new target country. While both of these scenarios allow companies to exercise maximum control over their operations and to decisively enter the target country's markets, they also expose the company to the highest level of political, environmental, legal, and financial risks.

For a comprehensive review of the advantages and disadvantages of all modes of entry discussed in this chapter, please see Table 11.1.

As global communication, travel, and trade have become increasingly easier and more widespread, many companies have found it possible and even beneficial to use more than one entry mode simultaneously. Such strategy is most often used for two main reasons: to enter several markets at the same time or to leverage the advantages of one entry mode before transitioning to another.

TABLE 11.1 **Advantages and Disadvantages of International Modes of Entry**

MODE OF ENTRY	ADVANTAGES	DISADVANTAGES
Exporting	Low risk Easy market entry or exit Gain local market knowledge Bypass FDI restrictions	Tariffs and quotas Transportation costs Possible distributor relationship issues
Licensing	Low risk Fast market access Bypass regulations and tariffs Gain local market knowledge	Less control over market and revenues Intellectual property concerns Potential problems with licensees/future competitors
Franchising	Low financial risk Bypass regulations and tariffs Keep more control Gain local market knowledge	Less control over market and revenues Some loss of control over operations Potential franchisee relationship issues
Contract manufacturing	Low financial risk Save on manufacturing costs Flexibility of short term commitment Emphasis on marketing/sales	Less control over operations Less knowledge about local market Potential damage to brand/finances if human rights issues arise
Management contracts	Insider access to market Emphasis on firm's expertise Low financial risk	Limited profits and market access Potential copyright and intellectual property issues
Turnkey operations	Access to FDI-unfriendly markets No long term operational risks Emphasis on firm's expertise	Some financial risks Potential issues with partners/infrastructure/ labor/profit repatriation
Joint ventures	Insider access to market High profit potential More control over operations Shared risks Gain knowledge from partner(s)	High investment of resources Potential issues between partners over control/ contributions/goals, etc. More management levels Potential intellectual property issues
Fully owned subsidiaries	Full market access/acceptance Full control over operations/profits Bypass tariffs Diversify operations	High financial/resources investment High political and environmental risks Potential profits repatriation issues More management levels

A medium-size financial services firm based in Florida used this twofold approach when it decided to expand its offering of Real Estate Investment Trusts (REITs) to international investors. The company used a quantitative approach to determine the most promising markets for entry, followed by a strategic analysis of its investment division against the backdrop of the global real estate environment.

Applying a factor weighting method that combined quantitative and qualitative factors provided a general framework for determining the four markets that showed the most promise for further evaluation. Each market was then investigated further to determine its specific domestic REIT environment, its regulatory environment, primary local competitors, tax ramifications and investment alternatives.

The company ultimately decided to enter its chosen international markets with a two-step plan. The first phase included using the resources of the firm's

Text Box 11.3 International Business Alliances

International alliances are defined as "relatively enduring inter-firm cooperative arrangements, involving flows and linkages that use resources and/or governance structures from autonomous organizations, for the joining accomplishment of individual goals linked to the corporate mission of each sponsoring firm." International strategic alliances are becoming a fast-growing method of foreign market entry. Compared with foreign direct investment, international strategic alliances embody a lower level of financial investment and risk, and allow for the pooling of resources, skills, and abilities across multiple firms with the goal of achieving a joint purpose. International strategic alliances, however, are not risk free. The different decision style of the alliance companies, the loose association that exists among the alliance firms, and the sharing of strategic resources exposes firms to potential failure and an unstable business environment in which one partner may take advantage of another.

Despite the risk factors associated with strategic alliances, this mode of entry into foreign markets has its advantages. For example, strategic alliances have the potential to lower the transaction costs, hedge against strategic uncertainty, acquire needed resources, allow firms to evade international barriers to entry, protect a firm's home market from international competition, broaden a firm's product line, allow firms to enter new product markets, and enhance resource use efficiency. Tallman argued that firms utilizing strategic alliances could enhance their firm-specific resources (e.g., physical assets, intangible property, patents and trademarks, human resources, complementary resources), technical capabilities (e.g., R&D, manufacturing, marketing, sales, market knowledge), and managerial competencies (e.g., management skills and abilities, value-added activities).

The advantages gained by using international strategic alliances depend on the type of industry and the way in which the alliance is structured. For example, some researchers contend that firms in a mature industry are more likely to benefit from strategic alliances, whereas others propose that technology-based alliances tend to benefit high-tech industries more than traditional industries.

Many different frameworks have been developed for the proper formation and execution of an international business alliance, including conducting SWOT, goal compatibility, and value-added analyses for participating firms, and/or examining their market power, efficiency, and competencies. Nevertheless, the most vital issues for a successful international business alliance remain selecting the right partner, developing trust, and developing appropriate contractual framework.

(From Alon, I. 2003. International Business Alliances: A Practical Perspective from the Packaging Industry. *Proceedings, Annual Academy of International Business, Southeast Meeting.*)

domestic financial partners who are active in these markets to build a local presence and brand recognition (international alliance). The second step revolved around the building of new distribution agreements with local, established brokers/dealers that could further expand the regional markets for the firm's REITs (direct exporting).

The first option, although limited in scope, allowed the company to leverage its existing relationships and enter international markets using a minimal amount of its resources and benefiting from the networks and market knowledge of its partners. The second option, although more expensive, provided a greater coverage and market penetration of the products, while capitalizing on the already existent name recognition and client base. By combining the international alliances and direct exporting modes of entry, this financial services firm was able to enter several markets simultaneously and safely while preserving its resources and gaining market intelligence that proved invaluable for the second, more aggressive step of their international market expansion.

SMEs tend to reflexively rely on nonequity modes of entry (exporting, licensing) because they would rather preserve capital and avoid high risks when moving into international markets. However, recent research suggests[8] that using transaction cost analysis to select an international mode of entry—a method usually associated with large corporations—can actually improve their chances of selecting the most efficient method for their specific organization. The authors of the study recommend that SMEs evaluate three specific transaction cost criteria:

- Level of investment required for each asset. If no particular asset requires a large investment, nonequity modes such as licensing or franchising may be suitable for market entry. If such entry requires a high level of specific-asset investment, equity modes of entry such as IJVs or fully owned subsidiaries may be more appropriate.
- Environmental factors of the target country. A more stable and economically and politically secure country would be more inviting to an equity mode of entry, whereas a country with political or social turmoil and frequent economic crises would be suitable for nonequity modes of entry.
- Status of internal control systems and processes. A business that is built on strong internal culture and regulations would be more comfortable upholding them in their new markets by entering through equity modes. On the other hand, a more open and flexible firm may be comfortable with relying on the controls of partners such as exporting agents or licensees.

SME decision makers can rely on transaction cost theory to make more informed decisions about the most appropriate mode of entry for their company. Decisions made using this method seem to lead to a better performance abroad, according to this limited study.

Whether a firm uses transaction cost analysis or any other accepted method to evaluate their international market strategy, the choice of entry mode should be carefully considered and planned to ensure smoother, more profitable operations abroad.

Discussion Questions

1. Describe some internal factors that need to be considered before deciding on the mode of entry for a company. How does a company's internal makeup affect the speed in which it goes global?
2. Describe some external factors that need to be considered before deciding on the mode of entry for a company. Be sure to include target country factors and domestic country factors in your answer.
3. As with all other forms of market entry, an entrepreneur who is considering exporting should do plenty of research and planning before committing to a market or a distributor. What indicators should be considered in selecting a distributor?
4. How does international franchising differ from contract manufacturing?
5. How do the environmental factors of a target country affect the mode of entry into that particular market?

Endnotes

1. Root, F. 1987. *Entry Strategies for International Markets. Designing Entry Strategies for International Markets*. MA: Lexington Books.
2. Moen, Ø., and P. Servais. 2002. Born global or gradual global? Examining the export behavior of small and medium-sized enterprises. *Journal of International Marketing* 10(3):49–72.
3. Deresky, H. 2000. *International Management: Managing Across Borders and Cultures*, 3rd ed. Upper Saddle River, NJ: Prentice Hall: 238–240.
4. Griffin, R. W., and M. W. Pustay. 2003. *International Business: A Managerial Perspective*, 3rd ed. Upper Saddle River, NJ: Prentice Hall: 326,346–348.
5. Welsh, D. H. B, and I. Alon, eds. 2001. *International Franchising in Emerging Markets. Central and Eastern Europe and Latin America*. Chicago, IL: CCH Incorporated: 33–34.
6. Daniels, J. D., and L. H. Radebaugh. 2001. *International Business: Environments and Operations*, 9th ed. Upper Saddle River, NJ: Prentice Hall: 495,496.
7. Beamish, P. W., Morrison, A. J., Inkpen, A. C., and P. M. Rosenzweig. 2003. *International Management*. New York: McGraw Hill Irwin: 122.
8. Brouthers, K. D., and G. Nakos. 2004. SME Entry mode choice and performance: A transaction cost perspective. *Entrepreneurship: Theory and Practice* 3:229–247.

Part Three

Area Studies

Chapter Twelve

ENTREPRENEURSHIP AND SECURITY:

THE STATE OF ENTREPRENEURSHIP IN EASTERN EUROPE

Barbara M. Weiss
The University of Tampa, Tampa, Florida

Learning Objectives

Upon completion of this chapter, students should be able to:

- Appreciate risk complexity in a dynamic global system.
- Analyze the effect of political, economic, and societal risk on global entrepreneurship.
- Assess entrepreneurial conditions in Eastern Europe.
- Explore the economic basis of security in a global age.
- Explain the difference between risk-managing and risk-taking capitalism.

Key Terms

economic participation
entrepreneurial capitalism
human security
market sustainability

political participation
risk analysis
risk taking
risk management

◎ Introduction

Entrepreneurship is not only characteristic of market capitalism, but is also an indicator of economic and political participation. The countries of Eastern Europe are moving in different directions in terms of their international relations and market economies. Romania entered the European Union (EU) in 2007, Belarus is merging with Russia, and Ukraine is somewhere in the middle. Poland, Slovenia, and Romania have entered the EU. Serbia, like other prospective EU members, faces the regional group's current enlargement limits and Russia's increasing political and economic influence. This installment of the discussion of global entrepreneurship is based on the notion that the increase of risk-managing capitalism, at the expense of risk-taking capitalism, is destabilizing the international system. It proposes that entrepreneurship, as a measure of economic participation, goes hand-in-hand with political participation. It introduces a market sustainability curve of an optimal environment for risk-taking entrepreneurship and market capitalism that is the economic basis of security.

Even though the interests of elites in industrialized and developing countries have coalesced in favor of globalization, the rest of the world's people are not nearly as unanimously in favor of it. Portfolio and derivative investments and a large share of foreign currency transactions in global financial markets are detached or disassociated from their transaction locus. Risk-managing investment and the securitization thereof effectively "de-link" investor interests from the locus of the investment and therefore the source of the investment's profit.[1] Managing pooled risk by hedging and transferring it through securitization has generated excessive negative risk externalities. If the locus of control over political, cultural, and economic matters shifts too far from the local level, it produces a risk externality, which destabilizes markets.

Globalization tends to be highly uneven in its consequences.[2,3] Many people are not participating in market integration. Globalization has been accompanied by the greater risk of dislocation and financial uncertainty for some workers, families, and communities across the world.[4] If the power of firms and state–firm cooperation becomes so great that it shuts out too many people who want to integrate into international markets, markets will continue to fail. Frequent financial crises of the magnitude of the crisis of 1997 to 1999 could lead to popular movements to limit interdependence, and to a reversal of economic globalization.[3] The shocks of 2001 risked worsening this long-standing marginalization.[5] The long-term effects of the current global economic crisis on market capitalism are unfathomable.

◎ Global Entrepreneurship

Market failure is unnecessary or at least largely avoidable. Sustaining globalization and market capitalism requires ever-broadening market access. Entrepreneurship is synonymous with risk-taking capitalism. Entrepreneurship is a source of long-term economic growth and a key determinant of international competitiveness. The extent to which entrepreneurship is allowed to flourish is akin to liberation. It is an indicator of economic and political participation. Entrepreneurs shape nations.[6] Therefore, the level of entrepreneurship is also indicative of a dynamic civil society and democratization.

The entrepreneurial spirit is innate in human nature. Entrepreneurial culture, and with it the potential for economic growth and development, is everywhere. But it is too often repressed, and risk-taking entrepreneurial capitalism is in short supply.[7] The governments of countries ruled by repressive regimes and their collusive economic interests fear them. Authoritarian regimes respond not only with onerous economic restrictions, but also with political repression, price controls, and expropriation of private assets and state ownership of them. The gain in power from techno-economic progress is being increasingly overshadowed by the production of risks.[8] The consolidation of firms in almost every industry, the resurgence of the state in the wake of market crises, and greater state–firm cooperation increase barriers to entry, reduce market access, and impede innovation.

Entrepreneurialism need not be engendered but unimpeded.[9] Knowledge is the basic ingredient of the innovative process.[10] Knowledge is inherently uncertain and asymmetric.[11] Profiting from it requires taking risk. Entrepreneurship capital is a conduit for knowledge.[11] However, the lack of financing presents an often insurmountable hurdle for start-up firms.

Risk and Human Security

Risk presumes a society that actively tries to break away from its past—the prime characteristic of modern industrial civilization.[2] Technological innovation and capital investment therein have accelerated the rate of economic, political, and social change.

> As the 1990s progressed, it became clear the international marketplace was fraught with economic risks that affected sales and even the most nimble companies found connecting with customers in local markets more challenging than expected. Local competitors proved much tougher than anticipated and local markets stubbornly resisted standardization.[12]

Risk is a complex and interactive phenomenon that involves both (bio) physical attributes and social dimensions.[13] Risk is symptomatic of a lack of knowledge about the course of future events. Human beings have invented the concept of risk to help them to understand and cope with the dangers and uncertainties of life.[14,15]

> Risks are a reflection of human actions and omissions, the expression of highly productive forces. That means the sources of danger are no longer ignorance but knowledge; not a deficient but a perfected mastery over nature; not that which eludes the human grasp but the system of norms and objective constraints established with the industrial epoch.[8]

Risk analysis requires an approach that is capable of illuminating risk in its full complexity, is sensitive to the social settings in which risk occurs, and also recognizes that social interactions may either amplify or attenuate the signals to society about the risk.[13]

A competing notion of "human security" is creeping around the edges of official thinking, suggesting that security be viewed as emerging from the conditions of daily life—food, shelter, employment, health, public safety—rather than flowing downward from a country's foreign relations and military strength.[16]

> With goods, capital, technology, and information now moving more freely, globalization has been proceeding with enormous momentum. At the same time, issues such as environmental degradation, terrorism, violations of human rights, transnational organized crime, illicit drugs, refugees, poverty, and infectious diseases such as AIDS are becoming more severe, moving across borders to directly threaten human survival, daily life, and dignity.[17]

Even in the realm of peace and security, new threats have emerged that go beyond traditional security threats.[18] Russian President Dmitry Medvedev describes corruption and poverty as the main threats to his country's national security.[19]

State security and human security have become intertwined.[20] Citizens bear the burden of war and are generally inclined toward caution; republics, in which citizens' opinions are represented, are therefore less war prone than other forms of government.[21] The basic notion of security is being redefined, placing much more weight on the needs and concerns of human beings and the quality of their environment.[22] Human security expands the traditional notion of security to include protection of human beings from threats. It is based on two premises: (1) freedom from want and (2) freedom from fear.[23] Three common characteristics of physical risks include surrounding uncertainty, significant consequences, and externalities.[24] Risk externalities are a source of uncertainty. The threat of deadly conflict must be tackled at every stage and conflict prevented through a combination of sustained economic growth and development and protection of human rights.[25]

Triangle of Social Space

Where do we look to for support of entrepreneurial capitalism for greater international security? The future does not rest in the state, regions, or globally, but in the minds of individual people everywhere. This is where we will turn next, to the locus of the entrepreneurialism—civil society.

Households own all resources either directly as workers or entrepreneurs or indirectly through their ownership of business corporations.[26]

> Households are the ultimate "shareholders" of the system . . . [They] have always been the ultimate bearers of financial and other risks.[27]

However, the rate of financial risk transfer, from the banking and financial sectors to individuals and families, has increased.[27,28]

International relations are not a matter of states alone; they are relations between peoples.[29] Globalization has brought with it a fundamental change in world politics: States, traditionally seen as the only legitimate players on the international states, have been joined by other stakeholders, such as international organizations, civil society organizations, business actors, and religious actors.[20] There are no dominant structures of cooperation and conflict in a polyarchic system; nation-states, subnational groups, transnational special interests, and communities all vie for the support and loyalty of individuals.[30] Functionalist integration organizes particular layers of social life in accordance with particular human requirements, thereby breaking down the artificialities of zoning arrangements associated with the principle of sovereignty.[31]

The triangle of social space, depicted in Figure 12.1, indicates that market integration is a complex process of state, firm, and civil society interaction that affects the global, regional, and local levels.[32] It traces interaction and locates risk. The vertical two-directional arrows in the triangle of social space traverse all levels to indicate that "all politics (and economics) is local." It opens avenues of participation that avoid pareto optimal redistribution of existing wealth through market access and the creation of new wealth.

Market Sustainability

Market stability and security are prerequisites for market sustainability. Risk reduction and crisis prevention stabilize markets. However, market crises increase the role of the state to stabilize them. In other words, the market's potential for affecting positive change may have the opposite effect—the resurgence of state intervention in the market. Figure 12.2, the market sustainability curve, is an adaptation of the Laffer Curve of the optimal level of taxation beyond which the

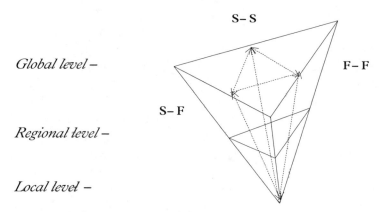

FIGURE 12.1 Triangle of social space

(Adapted from Stopford, J. M., and S. Strange. 1991. Triads of relationships. In Rival States, Rival Firms: Competition for World Market Shares. Cambridge: Cambridge University Press: 22; conceptualization of Sassen 1999; Sum 1999; Keohane, R. O., and J. S. Nye. 2001. *Power and Interdependence: World Politics in Transition*, 3rd ed. New York: Pearson Professional.

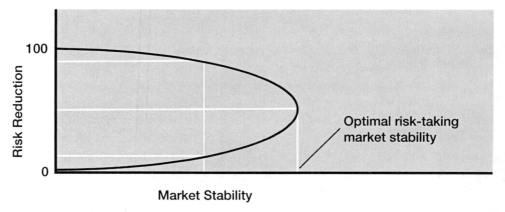

FIGURE 12.2   The Market Sustainability Curve

tax rate becomes a disincentive to work and thereby yields fewer taxes, even though the tax rate is higher.

This figure is another indicator of state presence in the market; in this case, the extent to which the state reduces risk to provide stable market conditions. The state reduces an optimal level of risk to yield the level of market stability at which risk-taking entrepreneurialism can take place. In terms of market access, there is also an optimal economic system for entrepreneurial capitalism, in terms of firm size, the level industry consolidation, barriers to entry, competition, and risk management. When the level of risk reduction exceeds the optimal level, the political and economic system becomes closed, repressive, authoritarian, and limits participation the further along the curve toward one hundred on the vertical axis.

European Entrepreneurship

Political, economic, and societal variables at different levels of the global system affect the level of entrepreneurship. Risk communities have emerged to cope with global financial crises. Policy considerations regarding the desirable risk profile of the household sector involve important cultural, social, and political issues, which are likely to be addressed differently across countries or regions.[27]

EU entrepreneurship has been lackluster because of restrictive government regulations and European workers place a premium on job security.[33] Only half the number of Europeans have thought about starting a business as have Americans.[34] Moreover, Europeans' fear of failure is over two times greater than Americans'.[34] Another limitation of European entrepreneurs is cultural. While the single market has all but eliminated transaction costs, language and consumer preference differences remain, making it international entrepreneurship from the get-go.[35] Lack of finance is another market barrier to European entrepreneurialism.[34] These barriers, together with country differences in the costs of doing business (e.g., business registration, tax rates), complicated legal codes, and an emphasis on risk prevention[36] indicate EU countries place too much emphasis on risk reduction, which threatens regional market sustainability.

Betwixt and Between National Sovereignty

Looking eastward in Europe complicates the regional entrepreneurship picture. The immediate post-Cold War period saw Central European and Asian countries, the former republics of the Soviet Union, reestablish their national sovereignty.

Ever since the collapse of communism in 1989, the eastern half of Europe has been struggling to reach the level of economic, social, and cultural development as the west. The ruinous legacy of one party rule and planned economies was daunting. Everything from the rule of law to competitive companies needed to be rebuilt (in the case of central European countries or constructed from scratch) for those whose pre-communist experience was of autocracy and feudalism.[37]

Map 12.1, Eastern Europe, outlines the seven Eastern European countries included in this discussion. They are, for the most part, located from north to south in the eastern part of Eastern Europe with the exception of Slovenia and Serbia. A number of these countries have not radically privatized—indeed, have renationalized—their economies.[38] It has yielded rent-seeking economic interests. State-owned enterprises (SOE) and collective agriculture remain dominant. An entrepreneurial culture exists, but has emerged with only varying degrees of success.

MAP 12.1

Eastern Europe.

Courtesy maps.com

Political Risk

The list of political risk variables in Figure 12.3, while not exhaustive, provides information about the current political systems in the seven Eastern European countries. Business Monitor International assesses short- and long-term economic and political risks. Slovenia has little political risk, although it is expected to increase in the long-term. Political risk in Poland and Romania is moderate in the short-term and expected to decline in the long-term. Russia's political risk is expected to increase in the long-term. Serbia and Ukraine, while relatively risky in the short-term, are not expected to change their political risk level in the long-run. The failed states index of 177 countries compiled by the Fund for Peace assesses the strength of state according to twelve indicators (four economic, two social, and six political) indicates the strongest states are the EU members, Slovenia, Poland, and Romania.[39] They rank 156th, 145th, and 128th, respectively. The weakest state is Belarus at 53rd. The remaining states, Serbia, Russia, and Ukraine rank 70th, 72nd, and 108th, respectively.

In terms of the economic aspects of political risk, the sovereign credit ratings (i.e., foreign and local currencies) of the seven countries are ranked by Moody's as at least "stable." Belarus and Ukraine have the lowest credit rating of B1. Next come Romania at Baa3 and Russia at Baa1. The most creditworthy country is Slovenia, followed by Poland. In terms of fiscal discipline, as measured by gross government general debt as a percentage of GDP, Slovenia and Russia have the leanest government budgets (data for Belarus is suspect) at 23 and 26% of GDP, respectively. The rest of the countries fared quite a bit worse at between 44 to 46% of GDP.

		Belarus	Rank	Poland	Rank	Romania	Rank	Russia	Rank	Serbia	Rank	Slovenia	Rank	Ukraine	Rank
Political Risk	Short-term	na		71.5	61	69.4	73	72.7	59	42.7	125	86.7	12	47.3	121
	Long-term	na		78.4	29	74.6	39	54.3	97	44.5	117	75.3	35	42.5	123
	Failed States Index	84.4	53	47.6	145	59.9	128	79.7	72	80.1	70	37.1	156	70.8	108
Soverign credit rating			Outlook		Outlook		Outlook		Outlook		Outlook		Outlook		Outlook
	Foreign currency	B1	Stable	A2	Stable	Baa3	Stable	Baa1	Positive	na		Aa2	Positive	B1	Stable
	Local currency	B1	Stable	A2	Stable	Baa3	Stable	Baa1	Positive	na		Aa2	Positive	B1	Stable
Fiscal Discipline	Gross General Government Debt [or Total Debt]/GDP	16.6	2006	44.2	2007	45.6	2006	26.3	2006	43.5	2006	23.4		46.3	2006
Corruption	Corruption Perception Index	2.0	151	4.6	58	3.8	70	2.1	147	3.4	85	6.7	26	2.5	134
Press Freedom		91	188 Not Free	24	51 Free	44	94 Partly Free	78	170 Not Free	39	84 Partly Free	23	46 Free	53	110 Partly Free

Risk rank	Group level	Low risk	1	2	Medium risk	3	4	5	High risk	6	7

FIGURE 12.3 Political Risk Variables

(From Political Risk (short- and long-term), http://www.businessmonitor.com; Failed States Index, The Fund for Peace—Failed States Index Scores 2008; Sovereign credit rating, "Sovereign Ratings List," http://www.Moodys.com, October 28, 2008; Fiscal discipline, World Bank—HNPStats—Country at; Corruption, http://www.transparency.org/policy_research/surveys_indices/cpi; Press Freedom, http://www.freedomhouse.org/uploads/fop08/FOTP2008Tables.pdf.)

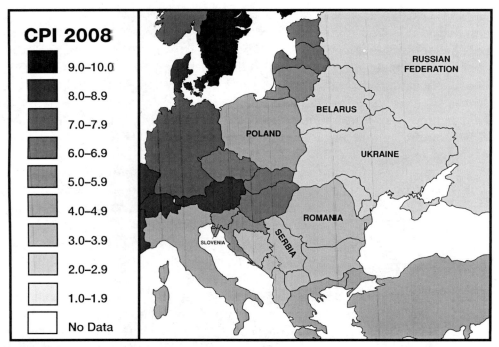

FIGURE 12.4 Corruption Perception Index

(Reprinted from Corruption Perception Index. Copyright 2008 Transparency International: the global coalition against corruption. Used with permission. For more information, visit http://www.transparency.org)

The next political risk variable in first table is the corruption perception index, which ranks the perceived level of corruption in 180 countries. Figure 12.4, the corruption perception index, listed above, indicates the disparity of the perceived level government corruption is widest in Eastern Europe.[40] Officialdom chokes business; corruption is stubbornly entrenched.[41] According to the Transparency International 2008 Survey, the farther east you go in Eastern Europe, the more corrupt the government is perceived to be. The Russian Federation, Belarus, and Ukraine are perceived to be the most corrupt, followed by Romania and Serbia, then Poland, and lastly, Slovenia.

The final political risk variable, the level of press freedom in 2008, as measured by Freedom House in 195 countries, is concerning. Media is restricted in every country except Slovenia and Poland. The press is partly free in Serbia, Romania, and Ukraine and not free in Russia and Belarus.

Pipeline politics have long affected countries in the region and their international relations, even when market prices did not affect the resource market.[42] The political risk of the resource industry risk is increasingly evident since the rise in energy prices since 2004. The closer to Russia and its natural gas and oil transit routes, the greater the overall (political, economic, and societal) risk. The map located on the International Energy Administration Web site shows the network of natural gas and oil pipelines in the region.*

---

*(From International Energy Administration, U.S. Department of Energy, EIA—International Energy Data and Analysis, Russia Energy Data, Statistics and Analysis—Oil, Gas, Electricity, Coal, Energy Information Administration, U.S. Department of Energy.)

The Druzhba (Friendship) oil pipeline, one of the world's largest and longest, began to deliver unrefined oil to Central Europe in 1962. Branches of the pipeline transit through Belarus and Ukraine. Belarus gets around 400,000 barrels per day (bbl/d) of Druzhba crude oil for its two refineries.[43] Eighty percent of Russia's natural gas bound for Western Europe flows through Ukraine.[44] Russia has cut gas and oil supplies to Europe via Ukraine and Belarus. The coming online of the North Stream Pipeline will divert gas flows away from Ukraine and Belarus to through the Baltic Sea directly to Germany.[45] This may portend lessening risk in Ukraine and Belarus.

Russia and Serbia are traditional allies. Russia's Gazprom supplies Serbia with 90% of its natural gas. It plans to make Serbia the hub of its South Stream Pipeline.[45] Gazprom, Russia's state owned monopoly, also plans to buy a controlling interest in Serbia's state oil and gas industry.[45]

Economic Risk

Table 12.1 shows the sectoral composition of the seven Eastern European countries. Eastern European economies are representative of newly developing economies. The service sector accounts for less than 70% of GDP, manufacturing for over 30% of GDP, and agriculture for over 5% of GDP. From this table it appears the Serbian economy has the largest agricultural and service sectors and the smallest manufacturing sector. Poland and Romania have relatively important service economies. Belarus, Russia, and Ukraine have similar economic structures. Belarus and Russia have comparatively small service sectors and the largest manufacturing sectors. Ukraine has more service industries and less manufacturing and agriculture than the other two countries. Slovenia has relatively strong manufacturing and service economies and the smallest agricultural sector. Poland and Russia also have small agricultural sectors.

Figure 12.5 continues the risk analysis begin in the first table. The *World Economic Outlook Database* reports the seven countries account for over 5% of the

TABLE 12.1 Economic Structure

	% OF GDP	AGRICULTURE	INDUSTRY	SERVICES
Belarus	2006	8.8	39.9	51.3
Poland	2007	4.3	29.9	65.9
Romania	2006	8.3	26.4	65.4
Russia	2007	4.8	38.6	56.7
Serbia	2006	12.0	20.0	68.0
Slovenia	2007	2.0	34.0	63.0
Ukraine	2007	7.4	32.1	60.5
Average		**6.8**	**31.6**	**61.5**

(From World Bank—HNPStats —Country at Corruption, http://www.transparency.org/policy_research/surveys_indices/cpi; Press Freedom, http://www.freedomhouse.org/uploads/fop08/FOTP 2008Tables.pdf.)

	Belarus	Rank	Poland	Rank	Romania	Rank	Russia	Rank	Serbia	Rank	Slovenia	Rank	Ukraine	Rank
PPP GDP (2008) Billions Current International Dollars	117.527		669.032		272.881		2,285.21		80.717		58.151		349.982	
World Share (%) (2008; 5.343%)	0.165		0.969		0.386		3.241		na		0.084		0.498	
Current Account/GDP (%), 2008	-5.943		-4.724		-13.802		6.482		-18.57		-4.694		-7.193	
Gross Domestic Savings/GDP	18.9	2007	20.5	2007	9.6	2007	33.0	2007	4.8	2007	na		18.8	
Gross Capital Formation/GDP	28.0	2007	21.5	2007	22.4	2007	24.5	2007	25.1	2007	na		22.4	
Economic risk Short-term	na		65.0	65	69.0	53	75.2	33	50.6	102	77.5	24	62.1	72
Long-term	na		63.8	47	60.5	60	73.5	14	47.8	97	69.8	31	60.2	61
Public sector	Q2'08	1Qt'08	9'08	1Au'08	2007		2007							
Reserves (US$ millions)	124.7	-334	74,226	-7,373	39,423	2007	476,391	2007	13,772	2007	993.05	Aug-08	28,426	2007
Private sector "Economic Freedom"	44.7	150	59.5	83	61.5	68	49.9	134	na	na	60.6	75	51.1	133
Ease of "Doing Business"		85		76		47		120		94		54		145
Registering Property		14		84		114		49		97		104		140
Getting Credit		109		28		12		109		28		84		28
Protecting Investors		104		38		38		88		70		18		142
Enforcing contracts		14		68		31		18		96		79		49

Risk rank **Group level** Low risk 1 2 Medium risk 3 4 5 High risk 6 7

FIGURE 12.5 Economic Risk Variables

(From PPP GDP and Current Account/GDP, WEO Database; Gross Domestic Savings/GDP and Gross Capital Formation/GDP, World Bank - HNPStats - Country at Corruption, http://www.transparency.org/policy_research/surveys_indices/cpi; Press Freedom, http://www.freedomhouse.org/uploads/fop08/FOTP2008Tables.pdf.) Economic Risk, http://www.businessmonitor.com—Public sector reserves, Central bank websites; "Economic Freedom," Index of Economic Freedom 2008, Heritage Foundation; "Ease of Doing Business, Registering Property, Getting Credit, Protecting Investors, Enforcing Contracts," Rankings—Doing Business—The World Bank Group.)

world's purchasing power parity gross domestic product (PPP GDP) in 2008. There is also great disparity in the relative economic size of the seven countries. The largest economy by far is Russia, followed by Poland, Ukraine and Romania, Belarus, Serbia, and Slovenia. Poland's economy is about a third the size of Russia's, Ukraine about half the size, and Romania about a third the size of Poland. Serbia and Slovenia are about 30% and 20% the size of Romania, respectively.

The countries with the largest current account deficits, in terms of GDP, are Serbia, followed by Romania, Ukraine, Belarus, Poland, and Slovenia. Russia has a substantial current account surplus. The level of domestic savings, as a percentage of GDP, is Russia, Poland, Belarus, and Ukraine, followed by Romania and Serbia. The rate of domestic capital investment is between 22% and 28% in the seven Eastern European countries. It is highest in Belarus, Serbia, and Russia, followed by Romania and Ukraine and Poland.

Business Monitor International's measure of short- and long-term economic risks tends to rank the economic risk of Eastern European market higher than in other emerging markets. Short-term economic risk is the lowest in Slovenia and Russia. The long-term economic risk of both countries is expected to decline a bit. The economic risk of the other five countries is higher and is forecast to remain almost the same in the short- and long-term.

The results of the World Banks' "Doing Business" 2009 survey of 191 countries between April 2007 and June 2008 continues to illustrate diversity among the seven Eastern European countries. While Romania and Slovenia are ranked overall as good places to do business, a closer look at individual variables (i.e., registering property, getting credit, protecting investors, and enforcing contracts) presents a different picture. Romania and Slovenia are not perceived to be good places to register property. Slovenia is not a very good place to enforce contracts or get credit. Perhaps surprisingly, Belarus and Russia are perceived to be good places to register property.

The United Nations Conference on Trade and Development (UNCTAD), *World Investment Report* (WIR), includes a transnationality index that measures the importance of inward foreign direct investment (FDI) to host country's economies (e.g., gross fixed capital formation, value added, employment). The transnationality index available on the UNCTAD.ORG Web site shows FDI was as important in Romania, Poland, Slovenia, and Ukraine as it was in the rest of Europe in 2005.* Only Serbia, Russia, and Belarus do not host FDI to the extent that it affects the domestic economy.

Societal Risk

Figure 12.6 provides insight into the lives of the citizens of these seven countries. The combined population of the seven Eastern European countries is under 270 million people. Their PPP GDP per capita is varied with the consumers of tiny Slovenia the most well-off. Poland and Russia follow with about 60% of the per capita GDP of Slovenia. Romanians and Belarusians have comparable annual GDP per capitas, at less than half of Slovenians'. Serbians earn about a third the income of Slovenians and the people of Ukraine receive only 25% of the per capita income of those in Slovenia.

	Belarus	Rank	Poland	Rank	Romania	Rank	Russia	Rank	Serbia	Rank	Slovenia	Rank	Ukraine	Rank
Population (millions)	9.7	2007	38.1	2007	21.5	2007	141.6	2007	7.4	2007	2.0	Oct-08	46.3	2007
PPP GDP per capita, 2008 (Current International Dollars)	12,344		17,560		12,698		16,161		10,911		28,894		7,634	
Unemployment rate (% of total labor force)	na		6.7	Aug-08	5.9	Q2 2008	5.3	Sep-08	18.8	Jul-08	4.2	Aug-08	1.8	Aug-08
Consumer Price Index (annual % change, 2008)	15.3		4.0		8.2		14.0		10.7		5.9		25.3	
Human Development Index (HDI)	0.804	64	0.870	37	0.813	60	0.802	67	na	na	0.917	27	0.788	76
Internal refugees	4.3		3.0		3.5		5.4		7.3		1.7		3.2	
Life expectancy	68.7	2001-05	75.2	2000-05	71.9	2000-05	65.0	2000-05	73.6	2000-05	77.4	2000-05	67.7	2000-05

Risk rank	Group level	Low risk	1	2	Medium risk	3	4	5	High risk	6	7

FIGURE 12.6 Societal Risk Variables

(Reprinted with permission of United Nations from World Investment Report.)

---

*(From WIR2008—Transnational Corporations and the Infrastructure Challenge. *World Investment Report 2008*. Geneva and New York: United Nations, 2008: 12, UNCTAD.ORG.)

The unemployment rate in Serbia was very high in September 2008, at almost 19%. Unemployment data was unavailable for Belarus and unreliable for Ukraine. Unemployment in the remaining countries ranged between 4.2% and 6.7% in the third quarter of 2008. The human development index (HDI) that weighs per capita GDP with qualitative indicators of development such as education, health care, life expectancy, etc., indicates the quality of life is very high in Slovenia, low in Poland, and much lower in Romania, Belarus, Russia, and especially Ukraine. HDI data for Serbia is not available. The highest life expectancy is not surprisingly in comparatively wealthy Slovenia.

A summary look at the color-coded group level political risk ranking in Figure 12.3 indicates that Slovenia and Poland are good business opportunities. A summary look at the color-coded group level economic risk ranking in the Figure 12.5 indicates that Russia and Poland are good business opportunities. A summary look at the color-coded group level societal risk ranking in Figure 12.6 indicates that Slovenia and Poland are good business opportunities. However, this is only a preliminary look at business opportunities in Eastern Europe.

In Russia, for example, risk analysis does not capture the full effect of its resource industry. Gazprom is Russia.[45] It provided a quarter of the 2007 state budget, supplies the country's reserves, and funds one of the world's largest sovereign wealth funds (SWFs). Gazprom was the world's third biggest company until the financial crisis, which cut its share value by about 75%.[45] It is the engine of Russia's foreign policy, especially the flow of energy supplies to Europe whether from Russia or elsewhere (i.e., the Caspian Sea region through Georgia and Libya).[46–48] Gazprom has blocked major foreign investment in its operations (even as it buys European utilities supplying gas directly to consumers).[45] It is also cultivating Western energy companies to act as lobbyists for Russian interests.[45]

The Case of Belarus

The hostile environment facing Belarusian entrepreneurs is well documented. The general consensus on entrepreneurship in Belarus is that it's hopeless, a basket case. The authoritarian rule and the highjacking of democracy have neither snuffed out market initiative, nor the will to take it. A visit from Belarusian entrepreneurs and the stories they told of overwhelming odds they face and yet persevere, attest to this.[49]

After an initial surge of capital reform from 1991 to 1994, including the privatization of state-owned enterprises (SOEs), institutions of private property, and development of entrepreneurship, Belarus under Lukashenko has greatly slowed, and in many cases reversed, its pace of privatization and other market reforms, emphasizing the need for a "socially oriented market economy."[50] Entrepreneurship represents a threat not only to large Belarusian economic interests, but also to political powers that be. Table 12.2 lists the responses to two questions in a 2007 survey conducted by the Institute for Privatization Management (IPM) in Minsk. The managers of small and medium enterprises, a proxy for entrepreneurship, prefer by more than 2:1, entry into the European Union (EU) to a closer partnership with Russia.

Belarus' first president, Alexander Lukashenko, a former state farm director, has been in power since 1994. He has long overstayed his welcome, according to constitutional term limits. President Lukashenko has steadily consolidated power in the executive branch through authoritarian means and dominates all branches of government.[51] Corruption, inefficiency, and political interference in the judiciary are prevalent.[52]

> The president appoints six of the 12 members of the Constitutional Court, including the chairman and the chairman of the Supreme Court and the Supreme Economic court. He also has the authority to appoint and dismiss all district and military judges.[53]

President Lukashenko has sought to develop closer ties with Russia for much of his career.[54] Minsk is the capitol of the Commonwealth of Independent States (CIS). An informal Russia–Belarus Union has been in effect since the 1990s. The Belarusian economy has been dependent on heavy discounts of oil and natural gas prices of imports from Russia and re-export of oil and natural gas at world market prices, using windfall profits to subsidize state enterprises.[50] Russia cut energy supplies to Belarus in 2006 until Minsk agreed with Russia's Gazprom in December 2006 to more than double the price it pays for Russian natural gas.[54] Belarus received a $1.5 billion stabilization loan from Russia.[50] Gazprom will, in turn, gradually acquire a 50% stake in Beltransgaz, the Belarusian gas pipeline firm.[50] According to a stated plan of the Belarusian government to pass along Russia's price rises to European customers, Belarus raised the prices for Russian oil transit to Poland, Germany, and Ukraine by 22.5% in January 2009.[55]

TABLE 12.2 IPM SME Survey Results—2007

RELATIONSHIP WITH RUSSIA	
Build a partnership while retaining national sovereignty	64.9%
Become a political and economic union of independent states	31.2%
Form a federation	3.2%
	99.3%

EU ENTRY	
Yes	67.6%
No	30.2%
	97.8%

(From Survey results. IPM Research Center. Research. Forecasts. Monitoring. Minsk. Belarus.)

TABLE12.3 Ethnic Composition

Belarusian	81.2%
Russian	11.4%
Polish	3.9%
Ukranian	2.4%
	98.9%

Data source: "Background Notes: Belarus," U.S. Department of State, Bureau of European and Eurasian Affairs, 2/08: 1.

Belarusian ethnicity is distinct from Russia (see Table 12.3). About 400,000 ethnic Poles live in the west of Belarus.[54] However, Belarus has a weak sense of national identity.[56] Even though Belarusians fear class division,[57] Belarusian society is oppressed. For example, all Internet service providers in Belarus operate through a state-controlled portal.[50]

Belarus was one of the most prosperous parts of the Union of Soviet Socialist Republics (USSR); its industry was relatively well-developed, it had a broad agricultural base, a high education level, and one of the highest standards of living.[50,54,58] But with independence in 1991 came economic decline.[54] Virtually unreformed, 75% to 80% of Belarus' economy is in state hands.[59] Belarus wants to avoid the mistakes made by neighboring Russia and Ukraine in the early 1990s, when hundreds of enterprises were asset-stripped and sold at bargain basement prices.[59] The government under Lukashenko has renationalized companies, including banks, which had been privatized after independence, using the so-called "Golden Share" mechanism.[54] Administrative price regulation continued in January 2008.[60] But later in the year, in an apparent policy reversal, the Belarusian government hosted its first Belarus Investment Forum in November 2008. The Belarusian Prime Minister, Sergei Sidorsky, announced a list of some 600 companies slated for privatization, as well as plans to streamline business regulations and reform the tax code.[59]

Belarus is a key transport hub, is a source of cheap and skilled labor and huge fresh water reserves, and prides itself on its organic way of life.[59] Its main industries are agricultural equipment (i.e., tractors), motorcycles, chemicals, fertilizer, textiles, and consumer goods. Its major trading partners are Russia, Germany, Ukraine, and Poland. Western investors are reportedly more eagerly awaited than Russian investors.[59]

Summary

Societies balance between tradition and change, confidence and uncertainty, tolerance and intolerance, competitiveness and complacency, security and insecurity. Innovation—"building a better mouse trap"—self-determination, independence, and living a better life motivate entrepreneurs as much as profit. Global entrepreneurship is vulnerable. Long-term market instability and marginalization and economic deprivation lead to a "crabs in a barrel" mentality and reactionary populism.

Political economies may teeter between being liberal and being controlled. The concurrence of economic and political participation implies the obvious: that political oppression suppresses risk-taking. The development and growth of a market economy, the point at which risk-taking entrepreneurship becomes central to the process of economic growth and development, flourishes in democratic political systems.

The current environment explains the problems of global entrepreneurship. Regional responses to global financial crises lead to risk communities. Globalization in an age of high energy prices, market crises, and power politics by states *and* firms is very evident in Eastern Europe. This survey of the state of entrepreneurship in Eastern European countries yields the full complexity of the risks of international business, especially global entrepreneurship. Assessing risk at the local level, as indicated by the level of entrepreneurship, is a complex and ongoing process. The accuracy, reliability, comprehensiveness, and timeliness of the data are all important. Ongoing, proactive, and objective "what-if" scenario and contingency planning are also necessary.

Political oppression and predatory capitalism—volatility-inducing speculation, oligopolistic/monopolistic market control, extortionist wealth maximization—threaten society in equal measure and are therefore threats that should be avoided everywhere and at all times. Finding the point where institutional constraints (i.e., political, economic, societal) give way to open markets is essential and therefore a goal of future research. Determining whether or not this is happening is also important. We will then be able to assess the viability and sustainability of a risk-taking society and democratic peace.

Discussion Questions

1. What is the relationship between entrepreneurship and globalization?
2. Describe market conditions and the "state of entrepreneurship" in Eastern Europe.
3. Rank each Eastern European country discussed here according to their respective levels of entrepreneurial business risk. Explain the criteria for the ranking. What are the opportunities and risks of entrepreneurship in the region in each country?
4. In which industries in Eastern Europe is it best to start a business?
5. How do the EU and Russia affect entrepreneurship in Eastern Europe?

Endnotes

1. International Monetary Fund. 2001. *International Capital Markets*. Washington, DC: International Monetary Fund.
2. Giddens, A. 2000. *Runaway World: How Globalization Is Reshaping Our Lives*. New York: Routledge.
3. Keohane, R. O., and J. S. Nye. 2001. *Power and Interdependence: World Politics in Transition*, 3rd ed. New York: Pearson Professional.
4. G8 Summit Communiqué. 1999. Köln, Germany. http://www.library.utoronto.ca/g7/summit/1999koln/finalcom.htm.

5. Economist 2/2/02, 66.
6. China startups: Five entrepreneurs shaping a nation. *NYSE* Second Quarter (2008): 14–21.
7. Personal communication. 2008. Jack Flynn, President, FGX International.
8. Beck, U. 1992. *Risk Society: Towards a New Modernity*. London, Thousand Oaks, and New Delhi: Sage.
9. Ireland, R. D., Tihanyi, L., and J. W. Webb. 2008. A tale of two politico-economic systems: Implications for entrepreneurship in central and Eastern Europe. *Entrepreneurship Theory and Practice* 32:107.
10. Dosi, G., Llerena, P., and M. S. Labini. 2005. Science-technology-industry links and the "European paradox": Some notes on the dynamics of scientific and technological research in Europe. LEM Paper 2005/02. Pisa: Laboratory of Economics and Management, Sant'Anna School of Advanced Studies.
11. Audretsch, D. B., Thurik, R., Kwaak, T., and N. Bosma. 2003. *SMEs in Europe 2003*. European Commission, Observatory of European SMEs 7.
12. Forteza, J. H., and G. L. Neilson. 1999. Multinationals in the next decade. *Strategy + Business* 16. http://www.strategy-business.com/best practice/99303/page1.html.
13. Kasperson, J. X., and R. E. Kasperson. 1996. The social amplification and attenuation of risk. In *Challenges in Risk Assessment and Risk Management*. Kunreuther, H., and P. Slovic, eds. Thousand Oaks, CA: Sage Periodicals Press: 95–105.
14. Kunreuther, H., and P. Slovic. 1996. *Challenges in Risk Assessment and Risk Management*. Thousand Oaks, CA: Sage Periodicals Press: 119.
15. Kunreuther, H., and P. Slovic. 1996. discuss risk in the context of decision-making by institutional risk managers (i.e., industry and government) on health, safety, and environmental issues.
16. Mathews, J. T. 1997. Power shift. *Foreign Affairs* 76: 50–66.
17. *Diplomatic Bluebook*. 1999. Tokyo: Japanese Ministry of Foreign Affairs (MOFA).
18. The Final Report of The Helsinki Process on Globalisation and Democracy: A Case for Multi-Stakeholder Cooperation. 3 October 2008, http://www.helsinkiprocess.fi/netcomm/ImgLib/33/257/HP08_report_web.pdf.
19. Corruption, Poverty Threatening Russia's Security: Medvedev. *ABC News*, 25 June 2008. http://www.abc.net.au/news/stories/2008/06/25/2286081.htm.
20. The Final Report of The Helsinki Process on Globalisation and Democracy: A Case for Multi-Stakeholder Cooperation. 3 October 2008, http://www.helsinkiprocess.fi/netcomm/ImgLib/33/257/HP08_report_web.pdf.
21. York: Macmillan, [1795] 1957: 12f, in Beate Jahn. 2005. Kant, Mill, and Illiberal Legacies in International Affairs. *International Organization* 59(40):180.
22. Development Assistance Committee (DAC) Report. 1995. Organization of Economic Cooperation and Development (OECD): 18.
23. We the Peoples: The Role of United Nations in the 21st Century. 2000. United Nations. http://www.un.org/millennium/sg/report/summ.htm.
24. Zeckhauser, R. J., and W. K. Viscusi. 1996. The risk management dilemma. In *Challenges in risk assessment and risk management*. Kunreuther, H., and P. Slovic, eds. Thousand Oaks, CA: Sage Periodicals Press: 144–155.
25. We the Peoples: The Role of United Nations in the 21st Century. 2000. United Nations. http://www.un.org/millennium/sg/report/summ.htm.
26. McConnell & Bure 2005, 36.
27. Groome, T., Blancher, N., Haas, et al. 2006. The limits of market-based risk transfer and implications for managing systemic risk. IMF Working Paper WP/06/217.
28. de Rato, R. 2007. Responding to Shifts in Financial Risk: The Need for Leadership. Speech to the Wharton School, University of Pennsylvania, 23 March 2007. http://www.imf.org/external/np/speeches/2007/032307.htm.
29. Annan, K. Address to the General Assembly. United Nations, 19 September 2006. http://www.un.org/webcast/ga/61/pdfs/sgstatement_to_the_ga06.pdf.
30. Brown, S. 1974. New Forces in World Politics. Washington, DC: Brookings Institution: 186 in Nye, J. S. 1988. Neorealism and neoliberalism. *World Politics* 40:236.
31. Claude, I. L. 1971. *Swords into Ploughshares: The Problems and Prospects of International Organization*, 4th ed. New York: Random House.
32. Weiss, B. *Risk and security*: The political economy of investment and market integration. Manuscript being revised for publication. The 'triangle of social space' figure is part of Chapter 3, States, firms, and market integration: Constructing international organization," which has been submitted for publication as a journal article.
33. Woolsey, M. 2005. Lackluster entrepreneurship in the EU. *Forbes* 10 October 2005. http://www.forbes.com/2006/10/09/france-germany-taxes-ent-fin-cx_mw_1010european.html.
34. Entrepreneurship survey of the EU (25 member states), United States, Iceland and Norway: Summary. 2007. Flash EB Series # 192. Organized and Managed by the Eurobarometer Team of the European Commission, Conducted by The Gallup Organization. Fieldwork: January 2007, Report: April 2007.

35. Attitudes towards the planned EU pilot project. Erasmus for young entrepreneurs. 2007. Flash EB Series # 212. Organized and Managed by the Eurobarometer Team of the European Commission, Conducted by The Gallup Organization. Fieldwork: October 2007, Report: November 2007.

36. Third Report on Economic and Social Cohesion: A New Partnership for Cohesion, Convergence, Competitiveness, Cooperation. Commission of the European Communities 18 February 2004: xxvi. http://ec.europa.eu/regional_policy/sources/docoffic/official/reports/pdf/cohesion3/cohesion3_conclusion_en.pdf.

37. Who's next? *Economist.com* 23 October 2008. http://www.economist.com.

38. Ivanova, Y. V. 2004. Belarus: Entrepreneurial activities in an unfriendly environment. *Journal of East-West Business* 10:30.

39. The Fund for Peace. Failed States Index, 2008. http://www.fundforpeace.org/web/index.php?option=com_content&task=view&id=99&Itemid=140.

40. Transparency International. Corruption Perception Index, 2008. http://www.transparency.org/policy_research/surveys_indices/cpi/2008.

41. The Economist 10/28/08.

42. Prybyla, J. S. 1963. Eastern Europe and Soviet Oil. *The Journal of Industrial Economics* 13:154–167.

43. Factbox—Russia's Druzhba Pipeline. *Reuters*, 8 January 2007. http://uk.reuters.com.

44. Feifer, G. Gazprom and Russia's Foreign Policy. National Public Radio, 5–7 January 2009. http://www.npr.org/templates/story/story.php?storyId=99026745.

45. Feifer, G. Gazprom and Russia's Foreign Policy. National Public Radio, 5–7 January 2009. http://www.npr.org/templates/story/story.php?storyId=99026745.

46. Kovalev, V. Gazprom's Power Play. *Business Week*, 6 March 2007. http://www.businessweek.com/globalbiz/content/mar2007/gb20070306_599860.htm?campaign_id=rss_daily.

47. Macalister, T. Russia's Power Play in Europe. *The Guardian*, 12 April 2007. http://www.guardian.co.uk/world/2007/apr/12/business.russia.

48. Gazprom and the Struggle for Power. *The Independent*, 7 January 2009. http://www.independent.co.uk/news/business/analysis-and-features/gazprom-and-the-struggle-for-power-1230068.html.

49. Women Entrepreneurs and Small Business Development: A Project for Belarus. International Visitor Leadership Program, Office of International Visitors, Bureau of Educational and Cultural Affairs, U.S. Department of State, 10–28 September 2007.

50. Background Note: Belarus. U.S. Department of State, Bureau of European and Eurasian Affairs, February 2008: 3–5. http://www.state.gov.

51. Background Note: Belarus. U.S. Department of State, Bureau of European and Eurasian Affairs, February 2008: 1. http://www.state.gov.

52. Country Report on Human Rights in Belarus. U.S. Department of State, Bureau of Democracy, Human Rights, and Labor, 11 March 2008: 4. http://www.state.gov.

53. Country Report on Human Rights in Belarus. U.S. Department of State, Bureau of Democracy, Human Rights, and Labor, 11 March 2008: 4. http://www.state.gov.

54. BBC news.

55. Belarus Raises Prices for Russian Oil Transit. Russia-InfoCentre, 8 January 2008. http://www.russia-ic.com/news/show/7631/.

56. Country Profile: Belarus. *BBC News*. http://newsvote.bbc.co.uk.

57. Miazhevich, G. 2007. Official Media Discourse and the Self-Representation of Entrepreneurs in Belarus. *Europe-Asia Studies* 59: 1338.

58. Although 70 per cent of the nuclear fallout from the Chernobyl, Ukraine nuclear power plant accident in 1986 landed on Belarusian territory and about 20% of Belarusian land remains contaminated. Background Note: Belarus. U.S. Department of State, Bureau of European and Eurasian Affairs, February 2008: 5. http://www.state.gov.

59. Denysenko, M. Belarus Comes in from the Cold. *BBC News*, 21 November 2008. http://news.bbc.co.uk/2/low/europe/7741201.stm.

60. Tochitskeya et al. 1/2008, 4.

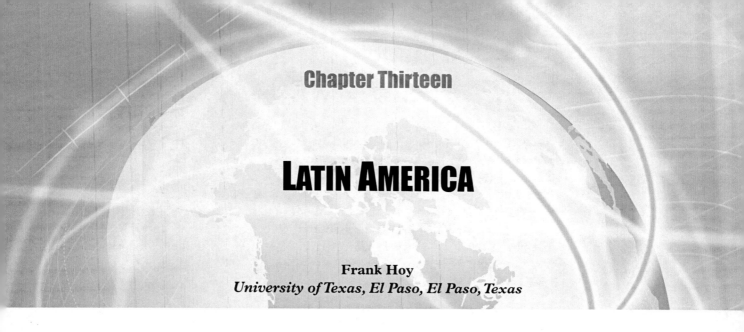

Chapter Thirteen

LATIN AMERICA

Frank Hoy
University of Texas, El Paso, El Paso, Texas

Learning Objectives

Upon completion of this chapter, students should be able to:

- Understand the environment presented to an entrepreneur interested in Latin America: history, geography, and language; government and legal system; economic structure; culture and religion; educational system; demographics and physical infrastructure; industrial structure; trade agreements and associations; and import/export information and small business practices.

Key Terms

CAFTA	neoliberalism
family roles	privatization
import substitution industrialization	property rights
NAFTA	

⊙ Introduction

Latin America is a region of great diversity, yet with some remarkable consistencies as related to political and economic history and conditions. Although other factors have been at play, it is primarily through politics, cultures, and economics that we can comprehend the environments for entrepreneurship across Latin America.

This is a region that stretches from Mexico, through Central America, into South America, and down to the Southern Cone. Many island countries of the Caribbean Basin are also considered part of Latin America due to historic colonization and language dominance.

History, Geography, and Languages[i]

Archeologists peg the first migrations from Asia to the Americas at approximately 35,000 years ago. Tribal groups concentrated in the Pacific Northwest for eons, with initial incursions into South America occurring 25,000 years later. Nomadic tribes began small crop development, eventually evolving into city and regional states in many areas. By the time of European colonization, two predominant empires had arisen: the Incas in what is now Peru and neighboring countries and the Aztecs in modern day Mexico.

The indigenous populations throughout were severely depleted following the European conquest beginning in the sixteenth century. War, disease, enslavement, and dislocation had disastrous effects. The early economies resulting from European settlement were labeled hacienda forms of land use. This practice combined Iberian and American Indian systems. Many pre-Columbian Indians were clustered in communal villages loosely governed by absentee aristocratic landlords. The Spaniards overlaid this system through huge royal land grants. They imposed taxes, but were expected to protect the natives and educate them in the Catholic faith.

Conquest and colonization were led by Spain and Portugal, countries speaking romance languages derived from Latin, hence the term Latin America. A third romance-language country, France, bequeathed its language to Haiti, French Guiana, and the French West Indies. Despite the decimation of the Indians described above, many tribal groups flourish to this day and use their native languages. At least fifty distinct language groups are identified in modern day Mexico alone.

The large landholding systems survived through revolutionary periods as the various colonies in Latin America won their independence from the Europeans. *Criollos*, American-born descendants of Europeans, emerged as the political and economic elite, controlling indigenous populations through the *hacienda* system.

---

i. Unless otherwise indicated, the source of information on Latin America is the *New Encyclopædia Britannica*, 2002.

Resources for export and domestic use were in the hands of large landowners. Eventually, industrialization began to change the political and economic environments of the continent in the nineteenth century.

The map showing the nations of Latin America looks today much as it did in the post-revolutionary period of the 1800s. There is extraordinary variation in the geography of the Americas. The Western Hemisphere from Mexico to Chile contains islands as well as the continental land mass. Beginning with oceans on both sides of the continent, to lowlands, high plains, volcanoes, highlands, and mountain ranges, the region consists of deserts, tropical rain forests, temperate zones, and more. Until recent advances in transportation, communication, and information technology, opportunities for entrepreneurs were defined and often restricted by the geography of the location of their enterprise. Even today, the dominance of the micro-enterprises in the small business sector results in local firms using local resources to satisfy local needs.

Government and Legal Systems

Following colonial exploitation, Latin America splintered into multiple nations, often controlled by political, military, and economic elites. There was a continuation of the suppression and deprivation of the indigenous populations. The earliest constitutions were adopted in the beginning of the nineteenth century and were designed for representative governments. The failures of these initial governments led to greater centralization of political power.

Latin American countries have been characterized by frequent changes in government, although the underlying political structures may have evolved in very different ways. For some, the shape of governance derived from revolution. Examples are Bolivia, Cuba, and Mexico. Others have been affected by extended periods of military rule. Some of the countries in this category are Argentina, Brazil, and Peru. A third force shaping political development is constitutional democracy, with Chile, Columbia, and Venezuela as examples.[1]

The global depression of the 1930s began a period of aggressive state involvement in economic systems that continues in many Latin American countries to the present. Political leaders expanded government functions to stabilize and improve their national economies. They also increased the role of the state in addressing social problems. In some countries this resulted in legislation that subordinated property rights to the social needs of the population.

The twentieth century saw a reduced role of the Church, increased nationalism, and experiments with various ideologies, including socialism, communism, and fascism. By the end of the century, some form of democracy prevailed in most countries, with the Communist dictatorship in Cuba an exception.

Two major factors discouraging entrepreneurs from creating and growing legitimate businesses are (1) the lack of access to capital due to extensive government debt, and (2) perceived unfairness of judicial systems. If a prospective business owner questions whether property rights will be protected and whether contracts will be upheld, the risk associated with the venture is magnified.

Economic Structure

Preceding the conquest, the Americas were sparsely populated with few cities of any size. Economies were primarily agricultural, with some nomadic tribes and hunter-gatherers. Although there were merchants who carried on trade among various peoples and across considerable distances, inter-tribal warfare was endemic and shaped many cultures and economies.

European conquerors introduced feudal economic systems through which they extracted resources for the benefit of the mother countries. Eventually, a merchant class began to emerge to provide a distribution system both for the silver trade[ii] and for the produce of the haciendas. Mercantile economies were built on the backs of slave labor, both Indian and African.

It is interesting to observe, in our current era of trade debate, that Spain instituted free trade throughout its possessions in the New World in the latter half of the 1700s. Commercial trade volume increased dramatically at this time, though cause and effect are not clear. Population grew considerably in the region and industrial growth was expanding the economies of Europe, creating markets for the materials from mines and farms.

It may be that the economic growth combined with English control of trade routes to Europe contributed to struggles for independence as the colonies engaged in greater commerce among themselves. The revolutions during the first quarter of the nineteenth century, however, had a devastating effect on the economies of the newly independent nations. Compounding the destruction of lives and property were the foreign debt burdens and lack of infrastructure. All this led to a shortage of capital for business investment. In the latter half of the century, the situation reversed with extensive foreign investment focusing both on technological advances for basic industries and on the export of raw materials. A negative consequence was the evolution of single-product economies in many countries.

According to Dietz and Street, the Great Depression of the 1930s was magnified in Latin America due to dependence on export and import markets.[2] Countries suffered successions of balance of trade crises. They responded by shifting their political and economic interests from the landed oligarchies toward production by incipient capitalists. Governments erected trade barriers as they instituted import substitution industrialization strategies. Figure 13.1 summarizes the stages of economic development for the region.

The regional commission of the United Nations, the Economic Commission for Latin America and the Caribbean, labeled the five decades of the second half of the twentieth century as indicated below[3,iii]:

- 1950s: industrialization through import substitution
- 1960s: reforms to facilitate industrialization
- 1970s: reorientation of development "styles" towards social homogeneity and towards diversification as a means of promoting exports

---

ii. For the Portuguese, the primary export was brazilwood, closely followed by sugar.
iii. In Spanish, the acronym is CEPAL, Comisión Económica para América Latina y el Caribe.

Mineral extraction; Hacienda production; Regional fragmentation; Easy ISI;

colonial plunder; ⮕ *criollo* control; ⮕ export orientation; ⮕ industrialization;

growth poles   greater trade   U.S. Investment   inward orientation

1500–1700	1700–1810	1825–1914	1915–1945

1810–1824
Wars of Independence

Source: Dietz and Street, 1987, p. 8.

FIGURE 13.1   Stages of Latin America's Development, 1500–1945

- 1980s: overcoming the external debt crisis through "adjustment with growth"
- 1990s: changing production patterns with social equity

The post-World War II years were generally good for Latin American economies. By the 1980s, however, what had been described as economic miracles were turning sour. Dietz and Dilmus[4] listed the following as the driving factors in economic development:

1. Science and technology
2. Debt crises
3. Neoliberalism
4. Economic slump

Dietz and Dilmus contended that governments and lenders over-expanded in unrealistic expectations of continued growth. They found that countries continued to be overly specialized in product categories (e.g., Brazil and Colombia in coffee, Chile in copper, Costa Rica in bananas, and Panama dependent on the canal). Academic studies in science and technology led to lower status careers than law and other professions. Thus, science and technology development were not supported from within, and talented individuals were not attracted to those fields. Spikes in oil prices in the 1970s helped some countries and hurt others, but in the longer term hurt all due to borrowing. The economic slump of the 1980s created debt crises, which were exacerbated by the protectionist policies focused on industrial development. Neoliberal policies included credit tightening, which in turn limited capital for prospective entrepreneurs and for business owners.

Many countries engaged in neoliberal approaches to managing their economies. While lifting trade barriers and encouraging foreign investment, some defaulted on loans and others rescheduled repayments. Interest rates were boosted to control inflation. State enterprises were privatized and regulations reduced on industries. Countries entered into free trade agreements. Economic conditions varied significantly among Latin American countries in the 1990s, but there was general growth corresponding to the strengthening of democratic political systems.

In the modern era, "Latin America's history is replete with economic reforms that have failed due to the lack of credibility."[5] Credibility has been lost by the reversals of reforms that have occurred with changes in governments and by the lack of internal consistency of some of the reform strategies. Continuing bottlenecks to economic development include inefficient supply systems for food products, rigidity in government tax and expenditure structures, insufficient internal savings, and the lack of supply of intermediate agricultural and industrial inputs. Some examples are fuels, fertilizers, transportation facilities, and credit availability. Additionally, there are many sections of Latin America that continue to be relatively closed market systems. These are typically geographically isolated areas in which residents communicate in local Indian dialects. The citizenry of these areas often lack education and are impoverished, limiting the interest by other groups in engaging them in trade.

One of the changes in direction of national governments in recent years has been the movement away from national control of industries. Several countries have experimented with privatization, much along the lines of the former Soviet Republics and Soviet satellite countries. For example, in Mexico there were almost 1,200 state-owned enterprises in 1982. By 1994, that number had been reduced to just over 200.[6]

In a study of Caribbean Island economies, Leo-Paul Dana reported that higher per capita income was associated with pro-business ideologies, as demonstrated by minimal regulation and intervention.[7] Unfortunately, economic development for most nations in Latin America is hindered by the following[8]:

1. a lack of legal guarantees for property rights;
2. the failure of judicial systems to enforce contracts;
3. absence of recourse resulting from damages or injuries associated with the informal sectors; and
4. inefficiencies of tax systems.

With the exception of Cuba, nearly all of Latin America can be described as functioning within capitalist systems. Key facilitators for entrepreneurs tend to be state enterprise privatization, low labor costs, and free trade opportunities. Factors hindering entrepreneurship in current economic environments include lack of capital for starting and growing ventures, low education levels, and dysfunctional political involvement in the private sector (fiscal and monetary policies as well as corruption in some countries). Additionally, the cultural and religious heritages of the region have not been as supportive of risk taking and innovation in the private sector as other parts of the world.

Culture and Religion

As evidenced in the section on history, the culture of the region has been heavily influenced by the countries of the Iberian peninsula. The native populations on islands and coastal areas were culturally assimilated by the conquerors in many cases. Interior and isolated tribes and communities retained more of their beliefs longer, including religious and marital practices. With these groups there has been more of a blending as many languages and traditions were retained.

Catholic priests and missionaries were major influencing factors in imposing European values on the indigenous populace. Representatives of the Church sometimes protected and sometimes abused their charges. They traveled incredible distances enduring incredible hardships, often sacrificing their lives in the years following the conquests. Many of the priests became the historians both of the European colonizers and of the Indians they sought to convert.

Over the centuries, Roman Catholicism waxed and waned in its influence, but by most objective measures would have to be labeled a powerful force across the continent. Historically, the Church played a conservative role and was aligned with social, political, and economic elites. In the twentieth century, evangelical Protestant denominations began having a more visible presence. Mainstream Catholicism continued to espouse traditional Church doctrine, but emphasized social advancement, criticizing dictatorial regimes and the failure of capitalism to result in more egalitarian societies.

In many Latin American countries, culture and traditions are succumbing to corruption and violence.[8] Public sector corruption extends from petty bribery of low level officials to indictments of elected officials at the highest levels for misappropriation of public funds and other crimes. Civil insurrections once associated with political ideologies have degenerated to acts of terrorism, often connected with drug trafficking.

Research suggests that entrepreneurial behavior in Latin America is deviant from mainstream society. Applying case study methodology to a sample of firms in Puerto Rico, Leonora Hamilton described findings regarding entrepreneurs and their ventures that are consistent of prior literature in other locales, suggesting that successful entrepreneurs and their ventures may be more similar across cultures than they are with other groups in their own cultures.[9-11] Hugo Kantis concluded that obstacles and facilitators for creating knowledge-based businesses in Latin America were similar to those of developing countries in other regions of the world.[12]

Despite the weakening influence of the Church, abuses in the public sector, and crime and insurgencies, various traditions and values continue to be deeply embedded in population groups in Latin America. Thomas Cochran contended that entrepreneurial activity is more a function of culture than economics.[13] He contrasted three Latin American countries with the United States to make his point. He argued that cultures in Latin America were less supportive of economic development, based on the following distinctions:

1. Family interests supersede profit maximization.
2. Social and personal interests take precedence over business obligations.
3. Nepotism preempts able top management.
4. Managers and workers are less accepting of constructive criticism.

Additionally, status in Latin American countries is more often associated with professional careers than with entrepreneurship. Earl Young supported Cochran's observations about the role of family as both facilitator and obstacle for entrepreneurship in his study of business owners in Mexico, one of the three countries Cochran examined.[14]

We see, therefore, that entrepreneurs are both affected by the cultural systems in which they abide and conduct business, and are also able to deviate from those traditions in order to innovate, create, and grow their ventures. In Latin America, entrepreneurs appear to have to operate counter to the risk aversion inherent in the religious and cultural mores that dominate the region. Perhaps the most critical obstacle to economic development through entrepreneurship in Latin America is the low level of educational achievement of the general population.

Educational Systems

Few dispute the promise of education in enhancing the quality of life in Latin America, yet the record is dismal by nearly any standard. Although there have been gains in universal access, quality suffers. Segments of the population are excluded from higher education by a primary and secondary school system that encourages repetition and dropping out rather than excellence. Public primary education has been emaciated as dollars are funneled into public university systems. Teachers are poorly trained and managed.[15]

According to United Nations' statistics, Latin American children average 4.2 years of education, with half the students completing less than sixth grade. The poorest 20% of the population are allocated 16% of total public spending, thus perpetuating inequality rather than promoting opportunity and class mobility. Economic progress is inhibited by the lack of a well trained labor force. Improvements in public education are being negotiated into free trade agreements, in particular the Free Trade Area of the Americas.

Educational systems in Latin America tend to be centralized under ministries of education. Problems that occur among multiple countries include lack of qualified instructors, high rates of illiteracy, inequality between rural and urban schools, political instability, and inadequate provisions for Indian tribes. Adult education is recognized as a critical need. Many countries experience difficulty keeping up with population growth and preparing students for the rapid technology changes that impact industries. Higher educational programs have been characterized by imbalances between the courses of study offered and the economic development needs of the countries.

Expectations have risen along with improvements in communication and transportation. As with developed countries, education is perceived in lesser developed Latin American nations as a requisite for good employment and improved status. Education programs for entrepreneurship came later to Latin America than to Europe and the United States. The focus of education to date has been primarily on micro-enterprises and self employment.

Thus, entrepreneurship in the region is constrained on two fronts. Because entrepreneurs have higher levels of education than the general population, the failure to educate larger segments of population reduces the supply of business owners. Second, an undereducated workforce limits the availability of a qualified labor force for starting and growing enterprises. The latter is compounded by global competitiveness. Other regions of the world are paying lower wages to workers whose skills exceed those of the Latin Americans.

Demographics and Physical Infrastructure

Latin America was one of the fastest growing regions of the world during the twentieth century, with an annual rate in excess of 3% in many years. As a percentage of world population, Latin America nearly doubled from 4.5% in 1900 to 8.6% in 2000.[16] The region's population was estimated in 2003 at 534 million. Growth rate declined in recent years to under 1.5%.

The twentieth century was also characterized by dramatic rural to urban migrations. From 1950 to 1980, per capita income rose 2.4% per year. Overall, however, the period of import substitution industrialization ended in massive devaluations and a fall in real wages. From 1960 to 1980, life expectancy in the region increased by ten years.[17]

Rapid industrial growth following World War II created huge demands for new and better roads, schools, telephones, and water and the government bureaucracies to oversee these expansions. This in turn led to tax increases. Tax increases in turn have generated increased tax avoidance by individuals and businesses. As a result, governments do not generate sufficient revenues to satisfy infrastructure demands caused by population growth and technological advancement.

Despite this bleak picture, wealth is being created in Latin America, though not evenly across the region. There are growing markets for entrepreneurs to penetrate. Multi-national corporations have recognized these opportunities by expanding their marketing efforts in many countries. Locally owned ventures are serving as suppliers and distributors for these foreign investments. Lagging infrastructure, however, handicaps entrepreneurial companies from expanding in the region.

Industrial Structures

As explained previously, the economies of Latin American countries were traditionally reliant on single products. The lack of export diversity resulted in declining productivity in industries that had diminishingly lucrative outputs.[2] Lip service was paid to free markets, but the political systems did not permit free labor organizations or free press. Until democratization movements took hold, the concentration of property and income were extreme. Transnational corporations held monopoly power in many industries.

A period of import substitution industrialization (ISI) was instigated by many governments beginning in the 1930s in an effort to stimulate the formation of domestic companies and reduce dependence on foreign investment and the implied external control associated with that investment. ISI policies typically involved the imposition of trade barriers and were accompanied by post-war decades of economic growth. Brazil applied this strategy in growing a minicomputer industry and an aeronautics industry. Immediately following World War II, some countries saw their imports increase due to pent up demand and dollar reserves having been accumulated. Local industries flourished, but needed more parts and materials and labor skills than the countries could supply. Attempts to protect local industries extended to suppliers, which had the downside of increasing costs because of inefficiencies.

Alternatively, the military governments of Argentina and Chile chose more open market courses. The policy of the regime in Chile was generally supported by the business community, whereas Argentina achieved less success and greater opposition from within. The Argentine government intervened in the private sector to the extent of dissolving associations of entrepreneurs in the 1970s.[18]

According to Dale Story, stereotypical industrial entrepreneurs in Latin America have been weak and dependent on the national government.[19] As a result, they are much at the mercy of governmental policies, such as when countries reacted to the oil price shock of the 1970s by heavy international borrowing to maintain and expand social programs.

It is difficult, if not impossible, for individual entrepreneurs to build successful businesses in industries that lack critical mass. Few start-ups can fulfill all the requirements of a supply chain. Government policies that concentrate on one or a small number of industries inhibit creativity and innovation in alternative arenas. Industrial policies to build complete supply chains for particular products actually foster inefficiencies in global competition, ultimately spelling doom for the smaller companies that may exist only to serve a declining industry. Free trade agreements may encourage greater diversity and support entrepreneurial development.

Trade Agreements and Associations

Trade agreements received attention in popular media in the 1990s with the formalization of the European Union and the North American Free Trade Agreement. As explained previously, however, inter- and intra-regional trade practices were issues in the Western Hemisphere even during the Spanish colonial period. Some of the more significant trade agreements and associations affecting Latin America in recent years include those enumerated below.

The Latin American Free Trade Association (LAFTA) was formed under the Treaty of Montevideo in 1960. Original members were Argentina, Bolivia, Brazil, Chile, Colombia, Ecuador, Mexico, Paraguay, Peru, Uruguay, and Venezuela. The purpose of LAFTA was to liberalize trade among the members, eventually leading to a Latin American common market. Progress lagged, and in 1980 LAFTA was replaced with the Latin American Integration Association (LAIA), which continued the goal to reduce trade barriers, but with no goal for a common market.

The Andean Community evolved from the Cartagena Agreement, signed in 1969. The Andean Community members are Bolivia, Colombia, Ecuador, Peru, and Venezuela. In 1993, all countries except Peru approved a free trade zone. Peru began phasing into the trade zone in 1997.

Mercosur is the common market of the Southern Cone. It originated with the Asunción Treaty in 1991. Members are Argentina, Brazil, Paraguay, and Uruguay. The participating nations agreed to move toward the free movement of goods and services among the members, the establishment of common external tariffs, the coordination of macroeconomic policies, and the harmonization of relevant legislation. Mercosur is the fourth largest economic bloc in the world. It has a bilateral trading agreement with the European Union, its principal trading and investment partner.

At the 8th Ministerial Meeting of the Free Trade Area of the Americas, held in Miami, Florida in October, 2003, representatives of thirty-four participating countries issued guidelines for continuing negotiations in an effort to achieve an area of free trade and regional integration. Setting a target date of January, 2005 for an agreement, the FTAA sought to foster economic growth, the reduction of poverty, development, and integration through trade liberalization.[20]

In December 2003, Mercosur and the Andean Community reached a trade agreement linking 350 million people in countries with more than $1 trillion in gross national product.[21] In the same month, El Salvador, Guatemala, Honduras, Nicaragua, and the United States concluded the Central American Free Trade Agreement (CAFTA), to reduce trade barriers, eliminate tariffs, open markets, and promote investment and economic growth among the signatories.[22]

Other trade groups include the Association of Caribbean States (ACS), the Caribbean Community and Common Market (CARICOM), the North American Free Trade Agreement (NAFTA), and the System of Central American Integration (SICA). Additionally, there are numerous bilateral agreements, associate memberships, and other associations among and between nations in Latin America.

Trade agreements and associations present both opportunities and threats to domestic entrepreneurs. The most severe threats are likely to be toward business owners in protected industries that cannot compete effectively in the global marketplace. Opportunities are associated with expanded markets and with exploiting the market inefficiencies in other nations.

Import/Export Information

Available trade information for FTAA countries from 1997 through 2001 can be accessed at http://ftaa-hdb.org/infocom.asp. Multiple interpretations can be drawn from these numbers. One is that the missing data suggest that many countries continue to have difficulty collecting information on trade transactions. Another is that the annual fluctuations may more reflect conditions within national economies than external trade practices. Alternatively, trade variations may be primarily a function of global economic trends rather than trade agreements. Finally, these numbers exclude the informal, unreported trade that is practiced internationally as well as domestically.

Small Business Practices

All environments present both opportunities and threats. As in other regions of the world, small businesses in Latin America have the advantage of flexibility— flexibility in both decision making and in production. Also as in other regions, the imposition of government (i.e., adherence to regulation) falls disproportionately on small firms. The Foundation for Development and Integration, located in Cali, Colombia, calculated that government compliance costs in that country resulted in losses of about 23% for small businesses.[23] Alternatively, Pier Abetti and Patricia Wheeler, in a study comparing France, Mexico, and the United States, found entrepreneurial success consistently in communities with governments that successfully build infrastructures for technological entrepreneurship.[24]

Another aspect of Latin American government involvement in the private sector has been the absorption of bank credit by the public sector. Because so many countries have undertaken heavy debt burdens, they divert capital that small businesses might otherwise borrow in order to form and expand.[25]

As the review of cultural influences suggests, family involvement in enterprises permeates the region. "The persistence of family-centeredness is a common feature of (Mexico and) other Latin American countries."[26] Another aspect of culture affecting entrepreneurship is risk avoidance. Albert Lauterbach observed almost forty years ago that "this attitude is a far cry from the Schumpeterian entrepreneur whom some contemporary observers consider the mainstay of economic development in less developed areas today."[27]

Studies have also found that entrepreneurs in Latin America have different demographic characteristics than the general populations of their countries.[28] They are more likely to be higher educated, from wealthier (predominantly middle class) backgrounds, and urban.

Lawrence Franko cited evidence in support of Schumpeterian economics in Mexico and in Colombia.[29] Reviewing historic economic patterns, he observed specific entrepreneurial breaks with the formation of new industries. For Mexico, disruptions occurred with sugar refining in 1901, textile mills beginning in 1906, and cement plants in 1909. The implication of this analysis is that countries with single industry dominance are still capable of innovating in other industries in which they may develop a competitive advantage.

One study found that important sources of capital and entrepreneurial expertise may come from expatriates.[30] These venturers typically have family business backgrounds. They are likely to be seeking quality of life and reduced initial investment. In their literature reviews of groups that generate entrepreneurial activity, Albert Shapiro, Lisa Sokol and Seymour Lipset gave examples from Argentina, Brazil, Colombia, Cuba, Mexico, and other countries that indicated migrant populations display a disproportionate degree of entrepreneurial behavior when compared with indigenous groups.[31,32]

Small firms are discovering that the global economy is real and affecting them directly. For example, special incentives for pharmaceutical manufacturers have brought foreign investment to Puerto Rico with accompanying local sourcing.[33] On the other hand, the expansion of Wal-Mart in Latin America is impacting smaller firms both positively and negatively. Opportunities are being created for local suppliers, but competitors are finding margins cut drastically.[34]

No discussion of the small business sector would be complete without addressing the economy sometimes labeled informal, extralegal, unauthorized, unlicensed, underground, or black market. It was recently estimated that in Mexico alone more than 10 million people were engaging in unreported business activity, particularly pirated merchandise.[35] In examining failures of capitalism in Latin America, Hernando de Soto recorded estimates that 60% to 70% of all construction in Brazil is never reported and that 80% of all real estate throughout Latin America is held outside of the law. He compared Latin America with Russia: both had strong underground economies, glaring inequalities, pervasive mafias, political instability, capital flight, and flagrant disregard for the law. De Soto concluded that these conditions limit the ability of national economies to produce and use capital efficiently.[8]

Many countries are proactively encouraging small business formation and development as part of their economic development strategies.[36] Examples include:

- Fostering technological entrepreneurship through the creation of a science park in Brazil[37];
- training students to start ventures and business owners to improve their firms' performance at an innovation and entrepreneurship development center in Honduras[38]; and
- counseling business owners and prospective business owners in basic financial, management and marketing skills through a network of small business development centers in Puerto Rico.

Fernando Quezada and Alvaro Mello cautioned, however, that greater trust is needed between the program delivery partners (i.e., government, industry, and universities) for these programs to be effective.[39] This comports with Utz Hoeser's investigation of incubators in Argentina, which he found to be unsuccessful, especially when compared to other countries such as Brazil.[40]

Summary

It would appear that a propensity for entrepreneurship exists throughout Latin America, but that several prerequisites are missing that would otherwise increase the number of start-ups and provide an environment for innovative and high-growth potential ventures. Obvious gaps are education, capital, and technological expertise. Expanding markets, reduced trade barriers, large labor pools, government support programs and other factors may provide stimuli for small business development in the future.

Discussion Questions

1. What are two major factors that discouraged entrepreneurs in Latin America from creating and growing legitimate businesses? Be sure to include the notion of property rights in your answer.
2. Dietz and Dilmus contended that governments and lenders over-expanded in unrealistic expectations of continued growth. In the late 1970s and through the 1980s what kinds of crises were created? What types of policies were they exacerbated by?

3. Thomas Cochran contended that entrepreneurial activity is more a function of culture than economics. Explain why, according to Cochran, Latin Americans were less supportive of economic development.

4. What are some of the limitations of the Latin American education system? How do local politics and class structure play a role?

Suggested Reading

De Soto, H. 2003. *The Mystery of Capital: Why Capitalism Triumphs in the West and Fails Everywhere Else*. New York: Basic Books.

De Soto, H. 2002. *The Other Path*. New York: Basic Books.

Gannon, T. A., ed. 1968. *Doing Business in Latin America*. New York: American Management Association.

Endnotes

1. Sigmund, P. E., ed. 1970. *Models of Political Change in Latin America*. New York: Praeger Publishers.

2. Dietz, J. L., and J. H. Street, eds. 1987. *Latin America's Economic Development: Institutionalist and Structuralist Perspectives*. Boulder, CO: Lynne Rienner Publishers.

3. ECLAC. 2003. Economic Commission for Latin America and the Caribbean. Web site: www.eclac.cl.

4. Dietz, J. L., and D. J. Dilmus, eds. 1990. *Progress toward Development in Latin America: From Prebisch to Technological Autonomy*. Boulder, CO: Lynne Rienner Publishers.

5. Edwards, S. 1991. Structural adjustment reforms and the external debt crisis in Latin America. In: *The Latin American Development Debate: Neostructuralism, Neomonetarism, and Adjustment Processes*. Boulder, CO: Westview Press: 158.

6. Rogozinski, J. 1999. *High Price for Change: Privatization in Mexico*. Washington: The Inter-American Development Bank and the Johns Hopkins University Press.

7. Dana, L-P. Introducing a model for the classification of entrepreneurial policy, case study: British Virgin Islands, Cayman Islands, Dominican Republic, Grenada, Puerto Rico and the U.S. Virgin Islands.

8. De Soto, H. 2003. *The Mystery of Capital: Why Capitalism Triumphs in the West and Fails Everywhere Else*. Jackson, TN: Basic Books.

9. Hamilton, L. C. 2001. SME's policy and practices: A comparative case study of success determinants in Puerto Rico's firms; the construction industry. International Council for Small Business World Conference, Taipei, Taiwan.

10. Hamilton, L. C., and L. R. Rivera. 2003. Is there potential to stimulating start-ups and strengthen SMEs competitiveness? International Council for Small Business World Conference, Belfast, Northern Ireland, United Kingdom.

11. Jansson, D. G., and R. D. Hisrich. 2003. Development of local entrepreneurship in Puerto Rico. *Frontiers of Entrepreneurship Research*.

12. Kantis, H. 2003. Knowledge based ventures: Empirical evidences in Latin America. International Council for Small Business. Belfast, Northern Ireland, United Kingdom.

13. Cochran, T. C. 1960. Cultural factors in economic growth. *Journal of Economic History* 20:515–530.

14. Young, E. C. 1993. Major elements in entrepreneurial development in Mexico. *Journal of Small Business Management* 31(4): 80–85.

15. Franko, P. M. 2003. *The Puzzle of Latin American Economic Development*. Lanham, England: Rowman & Littlefield Publishers: 374.

16. Population Reference Bureau, 2003.

17. Hartlyn, J., and S. A. Morley, eds. 1986. *Latin American Political Economy: Financial Crisis and Political Change*. Boulder, CO: Westview Press.

18. Ominami, C. 1991. Deindustrialization and industrial restructuring in Latin America. In: Meller, P., ed. *The Latin American Development Debate*. Boulder, CO: Westview Press.

19. Story, D. 1983. Industrial elites in Mexico: Political ideology and influence. *Journal of Interamerican Studies and World Affairs* 25:351–376.

20. Free Trade Area of the Americas. 2003. Ministerial declaration of Miami. Web site: www.ftaa-alca.org/ministerials/miami/declaration_e.asp.

21. *Wall Street Journal*. 2003. South American groups forge free-trade pact. December 17: A20.

22. Office of the United States Trade Representative. 2003. U.S. & Central American countries conclude historic free trade agreement. Web site: www.ustr.gov/releases/2003/12/03-82.pdf.

23. CIPE. 1993. Center for International Private Enterprise. Fostering entrepreneurship. *Prosperity Papers series*. Web site: http://www.cipe.org/publications/education/prosperity/ppl.htm.

24. Abetti, P. A., and P. A. Wheeler. 1990. Planning and building the infrastructure for technological entrepreneurship: Field studies in the U.S.A., France and Mexico. In: Churchill, N.C., Bygrave, W. D., Hornaday, J. A., Muzyka, D. F., Vesper, K. H., and W. E. Wetzel, eds. *Frontiers of Entrepreneurship Research*. Babson Park, MA: Babson College Center for Entrepreneurship.

25. Camp, R. A. 1989. *Entrepreneurs and Politics in Twentieth-Century Mexico*. New York: Oxford University Press.

26. Derossi, F. 1971. *The Mexican Entrepreneur*. Paris: Development Centre of the Organization for Economic Co-Operation and Development: 101.

27. Lauterbach, A. 1965. Government and development: Managerial attitudes in Latin America. *Journal of Inter-American Studies* 7:201–225.

28. Lipman, A. 1965. Social backgrounds of the Bogota entrepreneur. *Journal of Inter-American Studies* 7:227–235.

29. Franko, L. G. 1966. Politics and economics of joint ventures in Latin America. In *Entrepreneurship and Industrialization in Latin America: Three Essays*. Lawrence G. Franko, Michael Dixon, and Carlos Arturo Marulanda R. Austin, TX: The University of Texas.

30. Befus, D. R., Mescon, T. S., Mescon, D. L., and G. S. Vozikis. 1988. International investment of expatriate entrepreneurs: The case of Honduras. *Journal of Small Business Management* July:40–47.

31. Shapiro, A., and L. Sokol. 1981. The social dimensions of entrepreneurship. In: Kent, C. A., Sexton, D. L., and K. H. Vesper, eds. *Encyclopedia of Entrepreneurship*. Englewood Cliffs, NJ: Prentice-Hall.

32. Lipset, S. M. 2000. Values and entrepreneurship in the Americas. In: Swedberg, R., ed. *Entrepreneurship: The Social Science View*. London: Oxford.

33. Orengo Serra, K. L. 2003. The pharmaceutical firms and the development of Puerto Rico. International Council for Small Business, Belfast, Northern Ireland, United Kingdom.

34. Duggal, V. P. 2003. Small business versus big business—Amigo & mega retailer Wal-Mart. International Council for Small Business World Conference, Belfast, Northern Ireland, United Kingdom.

35. Maquila, P. 2001. More than 10 million Mexicans living off black market: Concamin. Weekly Bulletin 192. Web site: http://www.maquilaportal.com.

36. Mello, A. A. 1987. Patterns and profiles of Brazilian entrepreneurs: Data from entrepreneurship development programs sponsored by the empretec programme—United Nations and Sebrae—Brazilian agency for micro and small business assistance programme.

37. Filho, S. P., and S. R. Goulart, Jr. 1993. Planning and building the infrastructure for technological entrepreneurship: The case of São Carlos Science Park—Brasil.

38. Yu-Way, L., and Z. Martin. 1987. Innovation and entrepreneurship development center: Honduras. *Journal of Small Business Management* Oct:70–72.

39. Quezada, F., and A. Mello. 1987. Empirical observations of the new social entrepreneurship in Brazil.

40. Hoeser, U. 2003. The slow development of the Argentinean incubation sector. International Council for Small Business World Conference, Belfast, Northern Ireland, United Kingdom.

Chapter Fourteen

CHINA

Lan-Ying Huang, *National Changhua University of Education, Changhua City, Taiwan*
Shawn Carraher, PhD., *Cameron University, Lawton, Oklahoma*

Learning Objectives

Upon completion of this chapter, students should be able to:

- Underand the culture of China.
- Understand Guanxi and its importance in doing business in China.
- Understand foreign direct investment.

Key Terms

China
foreign direct investment
guanxi

◎ Introduction

With nearly one-quarter of the world's population and one of the fastest rates of economic growth, China is perceived as a golden opportunity for success and has become the target for business expansion by many foreign businesses. The record $319 billion inflows in Asia, more than a 300% increase over 1999, was primarily due to an unprecedented boom in foreign direct investment (FDI) in Hong Kong and China. In the current chapter we examine doing business in China with a special emphasis on the concept of *guanxi* and its impact on doing business or investing in China.

Guanxi

The Chinese word *guanxi* entails *guan* and *xi*. The Chinese meaning of "guan" is either "to connect" or "a gate/pass that can be closed."[1] "To connect" is to build a linkage between two independent individuals. The latter explanation meant a "door," and its extended meaning is "to close." Inside the door, you are "one of the group," but outside the door, you are barely recognized. *Guan* can also refer to "doing favor to someone." For example, *guan huai* means "showing care for someone." *Xi* means to tie up and extend into relationships. In addition, it can also refer to maintaining long-term relationships. Guanxi is so prominent in China that it leads scholars to term the arts of establishing and managing guanxi as "*guanxixue*" (relationology)[2] or the "Chinese gift economy."[1] To sum up, guanxi means to "doing favors for and maintaining a relationship with someone you recognized."

Many sociologists and anthropologists have attempted to define the nature of guanxi. Some qualify it as "particularistic ties" between individuals[2,3] based on trust and affection through which people exchange favors, while others view it as a kind of social networking.[1,2] Chien Chiao, a Chinese anthropologist, defines guanxi as "a status in which a person or an organization interacts with another person or organization, and in which they are mutually affected and enjoy mutual gains."[4] Pye defines guanxi as "friendship with implications of continued exchange of favors."[5] Scholarly descriptions of guanxi include "tight, close-knit networks,"[6] "interpersonal connections,"[7] and a "gate or pass."[6] Tsui and Farh remark "the literature shows no consensus in the translation or definition of the term guanxi."[8]

Guanxi refers to the concept of drawing on connections or networks in order to secure favors in personal or business relations. It is pivotal at all levels of societal functioning and in all kinds of dealings in the oriental country. Guanxi literally binds millions of Chinese firms into a social and business web. No company can go far unless it has extensive guanxi.[9] In fact, a new term has arisen in China: *guanxihu*. This term, applied to specially connected firms, refers to the bond between guanxi members that leads them to give highly preferential treatment to other members of their network.[10]

Guanxi, *renqing* (human feelings), and *mianzi* (face), are regarded as key building blocks of the Chinese culture. The three elements are viewed by anthropologists and sociologists as fundamental socio-cultural concepts which shape the social behavior and cognitive thinking of the Chinese.[2] Renqing, unpaid obligations to the other party as a result of invoking the guanxi relationship, is a form of social capital that provides leverage in interpersonal exchanges of favors.[1] When the Chinese people weave their networks of guanxi, they are also weaving a web of renqing obligations that must be repaid in the near future.[11] The person's face (mianzi) is also a key component in the dynamics of guanxi because one must maintain a certain level of prestige to cultivate and expand a viable network of guanxi connections.[6] Mianzi is an intangible form of social currency and personal status. It provides the leverage one needs to successfully expand and manipulate a guanxi network.

Characteristics of Guanxi   Guanxi is the word that describes the pervasive network of personal or business relations. It refers to a relationship between two people or organizations maintaining implicit mutual obligations and understanding the Chinese attitudes toward long-term social and business relationships. Its roots are deeply embedded in Chinese culture.[12] The following describes the different facets of the characteristics of *guanxi*.

First, guanxi is ego-centric. Chiao suggests that guanxi is "ego-centric."[4] King indicated that guanxi building is "an ego-centered social engineering of relation building." As observed by King, guanxi relations in China are "a form of interpersonal relationship which is predominantly based on particularistic criteria."[2]

Second, guanxi is transferable. Guanxi network refers to transactions between two persons, A and C, who are linked by their mutual relationship with a person, B, who acts as a facilitator. That is, if A has guanxi with B and B is a friend of C, then B can introduce A to C or vice versa. Otherwise the relationship between A and C is impossible.

Third, guanxi is reciprocal. Guanxi connotes an unspoken commitment of parties involved in the relations. They are supposed to share their resources and are obliged to help one another in an unlimited manner. Specifically, it concludes the notion of a continuing reciprocal relationship over an indefinite time period. Anyone who refuses to return favors will be condemned as untrustworthy and will lose their face in all connected networks.[13] The idea of enjoying the prestige of not losing face (mianzi) and at the same time saving other people's face is a key component in the dynamics of guanxi.[14] In a guanxi network relationship, both parties are required to commit to one another by an invisible and unwritten code of reciprocity and equity.

Fourth, guanxi is highly personalized. Guanxi network hinges upon personal connection among particular individuals. If one attempts to build a good network with another organization, one must first develop fine guanxi with key managers in the organization.[15] That is, guanxi between organizations is first established by and continues to build upon personal relationships; when the key individuals are gone, so goes the guanxi in the organization as well.

Fifth, guanxi is instrumental. Chiao proposes that the construction of guanxi is mainly to fulfill utilitarian objectives.[4] That is, the objective of networking in guanxi is to have mutual gains. This instrumental nature of guanxi is confirmed by King and Yang.[1,2] Yang indicated: "guanxixue is using people." Guanxi relations are built primarily on self-interest.

Finally, guanxi is dynamic. Chiao suggests that guanxi relations have to be alive and useful.[4] In other words, guanxi is a long-term nurturing process that requires enormous patience and time. Accordingly, relationships have a longevity dimension in the Chinese culture.

The Difference from Western Networking

Traditional Chinese marketing through guanxi (personal relationship) is similar to "relationship marketing" in the West. Ambler et al. compared relationships and guanxi (connections) in China with relationship marketing as it has emerged in the West.[16] The term guanxi goes beyond Western ideas of networking or business favoritism.[17] Favor exchanges that take place amongst members of the guanxi network are not solely commercial, but also social, with the involvement of renqing exchange and mianzi giving. The feature of favor exchanges often causes guanxi to be often named as "social capital." In contrast, networking in the West is a term virtually associated with commercial-based relations. In addition, Western networking emphasizes organizational commitment in the assessment of partner firm's effort to develop the relationship, whereas guanxi emphasizes on personal relationship creation and development. Only when the personal relationship is devoted to and used by the organization for whatever purposes, does guanxi then play a role at the organizational level.[18] More specifically, in China, transactions often follow successful guanxi, while in the West a relationship follows successful transactions.

Cultivating, Maintaining, and the Prominence of Guanxi in China Market

Linkage, a broad definition of family ties, is the core of social networks or ethnic ties in Chinese culture. Chinese networks stretch from the core of close family members, to distant relatives, to those who are connected to someone in one's family as peripherals, such as classmates, people from the same region, and friends. In other words, family is the most fundamental unit of the Chinese society. Individuals are embedded networks of family ties and family derived social relationships. People prefer to organize different forms of linkage in terms of commonness on some particularistic ties.

Guanxi, often translated as social connections or relationships with implications of a continual exchange of favors, plays an integral role in Chinese life and business. Its existence is a central concept for understanding Chinese networking strategies in economy and society. Chinese social connections can be built in two ways: group identification and altercastering. Group identification is a process by which commonality is cultivated among individuals. In a sense, the commonality is a base upon which guanxi connections are built, and it is termed as the "guanxi base."[3] In the literature, guanxi base is often formed through either an ascribed guanxi base founded on innate attributes among individuals or an achieved guanxi base built by shared experience. An ascribed guanxi base is often formed through kinship and locality. Kinship ties, members of a person's immediate and extended families, are supposed to be the most significant. Its significance is confirmed by Chu and Ju in which a higher percentage of respondents would offer help to a relative rather than to a friend (70.9% vs. 64.3%, respectively).[19] Locality guanxi base is formed through people who come from the same towns. Achieved guanxi bases are established through the shared experience among individuals, such as coworkers, classmates, sworn brothers, teacher-student relations, and many others.[4] Among these, coworkers and classmates have relatively more influence in guanxi building.[3]

Guanxi can also be established between strangers as long as there are intermediaries trusted by both sides. Altercastering is a term used for describing the establishment of guanxi between individuals who have no commonality.[11] The technique is commonly known in China as "*la guanxi*" (pulling social relationships). One effective way of accomplishing the linkage between two unrelated individuals is through an intermediary who is familiar to both parties.

A guanxi base alone is insufficient to establish strong guanxi. Alston noted, "guanxi ties have to be continuously reinforced."[13] Two of the most frequently used tactics to enhance guanxi in Chinese society are presenting a gift to and holding a banquet for the other party.[11] In a social exchange, according to Yang, when a gift has been received or a request for a favor has been granted, there is a symbolic breaking down of the boundaries between persons, thereby developing an unpaid obligation or liabilities that must be repaid at some point since guanxi is reciprocal.[1] This unpaid obligation or renqing is the first step in a series of exchanges. When the recipient repays the gift by giving out another gift, or the petitioner returns the favor by giving help in other ways, the indebtedness in the guanxi-based relation is cleared.

Another important dimension of guanxi is the degree of closeness, which is determined by *ganqing*, or affection. The experience of sharing and interaction through living, working, or studying together is a prerequisite in building up ganqing. Ganqing is a key determinant of the quality of guanxi. In addition, trust is essential to long-term guanxi maintenance. It exists only among in-group members who are supposed to fulfill the obligation of responding to the requests of other members in the same network. If individuals abide by the rules of the social interaction and fulfill the obligation, they are considered as reliable and trustworthy and are entitled to the benefits of guanxi.

Since China started economic reform and opened the door to the world in 1979, guanxi has acquired even more practical importance for the Chinese in both social and business settings.[20] Davies et al. survey of Hong Kong Chinese executives regarding the importance of guanxi relationships found that the businessmen believed that once good guanxi had been established, a number of benefits would follow.[21] Under a weak legal system in China, guanxi networks can be used as substitutes for institutional support such as obtaining scarce resources, mitigating various forms of governmental interference, and protecting property rights.[22] It compensates for systematic inefficiency and institutional weaknesses. In other words, guanxi connection is a very useful means of dealing with the Chinese bureaucratic maze because it balances the awkward Chinese bureaucracy by giving individuals a way to circumvent rules through the activation of personal relations. The formal bureaucratic rules often inhibit business dealings, while guanxi facilitates them.[13] Hence, guanxi improves efficiency, saves time, and eases the procurement of necessary production resources (e.g., government approvals, utilities, and local suppliers of labor and materials).[21] Developing, expanding, and maintaining one's guanxi network have become a form of social investment.[23]

On the other hand, a guanxi network is imperative for foreign firms that lack marketing experience, distinctive competencies, and distribution channels to cultivate guanxi networks to compensate for their deficiencies, to access and expand their local markets, and eventually to be able to compete.[24] Given the benefit of obtaining information on government policies, market trends, and business opportunities, guanxi networks help firms to reduce uncertainty.[21] Both Western investors and overseas Chinese firms strive to establish close connections with China government/partners in order to gain an edge over competitors. Therefore, as China continues to attract investors because of its economic perspective, guanxi utilization has become increasingly pervasive and has been deemed to have certain implications to international executives active in this economy.

To summarize, in the absence of adequate legal protection, foreign investors rely on guanxi to safeguard their property rights and contracts and to seek solution of investment disputes. Moreover, those who have strong connections in China actually take advantage of the weak legal system to obtain extra lucrative business opportunities for their own benefit. Foreign companies investing in China with varied sizes, sectors, and location all find informal transnational networks essential to protecting their interests. However, due to the heavy reliance on personal connections, guanxi has its limitations as a business strategy, especially in the long run.

While guanxi network is an effective alternative for foreign investors in China to obtain protection and benefits under the government bureaucracy, it is important to be aware of the limits of guanxi network. First, guanxi is not equally effective across areas and it cannot solve all the problems of a legal system. For example, large FDI projects involve many participants at many levels in China. The role of guanxi has been greatly exaggerated. It is impossible for any firm to build all the connections with all the actors since there is always the risk that other people may gang up and become more powerful.

In addition, because guanxi is so personalized, the participation of key people is constantly required. Therefore, maintaining guanxi connection can be very expensive and time-consuming. The networks hinge on personal connections. But given the lack of political institutionalization in China, the fate of individuals is hard to predict. If the key individuals change positions or lose power, FDI projects based on guanxi with them may suffer setbacks or be doomed altogether. Many business consultants realize this dilemma and build good relationships with as many officials in China as possible. But that is easier said than done. The guanxi evolution model presented on the next page (Figure 14.1) illustrates cultivating, maintaining, and benefits of a guanxi-based relationship. In short, guanxi involves cultivating personal relationships through the exchange of favors and gifts for the purpose of obtaining goods and services, developing networks of mutual dependence, and creating a sense of obligation and indebtedness.[1]

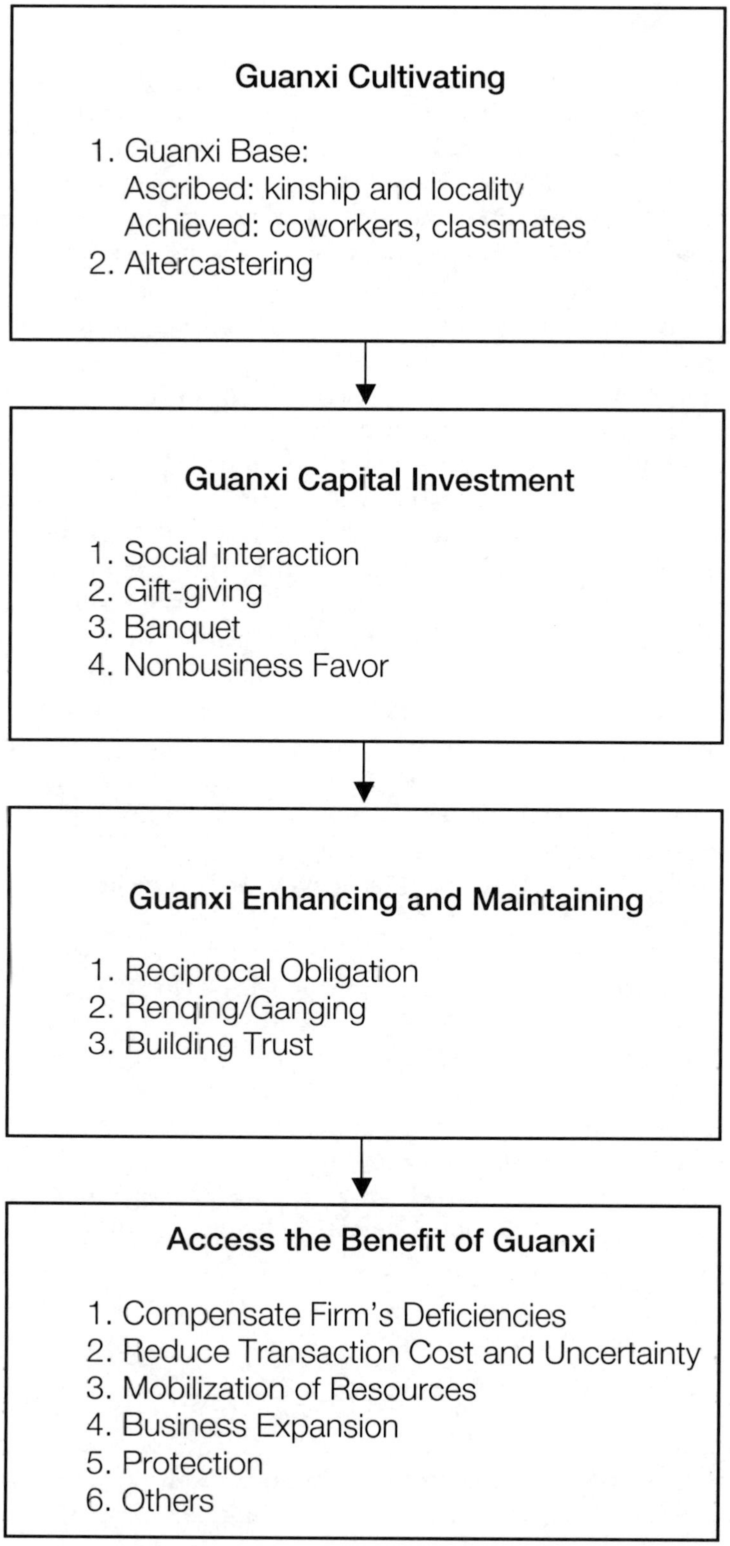

Guanxi Cultivating

1. Guanxi Base:
   Ascribed: kinship and locality
   Achieved: coworkers, classmates
2. Altercastering

Guanxi Capital Investment

1. Social interaction
2. Gift-giving
3. Banquet
4. Nonbusiness Favor

Guanxi Enhancing and Maintaining

1. Reciprocal Obligation
2. Renqing/Ganging
3. Building Trust

Access the Benefit of Guanxi

1. Compensate Firm's Deficiencies
2. Reduce Transaction Cost and Uncertainty
3. Mobilization of Resources
4. Business Expansion
5. Protection
6. Others

FIGURE 14.1 Guanxi Evolution Model

Guanxi as Social Capital

Social networks are sets of recurrent associations between groups of people linked by occupational, familial, cultural, or affective ties.[25] Many scholars have proposed that business and social networks can improve the allocation of resources and promote the trade in the international market.[26] Weidenbaum and Hughes use the term "bamboo networks" to describe the role of social networks in Chinese society.[17] Through these networks, trade and investment information is passed along, business introductions are made, and deals are done often on handshakes. Business transactions are often done through personal contacts and recommendations.

The development trend of ethnic economies has generated intense interest among sociologists and economists because it intersects the subjects of interest of economics and sociology.[25] They try to explain this phenomenon or influence of social networks and ethnic ties from the perspective of social capital. Social capital refers to the capacity of individuals to command scarce resources by virtue of their membership in networks or broader social structures.[25] That is, the resources themselves are not social capital; the concept refers to the individual's ability to mobilize them on demand. Resources acquired through social capital often carry the expectation of reciprocity at some point in the future. Pierre asserts that entrepreneurs try to build up and invest "social network capital" aimed at generating economic capital.[27] These social resources can then be transformed into firm level resources in the form of access to decision makers and their professional networks, intelligence about market opportunities, licenses, monopolies, rents, etc. Social capital and associated norms can increase productivity by reducing the costs of doing business as well as facilitating coordination and cooperation.

Portes criticize the drawback of social capital by saying that communities, groups or networks which are isolated, parochial, or working at cross-purposes to society's collective interests can actually hinder economic and social development.[25] However, in the case of doing business with Mainland China, social capital could be the most crucial competitive advantage of some of the foreign investors. While many Western investors treat social capital as their insurmountable obstacle to investing in Mainland China, some overseas Chinese investors have turned these problems to their advantage through informal channels such as personal contact and family connections. Hodder observed that informal connections have played a large role in transactions among overseas Chinese businesses.[28]

Guanxi and Business Networks

FDI theory does not account for the role and influence of social relationships in business transactions.[29] Alternatively, network perspective research draws on the theories of social exchange and resource dependency and focuses on firm behavior in the context of interorganizational and interpersonal relationships,[30] arguing that organizational boundaries incorporate both business (formal) and social (informal) relationships.[31]

According to Johanson and Mattsson, business networks are concerned with relationships among organizations and individuals, while guanxi networks govern interactions and transactions in particular between individuals.[31] However, organizations do not have guanxi; it is the employees of the organization who have guanxi. In practice, most Chinese cultivate intricate and pervasive personal ties, guanxi, which govern their attitudes toward not only social but also business relationships.[8] Hence, the Chinese guanxi network is more than merely a symbolic implication of individual and organizational ties. Most scholars agree that the social capital embodied in managerial ties and networks matters.[29,32] Building managerial ties centers on networking, which can be defined as both an individual's attempt to mobilize personal contacts in order to profit from entrepreneurial opportunities[29] and a firm's efforts to cooperate with others in order to obtain and sustain a competitive advantage.[33] Hamilton and others assert that business networks provide Asian firms with a wide range of competitive advantages in the form of social (relationship) capital based on interlocking connections (guanxi) to local or regional business partners, high ranking officials and local power elites, government entities, and so forth to get things done.[34]

Many researchers support the network perspective in the form of formal and informal relationships (relationships involving clients, competitors, colleagues, government, friends, and so forth) to the success in entering new international markets.[35] Coviello and Kristina and Coviello and Munro suggest that these network relationships influence initial market selection and also mode of entry.[36,37] Bjorkman and Kock conclude that key actors and their social networks and bonds with important international partners have significant impact on internationalization of service firms.[38] Fontes and Coombs found that firms established relationships with other organizations to complement their activities or compensate for deficiencies.[39] Zafarullah, Ali, and Young found that the engineering-consulting firms' networks go beyond ethnic ties, relatives, and friends to include more diverse and formal connections.[40]

It is widely recognized that guanxi is a key and practically significant business determinant influencing firm performance because the lifeblood of the Chinese economy and business conduct is guanxi network. Guanxi has a direct impact on the market expansion and sales growth of Chinese firms by affecting resource sharing and social, economic, and political contexts in inter-firm transactions. In a qualitative study by Ai, it was discovered that Canadian companies that had developed good connections with Chinese local parties achieved higher levels of business performance than firms that had not.[41] Abramson and Ai found that awareness of and experience with the changing Chinese business environment, guanxi relationships, and informal interaction patterns for obtaining information seemed to represent key success factors for Canadian companies in China.[42] Xin and Pearce found that private company executives made more extensive use of guanxi, and maintained deeper business connections as a way of reducing environmental uncertainty than did the more institutionally state-owned company executives.[22] Wank prioritizes various forms of guanxi on the basis that the more personal, and the longer it precedes the current business relationship, the stronger it is.[43] Luo and Chen explored the impact of guanxi on performance of firms operating in China from the strategic management perspective.[12] Their findings suggest that guanxi-based factors have a significant favorable influence on firm's profitability, asset efficiency, and market growth. This influence appears significant for both local Chinese and foreign ventures. Luo examined the relationship between guanxi-based business variables and the financial performance of foreign-invested enterprises (FIE) operating in China.[44] He found that guanxi has a significant and positive effect on FIEs' accounting and market performance. More recently, Ambler, Styles, and Wang have established that channel relationships and prior guanxi have a positive impact on the performance of inter-province export ventures within China.[16] Peng and Luo demonstrated that firm managers' micro interpersonal ties with top executives at other firms and with government officials help improve macro organizational performance.[45] Their findings show that managerial ties were necessary but insufficient for good performance. A number of traditional strategy variables also drive performance. Ewing, Caruana, and Wong's study empirically links guanxi to performance.[46] It would appear as if long-term success is still strongly influenced by personal connections and relationships resulting from guanxi. They agree with Kotler and his colleagues, who maintain that marketers practicing guanxi must honor their obligations, be good and loyal friends, and true co-regionals.[47] Park and Luo found that guanxi utilization is likely to have a positive effect on sales growth but no effect on profit growth.[48] Their results indicate that guanxi networks have a substantial impact on market expansion efforts, but less impact on accounting returns.

In sum, a firm can enhance its accounting and market performance by benefiting from the *guanxi* network it has established. In essence, this network constitutes a firm's core competency and distinctive competitive advantage that can lead to a high performance for the firm.

Who Needs Guanxi Most?

Yeung and Tung suggested that guanxi was needed by four main types of companies: (1) for firms which focus mainly on the China market; (2) for less-experienced executives who are more dependent on guanxi to break the ice; (3) for small- and medium-sized firms which tend to rely more on guanxi to obtain favorable arrangements and resources; and (4) for firms in tertiary sectors which need to rely more on guanxi.[6]

Because firms with different organizational dynamics vary in their capabilities to scan information, control uncertainty, and benefit from exchange favors, they have different levels of need and capacity to build and sustain guanxi network connections. In general, firms that lack organization capabilities tend to have increased need for guanxi cultivation. Additionally, in a transition economy with increasing competition and decreasing government protection, firms may need to invest even more in guanxi development to be able to continue to offer and exchange favors with their competitive forces and government authorities.

Xin and Pearce observed that private company executives made more extensive use of guanxi, and maintained deeper business connections as a way of reducing environmental uncertainty than did the state-owned company executives.[22] As Xin and Pearce found in China, smaller firms typically need to rapidly establish ties with other organizations.[22] However, Park and Luo proposed weak support for organizational factors as antecedents to *guanxi* utilization but found no differences between organizations with strong and weak organizational capabilities in terms of their attempts to develop *guanxi* networks. For example, they indicate that companies in China need to network actively with the business community and government authorities both to overcome the liability of newness and to ensure the survival and growth of older firms.[48] Firms in China develop and maintain good connections with government authorities regardless of their resources.

Investing in China

China's "open door" policy has captured enormous attention in the past fifteen years. One result of China's opening to the world is the inflow of FDI from developed countries, newly industrialized countries (NICs), and some developing countries, because China's opening to the world has provided many opportunities to many, and has exerted noticeable impact on the world. The presence of FDI in China, which is mainly from the NICs and the West, creates a unique area of study within the domain of international production. What is so special about China is that it has been a planning economy. Hence, doing business in China is more complex than in other countries. In China, guanxi is an important resource for individuals and firms to induce cooperation and govern relationships efficiently. Guanxi networks might be viewed as significant factors for firms investing in China.

FDI in the global economy has increased dramatically since the early 1980s. FDI flows to China, at $81.1 billion in the first ten months of 2008, grew at a rate of 35.1%.[49] China, with Hong Kong, is the single largest FDI recipient in Asia. It is noteworthy that the portfolio of FDI in China has been broadening over the past twenty years. In its effort to become a member of World Trade Organization (WTO), China is considering adopting a number of new policy measures relating to FDI.

China presently constitutes the largest FDI absorption territory, and one of the major sources of outward FDI in the world since its open-door policy began in 1979. Many foreign investors are eager to gain a foothold in this populous market. However, doing business in China is complicated and can be particularly difficult. Foreign investors can be confused and irritated by the long negotiation process, government hierarchy, and the distinctive practices that they meet in China.[50] Instead, foreign investors depend on personal connections (guanxi) with regional authorities, bureaucracies, and individuals in China to safeguard and enhance their business interests. Therefore, in addition to the advantages firms possess, both Western and overseas Chinese firms strive to establish close connections, guanxi, with Chinese government/partners in order to gain an edge over competitors.

Guanxi as an Advantage in China Market

As mentioned previously, guanxi is an important resource for individuals and firms in China to induce cooperation and govern relationships efficiently. *Guanxiwang* is the network of these continuing relationships used to secure favors in personal and organizational relations.[1] The underlying premise is that Chinese firms utilize guanxi to manage organizational interdependence, and to mitigate institutional disadvantages, structural weaknesses, and other environmental threats.[48] With guanxi, one is an "insider": negotiations proceed smoothly and much can be accomplished. Without it, one is an "outsider" with little chance of success. As China continues to attract investors because of its economic perspective, guanxi utilization has become increasingly pervasive and has been deemed to have certain implications for international executives active in this economy.

In Chinese culture, guanxi, or connections, have historically been critical to facilitating business.[51] Nowadays, the art of guanxi is essential for obtaining scarce resources as well as dealing with the bureaucratic maze in China. In the business arena, there is a well-accepted "motto" among non-Chinese investors in China: "Who you know counts more than what you know." It is not only the products that make the deal, but the relationship.[52] Chinese firms develop guanxi as a strategic mechanism to overcome competitive and resource disadvantages by cooperating and exchanging favors with competitive forces and government authorities. These informal social networks are developed through natural relationships such as family, marriage, schooling, and work.[44] Whereas overseas Chinese businesses—particularly those from Hong Kong and Taiwan—have contributed greatly to the improvement of China's economy in general. Many believe that the overseas Chinese have an inherent advantage over Western investors because of their shared culture, ethnics, and language. Although managers all over the world devote a considerable amount of time and energy in cultivating interpersonal ties,[53] Chinese managers perhaps "rely more heavily on the cultivation of personal relationships to cope with the exigencies of their situation."[54] *Guanxi* is an important asset for overseas Chinese businesses in competing with Western rivals in China.

Foreign Investments in China

Ever since China engaged in economic reforms and adopted an open door policy, their society constituted the largest FDI absorption territory. According to UNCTAD, China is the single largest FDI recipient in the developing world. In 2007, FDI in China reached a record high $83.5 billion.[55] These foreign funds flowed into China from different source countries and were distributed in highly unequal amounts to different regions across the country. Whereas FDI in many parts of the world has declined it has continued its increase in China since 2008.

Prior to the period of the open door policy, political conflicts and power struggles often hindered China's economic development. China has experienced several stages in its efforts to attract foreign direct investment. From 1979 to 1985, China invited FDI for purpose of export expansion; however, the policy had many limitations for foreign investors intending to sell products to the local market. From 1986 to 1989, China broadened investment opportunities by allowing more manufactured products to enter its domestic market. In the last decade, in an attempt to absorb more investment from Taiwan and other large multinational companies from the developed countries, China improved its investment environment and allowed foreign investors to enter financial and service sectors. Special economic zones (SEZs) in two southeastern provinces, Guangdong and Fujian, offering special incentives and infrastructural advantages, also attracted many mature export-oriented firms.

Current Chinese foreign investment policy encourages export-oriented foreign enterprises and high technology enterprises. Chinese authorities usually emphasize the desirability of attracting FDI that brings in high technology, increases exports, and develops infrastructure. In general, during the past two decades, FDI has been the dominant economic element and has generated special and significant effects on the growth of national income and export performance in the SEZs.

While China's market and its rapid economic growth rate are very attractive to multinational corporations, the present economic retrenchment and other constraints inherent in its legal framework create many uncertainties for foreign investors. Indeed, the booming economy offers foreign investors many attractive business opportunities to access the Chinese vast market and exploit its potentialities. However, China is a country where information exchange through official channels is limited and the legal system and various intergovernmental mechanisms do not provide adequate protection of foreign property and contracts. Foreign investors may face additional difficulties if they are unfamiliar with China's unique business environment. Moreover, language and cultural barriers and omnipresent and burdensome Chinese bureaucracy also present additional difficulties to foreign (especially Western) investors. A most striking feature of Chinese business environment and one likely to confuse newcomers is the importance of personal connections (guanxi) with regional authorities, bureaucracies and individuals in conducting business operations.

While many Western firms—especially small- to medium-sized entrepreneurial organizations—balk at seemingly insurmountable obstacles, some overseas Chinese firms have managed to get around them and turn these problems to their advantage through informal channels such as personal contact and family connections. Through these networks, trade and investment information is passed along, business introductions are made, and deals are done often on handshakes. Gao investigated whether overseas ethnic Chinese play a positive role in FDI in China and how important this role is quantitatively.[56] Ethnicity, common language, and many other factors may have contributed to the large FDI flows from Hong Kong and Taiwan into China. It is natural for businesses in these two regions to turn to a neighbor such as Mainland China that offers both unlimited supply of cheap labor and a potentially large market. Geographic proximity, labor costs, and market potential can all play a role in the large inflows of FDI in China from Hong Kong and Taiwan. When seeking to do business in China it is important to remember the importance of guanxi and be patient when working through the mazes of the government bureaucracy.

Summary

With 1.3 billion people China has nearly one-quarter of the world's population and continues to be an economic giant that is continuing to grow while much of the rest of the world continues to contract. At the core of the Chinese business world is the importance of guanxi, a multidimensional construct dealing with social interactions and relationships. Foreign direct investment has continued to increase in China and, while expected to slow down during times of recession, it is expected to continue to increase as happened in the downturn of 1999 to 2000.

Discussion Questions

1. Define renqing (human feelings) and mianzi (face) and how they play a part in guanxi.
2. Explain what is meant by the guanxi being reciprocal. What unspoken rules are implied between parties?
3. Describe group identification and altercasting as ways to build guanxi.
4. Describe Chinese economic development prior to its period of "open door" policy.
5. Other than geographical proximity, why would countries like Hong Kong and Taiwan invest heavily in China?

Endnotes

1. Yang, M. 1994. *Gifts, Favors, and Banquets: The Art of Social Relationships in China*. New York: Cornell University Press: 49.
2. King, A. 1991. *Guanxi* and network building: A sociological interpretation. *Daedalus* 120(2):63.
3. Jacobs, B. J. 1979. A preliminary model of particularistic ties in Chinese political alliances: Kan-Ching and Huan-His in a rural Taiwanese Township. *China Quarterly* 78:237–273.
4. Chiao, C. 1982. *Guanxi*: A preliminary conceptualization. In: Yang, K. S., and C. I. Wen, eds. *The Socialization of Social and Behavioral Science Research in China*. Taipei: Academia Sinica: 345–360.
5. Pye, L. W. 1982. *Chinese Commercial Negotiating Style*. Cambridge: Gunn & Hain Publishers Inc.
6. Yeung, Y., and R. L. Tung. 1996. Achieving business success in Confucian societies: The importance of guanxi (connections). *Organizational Dynamics* 25(2):54–65.
7. Xin, K., and J. L. Pearce. 1996. *Guanxi*: connections as substitutes for formal institutional support. *Academy of Management Journal* 39(6):1641–1658.
8. Tsui, A. S., and J. L. Farh. 1997. Where guanxi matters: Relational demography in the Chinese context. *Work and Occupations* 24:56–79.
9. Campbell, N. 1987. Experiences of Western companies in China. *Euro-Asia Business Review* July:35–38.
10. Pearce, J., and R. Robinson, Jr. 2000. Cultivating guanxi as a foreign investor strategy. *Business Horizons* January–February:31–38.
11. Hwang, E. R. 1987. Face and favor: the Chinese power game. *American Journal of Sociology* 92:35–41.
12. Luo, Y., and M. Chen. 1996. Managerial implications of guanxi-based business strategies. *Journal of International Management* 2(4):293–316.
13. Alston, J. P. 1989. Wa, gianxi, and inhwa: managerial principles in Japan, China, and Korea. *Business Horizons* March–April;26–31.
14. Redding, S. G., and M. Ng. 1982. The role of face in the organizational perceptions of Chinese managers. *Organizational Studies* 3;204–209.
15. Luo, Y., and M. Chen. 1997. Does guanxi influence firm performance? *Asia Pacific Journal of Management* 14:1–16.
16. Ambler, T., Styles, C., and X. Wang. 1999. The effect of channel relationships and guanxi on the performance of inter-province export ventures in the People's Republic of China. *International Journal of Research in Marketing* 16(1):75–87.

17. Weidenbaum, M., and S. Hughes. 1996. *The Bamboo Networks*. New York: Martin Kessler Books, the Free Press.

18. Luo, Y. 1997. Pioneering in China: Risks and benefits. *Long Range Planning* 30:768–776.

19. Chu, G. C., and Y. Ju. 1993. *The Great Wall in Ruins*. Albany, NY: State University of New York Press.

20. Chen, M. 1994. *Guanxi* and the Chinese art of network building. *New Asia Review*. Summer:40–43.

21. Davies, H., Leung, T. K., Luk, S. T., and Y. Wong. 1995. The benefits of "*guanxi*." *Industrial Marketing Management* 24(3):207–214.

22. Xing & Pearce, 1996.

23. Wall, J. A. 1990. Managers in the People's Republic of China. *Academy of Management Executive* 4;19–32.

24. Tao, J. 1988. Cooperative joint ventures in China. *International Financial Law Review* 7(10):34–36; Punnett B. J., and P. Yu. 1990. Attitudes toward doing business with the PRC. *International Studies of Management and Organization* 20:149–160.

25. Portes, A., ed. 1995. Economic sociology and the sociology of immigration: A conceptual overview. *The Economic Sociology of Immigration*. New York: Russell Sage Foundation: 1–41.

26. Rauch, J., and A. Casella. 1998. Overcoming informational barriers to international resource allocation: Prices and group ties. NBER Working Paper No. 6628.

27. Pierre, B. 1986. The forms of capital. In: Richardson, J. G., ed. *Handbook of Theory and Research for the Sociology of Education*. New York: Greenwood Press: 241–258.

28. Hodder, R. 1996. Far Eastern Economic Review. *Hong Kong* 159(5):28.

29. Granovetter, M. 1985. Economic action and social structure: the problem of embeddedness. *American Journal of Sociology* 91:481–510.

30. Axelsson, B., and G. Easton. 1992. *Industrial Networks: A New View of Reality*. London: Routledge.

31. Johanson, J., and L. Mattsson. 1985. Marketing investments and market investments in industrial networks. *International Journal of Research in Marketing* 2(3):185–195.

32. Burt, R. 1997. The contingent value of social capital. *Administrative Science Quarterly* 42:339–365.

33. Powell, W. W. 1990. Neither market nor hierarchy: Network forms of organizational. In: Staw, B. M., and L. L. Cummings, eds. *Research in Organizational Behavior*. Vol 12. Greenwich, CT: JAI Press: 295–336.

34. Hamilton, G. 1991. *Business Networks and Economic Development in East and Southeast Asia*. Hong Kong: Centre of Asian Studies, University of Hong Kong.

35. Ford, D. 1984. Buyer seller relationships in international industrial markets. 13:101–112.

36. Coviello, N. E., and M. Kristina. 1999. Internationalization of service SMEs: an integrated perspective from the engineering consulting sector. *Journal of International Marketing* 7(4):42–66.

37. Coviello, N., and H. Munro. 1995. Growing the entrepreneurial firm: Networking for international market development. *European Journal of Marketing* 29(7):49–61.

38. Bjorkman, I., and S. Kock. 1997. Inward international activities in service firms—illustrated by three firms from the tourism industry. *International Journal of Service Industries Management* 8:362–376.

39. Fontes, M., and R. Coombs. 1997. The coincidence of technology and market objectives in the internationalization of new technology-based firms. *International Small Business Journal* 15(4):14–35.

40. Zafarullah, M., Ali, M., and S. Young. 1998. The internationalization of the small firm in developing countries: Exploratory research from Pakistan. *Journal of Global Marketing* 11(3):21–40.

41. Ai, J. 1994. *Canadian companies doing business in China—key success factors*. Unpublished MBA thesis. Simon Fraser University.

42. Abramson, N. R., and J. X. Ai. 1999. Canadian companies doing business in China: Key success factors. *Management International Review* 39(1):7–35.

43. Wank, D. 1996. The institutional process of market clientelism: *Guanxi* and private business in a South China city. *The China Quarterly* 147:820–838.

44. Luo, Y. 1997. *Guanxi* and International joint venture performance in China: An empirical inquiry. *Management International Review* 37:20–39.

45. Peng, M. W., and Y. Luo. 2000. Managerial ties and firm performance in a transition economy: the nature of a micro-macro link. *Academy of Management Journal* 43:486–501.

46. Ewing, M., Caruana, A., and H. Wong. 2000. Some consequences of guanxi: a sino-Singaporean perspective. *Journal of International Consumer Marketing* 12(4):75–89.

47. Kotler, P., Ang, S. W., Leong, S. M., and C. T. Tan. 1996. *Marketing Management: An Asian Perspective*. Singapore: Prentice-Hall Pergamon, Oxford.

48. Park, S. H., and Y. Luo. 2001. *Guanxi* and organizational dynamics: organizational networking in Chinese firms. *Strategic Management Journal* 22:455–477.

49. China says foreign direct investment up 35.1 percent. *The China Post*. November 13, 2008.

50. Davies, H. 1995. *China Business: Context and Issues*. Longman Asia Ltd., Hong Kong.

51. Tsang, W. K. 1998. Can *guanxi* be a source of sustained competitive advantage for doing business in China? *Academy of Management Executive* 12(2):64–73.

52. De Keijzer, A. J. 1992. *China: Business Strategies for the 90s*. Berkeley, CA: Pacific View Press.

53. Mintzberg, H. 1973. *The Nature of Managerial Work*. New York: Harper & Row.

54. Child, J. 1994. *Management in China During the Age of Reform*. Cambridge, England: Cambridge University Press: 150.

55. UNCTAD. World Investment Report 2008.

56. Gao, T. 2000. Ethnic Chinese networks and international investment evidence from inward FDI in China. September.

Part Four

International Case Study

Chapter Fifteen

DIRECT SELLING WORLDWIDE:

THE MARY KAY COSMETICS STORY

Dianne H. B. Welsh, *The University of North Carolina, Greensboro*
Yvonne Pendleton, *Director, Corporate Heritage Mary Kay Inc.*

Learning Objectives

Upon completion of this chapter, students should be able to:

- Understand the history of Mary Kay, Inc. and how Mary Kay Ash's basic guideposts on the human spirit and her belief in the abilities of women in particular have made the company a worldwide success.
- Understand the strategy behind their expansion around the globe.
- Understand the beliefs, norms, values, and culture that has made Mary Kay, Inc. one of the strongest direct selling companies in history.

⊙ Introduction

Mary Kay, Inc. had achieved prominence as a U.S. cosmetics company and direct seller, but the company had not even reached its tenth year when international opportunities knocked on its Dallas door. The year was 1971 when a couple of Australian entrepreneurs—so impressed by what they had seen and read of the company—persisted to get Mary Kay's first international outpost in this faraway land down under. That's how it came to be that Mary Kay was in Australia before it was anywhere else outside the U.S. The company now has a presence in more than thirty international markets on five continents and the focus for expansion is clearly on those places where the opportunity will be most appealing to entrepreneurial women.

What has transpired throughout the world is the creation of an interpersonal business model that seems to translate into a language and economic opportunity that women understand. Mary Kay's history illustrates how an American company can expertly tailor its marketing plan to emphasize specific market strengths. In regions where women are even more under-employed than they were in the United States of the mid-sixties, Mary Kay can be the great equalizer, the quintessential micro-entrepreneurial opportunity that has the potential to bring an entire family up from poverty or dire straits. Even in countries where infrastructures are far inferior to those of the United States, the company has experienced the great loyalty of women who—once they are exposed to the company philosophy and possibilities—will go to great lengths to make it work for their lives, in their market. According to company president and CEO David Holl, it is in developing an independent sales force and a corporate staff that understand the importance of Mary Kay's culture that the company's global development plan has the greatest chance for success. When the culture is understood and acted on, Mary Kay has seen success. Where it is not understood or embraced, the company has experienced difficulty.

The same year that Australia opened was coincidentally also the year that the company took another measure that would have far-reaching effects on the culture and the company's success.

In 1971, it named the first two Mary Kay Independent National Sales Directors—establishing an extremely prophetic leadership role that would come to be viewed as one of the smartest succession plans in the business world. It was pure and simple a strategic move—instigated by Mary Kay Ash herself—that has fostered female entrepreneurs like few others. It has been generally accepted that no one would ever replace the dynamic and charismatic company founder, but the founder had embarked, in establishing this position, upon a program where she could encourage leaders of hers and of succeeding generations to create new leaders. The prospect of achieving this pinnacle has greatly enhanced the appeal of the organization worldwide to entrepreneurial women aspiring to leadership.

Texas entrepreneur Mary Kay Ash founded her company on a shoestring in a small Dallas office center after vowing to create a company where women were provided opportunities long denied them in the workplace. She always said that she never imagined her cosmetics company would make it much outside Dallas city limits, let alone to nearly every time zone in the world. What the illustrious company founder did realize was that—just like in the America of the 1960s—the carving out of opportunity reverberates extremely well throughout every culture and language. "We discovered that all women want the same thing," Mary Kay Ash once said. "They want a better life for themselves, their families, and their countries. And they are willing to work for that."

Perhaps it is that common thread—paired with Mary Kay's 1963 founding belief that she wanted to create opportunities for women—that has contributed most to the company's fame as well as its growth as a company whose mission is to "enrich women's lives."

Corporate employees of Mary Kay, including the founder's own grandson, attest that seeing this mission to fruition in the United States is exhilarating. However, it is in the witnessing of this phenomenon outside the United States that they come to understand the strength, stability, and long-term possibilities of the company's mission. After a forty-five-year run, the potential for Mary Kay remains huge.

The Americas

By 1976, when the company's stock was first listed on the New York Stock Exchange, it had already opened three U.S. distribution centers in the South and on the East and West Coasts when a major opportunity arose. That was Canada, where in 1978 Mary Kay Ash answered repeated requests from its neighbor to the north. Canadians love to relate the cosmetic icon's first visit to their country. It was in the midst of a deadly winter storm that the petite dynamo came, sans boots, to meet and rally the Canadian independent sales force. Despite radio safety warnings to stay at home because of difficulty traveling, Canadian women came out to meet and greet Mary Kay in a hotel ballroom. It was said to be so cold there was ice forming inside the ballroom windows, yet Mary Kay's magnetism warmed the crowd. They definitely warmed to her message. That began a lifelong mutual admiration between the Texan and her Canadian operation. One executive who traveled with Mary Kay Ash on several subsequent visits said, "She was the consummate hands-on leader and that made a real impression with the women of Canada." Mary Kay never hesitated to get out from behind her desk and go up close and personal to disseminate her caring leadership style.

A *Reader's Digest* article, "Mary Kay's Sweet Smell of Success," appeared in late 1978, and just one year later the company and its founder were profiled on television's *60 Minutes*. This latter 1970s media attention would, coincidentally, set the stage for a continued bright future for the company, both domestically and globally.

Mary Kay expanded to Argentina in 1980. In 1986—shortly after the company was returned to private ownership—the first European operation, Mary Kay Germany, was established. Expansion to Asia didn't begin in earnest until the 1990s.

Argentina and Mexico offer two great examples in the Americas region that validate and provide insight into how closely the company's global success is aligned to its culture. Both countries have weathered economic crises that—rather than rocking them—only solidified Mary Kay's position in those markets. Argentina came on board in 1980 but it wasn't until 2001 that its staying power was proved. There was an economic crisis that year that saw a blistering 300% currency devaluation as well as a financial collapse. According to Mary Kay Latin American President Jose Smeke, even amidst these dire straits, "Our sales force count nearly doubled from 12,000 Independent Beauty Consultants to 20,000. There was a 28% sales increase in local currency." Why? How? Smeke says Mary Kay Argentina knew what to do in 2001 during this economic crisis because one of its most successful sister subsidiaries, Mary Kay Mexico, founded in 1988, had survived and thrived through a similar economic crisis in 1994. In Mexico that year, there was a currency devaluation of more than 150% in one day, a 20% unemployment rate, political uncertainty, and price increases of up to 60%.

"We faced daunting obstacles, but we had a commitment to our independent sales force and their families, and so we took some risks for them," says Smeke, who believes the appreciation and support of Mary Kay Inc. to Mary Kay Mexico at that time (and to Argentina seven years later) provided the trust and confidence that would see sales increase by 80% by the end of 1995, as well as a 35% increase in consultant count. "We had," Smeke recalls, "a sales force in very high spirits. Their accomplishments proved that during a crisis a direct selling company can be a very good option for women who need to help support their families." In Mexico and elsewhere in the Mary Kay world, one key most certainly makes a huge difference. "We always said to these small business owners, 'you are in business *for* yourself, but not *alone*,'" explains one corporate veteran.

The company's fortunes are closely tied to the performance of its independent sales force. Mary Kay Mexico had opened in 1988 when the U.S. parent company was twenty-five years old. In Mexico, Mary Kay has already celebrated its twentieth anniversary with an independent sales force of more than 250,000. There, as well as elsewhere in the region, there are dramatic and life-changing stories of triumph over illiteracy, poverty, and even war. Who are the women of this sales force? Throughout the world, their backgrounds and lifestyles are as varied as they are in the United States. Their stories portray the Mary Kay mission to enrich women's lives extremely poignantly. When Mary Kay Mexico published a call for stories to celebrate its fifteenth anniversary in 2003, hundreds of stories poured in. The best of those stories would be published in *Reader's Digest Mexico*. Among them were numerous stories like that of the fruit store merchant who had worked long hours with little to show. Without a car, but with the mentoring of her Independent National Sales Director, she decided to devote as much time to her Mary Kay business as she had to her fruit stand. She is now a successful Mary Kay Independent Sales Director in Mexico, planting many more fruitful seeds for growth than her produce stand ever would or could have provided.

Even husbands of sales force members, on occasion, will testify to the life-changing potential they have seen this opportunity offers their wives and their families. One of the things they always express appreciation for is the Mary Kay emphasis on family and balance, which resonates particularly well in these cultures. The company is proud of the twelve shelters it has helped fund across Mexico for women and children who are victims of domestic violence.

Mary Kay Ash saw the huge potential of changing women's lives in Mexico very early on. Not only did she enroll in Spanish classes, she often spoke to Spanish-speaking leaders in their native language. Even though in Mexico she was known to have ordered "a grandfather" once in a restaurant when she wanted a glass of milk, Mary Kay's love for the language and the culture was always a source of great pride to her Spanish-speaking "daughters" as she called them. The first Independent National Sales Director in the United States of Spanish descent was an immigrant who had been airlifted from Cuba to the United States with parental consent in 1961 to prevent her indoctrination into communism. By 1975, she was enamored with the thought that she could earn the use of a pink Cadillac like the one she had seen in Mary Kay literature. By 1977, she had her first of many pink Cadillacs, and in 1991 was named a Mary Kay Independent National Sales Director.

Mary Kay Brazil celebrated its tenth anniversary in 2008 with impressive increases in growth as well as sales. The seeds of entrepreneurship also flourish today in Brazil, where an American woman of Brazilian descent decided to take her knowledge and skills as a Mary Kay Independent Sales Director and start over in the land of her forebears. With eighteen years of Mary Kay business experience in the United States, she knew the huge potential Brazil would have for this company and its mission to enrich women's lives. She took a giant leap of faith, returning to Brazil to begin a new Mary Kay chapter in her life. It paid off. Only four years after starting over, this woman became Brazil's first Independent National Sales Director in August 2003—just five years following Mary Kay's opening in Brazil.

Mary Kay's General Manager in Brazil says that this woman's successful journey represents a true milestone. "Other women have started to see everything that's possible. She is, they reasoned, 'just like me' and so they came to understand how they could do the same."

Europe

The company had celebrated its thirtieth anniversary and had crossed the threshold as a billion dollar business at retail by the time Mary Kay Russia opened in 1993. By 2008, this market continued to grow in sales and profitability with a remarkable compounded annual sales growth rate over 35%. Not only has it become a pillar of strength, it is clearly among the best places on the globe to see the power of success potential that results from entrepreneurs with a penchant for hard work. Looking at Russia and the surrounding nations, it's apparent that the principles, career path, and products of this Dallas company have made the transition into an international opportunity that transcends generations, language and culture. Today, there are more than 380,000 Independent Beauty Consultants in Russia and some sixty women in Russia have ascended to the most prestigious sales force position of Independent National Sales Director. Mary Kay Russia also symbolizes that it is possible to transcend weather and wartime.

The story of one Independent National Sales Director from a region in the far east of Russia illustrates how enterprising women can overcome economic woes and a severe climate. For this woman, building her business often necessitated month-long waits for products to arrive when inclement weather would prohibit air travel to and from the area. She built it anyway. So intent was another woman to get her products to her market that she would routinely fly in the cargo hold of an airplane in order to make the nine hour trek to the distribution center.

Another Independent National Sales Director hails from Chechnya, a region torn by wars since the time of the czars through the Soviet period and even today. This former music teacher left Chechnya for Moscow to discover the only work she could find was cleaning floors. Her Mary Kay business brought a radical lifestyle change, affording her the luxury of owning her first car in the mid-1990s and the financial ability to unite her family, long separated by poverty and unrest at home.

Mary Kay has also been an important phenomenon during the second phase of "perestroika"—the end of the USSR and the start of privatization and reform.

The president of Mary Kay's Europe Region, Tara Eustace, resides in Russia where she says she has seen Mary Kay contribute to a better way of life, a change of thinking, and many positive influences. She recalls how Mary Kay Ash was overjoyed and proud to bring the Mary Kay opportunity to the former Eastern Bloc countries. Many in the Mary Kay world fondly recall the founder's visit to Germany shortly after the fall of the Berlin Wall. Germany had come on board in 1986 but shortly after reunification of East and West Germany, a newly free East German Independent Beauty Consultant just couldn't contain her enthusiasm when she walked across the stage to shake the hand of Mary Kay Ash. She grabbed the microphone and proclaimed, "First we get freedom, and then we get Mary Kay!"

Eustace says Europe has followed the Mary Kay model very closely. Russia in particular has adapted to the lack of infrastructure (post, delivery, poor phone lines, emerging bank infrastructure, lack of personal check or credit card systems) by developing a customer service operation center where placement and payment for orders as well as education can take place. Some of the largest recognition meetings for Mary Kay Russia have been held at the Kremlin, which at one time was one of the few venues large enough.

Eustace believes that often the most effective way to deal with a less than positive impression of the direct selling model is by careful attention to teaching and focusing first on quality rather than quantity. "A great Mary Kay staff," she concludes, "helps the new market attract and teach those very first vital Independent Beauty Consultants. Together they will build the opportunity in their country."

Eustace recalls hearing the poignant story of a woman from Odessa who is an Independent National Sales Director in the Ukraine. The home she lived in had no plumbing and no water. Today the woman recounts how one hot summer day she and her young son were dust-covered from hitchhiking along the motorway. "I was angry at myself and my miserable life," she writes, "when suddenly in the row of dusty cars, I see a white, clean Mercedes. That Mercedes became my dream." Today the woman drives a pink Mercedes courtesy of Mary Kay. She and her family vacation at the best international seaside resorts; her son studies at the most prestigious school and attends the finest sports club. "And owing to Mary Kay, I managed to make my dreams real," she says.

The entire Europe region is filled with stories of dreams come true and lives changed. Mary Kay Europe covers thirteen time zones and occupies eleven main offices and warehouses in the region. Its independent sales force numbers nearly 700,000.

Asia Pacific

If the prospect of a recognition and rally meeting of a U.S.-based capitalist company taking place at the Kremlin isn't enough of a contrast, imagine then that kind of a rally taking place in China. It is in this ancient land that Mary Kay has seen wonderful success. China, today the eighth largest consumer of cosmetics, is Mary Kay's most profitable subsidiary. It is also recognized by the business community. *Fortune China* named Mary Kay one of the top ten companies to work for in China for three years running. Not only is the marketing plan successful, Mary Kay manufactures its products at its facility in Hangzhou, and was the first cosmetics company that China granted a quality control and guarantee system certificate in 1998, just three short years after Mary Kay opened for business in China. Perhaps even more significant is the impact that the venerable culture of this American company has had on the historic land and its people. K. K. Chua, president of Mary Kay Asia, says he knew from the beginning that Mary Kay principles would transfer well into Chinese culture. "Confucius taught if you want others to treat you well, you must first treat others the same." As we examine the various components of what constitutes the Mary Kay culture, it is closely aligned with the Asian culture.

The region has not been an easy one to excel in. Mary Kay China faced daunting obstacles including a government ban on direct selling shortly after it opened. During the six months of the ban, more than 4,000 Mary Kay Independent Sales Force says Chua, "refused to go away." By the time Mary Kay was back in business, these faithful sales force members were ready to carry China to its current status as the company's largest subsidiary.

In addition to many inspiring stories, Chua points out that Mary Kay has made its way in China by following yet another of the founding principles. The belief in giving back to the communities has taken root in reinvesting part of its profits into the lives of the country's women. There is a micro credit fund for female workers, schools in mountain regions where female children have been too poor to attend school, scholarships for female students at two prominent universities, and youth projects emphasizing skills training. The most telling of the impact of Mary Kay Ash on a culture so far removed from her own is the small rose garden outside a maternity hospital in Shanghai. It commemorates Mary Kay's life and philosophy and this Mary Kay garden honors the fact that this American woman's legacy is firmly established in China.

Equally heartwarming is a painting that hangs in the Mary Kay Museum at the world headquarters in Dallas. The Chinese street scene was painted by a renowned Chinese artist as a thank you to Mary Kay Ash. The artist paid tribute to this American businesswoman who had provided her a first chance at developing her personality. In the tribute letter, she poured out the heartwarming story of never having spoken until her teens. Although recognized as an artist she was extremely uncomfortable around people until her own Mary Kay network gave her the confidence among people that had eluded her for her entire adult life.

Another strong testament comes from the woman who ranks among the top Independent National Sales Directors in international operations. In China, she was one of the fifteen pioneers in the Mary Kay Independent Sales Force—one whose fierce determination to excel at her Mary Kay business could not be dampened. By her late twenties, she had attained the prestigious Independent National Sales Director position and in her mid-thirties, ascended to first place among international Independent National Sales Directors. A medical doctor and National Sales Director told of never having worn makeup before she was thirty years old. Her mother believed only "bad girls" wore cosmetics. She came to know the company through its products and eventually left the medical profession to pursue a Mary Kay business. She says today, "In my mind, Mary Kay is a footstone. On this base, women's dreams could come true: beautiful appearance, harmonious family, bright life."

Another National Sales Director in China today has difficulty believing how her life has changed since she first began her Mary Kay business. She fondly recalls how she would regale her skin care class participants by telling them about the Texas-based legend and those infamous pink cars of the Mary Kay world. She went on to qualify, in 2000, for the first pink car in China. Having gone from being a jobless, homeless, and poverty stricken divorced mother to becoming an international success story is indeed a powerful journey. It is a journey that breathes belief into other women aspiring for their own brand of Mary Kay success. It is a confidence-inspiring journey that Mary Kay's history has proven others will emulate.

The Asia Pacific region is Mary Kay's largest outside the United States and encompasses nearly half the world's population, making it instrumental in the company's long range growth vision. In 2007, Mary Kay opened a subsidiary in India, where according to Chua, the company anticipates generating the same success experienced in other Asia Pacific markets, a region where there are more than 365,000 Independent Beauty Consultants.

Summary

The culture and principles of Mary Kay shape the heart of the company, no matter its location worldwide. Mary Kay is intent upon continuing its success and, in fact, achieved six years early an internal corporate challenge that by the company's fiftieth anniversary in 2013 international sales as well as the international independent sales force would exceed that of the United States. By 2004, the international business sales projection was expected to exceed what the entire United States did in the year 2001, and the company had targeted a new growth goal of five by fifty: $5 billion in revenues by its fiftieth anniversary in 2013.

With its vision to enrich women's lives, the company has gone to extra lengths to make the heart of the company the focus of international education and development. While the lucrative nature of the Mary Kay marketing plan and the staying power of a recognized brand would seemingly be sufficient, that's not enough. It's not enough, Holl says, that a woman can earn potentially at one hundred times the average per capita income of her country. This success works so much better and lasts longer when it is applied according to Mary Kay's founding principles. In 1963 when Mary Kay Ash stressed her Golden Rule style of doing business, it was a foreign concept to even a U.S.-based company. Today, that style is so celebrated that a recent newsletter took the time to spell out how the Golden Rule translates into all the major cultures and faiths of the world, and Mary Kay has adapted Golden Rule Customer Service as one of its most important platforms. There is always the emphasis on what Mary Kay saw as, "belief in the beautiful potential of women" that also drives Mary Kay's global success. Once the sales force understands the Mary Kay culture, adapting business systems to the customs and mores of each new country becomes a much simpler process. But it is never simple.

Mary Kay's international staff will talk of a starter kit designed for the tastes of Western women who drive their cars everywhere and how its size wreaked havoc on women in Asia who typically walk and take bicycles or buses everywhere. They will allude to how much more "global" the color palette and formulas of Mary Kay brands are today as they routinely conduct product focus groups on a multitude of skin tones and in nine languages. Even a recent new Independent Sales Director education session in Dallas featured fully one-tenth of the attendees needing translation into languages such as Polish, French, Cantonese, and Spanish. But more important than the language is the common and shared experience all women relate to. That will, in summary, make the difference for this American company. When accepting the posthumous academic award given Mary Kay Ash as "Greatest Female Entrepreneur in American History," her grandson and company executive Ryan Rogers said, "Mary Kay tapped into one of the greatest under-used natural resources this nation had to offer—the hearts and minds of its women." It is much the same today throughout the more than thirty markets where Mary Kay has a presence, and in those parts of the world that women have even fewer opportunities.

Direct selling is one of the only forms of retailing that can adapt to virtually any conditions or circumstances and Mary Kay is a great example of this. Entrepreneurs and capitalists alike have come to see that when direct selling operates by the highest of standards, it can make amazing strides in contributing toward solid world economies. Mary Kay, Inc. believes so strongly in the business principles established by Mary Kay Ash that, in 2008, it released an updated version of the founder's 1984 best seller, her only book about the business, now titled, *The Mary Kay Way: Timeless Principles from America's Greatest Woman Entrepreneur* (Wiley). Mary Kay, Inc. follows the ethical standards set by the Direct Selling Association (DSA), and was instrumental in seeing the document to fruition in the 1970s and strengthening it in the 1990s and again in 2007 when two of its top corporate officers chaired the DSA. The DSA is the industry trade organization comprised of 150 direct selling member companies worldwide and has been an advocate of ethical business practices and consumer services. The DSA Code of Ethics has served the industry well, an industry now comprised of some 15 million independent sales people.

The culture of Mary Kay, Inc. reflects today the caring attitude its founder, Mary Kay Ash, established at the outset. David Holl, president and chief executive officer, believes that, "A fiscally sound company can also be a nurturing and caring company. We have a larger goal than selling a product. I have seen firsthand the stories of self-esteem and personal growth that abound throughout the Mary Kay world. I know nothing would please our founder more." Holl continues, "We have experienced in more than four decades that the businesses that succeed the most in Mary Kay are those built and based on the number of lives touched. Having someone in your market break a belief barrier is extremely important. Having them succeed by following Mary Kay principles is even more important."

◎ Acknowledgment

The authors would like to thank Robin Diamond, Direct Selling Educational Foundation (DSEF), the employees of Mary Kay, Inc., and Joan Gillman, University of Wisconsin, for their assistance. A previous version of this case was presented at the International Council for Small Business (ICSB) Conference in Washington, DC, in June 2005.

GLOSSARY

Achievement vs. Ascription: Achievement-oriented type in negotiations tends to have characteristics similar to those associated with high individualism, masculinity, and short-term orientation. Ascription cultures are likely to be associated with the characteristics of collectivism, femininity, and long-term orientation.

ATLAS (Automated Trade Locator Assistance System):   Assists the entrepreneur considering exporting by identifying the largest potential markets for their products and/or services using a variety of criteria (including sales and dollar volume).

Body Language: Surrounding events and circumstances, facial expression, and other unintended and informal communication aspects beyond the message itself.

Born Global Entrepreneurs: Early adopters of internationalization; they apply knowledge-based resources to sell output in multiple countries from at or near their founding.

CAFTA (Central American Free Trade Agreement):   A trade agreement linking 350 million people in countries with more than $1 trillion in gross national product, in order to reduce trade barriers, eliminate tariffs, open markets, and promote investment and economic growth among the signatories.

China: A country with one-quarter of the world's population and one of the fastest rates of economic growth.

Comparative Entrepreneurship: The study of how entrepreneurial practice differs across nations, and investigates the similarities and differences between international entrepreneurs base on their country of origin.

Contingency Theory: A theoretical perspective which concludes that the most profitable firms are likely to be those that "fit" with their environments. An entrepreneurial strategy is more likely to be successful when it is consistent with the organization's mission, competitive environment, and resources.

Contract Manufacturing: The arrangement of using cheaper overseas labor for the production of finished goods or parts by following an established production process.

Crisis Management: The process of planning for and implementing the response to a wide range of negative events that could severely affect an organization.

Cross-Cultural Communication: An entrepreneur from Culture A may initiate his/her international business venture by sending ideas, inquiries, intentions, proposals, descriptions, samples, etc. to an individual from Culture B.

Cross-Cultural Dimensions: Power distance, individualism, masculinity, uncertainty avoidance, long-term orientation, universalism, neutrality, specificity, achievement orientation, time orientation, view of environment,

Cultural Awareness: Comparing individual cultures to other cultures to not only learn about similarities and differences, but also about whom they are in comparison to others; and to gain specific knowledge about working and living in other countries and how to manage cultural differences.

Culture: A society's norms, beliefs, and values.

Culture: The collective programming of the mind that distinguishes the members of one human group from another, also viewed as a system of ideas and norms that are shared among a group of people and that when taken together constitute a design for living.

Demand Side Perspective: The rates or the context in which entrepreneurship occurs. It deals with sources of opportunities and the entrepreneurial roles that need to be filled in an economy.

Direct Communication: Preference for explicit one or two-way communication, primarily in words, including identification, diagnosis, and management of conflict.

Direct exporting: Products distributed directly through agents and/or distributors in the target country.

E-commerce: Helps businesses compete in an increasingly demanding marketplace with a wide scope of domestic and international exposure by improving operations, decreasing costs, increasing sales, and facilitating communication with customers, partners, and employees.

Economic Factors: Indicators such as physical and financial infrastructures, access to capital, gross national product, balance of payment and balance of trade situation, debt and servicing costs, inflation rate, interest rate, exchange rate, and exchange rate stability influencing entrepreneurship in an economy.

Economic Participation: Among the central tenets of market capitalism defined as freedom to pursue individual well-being (i.e., freedom of enterprise), private ownership of resources including property rights, market access, low barriers to entry, and competitive markets.

Economies of (global) scope: When a firm produces more it increases production levels, thereby fostering standardization and economies of scale. The company may also enjoy greater efficiencies in marketing and distribution.

ELAN (Export Legal Assistance Network): Connects the entrepreneur with experienced international trade attorneys to address issues such as contracts, agreements between parities involved in the various aspects of exporting, and payment resolution matter.

Emerging Markets: While there is no consensus definition for the term "emerging markets" Czinkota and Ronkainen (1997) identified three characteristics associated with an emerging economy: Level of Economic Development, Economic Growth, and Market Governance.

Entrepreneurial Capacity: The ability of entrepreneurs to respond to new opportunities.

Entrepreneurial Capitalism: Risk taking entrepreneurial spirit in which an individual or company seeks the potential for economic growth and development and profit.

Entrepreneurial Culture: When opportunities are declined within the strategic vision of a corporation, many bright minds either become an extension or leave the organization to build their own organization of leadership and vision.

Entrepreneurial Opportunity Environment: The in-country conditions that create opportunities for entrepreneurs.

Entrepreneurial Support Organizations: Resources the entrepreneur may call upon to assist him or her in the entire export process, particularly in the analysis of foreign markets. These resources help the entrepreneur better identify a foreign market and determine whether or not it will be a viable market for the entrepreneur.

Ethnic Culture: Distinctive ethnic groups populating a nation.

Expatriate Assignment: Students work in organizations as expatriates and after that experience, use their learning to turn to entrepreneurship later in their lives as a means to self-development and economic progress.

Export Costs: Licenses, fees, insurance, overseas shipping, customs agents, bills of lading, and a large investment of entrepreneur's time.

Export Management Company: An organization that assists in the export of the product/service of the business that is seeking to export its items to an international market.

Export Trading Company: A trade intermediary that purchases the product or service from the entrepreneur's business and then proceeds to transport and sell the item in an international market(s).

Exporting Mindset: An assessment of the enterprise and of the entrepreneur to determine the export readiness and what skills/abilities of the firm and the entrepreneur could benefit from training/assistance from an export specialist. It is a planned activity with a recognized commitment of the resources of the entrepreneur and his or her firm.

External Factors: Factors that affect a company's choice to enter a foreign market but are independent of management's decisions.

Family roles: Strong family influences on the mission and values of business enterprises. Family goals may override those of the company even for relatively large firms.

Financials: Financial data which reports a company's performance including profit and loss, cash flow forecast, balance sheet, break-even analysis, assumptions and comments.

Financing Options: The U.S. Small Business has three loan packages for entrepreneurs participating in exporting seeking financial and technical assistance: SBA Export*Express*, The Export Working Capital Loan, and the International Trade Loan.

Foreign Direct Investment: Foreign funds flowing directly into a country's economy, bringing in high technology, increased exports, and develops infrastructure and has significant effect on the growth of national income and export performance in the Special Economic Zones (SEZs).

Formal Communication: Places high emphasis on following protocol and social order.

Freight Forwarder: An organization that will transport the items of the exporting organization to the international destination.

Fully-owned Subsidiaries: Involves buying an existing business or building new facilities in a new target country. Allows companies to exercise maximum control over their operations and to decisively enter the target country's markets, they also expose the country to the highest level of political, environmental, legal and financial risk.

GATT (General Agreement on Tariffs and Trade): Expanding over 110 nations and over several decades, this cooperative agreement between several countries assists in relaxing quota and import license requirements, introducing fairer customs evaluation methods, and establishing a common mechanism to resolve trade disputes.

GEM Global Entrepreneurship Monitor: Systematic approach to comparing entrepreneurship across nations by measuring differences in the level of entrepreneurial activity among countries, uncovering factors determining the levels of entrepreneurial activity, and by identifying policies that may enhance the level of entrepreneurial activity.

Global Market Integration: When countries increase the flexibility of their economies through structural reforms and speed up their economies through their own integration into the global economy.

Guanxi: The Chinese meaning of "Guan" is either "to connect" or "a gate/pass that can be closed." To connect is to build a linkage between two independent individuals. The latter explanation meant a "door" and its extended meaning is "to close." Inside the door, you are "one of the group," but outside the door, you are barely recognized. "Xi" means to tie up and extend into relationships. To sum up, guanxi means "doing favors for and maintaining a relationship with someone you recognized." Particular ties between individuals based on trust and affection through which people exchange favors, social networking. "A status in which a person or an organization interacts with another person or organization, and in which they are mutually affected and enjoy mutual gains."

High Content/Low Context Communication: High content stresses straight forward exchange of facts in communication. Information is given primarily in words, and the meaning is expressed explicitly, often in writing: the entrepreneur says what is meant and means what is said. High content cultures tend to emphasize an intended content put in a structured, straightforward format.

High Context/Low Content Communication: Shared experience and established personal relations make certain things well understood without them needing to be stated explicitly (people can read between the lines and understand each other's "body language." Rules for speaking, keeping silence, and behaving are implicit in the context.

Hofstede Study: Reduced the world's vast cultural variety to five universal dimensions allowing for international comparisons in managerial patterns: power distance, individualism, masculinity, uncertainty avoidance, and long-term orientation.

Human Security: Security viewed as emerging from the conditions of daily life—assurance of civil liberties, food, shelter, employment, health, public safety, freedom from fear—rather than flowing downward from a country's foreign relations and military strength.

Import Industrialization Strategies: Shifting Latin America's political and economic interests from landed oligarchies toward production by incipient capitalists.

Incoterms: A common set of rules and terms used to describe terms of trade associated with international trade. The objective of Incoterms is to mitigate the confusion over the control and insurance products at the various stages of the shipping process.

Indirect Communication: Preference for implicit communication and conflict avoidance; expressive (emotive) and personal communication style with high degree of subjectivity, stress on relationships.

Indirect Exporting: Exported products sold overseas by intermediaries who specialize in entry modes activity from the home base.

Individual vs. collectivism: Individualism leads to reliance on self and focus on individual achievement; the extent to which individuals or closely knit social structures such as the extended family (collectivism) are the basis for social systems.

Industrial Organization: A branch of microeconomics, which emphasizes the influence of the industry environment upon a firm. A firm must adapt to influences in its industry to survive and prosper; its financial performance is primarily determined by the success of the industry in which it competes.

Industrialized Markets: Industrialized countries are developed countries with a high GDP per capita.

Informal Communication: Stress on dispensing with ceremony and rigid protocol.

Institutional Factors: Laws, policies, and regulations that promote and support entrepreneurial development.

Intelligent Career Model: DeFillippi and Arthur's model of education which focuses on developing students' individual competencies so that they may identify and act upon entrepreneurial opportunities. In business they advocate a learning-centered approach that reflects the shifts from employees' assumed long term commitment to a firm, in which competencies were built according to organizational needs to a model of occupational excellence, wherein employees seek to continually upgrade skills valuable to the global marketplace.

Internal Factors: A firm's resources, overall strategy, management mindset, time commitment and, very importantly, types of products or services considered for international markets. Key issues include: Financial Resources, Human Resources and types of products/services.

International Entrepreneurship: The discovery and evaluation of opportunities and the organization of resources to exploit opportunities across national borders to create fundamentally new goods and services.

International Franchising: A form of licensing that eliminates some of the concerns associated with technology, trademarks, patents and other intellectual property by giving more control to the franchisor company over the franchisee who has licensed the company's trademarks, products and/or services and production and /or operation processes.

International Franchising: Franchising which allows firms to achieve the expanded reach and efficiencies associated with internationalization more rapidly and effectively than firms could have on their own. The system of franchising used around the world sells over one trillion dollars worth of goods and services.

International Joint Ventures: A method for entering international markets when two or more companies share ownership of a third commercial entity and collaborate in the production of its goods and services.

International Licensing: The process of transferring the rights to a firm's products to an overseas company for the purpose of producing or selling it there.

International Negotiations: Business parties learn about the venture itself, the surrounding business environment, and of utmost importance, building trust while trying to strategically protect themselves.

Internationalization: The transformation of a domestic entrepreneur into one who does business in more than one country. A business response to globalization that occurs when a domestic firm begins to sell or operate across national borders.

Internationalized: When a firm moves from being a domestic firm to providing goods or services overseas.

Intrapreneurial Culture: Formulated strategies with a positive outlook towards global expansion for many multinational corporations.

Knowing Competencies: Reflects a person's values and motivation and relates to a person's identity and the fit between this identity and choices made relative to tasks, projects, organizations and countries, in addition it refers to the skills and knowledge needed for performance on the job, and the person's level of expertise.

Level of Economic Development: Measured in terms of GDP (Gross Domestic Product) per capita.
Economic Growth—Usually measured in terms of the country's GDP growth rate.
Market Governance—The extent of free market government control of key resources, stability of the market system, and the regulatory environment.

Liberalization: The decreased role of government in the economy, such as the privatization of government owned industries.

Long-Term Orientation: The extent to which people focus on past, present, or future. Present orientation leads to a focus on short-term performance.

Management Contract: A company in one country can utilize the expertise, technology, or specialized services of a company from another country to run its business for a set time and fee or percentage of sales.

Market Sustainability: The optimal level of government policy that fosters long-term economic growth as illustrated by the Market Sustainability Curve.

Marketing: The blueprint or description of products and services offered that keeps a company building upward toward customer satisfaction and business success. In involves tailoring product, price, packaging, position, and presentation based on industry analysis, competitive analysis, and customer analysis.

Masculinity vs. femininity: The extent to which assertiveness and independence from others is valued. High masculinity leads to high sex-role differentiation, ambition, and material goods.

NAFTA (North American Free Trade Agreement): A trilateral trade block consisting of Canada, Mexico and the United States. NAFTA seeks to strengthen cooperation, expand trade, and promote development among the three nations.

National Culture: Comprised of different subcultures existing in a nation along the lines of its ethnic groups, regions, industries, firms, social/interest groups, business firms, and individuals.

Necessity Entrepreneurs: Entrepreneurs who create ventures for self-employment to make up for the lack of other job opportunities in their environment.

Neoliberalism: An economic philosophy blending concerns for social justice with an emphasis on economic growth.

Neutral vs. emotional: Interactions are based on objectivity and neutrality, or they are based on emotional bonds.

OPIC (Overseas Private Investment Corporations): A U.S. governmental development agency that works to encourage economic growth and development in emerging markets principally by issuing insurance programs designed to mitigate the risk a business may encounter in international trade especially as related to political instability and market reforms.

Opportunity Entrepreneurs: Entrepreneurs who form new ventures because they see the opportunity for potential rewards.

Opportunity Environment: The in-country conditions that create opportunities for entrepreneurs.

Organizational Culture: External vs. internal, task vs. focus, conformity vs. individuality, safety vs. risk, ad-hoc vs. planned, industry-based specifics, company size, community impact and other.

Outsourcing: Contracting out a firm's non-core, non-revenue-producing activities to other organizations primarily (but not always) to reduce costs. When implemented properly, outsourcing can cut costs, improve performance, and refocus the core business.

Planning: The act that makes all subsequent action go well.

Political Participation: Civil society of a state enjoying the right to elect public officials (i.e., representative democracy) and their public opinion affecting governance.

Political Stability: The lack of external and internal conflicts in a country.

Power Distance: The extent to which people accept unequal distribution of power. In higher power distance cultures, there is a wider gap between powerful and the powerless.

Privatization: The process of transferring a government function to private enterprise.

Proactive efforts in exporting: A concerted effort to search, identify, and explore foreign market(s).

Property Rights: The exclusive and legal right to own, enjoy and dispose of real property and to keep income earned from that property.

Protectionism: Helps nations utilize legal barriers, exchange barriers, and psychological barriers to restrain entry of unwanted goods. It is established to make global markets conscious of their worldwide shortage on raw materials and natural resources.

Reactive efforts in exporting: When a firm responds to product inquiries from foreign consumers and has not employed or actively searched for (new) foreign markets or demand for the entrepreneur's goods.

Resource-based View: The perspective that an organization's resources are the primary drivers of firm performance. These resources include all of a firm's tangible and intangible assets, such as capital, equipment, employees, knowledge, and information.

Risk: A complex and interactive phenomenon that involves both (bio) physical attributes and social dimensions. It is symptomatic of a lack of knowledge about the course of future events. Human beings have invented the concept of risk to help them to understand and cope with the dangers and uncertainties of life.

Risk Analysis: Illuminates risk in its full complexity, and is sensitive to the social settings in which risk occurs, and also recognizes that social interactions may either amplify or attenuate the signals to society about the risk.

Risk Management: Managing existing risk (i.e., risk that has already been undertaken) to yield a rate of return; usually a portfolio of financial assets.

Risk Taking: Measures taken to reduce future uncertainty; the essence of entrepreneurial capitalism.

SBDC (Small Business Development Centers), **SBI** (Small Business Institutes), **SCORE** (Service Corps of Retired Executives).

Self-reference Criterion: When a company or manager believes that the leadership styles and organizational culture that work in their home country should work elsewhere, however, organizational values and norms must be tailored to fit the unique culture of each country in which the organization operates.

Service learning projects: A form of experiential learning in which students, often working in teams, use their business skills to benefit the community.

Strategic Control: Consists of determining the extent to which the organization's strategies are successful in attaining its goals and objectives.

Supply Side Perspective: The individual traits, attributes, and characteristics of entrepreneurs in relation to entrepreneurship.

Technological Effect: A key factor to help moving products from the manufacturer to the end-user, providing local inventory, technical product support, sales, and service. The global competition challenge for entrepreneurs requires them to adapt with broad skills and an incredible ability to learn at faster paces than in previous decades of the technology workforce.

Trade Intermediaries: A third party to conduct the distribution and sale of the entrepreneur's product/service in an international market.

Trade Liberalization: Policies that reduce government interventions into trade, such as the removal of tariffs or other trade barriers.

Turnkey Operations: Involves the design, construction, equipment, and, often the initial personnel training of a large facility by an overseas company which then turns the key to the ready-to-run facility over to the purchaser.

Uncertainty Avoidance: The extent to which the culture tolerates ambiguity and uncertainty. High uncertainty avoidance leads to low tolerance for uncertainty and to a search for absolute truth and predictability.

Universalism vs. particularism: Universalistic cultures develop rules that apply to all relationships and situations. Particularistic cultures focus on the uniqueness of each situation.

Uppsala Model: Named after the Swedish University where researchers Johansen and Vahlne developed a process of theory internationalization. In their model, business progress through a series of discrete steps as a company evolves from a domestic to an international firm.

USAID (U.S. Agency for International Development): The federal agency that focuses on the delivery of the U.S. Foreign Economic Assistance Program.

WTO (World Trade Organization): An international body designed to supervise and liberalize global trade. Launched in 1995, it has over 150 nation members representing an estimated 95% of world trade. WTO agreements attempt to forge common ground in trading requirements across nations.

INDEX